MW00773958

Spirit Releasement Therapy

A Technique Manual

SPIRIT RELEASEMENT THERAPY: A Technique Manual Second Edition
by William J. Baldwin, DDS, PhD

©1992 Center for Human Relations
©2002 Center for Human Relations
©2005 Judith Baldwin, LLC
©2009 Judith Baldwin, LLC
©2012 Judith Baldwin, LLC

All Rights Reserved. No part of this work may be reprinted in any form or by any means without permission in writing from the publisher, Headline Books. Functioning solely as a publisher, Headline Books is not in a position to and has not sought to verify the author's data or conclusions. Headline Books therefore disclaims any representations herein and does not in any manner warrant sufficient detail in the Manual to support qualified professionals, both to replicate the procedures and to make informed assessments of the results.

The term Spirit Releasement Therapy was trademarked in 1993 by The Center for Human Relations. For convenience and clarity, the superscript ™ is not used in the text of this book. Any use of the term, Spirit Releasement Therapy™, must have written permission by The Center for Human Relations and/or Judith Baldwin, L.L.C.

Headline Books
P. O. Box 52
Terra Alta, WV 26764
www.HeadlineBooks.com
mybook@headlinebooks.com

Printing History:
First Printing February 1991 as:
Regression Therapy / Spirit Releasement Therapy A Technique Manual
Second Printing: First Revision, May 1992
Third Printing: Second Edition, May 1993
Fourth Printing: Second Edition, June 1995
Fifth Printing: Second Edition, April 1997
Sixth Printing: Second Edition, June 1999
Seventh Printing: Second Edition, January 2001
Eight Printing: Second Edition, June 2002
Ninth Printing: Second Edition, August 2004
Tenth Printing: Second Edition, December 2005
Eleventh Printing: Second Edition, March 2009
Twelfth Printing: Second Edition September 2012

ISBN: 0-929915-16-X
ISBN 13: 978-0-929915-16-6

Library of Congress Control Number: 2009923118

Baldwin, William J. D.D.S., Ph.D.
 Spirit releasement therapy: a technique manual / by William J. Baldwin, D.D.S., Ph.D.
   p. cm.
  ISBN 978-0-929915-16
 1. Psychology counseling. 2. Spiritual healing and spiritualism. 3. Spirit possession.
 4. Religious studies. 5. Personal transformation. 6. Exorcism. I. Title

                    2009923118

PRINTED IN THE UNITED STATES OF AMERICA

SPIRIT RELEASEMENT THERAPY

A Technique Manual

second edition

REGRESSION THERAPY
PRESENT LIFE RECALL
BIRTH REGRESSION
PAST LIVES THERAPY
RECOVERY OF SOUL-MIND FRAGMENTATION
SPIRIT RELEASEMENT THERAPY
REMOTE SPIRIT RELEASEMENT THERAPY
TREATMENT OF THE DEMONIC

by

WILLIAM J. BALDWIN, D.D.S., PH.D.

HEADLINE BOOKS, INC.

In The Spirit of Science

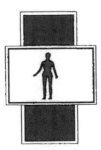

Table of Contents

Dedication

To you my beloved Judith, I express my deepest gratitude for your emotional support, your commitment and your faith in me. To you I dedicate this work as an expression of our love.

Acknowledgments

I wish to thank all of those who have helped to get this book produced and published, especially Dr. C. B. Scott Jones, president of the Human Potential Foundation, Inc. who first published the second edition in 1992, and C. Richard Farley, our liaison at HPF at that time, who told Scott, "We can do this."

My continuing thanks to Bob and Cathy Teets of Headline Books, Inc. for their tireless efforts in designing and producing the second edition of the book, their marketing skills and efforts, and for their assistance and guidance in publishing this fourth printing of the Technique Manual. At this time, the book is being used in sixteen countries and is under consideration for translation into at least six languages. The problem of spirit interference is universal in the human condition.

Reverent appreciation and deep, abiding love also goes to our unseen friends in the spirit world who assist in this work. Though I don't see them, I have absolute faith and trust in their partnership. I have seen the fruits of their efforts.

I extend my warmest appreciation to our clients who have been the greatest teachers along the way, and continue to be.

And to you, my beloved Judith, my partner in this life and many others, my confidant and constant, loving companion, my co-explorer on this journey in consciousness, I again dedicate this volume.

W.J.B.

Foreword

When Dr. Baldwin asked me to write the foreword for the *Spirit Releasement Therapy Technique Manual*, I accepted immediately because I have respected his work in this area for years. His *Manual* is greatly needed to guide therapists new to this material as well as those of us with years of experience in helping people who suffer from the attachment of earthbound spirits.

Dr. Baldwin assigned himself a monumental task with his *Manual*! He covers not only Spirit Releasement Therapy, but Past Life Therapy and therapy for those suffering from Multiple Personality Disorder. Besides carefully and thoroughly detailing the techniques of each, he illustrates his methods with verbatim material from his case files. The student is given the exact wording that can be used in the therapies.

When one finishes the *Manual*, one has at one's fingertips up-to-date knowledge of how to actually use the procedures that are described. Besides these invaluable tools, the therapist has been given clear and logical explanations of why they work. Dr. Baldwin includes discussion of the historical background of these therapies from ancient times through the latest literature on the subjects.

Dr. Baldwin casts much light on the issue of differential diagnosis, the starting point of any therapy in these fields. Without this, an unsuspecting therapist might go off in the wrong direction.

One of the aspects of Dr. Baldwin's work that sets him apart from many of us who work along similar lines is his expertise in the area of non-human entities. His fearlessness and years of experience now offers the reader excellent descriptions of these beings and the various categories involved as well as a step-by-step how-to approach to freeing the client from their grip.

The *Manual* is a true contribution to the field of healing. The reader comes away enriched and with a deep respect for Dr. Baldwin's work, knowledge, personality and spirit. And hopefully it will help thousands of therapists and therefore many thousands of clients. Bravo, Bill!

Edith Fiore, Ph.D.
Squaw Valley,
February 10, 1991

Preface

This Technique Manual developed from practical clinical experience. I was encouraged by many requests to produce such a book and compelled by my own inner knowing that the information must be committed to paper. It has been a labor of unconditional love. Many traditional therapists reject the notion of past life therapy, partly because it is based on the questionable philosophy of reincarnation. Both traditional and unconventional therapists, as well as many past life therapists, reject the notion of Spirit Releasement Therapy because it is based on the objectionable and, to many people, frightening possibility of spirit possession. Yet in clinical practice the open minded therapist with an awareness of the spiritual dimension and a working knowledge of these modalities will find evidence of both conditions; past life recall and spirit attachment. The purpose of this Technique Manual is to serve as a guide for those who wish to pursue the possibilities for spiritual healing in a clinical setting.

In 1970 I graduated from dental school and began my career in Southern California. As an adjunct to my dental practice, I pursued several courses of training in hypnosis. This training went beyond the field of dentistry. My experience of past-life regression therapy began when I experienced my first past-life exploration in 1977 and expanded later with group regressions, spontaneous past life memories, and many individual sessions.

In 1980 Dr. Edith Fiore gave a lecture at my local Society of Clinical Hypnosis. The subject was past-life therapy. During her presentation Dr. Fiore mentioned the problems caused by spirits of deceased human beings interfering with living people. I was incredulous. She was serious. Spirit possession was real and she treated the condition in her psychotherapy practice. She recommended a book by Anabel Chaplin entitled *The Bright Light of Death*, which described this condition from the viewpoint of a psychotherapist. The book changed the course of my life and my work.

I trained with Dr. Fiore and Dr. Morris Netherton and was certified in the Netherton Method of Past Lives Therapy. With this training and my own extensive reading and research, I felt comfortable conducting past-life regressions and I began seeing clients for past-life regression therapy in March 1981.

Most of the people I saw in session were dental patients who had enjoyed the benefits of hypnosis in my dental office. I learned a great deal as I conducted these first regressions. There was no way to prove the validity of the past life experiences described, and yet the clients benefited as a result of the sessions. What proved to be true was the fact that thousands of people were able to recall what seemed to be memories of other existences, that is, prior incarnations. Some people interested in research and documentation have been able to verify names and dates of the personalities of earlier lifetimes. Skeptics have put forth various explanations for these memories, attempting to explain away the apparent experience of reincarnation.

After the first few months of doing past life regression work, I recognized that more than half my clients showed signs of spirit interference. Within a few years, as I learned to recognize the signs and symptoms of spirit interference, it became overwhelmingly clear that nearly everyone is influenced by non-physical conscious beings at some time in their life, to some degree, for varying time periods.

While there were several books on past-life therapy by that time, there were precious few on the subject of a clinical approach to relieving the condition of spirit possession. Religious texts assumed a preconceived notion that all spirits are demonic, and took the classic adversarial approach to exorcism steeped in ritual, fear and superstition. This widely accepted method of exorcism seemed violent and without compassion, thus I rejected the traditional religious approach.

As I continued my search for information and precedent in this field, I discovered a book by psychiatrist Carl Wickland entitled *Thirty Years Among The Dead* which was published in 1924. The discarnate earthbound spirits which afflicted his patients were channeled through his wife, Anna, a gifted trance medium. His conversational approach with these intruding spirits was practical, methodical and compassionate. Invisible helpers from the spirit world assisted these lost and confused souls to find their rightful place in the Light. Wickland's methods became the basis for the techniques I have developed. While perusing a used book store I found a hardcover copy of Wickland's book. Inside the front cover, inscribed in his own hand, were these words:

"Truth wears no mask
Bows at no human Shrine
Seeks neither place nor applause
She only asks a hearing."
        Sincerely, The Author
        Carl A. Wickland M.D.
Los Angeles, Calif.
January 26, 1929

These words still thrill me whenever I read them. It feels somehow as if he were reaching out to me across the decades with an invitation to continue the work. I have accepted the invitation. It has become my work.

In the fall of 1982 I left the practice of dentistry and six months later enrolled in a doctoral program in clinical psychology. I graduated in 1988. My dissertation was entitled Diagnosis and Treatment of the Spirit Possession Syndrome. The dissertation is the basis of this Technique Manual. The material has been presented in lectures, workshops and training classes across the United States and several other countries. The basic training class offers "hands-on" experience, and demonstrations of the techniques included in the Manual.

Psychologists, psychotherapists, mental health practitioners, psychiatrists and members of the clergy have attended the trainings and now use the techniques in their private therapy and counseling practices. For many people there is a deep awareness that there is truth in these concepts, and that this is another avenue of healing too long ignored.

The subjects covered in the Manual are arranged in a systematic fashion, meant to be read the first time in the order presented, although there is no set order in the clinical application of the techniques. Within some sections there are references to information in prior and succeeding sections. The therapeutic questions presented in the technique sections are to be used verbatim in sessions. The specific wording has evolved and developed in actual practice. It is this specificity which is essential to success with this methodology. It works!

The best way to learn the material is firsthand as a subject, then as an observer and finally as a facilitator. In the training classes participants volunteer as demonstration subjects. Observing a number of demonstration sessions gives a working knowledge of the techniques, and how they are used together in an actual clinical session. The case histories in the text clearly reveal that more than one issue may surface in a session for healing. Several techniques may be used together when appropriate. Consequently the therapist must be proficient in all the subject areas and treatment approaches as any or all may be needed in a given session. With practice the therapist will be able to move smoothly from one technique to another as the situation demands in an actual session. As in any learned skill, proficiency and confidence in the work will develop with continued practice.

After more than twelve years of pioneer work in this field it has become apparent that the condition of spirit interference, spirit possession, or spirit attachment is almost universal in the human population. Other practitioners of the modality of Spirit Releasement Therapy, or clinical depossession, as it is also termed, have discovered the same prevalence. If spirit interference is a normal condition it must be studied and understood. If it is an actual intrusion into the human system by unwelcome non-physical parasites, then it is essential that people be made aware of it and that more practitioners, both in the mental health professions and in the clergy, be trained to use the appropriate techniques to relieve this affliction. Thus another purpose of this book is to dispel the myth and superstition regarding spirits and spirit possession, more appropriately termed spirit attachment.

William J. Baldwin
Carmel Valley, California
February 14, 1991

About This Technique Manual

This manual has developed out of ten years of clinical experience and the Spirit Releasement Therapy Intensive Training, formerly called the Regression Therapy Intensive Training. The training class presents a basic explanation of the subjects and techniques included in the manual. Some of the techniques are described in various ways and may be found in several places in the manual. The repetition may assist in clarifying some items. There are many cross references to other sections and techniques, with page numbers. The table of contents and index provide quick references to topics. Subject headings in the table of contents are not listed specifically in the index.

Beginning with Section I the headers on the even number pages indicate the major section title: Introduction, Regression Therapy, Recovery of Soul-Mind Fragmentation, Spirit Releasement Therapy, and Discussion. The headers on the odd number pages indicate the subsection titles. The page numbers appear with the headers to allow for quick access to any page or section when "thumbing through" the Manual.

The continuing dilemma of which third-person pronoun to use in written text has not been resolved. The pronouns he, she, him, her, they and them are used regularly. Gender bias is neither intended nor implied and need not be inferred.

Many people gladly gave permission to use the material of their sessions in any manner. Names and identifying circumstances have been changed. Session dialogues have been edited for the sake of clarity only. Nothing of value has been changed, deleted or embellished. Many sessions are described rather than transcribed. A two-hour session covers about 45 written pages.

The word "therapist" is used extensively in the text. The terms "guide," "practitioner" or "facilitator" could be used interchangeably with "therapist." Although the work may be done by many untrained people, the presentation of this book presupposes some training in psychology, hypnotherapy and counseling.

The word "light" is used in several contexts. Light with a capital letter "L" can be substituted for the name of Jesus Christ, if there is some sensitivity or philosophical or religious aversion to the name. The Light is the energy which comes at the time of death. It is the next step in the spiritual evolution of a being after death of the physical vehicle, the human body. A tunnel, a doorway, a stairway opens toward the Light, also called heaven. It is the level of the recycling process for the earth-level reincarnational wheel of rebirth. Visualizations of light with a small letter "l" are used often for meditation, guided imagery and self protection.

Case histories are set off from the remainder of the text by a one-line space. Descriptions of case histories are not separated from the rest of the text. These cases and descriptions are meant to clarify a part of the text or to exemplify a specific point. However, these brief descriptions lose the subtleties of the actual session. There is no way to capture in writing the infinite fluctuations of the human psyche that occur in the course of a two-hour session. The richness of the human interaction is left for the practitioner to discover and experience during the practice and application of the techniques described in the manual.

The designation Spirit Releasement Therapy is a registered trademark. Though it is now used widely, it is not in any dictionary as yet. The term is used in the Manual without the superscript ™ or ® to avoid clutter.

There is one established fact which remains unchangeable: The client has the answers to all of his or her own problems. The solution lies within each person. It is the therapist's job to assist in the discovery.

The Truth

After God created the world and settled Man and Woman there, He wanted to place the Truth somewhere in the world where humans would eventually find it, but not before they attempted to figure it out for themselves. He asked the Archangels for advice. One Archangel suggested that the Truth be placed at the top of the highest mountain. A second Archangel cautioned that man would quickly crown the highest mountain peak. The first Archangel suggested placing the Truth at the bottom of the sea. The second Archangel again cautioned that man would soon fathom the deepest ocean. Suddenly inspired, the third Archangel enthused "Let's place the Truth deep inside every person. They won't look there for a long, long time."

And that's exactly what He did.

Navajo Creation Myth

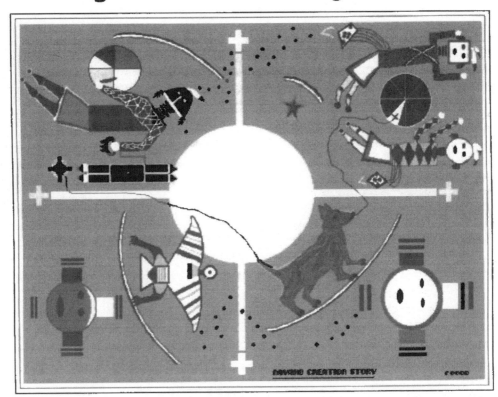

"Navajo Creation Myth," by Rocco Tripodi. Cayote steals fire from the great Spirit and travels around the sun to bring it to the first man and woman. Computer graphics courtesy of the artist.

Introduction

Notes

Quick Guide to Section I

From, *The Sacred Tree*
©1988 Four Worlds Development
Project, Illustration by Patricia Morris

Introduction

The mysteries of Death have always frightened and fascinated people, perhaps as long as there have been people to consider it. Ancient and modern religious literature contain many references to the afterlife and the process that happens to humans after the transition of death. Several books have been written in recent years recounting the "near-death experience," or NDE, in which a person "dies" and is consequently resuscitated (Kübler-Ross, 1969; Moody, 1975; Osis and Haraldsson, 1977; Ring, 1980; Sabom, 1982).

After recovering from near death, many people can accurately describe nearby events which occurred while the body was clinically dead, including the activities of the medical personnel during the resuscitation attempts. It seems as if the consciousness separates from the body, remains fully aware, and "sees" (that is, perceives) everything in the vicinity in precise detail, usually from a vantage point near the ceiling.

Many report being greeted by friends and relatives who are no longer living. Often such people encounter a tunnel and a brilliant Light, and sometimes a figure of religious importance, usually Jesus. At first the Light seems to attract the newly deceased spirit, but at some point the religious figure indicates that it is not yet time to come into the Light, that there is more work to do in the physical body in the earthlife. The spirit of the person then rejoins the body, often much to the surprise of the people nearby.

Those who have been resuscitated report that some being or voice told them to return to the body. The Light is so totally peaceful, so indescribably beautiful, that many returnees resent the need to return. More than eight million Americans have gone through the near-death experience (Gallup, 1982).

Marion was in her late thirties. Several years prior to her session, she was involved in a motor scooter accident while vacationing out of the country on a small Caribbean island. Her right leg was severely damaged. After being taken to a small hospital in the island community which did not have the facilities to treat her, she was flown by helicopter to a large hospital on the mainland. By the time she was finally moved into surgery, she had lost considerable blood. She died on the table.

Moving out of her body, she drifted through the corridor to where her children waited. As she floated close to them, she observed her physician coming toward them to tell them about her death. Angry at him and concerned for her grieving children, she managed to rejoin her body successfully. The surprised surgeons could not save the leg.

Another case was described by a skeptical surgeon who had a patient who succumbed on the operating table. Several anxious minutes passed before resuscitation attempts proved successful. Later, the patient described exactly what the surgical team was wearing, the instruments they were using, the equipment in the room, and a number of accurate details about the adjoining rooms. Physicians often attribute such accounts to drug toxicity and hallucination. However, this patient was accurate in the details of her description—and she was totally blind. Although still skeptical, the surgeon did acknowledge that something had occurred which was above and beyond his belief systems about reality.

Not everyone who survives a near-death experience reports seeing the Light. Some people perceive a very hellish scene (Gallup, 1982, pp. 73-87). Some simply wander about observing the activities of the living (Ritchie, 1978). The level of such activity is said to be the Lower Astral plane. This includes the outer darkness, the place of "gnashing of teeth" referred to in the Bible. The Lower Astral is the place of demons, the dark-energy beings which are the minions of Lucifer, other mischievous spirits, and lost earthbound discarnates. Many of these spirits actively seek some unsuspecting and naive person to attach to for their own selfish purposes.

The undeniable implication of the NDE is that the individual personality survives physical death fully aware and conscious as a discrete entity, a spirit. The speculation naturally arises about the existence of this spirit before embodiment, prior to conception and birth. Where did it come from and where will it go? The Ancient Wisdom offers one possible explanation: reincarnation.

REINCARNATION

In the beginning there was the Source, the All That Is, the Totality of all and everything. Within this original Source, there was consciousness of being, self-awareness, that which has been called God, Goddess, All That Is, the I Am that I Am. In this state of total peace, unadulterated perfection, unmoving bliss, there seemed to develop a feeling of boredom, a longing for something else.

This urge for something else impelled Source to split off individual sparks of consciousness in order to explore itself in all dimensions, to experience what there was to experience, and finally to rejoin, enhancing the original Source with the gathered experience. Each spark of this Oneness has a slightly different and recognizable vibration. Each is individual yet an integral and essential part of the Oneness, the Totality.

Each particle, or spark of the original Totality, is termed a "monad." Like the parts of a hologram, each fragment of the whole contains a complete replica of the Totality when it was in its perfect state. The monad is endowed with an urge to return to this perfect state, which keeps it in perpetual motion toward eventual reunion with God (Bletzer, 1986, p. 408).

The terms soul and spirit are often used interchangeably, yet there is a conceptual difference. Spirit is the pure essence, the God force and the spark of God-consciousness is one fragment of that Totality. The soul is a spark of spirit that is individual consciousness, experiencing and growing with each experience. The soul-mind retains the memories of all experiences gathered by the soul, such as physical incarnation in the earth plane.

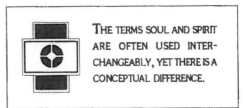

THE TERMS SOUL AND SPIRIT ARE OFTEN USED INTERCHANGEABLY, YET THERE IS A CONCEPTUAL DIFFERENCE.

Twin souls or twin flames are said to be the two halves of a monad, the God created spark of spirit, each experiencing on its own, yet connected in consciousness. The two will reconnect before the monad rejoins the Oneness. The two will follow separate, individual paths of spiritual growth, perhaps in order get the job done more quickly than one could do alone. They may or may not incarnate on earth at the same time. If they are incarnated in human form at the same time, they may or may not meet. Their purpose is not to be together in romantic relationship in physical bodies, but to grow spiritually toward eventual reconnection with each other and rejoining with Source.

It is also said that in the end times of any great age on earth, such as the present transition from the Piscean age to the Aquarian age, many twin souls will find each other for the spiritual work necessary during these times, both for their own soul growth and for the purpose of assisting others in preparing to move on to higher vibrational levels of existence.

When an individual spark of God-consciousness, the spirit being, chooses to come into the earth plane from unmanifest or non-physical consciousness, some preparation is required. There is a level of the spirit realm, described as the Light, which seems to be near the earth but in a higher frequency or vibrational rate and invisible to most people. In esoteric literature it has been called the Astral Plane. It is made up of Lower, Middle, and Upper levels, each level being further divided into sublevels. There is a portal, or entry station, through which a spirit being initially must pass in order to arrive at the specialized area of preparation in the Middle Astral (Monroe, 1985, p. 128).

In the Middle Astral there are great Halls of Learning where a being can prepare for earthly life. There is a Planning Stage where the being develops the Life Plan, the schedule of events and opportunities in the life to come. This place is often perceived as resembling a corporate board room with a large table, around which sit all the beings who will participate in the coming earth sojourn. In this Planning Stage all possible interactions with the others will be negotiated, agreed to, and arranged (Wambach, 1979; Whitton and Fisher, 1986).

In the Planning Stage, counselors (usually three to seven in number) assist the being in recalling and reexamining the unfinished business and unresolved emotional conflicts from other times, other places and other earth lifetimes. The being makes choices regarding elements of the coming life—for example, gender; race; health; parents; life circumstances, such as geographical location, affluence or poverty; marriage partners; and children. The entire range of learning opportunities for the coming life is developed in this stage.

Events and opportunities are arranged which will give everyone involved the opportunity to resolve conflicts and balance the remaining karmic debts. This is the foundation for the concept of Karma, the law of cause and effect: For every action there is an equal and opposite reaction. In the Christian tradition it is represented by the phrase, "As you sow, so shall you reap."

The Ancient Wisdom holds that there are three aspects of Divine Essence which shine forth to create, qualify, condition and govern all forms in the physical universe. The first, Will or willpower, is the propellant of existence. Love is the second aspect. It modifies the impact of Will and blends with Active Intelligence to produce wisdom. Active intelligence is the third aspect, the Mind of God which overshadows all substance. Spiritual maturity of the human race will see these three qualities fully evolved and manifesting. The final focus of our spiritual learning is love. The bottom line of healing is love. Love without object, unconditional love, love which neither demands nor expects anything in return (Fisichella, 1985, pp. 29-36).

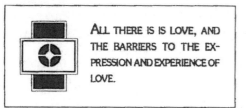

ALL THERE IS IS LOVE, AND THE BARRIERS TO THE EXPRESSION AND EXPERIENCE OF LOVE.

All there is is love, the expression of love as one person loves another, the experience of love as one person is loved by another, and the barriers to the expression and experience of love. The barriers to love between people are the mental and emotional residues which are carried from lifetime to lifetime. This is a basic tenet of past-life regression therapy and spirit releasement therapy.

As the designed events unfold in the lifetime, each involved being has the right of free will to choose any possible course of action, including the one which will lead to forgiveness, resolution and balancing past karmic debts. If the being makes an alternative choice, there is no punishment, recrimination, or judgment, just a different outcome. There will be another opportunity to balance the ledgers of the past. Within the framework of eternity, every injustice, every indiscretion, every sin of omission and commission, every jot and tittle will be balanced; nothing will be left undone or unresolved. When that total balancing is accomplished, all beings will rejoin Source. All will return Home. No being will be left behind, none will be left out.

An important aspect of the Planning Stage is the design of the lifeline, extending from conception to the maximum age attainable, which includes all possible choice points for choosing death and checking out of the lifetime. The checkout points might include terminated pregnancy, childhood illness, teenage suicide, battlefield death for a man, death in childbirth for a woman, auto accident, drug overdose, surgery, heart attack, murder, or death by natural causes at the maximum possible age on the lifeline. A spirit being plans all possible points of departure or death. No one is ever responsible for someone else's death. There is always something to be learned by the death of a person at any one of the checkout points, both for the person who chooses to depart from the physical body and for those who are left behind.

From this Planning Stage the spirit comes into the manifest or physical universe and the earth plane. The being will find its place, wherever that might be. A portion of the consciousness engages with the physical level at the moment of conception and remains with the developing fetus, recording all surrounding stimuli as though directed at itself. This portion of consciousness seems to be related to the subconscious, which records without discrimination, judgment or discerning filter of any sort everything which transpires nearby. This function of mind does not sleep and is apparently similar to, if not identical with, the hidden observer, the mechanism which records the experience of a person while under anesthesia or hypnosis (Hilgard, 1986).

The remembered information includes most prominently the emotions and communication of the mother, the father, and, to a lesser degree, others in the vicinity. This certainly includes the conversations and emotions surrounding the birth experience (Netherton, 1978; Verney, 1982, 1987; Grof, 1985; Chamberlain, 1988).

An essential accessory for the physical life experience is the conscious judging mind. The mind constantly assesses the environment for real or imagined threats to survival, and it finds many. The original design function of the mind was survival of the being, or of whatever the being considers itself to be. The pure being, or spirit, is passive in its embodied manifestation here on the physical plane. The aspect that becomes involved with other personalities in emotional interactions is the personality.

THE DESIGN FUNCTION OF THE MIND IS SURVIVAL OF THE BEING, OR WHATEVER THE BEING CONSIDERS IT- SELF TO BE.

Soon after conception, the being seems to forget who it is and whence it came, in time coming to presume that it is the physical body. Thus, survival of the body becomes the goal of the mind. As the personality develops, the being identifies with the personality and the mind itself. Since the function of the mind is survival of whatever the being considers itself to be—and since the being has come to consider that it is the mind—the function of the mind perpetuates its own concern with survival. The result is ego. This error of mind, this refocusing of its own function, leads to the unnecessary mental and emotional residues in the individual, and to much of the seemingly endless human suffering on the planet.

The ego seeks to survive by competing, by validating its own viewpoint and invalidating the viewpoint of other people, by making itself right and others wrong, (often at the expense of denying truth) and by justifying its own actions and behavior while judging the behavior of others; in short, by self-aggrandizing. The judgments, assumptions, conclusions and decisions are the mental residue on which the ego acts in successive lifetimes or incarnations.

Personal survival becomes the prime motivator for behavior, decisions, actions and interactions with others. Every real or imagined threat to survival which the ego successfully meets or overcomes without death establishes a survival mechanism. This mechanism can be called into operation in any future crisis that it perceives as a similar threat to survival. In any threatening situation, if any element of the situation at all resembles an earlier, similar situation, the survival mechanisms which seemed to be successful in the earlier situation will be reactivated. This is the cause of many irrational and inappropriate reactions to present situations.

In a stressful situation, people most often *react*—they revert to an earlier action or mode of behavior that was appropriate to an earlier, similar stressful situation but is not necessarily appropriate now. Usually, not only is the earlier behavior inappropriate to the present situation but it is often detrimental.

More positively (and occurring less often), people *respond* to a present emergency—they come up with an answer or reply that is appropriate and timely to the present stressful situation.

This defense mechanism occurs in reference to personal situations. In emergency situations, however, immediate appropriate reaction is purposely trained into emergency service personnel, such as firemen, police officers, and medical emergency room attendants.

The ego is constantly judging everything and everyone, including itself and its own behavior. The purpose of this judging is to survive by being right, although not necessarily responsible. The ego defends itself against other egos by considering itself right and making others wrong, by validating its own opinion and position and invalidating the opinions and positions of others, by avoiding domination by others while attempting to dominate others, and by other mechanisms designed to ensure one's own survival at all costs (Rinehart, 1976, pp. 165-187).

However, these self-deceiving mechanisms have a major personal cost: they deny one's self-responsibility, especially responsibility for one's own motives, intentions, emotions, desires, behavior and actions. This avoidance of responsibility leads to the further self-deception of falsely blaming others for one's own misfortunes and assuming false guilt for the suffering of others.

The ego is proficient at denying its own failings and inferiorities, suppressing these rejected aspects in the unconscious mind and thus denying them expression. However, this darker side, termed "the shadow," does find an avenue of expression, particularly in projections (Singer, 1973, pp. 209-228). Projection of the shadow onto another person or group of people often leads to prejudice, conflict and violence. This is one function of the ego which distorts the purpose of the reincarnation

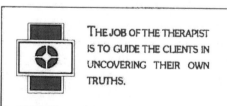

THE JOB OF THE THERAPIST IS TO GUIDE THE CLIENTS IN UNCOVERING THEIR OWN TRUTHS.

cycle as a process of spiritual evolution.

Responsibility begins with the willingness to acknowledge oneself as cause in any situation. This precludes blame, shame, guilt, resentment and remorse. It is always false, in a larger sense, to blame another person for one's own troubles or to feel guilt over perceived self-blame. Misperceptions and misinterpretations of human interactions lead to false decisions, assumptions, conclusions and judgments.

The emotional and mental residues thus engendered, and the deep spiritual need to achieve balance, can lead to unnecessary reembodiment in the reincarnation cycle. Discovering the truth of any situation and clarifying the distortions of mind will bring freedom from these destructive emotions and mental programming. This is the aim of past-life therapy and spirit releasement therapy. The client has his or her own answers, the truth of any situation, past or present. The task of the therapist is to guide the client in discovering these truths.

As a spirit being comes into this earth sojourn, It acts and behaves according to inner motivation, intention and desire, with the scope of the Life Plan as a silent background, the guideline, the stage for the drama of the life. The being does not judge, it simply observes. Once the being is embodied in the physical level, the ego's motives and desires seem to overwhelm the being's plan.

Ego judges itself for its own actions against a hidden standard of comparison, which is perfection—the perfection of the being or spark of God-consciousness. The ego builds up emotional residues of anger, resentment, guilt, remorse, disgust, fear, feelings of lack and scarcity, obligation or debt, when it does not meet its own expectations or live up to its own standards.

The ego is thus burdened with the residue of its own self-judgments. This residue, maintained in the soul-mind, is the burden, the unresolved conflict, that brings a being back into future lifetimes with the intention of resolving and balancing karmic debts. It is also the burden which holds some spirits close to the earth plane, that is, earthbound, after physical death in a compulsive effort to maintain the conflict situation.

However, earthbound spirits remain here not because they are attempting resolution but because they are arrested in the timelessness of the spirit realm, perpetually reexperiencing the mental, emotional and physical trauma of their death. Just as many human beings are stuck or fixated in their birth trauma, so earthbound spirits are often stuck in the death trauma.

Finding themselves involved in the physical world—where time seems to pass, expansion and contraction occur, and there is growth and decay of all physical objects and structures—they experience confusion. No longer governed by the timestream of the physical world, they often perceive events as moving in fast-forward motion.

The earthbound spirit is driven by the memories, needs, desires, appetites and emotions at the ego level and attempts to continue to interact with physical objects, substances and people. The poor soul has lost sight of the purpose of its incarnation, the path of resolution and spiritual evolution designed by the being, the spirit, the eternal spark of God.

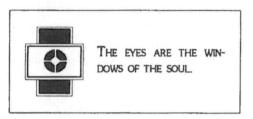

THE EYES ARE THE WINDOWS OF THE SOUL.

At the time of physical death the supraphysical body (also called the "etheric body" or "subtle body") lifts out of the physical shell. Contained within the subtle body are the energetic patterns of the emotional and physical residue of the experiences of the life (Kelsey & Grant, pp. 57-113; Woolger, 1987, pp. 161-188). Still encased in this subtle body, the being moves toward the Light, which—though sometimes close and sometimes a distance away—is always present at the time of death.

Guiding spirits come to assist. They may look like angels without wings, dressed in white robes. They may appear as shining lights. Spirits of deceased relatives or loved ones may arrive to guide the newly deceased person home to the Light. Even though they are without visible form, the newly deceased personality perceives and recognizes them through the vibration or feeling of their soul essence. If the one who comes does not have a perceivable form, then the eyes, considered to be the windows of the soul, will offer the key to such recognition.

There is a gateway or some kind of barrier through which one must pass to be fully in the Light, leaving the physical body behind, dead. If the departing spirit moves through whatever may be the last barrier and into the Light, then Death is final. The silver cord connecting the spirit to the physical body is finally and completely severed.

Once fully in the Light, the being will be in the vibrational level called the Middle Astral. Religious texts refer to this level as Heaven. During this Resting Stage, the being can rest for as long as it wants. (The neuter pronoun, "it," is used because there is no gender in spirit.) Spirit hospitals are available for healing to take place. After the Resting Stage comes a Review Stage, during which the being assesses (with the help of counselors) what was accomplished, what was not completed or resolved, and what needs to be examined in the Planning Stage for inclusion in a future embodiment (Whitton and Fisher, 1986). There are great Halls of Learning where a being can prepare for the ensuing lifetime. Finally comes the Planning Stage once again, then conception and the commencement of another physical life.

This is a simplified outline of the concept of reincarnation, the wheel of rebirth, the repeated physical embodiment of a spirit being.

SPIRIT POSSESSION SYNDROME

The condition of spirit possession—that is, full or partial takeover of a living human by a discarnate being—has been recognized or at least theorized in every era and every culture. In ninety percent of societies worldwide there are records of possession-like phenomena (Foulks, 1985).

Extensive contemporary clinical evidence suggests that discarnate beings, the spirits of deceased humans, can influence living people by forming a physical or mental connection or attachment, and subsequently imposing detrimental physical and/or emotional conditions and symptoms. This condition has been called the "possession state," "possession disorder," "spirit possession syndrome," "spirit obsession," or "spirit attachment." (Hyslop, 1917; Wickland, 1924; 1934, Allison, 1980; Guirdham, 1982; McAll, 1982; Crabtree, 1985; Fiore, 1987).

Earthbound spirits, the surviving consciousness of deceased humans, are the most prevalent possessing, obsessing or attaching entities to be found. The disembodied consciousness seems to attach itself and merge fully or partially with the subconscious mind of a living person, exerting some degree of influence on thought processes, emotions, behavior and the physical body. The entity becomes a parasite in the mind of the host. A victim of this condition can be totally amnesic about episodes of complete takeover.

A spirit can be bound to the earth plane by the emotions and feelings connected with a sudden traumatic death. Anger, fear, jealousy, resentment, guilt, remorse, even strong ties of love can interfere with the normal transition. Erroneous religious beliefs about the afterlife can prevent a spirit from moving into the Light because the after death experience does not coincide with false expectations or preconceived notions of the way it is supposed to be.

Following death by drug overdose, a newly deceased spirit maintains a strong appetite for the drug, and this hunger cannot be satisfied in the non-physical realm. The being must experience the drug through the sensorium of a living person who uses the substance. This can only be accomplished through a parasitic attachment to the person. Many drug users are controlled by the attached spirit of a deceased drug addict.

Many spirits remain in the earth plane due to a lack of awareness of their passing. At the time of death several choices are available for the newly deceased spirit. It can follow the direct path to the Light described in the near death experience (Moody, 1975; Ring, 1980). If there is an attached spirit the process may be more difficult. The newly deceased being can carry the attached earthbound to the Light thereby rescuing this lost soul. Often, the deceased is able to break away from the attached earthbound spirit and go to the Light alone.

After this separation occurs the earthbound can be lost again, wandering in the lower astral plane, often described as the gray place or the intermediate place. It can await the next incarnation of the being to whom it was attached. The entity can locate the being in the new incarnation and reconnect. This repeated attachment can occur for many lifetimes of the host. However, the earthbound can just as quickly attach to another unsuspecting person after separating from the former host at the time of death.

If the newly deceased spirit cannot break away from the attached spirit or hasn't strength enough to carry it into the Light, it can become earthbound also, with the original earthbound still attached to it. This pair can then attach to another living person. After death, the spirit of this person also may be prevented from reaching the Light due to the nested, or layered, attached spirits. This spirit becomes part of the chain of earthbound spirits that can compound until it numbers in the dozens, even hundreds.

An attachment can be benevolent in nature, totally self serving, malevolent in intention, or completely neutral. Attachment to any person may be completely random, even accidental. It can occur simply because of physical proximity to the dying person at the time of the death. In about half the cases encountered in clinical practice it is a random choice with no prior connection in this or any other incarnation. In the remainder some connection can be found, some unfinished business from this or another lifetime.

 SOME INVESTIGATORS IN THIS FIELD ESTIMATE THAT BETWEEN 70% AND 100% OF THE POPULATION ARE INFLUENCED BY ONE OR MORE DISCARNATE SPIRIT ENTITIES AT SOME TIME IN THEIR LIFE.

Even if there is some prior interaction between the host and the attaching entity, the attachment only perpetuates the conflict and carries little possibility for resolution, though every experience has the potential for learning of some kind.

Most people are vulnerable to spirit attachment on many occasions in the normal course of life. Some investigators in this field estimate that between 70% and 100% of the population are affected or influenced by one or more discarnate spirit entities at some time in their life (Berg, 1984, p. 50; Fiore, 1987b).

Any mental or physical symptom or condition, strong emotion, repressed negative feeling, conscious or unconscious need can act like a magnet to attract a discarnate entity with the same or similar emotion, condition, need or feeling. Anger and rage, fear and terror, sadness and grief, guilt, remorse or feelings of the need for punishment can invite entities with similar feelings.

Severe stress may cause susceptibility to the influence of an intrusive spirit. Altering the consciousness with alcohol or drugs, especially the hallucinogens, loosens one's external ego boundaries and opens the subconscious mind to infestation by discarnate beings. The same holds true for the use of strong analgesics and the anesthetic drugs necessary in surgery. A codeine tablet taken for the relief of the pain of a dental extraction can sufficiently alter the consciousness to allow entry to a spirit.

Physical intrusions such as surgery or blood transfusion can lead to an entity attachment. In the case of an organ transplant the spirit of the organ donor can literally follow the transplanted organ into the new body. Physical trauma from auto collision, accidental falls, beatings or any blow to the head can render a person vulnerable to an intrusive spirit.

The openness and surrender during sexual intercourse can allow the exchange of attached entities between two people. Sexual abuse such as rape, incest or molestation of any sort creates a vulnerability to spirit invasion. Violence during the sexual abuse increases the likelihood of intrusion by an opportunistic spirit.

A living person can have dozens, even hundreds of attached spirits as they occupy no physical space. They can attach to the aura or float within the aura, outside the body. If any part of the body of the host has a physical weakness the earthbound can attach to that area because of a corresponding weakness or injury to the physical body of the spirit prior to death. A spirit can lodge in any of the chakras of the host, drawn by the particular energy of the chakra or by the physical structures of that level of the body.

Connection with an earthbound spirit may be established by the purposeful choice of either the spirit or the living human due to a strong emotional bond between them in this life or in a previous lifetime together. A grieving person can welcome the spirit of a dear departed one only to find the consequences unbearable.

A living human can be affected by an attached spirit in many different ways. The discarnate entity retains the psychic energy pattern of its own ailments following death and can produce in the host any mental aberration or emotional disturbance and any symptom of physical illness.

Erratic or inconsistent behavior can result from a shifting of control between separate entities. This behavior is similar in appearance to the phenomenon of switching between alters in multiple personality disorder (MPD). This condition can be extremely confusing and frightening for a person and for their family.

An attached entity can be associated with any emotional track of a living person such as anger, fear, sadness or guilt. The emotional energy of the entity intensifies the expression of a specific emotion, often leading to inappropriate overreactions to ordinary life situations.

A subpersonality, that is a splinter or subordinate personality, can maintain a connection with an entity who came in at the chronological age when the subpersonality splintered away from the main personality due to a traumatic experience. The discarnate spirit may have joined at the time of the emotional trauma to help the child in the time of need. The continued connection with the entity prevents healing and integration of this subpersonality into the main personality system.

The mental, emotional and physical influence of an attached entity can alter the original path of karmic options and opportunities of the host. It can disrupt the planned life line by hastening death or prolonging life, thus interfering with any specific checkout

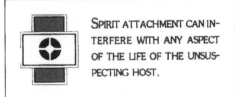

SPIRIT ATTACHMENT CAN INTERFERE WITH ANY ASPECT OF THE LIFE OF THE UNSUSPECTING HOST.

point. An entity of the opposite gender can influence the sexual preference and gender orientation. An attached entity can influence the choice of marriage partners and the choice of a partner for an extra-marital affair.

Many areas of a person's life can be influenced by one or more attached entities. In short, spirit attachment can interfere with any aspect of the life of the unsuspecting host.

The host is usually unaware of the presence of attached spirits. The thoughts, desires and behaviors of an attached entity are experienced as the person's own thoughts, desires and behaviors. The thoughts, feelings, habits and desires do not seem foreign if they have been present for a long time, even from childhood. This is a major factor in the widespread denial of the concept and lack of acceptance of the phenomena of discarnate interference and spirit attachment, obsession or possession. This is equally true for people in general and for professional therapists.

In most cases, a person can only experience and acknowledge the reality of the condition after an attached entity has been released. The realization may come some months after a releasement session as the person suddenly notices the absence of a familiar attitude, desire, addiction or behavior.

The symptoms of spirit attachment can be very subtle. An attached spirit may be present without producing any noticeable symptoms. Yet attached entities always exert some influence ranging from a minor energy drain to a major degree of control or interference. Complete possession and takeover can result in suppression of the original personality. The earthbound spirit does not replace the rightful spirit in the body in such a case, it just usurps control. An attached earthbound spirit cannot maintain life in a human body after the original spirit being has separated from the body in the transition of death.

A newly formed spirit attachment is usually more obvious to the

SPIRIT ATTACHMENT DOES NOT REQUIRE THE PERMISSION OF THE HOST. PEOPLE CREATE THEIR OWN VULNERABILITY AS PART OF THEIR REALITY.

unfortunate host. An attached entity can cause any of the following signs and symptoms: sudden onset of drug or alcohol usage; unusual and inappropriate speech, accent or foreign or unknown language, any behavior patterns inconsistent with normal conduct; unfamiliar reactions to familiar situations; repetitive and unusual movements of the body which are experienced as beyond one's control; unusual physical sensations or symptoms in the absence of a medically sound organic cause; loss of the normal sense of one's personal identity; a feeling that a spirit of some kind or another person has taken over control of one's mind and/or body; noticeable personality changes, however slight, following surgery, organ transplant, accident, emotional upset or moving into a new home.

As a result of a newly formed spirit attachment or possession, physical appetites for food, sex, alcohol or drugs can increase drastically. Personal attitudes and beliefs can suddenly change as can taste in clothing. The voice and even facial features and appearance can alter dramatically.

These sudden changes in behavior can be a factor in convincing the most skeptical person that there is an attached entity. Many people have the mistaken notion that there must be some bizarre outward signs caused by an interfering spirit such as depicted in the movie *The Exorcist*, based on the book of the same name (Blatty, 1971). The movie depicted a true case, but some symptoms and behaviors of the girl actually came from two other cases,

IT IS FASHIONABLE TODAY AMONG MANY "NEW AGE" ENTHUSIASTS TO ATTEMPT TO CHANNEL SOME HIGHER POWER, A SPIRIT TEACHER OR MASTER WHO WILL USE THE VOICE MECHANISM OF ANY WILLING PERSON TO SPEAK "WORDS OF WISDOM." ... THIS ACTIVITY CONSTITUTES PERMISSION AND WELCOME FOR A DISCARNATE SPIRIT.

added for dramatic impact. The incidence of such violent possession is rare.

Spirit attachment does not require the permission of the host. This seems to be a violation of free will. It also appears to refute the popular notion that each person is totally responsible for creating his or her reality and that there are no victims. The apparent conflict here stems from the definitions of permission and free will choice. Ignorance and denial of the possibility of spirit interference is no defense against spirit attachment. Belief or lack of belief regarding the existence of intrusive entities has no bearing on the reality of these beings and their behavior.

In denial and ignorance, most people do not refuse permission to these non-physical intruders. Individual sovereign beings have the right to deny any violation or intrusion by another being. With limited, if any, knowledge and distorted perceptions of the nature of the spirit world, the non-physical reality, many people leave themselves open and create their own vulnerability as part of creating their own reality. It is fashionable today among many "New Age" enthusiasts to attempt to channel some higher power, a spirit teacher or master who will use the voice mechanism of any willing person to speak "words of wisdom." Some use the terminology "for my highest good" when calling for a spirit to channel through. This activity constitutes permission and welcome for a discarnate spirit. The identifiers such as "master" and "teacher" and qualifiers such as "for my highest good," will be claimed by the entities as personally valid identifications, qualities or attributes. Unfortunately, some opportunistic spirits who respond to this invitation refuse to leave at the end of the channeling session.

Scanned reproduction of, "Saul and the Witch of Endor," (*Samual, 28:16-17*), *Pictorial Bible*, circa 1882

An afflicted person may report hearing voices, internally or externally, or having spontaneous visual images of bizarre or frightening faces or figures. Recurring dreams of being chased, being urged to commit suicide by someone, often a loved one who was a victim of suicide, may suggest the presence of an entity. A dream image of a person injecting something into the veins of the arm may be an attached entity's recall of the last memories before death.

During a session, a client described awakening suddenly from a vivid dream in which she was a man who was shot by another man. Unlike most dreams of death in which the person emerges from the body before the moment of death by falling, crushing, or auto accident, in this dream, she, as the man, saw the gun fire, felt the pain of the bullet impacting the chest, fell to the floor, then stood up out of the dead body. He was very angry. This was the entity's experience.

The clinical procedures and interventions of Spirit Releasement Therapy seem to facilitate the release of the attached spirit entity. After successful completion of the process, the imposed symptoms are alleviated partially or fully, often immediately and permanently.

The following case is an example of a phobia imposed by an entity. The woman was a child of ten at the time of the attachment. This session was done as a demonstration before a hypnosis training class.

At 40, Amy suffered terribly from the fear of flying. She had come by ground transportation to the class, which was held in a location over a thousand miles from her home. At one time she would vomit if she even had to drive to an airport, but with hypnotherapy she released that problem. Still, she could not get near an aircraft. Hers was a severe case.

Client: "Well, I have this terrible fear of flying." The panic showed in her eyes as she described the feeling.

Therapist: "What happened."

C: "I was maybe ten years old and I was at an airshow. And a helicopter crashed just a hundred feet in front of me. I watched the pilot burn. It was the first time I realized I was psychic. As he came over the top of the curve to come down in this maneuver I saw that he wasn't going to make it and I yelled at him in my mind. 'Pull out! Pull out! You're going to crash!' And he did, the helicopter just crashed right there in front of me!"

T: "Is the pilot still here? Is the pilot still here now?"

C: "No, he died. I was ten years old."

T: "I know. Is the pilot still here now?"

C: (pause) "Well, maybe he is."

T: "How do you feel, as you think about flying?"

C: "I get a queasiness in my stomach."

T: "If that queasiness could speak, what would it say?"

C: (shouting) "I can't get out! I can't get out! I can't get out! I can't get out! I can't get out! I can't get out!" (pause)

T: "What's happening?"

C: "I can't get out. They can't get me out." (pause)

T: "What's happening now?"

C: (more calmly) "Well, I'm outside watching my body burn. They couldn't get me out. The controls were shoved in my gut, I couldn't get out."

T: "What's your name?"

C: "Robert."

Robert had followed Amy home because she was very upset. He had a daughter her age and he understood the anguish she felt. So he followed her home to comfort her. As he reached his hand out to her to soothe her, he just slipped inside. He was attached and couldn't leave. Soon, Robert was trying to run the household.

C: "She was lazy. I wanted her to work more. I tried to get her to do her school work more. Her dad was a real..., he was a real jerk. Boy, I would have hit him, if I could. (pause) But now, she works too hard."

In this statement, Robert revealed his vulnerability. He was tired of his situation. The therapist recognized this vulnerability and used it as the entry point for the release procedure.

T: "Robert, you sound like you're very tired."

C: "Yeah, I really am."

When directed to focus his awareness upward, Robert quickly perceived the Light and he went into it, taking with him the physical sensation of queasiness from Amy's guts. This had been the residue of the crash when the controls rammed into his belly.

One of the class participants asked Amy, "How is your fear of flying now?"

C: "I think it's gone.... I think I'll fly home."

The phobia disappeared with the entity who had brought it as he went home to the Light.

Many people experience automatic writing, during which the hand and arm seem to be under separate control by an outside force. Mediumship or channelling presents the phenomenon of control by a separate consciousness, often speaking with a voice that is distinctly different from the persons normal speaking voice. Several other behaviors considered as psychotic or drug-induced symptoms by the American Psychiatric Association are specific signs and symptoms of spirit attachment and can often be eliminated by releasing the attached spirit.

A diagnosis of schizophrenia is based on certain symptoms defined as psychotic. This includes delusional thinking such as: thought broadcasting, the belief that one's thoughts can be heard by others; thought insertion, the belief that someone else has inserted thoughts in one's mind; hallucinations, some visual, more commonly auditory such as hearing voices; being under the control of a dead person or other outside force. (American Psychiatric Association [APA], 1987, pp. 187-198).

Multiple personality disorder and schizophrenia are distinctly different conditions. Delusional thinking is absent from the diagnostic criteria for MPD. The essential features of MPD include a disturbance of identity and memory and the presence of two or more distinct personalities within the person. These personalities may claim different gender, race, present different IQ, age, even specific mental disorders, and claim a different family of origin. The belief that one is possessed by another person, spirit or entity may occur as a symptom of MPD. The separate personalities may be able to function individually and be totally unaware of the others (APA, 1987, pp. 269-272).

Psychiatrist Scott Peck seems to confirm the condition of demonic possession in some of his patients. He calls for another diagnostic category for these people he feels are evil to be included in the Diagnostic and Statistical Manual of Mental Disorders of the American Psychiatric Association (Peck, 1983).

In a 389-page doctoral dissertation, Craig T. Isaacs (1985) states that present DSM-III categories of psychopathology are inadequate to describe the cases of demonic possession that he studied and described.

The differential diagnosis of these three conditions requires an intelligent assessment of the signs of MPD, a critical evaluation of the ostensible psychotic symptoms that partially define schizophrenia, and also must include the consideration of discarnate influence or spirit obsession, possession or attachment as a factor. Certain manifestations of the three conditions are similar enough to appear identical. The etiology and history of the afflictions are vastly different. The outcome and prognosis depend on the correct diagnosis and appropriate treatment.

Some interesting similarities become obvious when comparing spirit possession syndrome, or SPS, and multiple personality disorder, or MPD. An earthbound spirit attachment can develop at any point after a being leaves the planning stage in the Light, even prior to conception, at any time during a lifetime, and before arriving at the review stage in the Light after death. Dissociation and formation of alter personalities in MPD is nearly always the result of childhood trauma.

Though some steps in the therapeutic process are similar, the final goals of treatment of the two conditions are distinctly different.

MULTIPLE PERSONALITY DISORDER

The concept of divided or multilevel consciousness has been studied extensively in recent years. Ego states, subordinate personalities, or "subpersonalities" are active in the daily functioning of a healthy individual. However, an emotional trauma can cause "parts" or "fragments" to split from a normal personality. These partial personalities, or sub-personalities, retain the person's age and characteristics at the time of the split. They strive to fulfill the unfulfilled need that led to the split, and continue to maintain the emotional mood of the traumatic event. These subpersonalities are literally stuck or frozen in the incident.

Subpersonalities do not become the personality in charge nor do they take control of the behavior. Rather, they manifest as subconscious urges, and can cause variations in mood, physical energy, sociability, likes and dislikes in food and drink, unusual eating habits, and many other aspects of physical and emotional conditions and behavior (Assagioli, 1965; Watkins, 1978; Ferrucci, 1982; Brown, 1983; Stone & Winkelman, 1985, 1990).

In cases of extreme physical, emotional, or sexual abuse during childhood years, the dissociation can become complete, resulting in two or more separate and distinct personalities. The alter personalities "switch" as each recurrently comes out and takes full control of the person's behavior. This condition is termed multiple personality disorder, or MPD (APA, 1987, p. 269). Between 95% and 100% of diagnosed multiple personality cases have a history of childhood incest, torture or other abuse (Putnam, 1985, p. 11).

Only in recent years has the brutal reality of child molestation, incest and Satanic cult ritual abuse come into public and professional awareness. Pavelsky (1984) and others estimate that one out of three females and one out of six males are sexually molested by age eighteen. Coincident with the increasing recognition of widespread child abuse is the growing acceptance of MPD as a tragic consequence in many cases of this trauma. Currently, the condition is more often recognized, correctly diagnosed, and successfully treated as a specific mental disorder.

In the dissociation of MPD, reality contact is maintained through either the central or primary personality or an alter personality. The split is said to be massive or molecular; that is, each alter personality is complete, or nearly so, with the memory of its own history and relatively distinct and integrated behavioral and interpersonal patterns (Campbell, 1981, p. 458).

Each alter personality has its own psychophysiological profile, which may include pain response; handedness; ability to heal and rate of healing; response to any given medication; allergic reactions; eyeglass prescription; diseases such as diabetes, epilepsy, and arthritis, including swollen joints; appetites; and tastes in food and drugs (APA, 1987, p. 269-270).

In rare cases, one or more of the alter personalities speak and converse in a foreign language, modern or archaic, totally unknown to the primary personality. These cases are labeled responsive xenoglossy and suggest an intrusion by a discarnate personality (Stevenson, 1974a, 1984).

Dissociation is considered a coping mechanism for a traumatic or overwhelming, stressful situation. Not all people who suffer this kind of abuse develop MPD. It seems to depend on the capacity to dissociate in response to the post-traumatic stress of the abuse.

Dr. Richard Kluft (1986, pp. 87-89) has developed a "four-factor theory" of the etiology of MPD. The four factors he deems necessary for the development of multiple personality are:

1. A biological capacity for dissociation.
2. A history of trauma or abuse.
3. Specific psychological structures or contents that can be used in the creation of alternate personalities.
4. A lack of adequate nurturing or opportunities to recover from abuse.

Dr. Bennett Braun (1986, pp. 5-9) has proposed the 3-P model of the development of the disorder:

1. Two Predisposing factors are hypothesized as necessary: an inborn biological/psychological capacity to dissociate, and repeated exposure to an inconsistently stressful environment.
2. A Precipitating event must occur—a specific overwhelming traumatic episode to which the potential MPD patient responds by dissociating.
3. The Perpetuating phenomena are interactive behaviors, usually with the abuser, that continue for an unspecified time and are

beyond the control of the abused.

Hypnosis is presently the most reliable and efficient way of discovering, diagnosing and treating MPD. This treatment modality was fully accepted as a valid therapeutic modality by the American Dental Association and the American Medical Association in 1958, and by the American Psychiatric Association in 1962. However, its revival and general acceptance have been slow in coming. The stigma of Franz Anton Mesmer ("mesmerism") and the acrimony surrounding the birth of modern hypnosis still cloud the image of hypnotherapy, as does the indiscriminate display by stage hypnotists. The modern use of hypnosis is little understood by most psychotherapists, physicians and psychiatrists. Only about 10% of practicing mental health professionals utilize this technique.

Many professionals still deny the existence of MPD, or explain it away with some other diagnosis (Goodwin, 1985). Two separate studies have shown that correct diagnosis of MPD is established an average of 6.8 years after the patient first enters therapy (Braun, 1986, pp. 4-5).

SIMILARITIES BETWEEN MPD AND SPS

The study of Multiple Personality Disorder cannot be complete without a serious examination of the condition known as Spirit Possession Syndrome. Comparison of MPD and SPS reveals some indisputable similarities Some signs and symptoms of the two conditions are quite similar, some are distinctly different. Most mental health professionals have considerable skepticism regarding both conditions.

The classic symptoms of MPD may be muted and attenuated in childhood. The condition is often ignored, misunderstood, misinterpreted or misdiagnosed. A child's complaints and behavior are frequently disbelieved or passed off as childhood fantasy, and may lead to punishment.

Recognizable symptoms may begin to manifest in the late teens, but the condition is often not discovered and accurately diagnosed until the mid to late thirties. Approximately 65% of cases are found between the ages of 20 and 40 (Kluft, 1985a, p. 215). The condition has a natural history from the original traumatic episode(s) to full manifestation of symptoms of MPD. The person with MPD usually holds a poor self-image of mental and physical health. Cases of MPD in the United States may number in the thousands (Putnam, 1989, pp. 54-55).

The earthbound spirit of a deceased human can form an attachment to a living person at any point between conception and death. The mental, emotional and physical health of the host has no bearing on the potential for an attachment. Many cases of SPS are discovered in therapy while searching for the cause of a chronic problem or unexpected new conflict in the life of the client.

Some phases of the treatment of MPD and Spirit Releasement Therapy have a parallel intention, yet the final goal is totally different. For the alter personalities in MPD, the final step is either integration and fusion or at least cooperation and co-consciousness (Braun, 1986). For the condition of spirit attachment, only the release of the spirit can bring relief of the symptoms

(Wickland, 1924; Fiore, 1987a).

William James spoke on "Demoniacal Possession" in his 1896 Lowell Lectures. Recapitulating his previous lecture, "Multiple Personality," he mentioned three types of mutations in the sense of self: insane, hysteric, and somnambulistic. The fourth type, he said, is spirit control, or mediumship, which in the past had been equated with devil worship and pathology. He continued:

> History shows that mediumship is identical with demon possession. But the obsolescence of public belief in the possession by demons is a very strange thing in Christian lands, when one considers that it is the one most articulately expressed doctrine of both Testaments, and...reigned for seventeen hundred years, hardly challenged, in all the churches. Every land and every age has exhibited the facts on which this belief was founded. India, China, Egypt, Africa, Polynesia, Greece, Rome, and all medieval Europe believed that certain nervous disorders were of supernatural origin, inspired by gods and sacred; or by demons—and therefore diabolical. When the pagan gods became demons, all possession became diabolic, and we have the medieval condition (Taylor, 1984, p. 93-94).

In James' day, there was "...much alarmist writing in psychopathy about degeneration," and he suggested that "...if there are devils, if there are

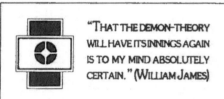

"THAT THE DEMON-THEORY WILL HAVE ITS INNINGS AGAIN IS TO MY MIND ABSOLUTELY CERTAIN." (WILLIAM JAMES)

supernormal powers, it is through the cracked and fragmented self that they enter." (Taylor, 1984, p. 110). Referring to the spiritualistic activities of Boston and New York in 1896, James states that the diabolic nature of demon possession now "...has with us assumed a benign and optimistic form, [in which] changed personality is considered the spirit of a departed being coming to bring messages of comfort from the 'sunny land'" (Taylor, 1984, p. 94).

James (1966) further stated that:

> The refusal of modern "enlightenment" to treat "possession" as a hypothesis to be spoken of as even possible, in spite of the massive human tradition based on concrete experience in its favor, has always seemed to me a curious example of the power of fashion in things scientific. That the demon-theory will have its innings again is to my mind absolutely certain. One has to be "scientific" indeed to be blind and ignorant enough to suspect no such possibility.

James' prescient forecast concerning the "demon-theory" is proving true. Dr. Ralph Allison (1985), considered a pioneer in the modern treatment of MPD, says bluntly that many of his multiple personality patients have exhibited symptoms of possession. He has described his encounters with aspects of their personalities which were not true alters. He found it difficult to dismiss these bizarre occurrences as delusion. With no "logical" explanation, he has come to believe in the possibility of spirit possession. (p. 12)

Allison (1980) describes numerous cases of apparent spirit possession in MPD. He has developed a conceptual scheme which distinguishes five levels or types of possession:

1. Simple obsessive compulsive neurosis.
2. Thought forms and created beings.
3. An aspect or fragment of the mind of a living person.
4. The earthbound spirit who once lived as a human being.
5. Full demonic possession.

Dr. Allison states that he has corresponded with many professionals who have come to similar conclusions about the origin and purpose of alter personalities. (1985).

Arthur Guirdham (1982), an English psychiatrist who is also psychic, has been in practice more than 50 years and refuses to consider the possibility of MPD as a viable diagnosis. He considers the condition to be possession by one or more spirit entities. He considers psychic influence or spirit possession to be the cause of many kinds of illness, mental and physical and other conditions such as sleepwalking and addictions.

It is interesting to note that the three subjects—hypnosis, spirit possession, and multiple personality disorder—were quite prominent at the turn of the century, then faded almost simultaneously into obscurity. With the publishing of the book, *The 3 Faces of Eve*, MPD once again came into public awareness (Thigpen and Cleckley, 1957). Hypnosis was accepted by the health professions in mid-century. Treatment of spirit possession never ceased but continued quietly through the years without much publicity.

The connection between spirit possession and MPD was brought back into public and professional awareness by psychiatrist Ralph Allison (1980). Included in his book is a chapter entitled, "Possession and the Spirit World." He describes the effects of spirit interference and the process of releasing the discarnates. Though considered an expert in the field of MPD, he has been criticized by many of his colleagues for considering the spiritual approach to the clinical treatment of MPD.

Dr. Richard Kluft (1985b) has coined the term *co-presence*, meaning an alter's ability to influence the experience or behavior of another personality. This describes precisely the effect of an attached earthbound spirit on the host.

Walter Young (1987) described a case of ostensible adult onset of MPD. Duane, a veteran of World War II, began having dissociative episodes after being discharged from the navy. Duane did not drink or use drugs. He described an inner voice that had been present since the war which sometimes advised suicide.

Duane had an unhappy childhood but there were not the usual precipitating factors leading to MPD. Duane and a friend named Max joined the navy together. In a tragic episode, Duane ordered Max to stand Duane's gunnery watch. A Japanese plane strafed the area and Max was fatally wounded. Duane was with Max in the last moments and heard Max promise, "I'll never leave you." Duane felt responsible for the death of his friend.

With Duane under hypnosis, "Max" claimed to have entered Duane because Max held Duane responsible for his death. He claimed that he had a score to settle with Duane because "it wasn't my time to die." He denied the presence of any other alters. He acknowledged that he was the "voice" that Duane heard. He took control occasionally and Duane was amnesic during these periods. Max lived a hedonistic lifestyle when he was in control of Duane's body, riding motorcycles, having affairs with women, and urging Duane to leave home on repeated trips. This fits the definition of co-presence described above.

Previous psychiatric records revealed that a dissociative condition was suspected. Max revealed that the former psychiatrist knew of his presence and had attempted to "banish" him. He just went away briefly and returned after the psychiatrist was gone. This is the result of inadequate knowledge of the releasement process.

Duane left therapy with Dr. Young after three months. His anxiety increased as hypnotic sessions were pursued with the intention of exploring the war and early life experiences.

In the discussion, Dr. Young suggests several unusual aspects of the case. Adult onset of MPD is little studied, little understood and considered rare. A single alter in a case of MPD is highly unusual. His discussion attempted to explain the case in psycho-analytic terms but without concrete conclusions.

The description of the case of Duane and Max is typical of spirit attachment. There are many specific indications, including the following:

1. There was no history which would indicate the antecedents of MPD.
2. The two were friends.
3. Duane was present at the time of Max's death.
4. Duane felt guilt, Max felt blame. This is an exact fit of emotions.
5. Max promised, "I'll never leave you."
6. Max stated that he had entered Duane. This is a clear description which the therapist must accept as valid.
7. The voice urged suicide as a way of assuaging the blame and guilt and achieving peace for both. This is typical of the influence of the dark beings exacerbating the feelings of revenge. The idea of achieving peace is a manipulative deception.
8. With Max in control, Duane was amnesic of the lifestyle adopted by Max. This is a case of occasional complete takeover.
9. Max knew he was a separate being and resisted the former psychiatrist's efforts to banish him. Max was not at all confused

by the situation.

10. The situation worsened with further inadequate and inappropriate treatment. Psychiatric intervention was obviously the wrong treatment approach for the condition.

Spirit attachment, or possession, is not affected by standard medical treatment, and traditional psychotherapy simply does not apply. Psychiatric intervention, especially the use of mind-altering drugs, can exacerbate the condition. A process of releasing the attached entity is the treatment of choice and indeed the only successful method of alleviating the problem. The process is gentle, logical, methodical, systematic and grounded in sound psychotherapeutic principles.

Depossession, disobsession, minor exorcism, or spirit releasement procedures are not dangerous or frightening, once a client is aware of the reality of the situation, and the therapist harbors no fear of the subject. The condition of spirit attachment, if properly treated, can be cleared immediately. However, hypnotic suggestion can mask organically caused symptoms, behavior can be altered by post-hypnotic suggestion, and the placebo effect of any kind of treatment ritual is well known (White, Tursky and Schwartz, 1985). For these

SPIRIT RELEASEMENT THERAPY IS NOT A SUBSTITUTE FOR APPROPRIATE MEDICAL OR PSYCHOLOGICAL TREATMENT.

reasons a psychological evaluation is recommended prior to the intervention and a thorough medical examination is necessary if there are physical symptoms. This treatment cannot be considered as a substitute for appropriate medical or psychological treatment.

BACKGROUND AND HISTORY

The first written accounts of the treatment of illness were deciphered from the cuneiform texts of Assyrian tablets dating from about 2500 B.C. Eloquent incantations and prayers to the tribal gods were interspersed with direct challenges to the demons that imposed disease of every description (Ehrenwald, 1976, pp. 27-29). Through the centuries, mental illness has been attributed to spirits, animal bites, phases of the moon, humors of the body, and many diverse causes. Transformations of personality, as evidenced in trance mediumship and multiple personality disorder, have occurred throughout history. Dual or multiple personality has been recognized and described only in the last two centuries. The diagnosis of multiple personality disorder is still not widely accepted in the mental health professions.

Through the annals of human experience, people have believed that there was a non-physical existence parallel and coexistent with the physical universe. People considered this world to be filled with spirits. In this belief system, termed animism, everything was imbued with spirits, including the air, earth, water, fire, storms, lightning, earthquakes, plants, animals, the wind, and their own physical bodies. This belief held that good fortune and bad were under the influence of non-physical intelligence. The ancients believed that most sickness was caused by evil spirits (Hoyt, 1978, p. 6).

The early writings of the Chinese, Egyptians, Hebrews, and Greeks show that they generally attributed mental disorders to demons that had taken possession of an individual. Hippocrates (460-377 B.C.), the great Greek physician, has been called the "father of modern medicine." He denied the possibility of intervention of deities and demons as the cause of disease. Further, he insisted that mental disorders stemmed from natural causes and, like other diseases, required more rational treatment. He agreed with the earlier view of Pythagoras that the brain was the central organ of intellectual activity and that brain pathology led to mental disorders. Plato (429-347 B.C.) and Aristotle (384-322 B.C.) studied and wrote about mental disorders. Both considered the cause to be natural, not supernatural.

The physician Galen (130-200 A.D.) studied and described the anatomy of the nervous system. He also elaborated on the Hippocratic tradition, compiling and integrating the existing material on the descriptions of mental disorder. Among the causes of mental disorders he listed the following: injuries to the head, alcoholic excess, adolescence, fear, shock, menstrual changes, economic reverses and disappointment in love.

With Galen's death in 200 A.D., the contributions of Hippocrates and later Greek and Roman physicians were lost in a resurgence of popular superstition. There was a return of the belief in demonology as the source of illness. Not until the sixteenth century did another prominent physician, Paracelsus (1490-1541), reject demonology as the cause of abnormal behavior. He defied the medical and theological traditions of his time, for which he was hounded and persecuted until his death. Also ahead of his time was Johann Weyer (1515-1588), one of the first physicians to specialize in mental disorders. His progressive views and wide experience in the field led to his reputation as the true founder of modern psychopathology.

The attitude of scientific skepticism developed rapidly in the sixteenth century, as illustrated in the works of Reginald Scot (1538-1599). Oxford educated and the author of a book entitled *Discovery of Witchcraft*, Scot devoted his life to exposing the fallacies of demonology and witchcraft. None other than King James I of England came to the support of demonology and ordered Scot's book seized and burned. During this period, a few churchmen were also beginning to question demonology and the practices of the time. St. Vincent de Paul (1576-1660) questioned and openly challenged the belief that spirit forces were the cause of mental illness.

In the face of this ongoing dissent, demonology lost ground. Reason and the scientific method gradually led to the development of modern clinical approaches to mental illness. Even so, the belief in demonology was still widespread. In 1768, the Protestant John Wesley declared that "The giving up of witchcraft is in effect giving up of the Bible."

In 1792, Phillipe Pinel brought reform to La Bicêtre, the hospital for the insane in Paris. He was later given charge of the Saltpêtrière and established similar reforms in that institution. Concurrently, William Tuke established the "York Retreat" and ushered in the era of humane treatment of hospitalized mentally ill patients in England.

The success of these more humanitarian methods was reflected in the United States in the work of Benjamin Rush (1745-1813), the founder of American Psychiatry. Rush was associated with the Pennsylvania Hospital in 1783, and encouraged more humane treatment of the mentally ill. Still, the established beliefs of the time affected Rush. Astrology influenced his medical theory and he used bloodletting and purgatives as his principal remedies. Even so, he is considered an important transitional figure between the old era and the new.

Mental illness and demonology—the study of spirit possession—have been inseparably linked through the tortuous course of history (Coleman, Butcher, & Carlson, 1980, pp. 25-44).

MPD and SPS

In eighteenth-century Europe, the concepts of possession and exorcism were eclipsed by the rise of rational philosophical and scientific inquiry. Franz Anton Mesmer, considered by many to be the father of modern hypnosis, was instrumental in this process. Through the application of his theory of *animal magnetism*, he was able to duplicate the curing feats of the popular and successful healer-exorcist, Johann Gassner (1727-1779), thus undermining religious authority.

Gassner received his ordination into the priesthood in 1750, and carried out his ministry in a small Swiss village beginning in 1758. A few years later, he began to suffer dizziness, violent headaches and other disturbances that worsened during the celebration of Mass. He suspected interference by "the Evil One," and sought relief through the Church's exorcism and prayers. The disturbances disappeared. Gassner began to use the practice of exorcism with good results, healing all sorts of ailments. His fame spread.

Though the Church held a firm grip on the lower and middle classes, Europe at this time was swept with the new philosophy of Enlightenment. Reason was expected to prevail over ignorance and superstition. As the result of an inquiry ordered by the Prince Bishop of Regensburg, Gassner was advised to reduce his healing activity and restrict the practice of exorcism to the patients referred by their church ministers.

In Munich, the Prince-Elector Max Joseph of Bavaria also ordered an inquiry, to which he invited Dr. Mesmer. Mesmer gave demonstrations in which he elicited various symptoms from subjects, and dispelled symptoms and behaviors such as convulsions and epileptic seizures simply by a touch of his finger. He achieved success similar to that evidenced by the exorcism procedures of Gassner, without the attendant ritual and superstitious trappings.

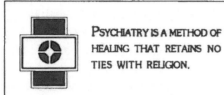

PSYCHIATRY IS A METHOD OF
HEALING THAT RETAINS NO
TIES WITH RELIGION.

The year was 1775 and the clash between these two men—Gassner, an unselfish man of great and recognized piety, and Mesmer, a son of the "Enlightenment"—represented the struggle between the forces of tradition and the principles of the new Enlightenment. This triumph of reason over tradition contributed to the rise of dynamic psychiatry, a method of healing that retained no ties with religion. In Rome, Pope Pius VI looked into Gassner's activities and decreed that the religious, ceremonial, ritualistic approach of exorcism must be performed with discretion and strict adherence to the code of the Roman Ritual.

It seems that healing is not enough. Curing the sick must be accomplished with methods that are acceptable to the community. The spiritual aspects of mental and physical illness were consequently ignored, and spiritually oriented methods of healing were swept into obscurity (Ellenberger, 1970, pp. 53-57).

Though an official committee of inquiry later discredited Mesmer, his theories form the basis of the current form of hypnosis. Today, hypnosis is the primary approach to the diagnosis and treatment of MPD.

After the time of Mesmer, occasional brief reports of multiple personality appeared in the medical literature. In 1791, German physician Eberhardt Gmelin reported a case of "exchanged personality." In 1811, Erasmus Darwin mentioned a case of a woman "possessed of two minds." Dr. Benjamin Rush described several cases in 1812. Around 1816, John Mitchell reported a case involving a young woman named Mary Reynolds. In 1840, French physician Despine published the case of successful treatment of Estelle, a young Swiss girl with dual personality. The case of Ansel Bourne, a man who experienced a total change of personality and life circumstances in the beginning months of 1887, was described by William James (1950, pp. 391-393).

The period from 1880 to 1910 was an era of great theoretical contributions to the study of dissociation. Among the foremost investigators of this era were Pierre Janet, Jean Charcot, Etienne Azam and Alfred Binet in France; Frederick W. H. Myers in England; and Morton Prince, Boris Sidis and psychologist William James in the United States (Putnam, 1989, pp. 1-4). Charles Cory of Washington University published an account of a case of alternating personality in 1919 (Crabtree, 1985, pp. 35-44).

Janet first used the term *désagrégation*, then later adopted the word *dissociation* (the translation used by William James) to describe the symptoms of hysteria. Janet proposed that a system of ideas can be split off from the major personality and exist as a subordinate personality, unconscious yet accessible through hypnosis. Too, he introduced the term *subconscious*, referring to a level of cognitive functioning that is out of normal awareness, but can occasionally become conscious. Morton Prince introduced the term *co-conscious* to indicate the result of splitting of normal consciousness into separate parts (Hilgard, 1986, p. 5).

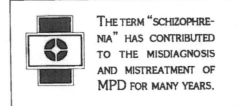

THE TERM "SCHIZOPHRENIA" HAS CONTRIBUTED TO THE MISDIAGNOSIS AND MISTREATMENT OF MPD FOR MANY YEARS.

By the end of the first decade of the twentieth century, hypnosis had fallen out of favor and popular usage, hastened by Freud's disenchantment with it. Clinicians, deprived of the use of hypnosis in diagnosing and treating MPD, reported fewer cases and interest waned. Bleuler introduced the term "schizophrenia" in 1910, replacing the older term "dementia praecox." This one act may have contributed to the misdiagnosis and consequent mistreatment of MPD for many years. It is well documented that MPD patients are still trying to escape this "schizophrenic net" (Putnam, 1986, p. 178).

Three popular books (the first two of which were made into popular movies) kindled a renewed interest in multiple personality disorder, though professional skepticism has not abated. *The Three Faces of Eve* (Thigpen & Cleckley, 1954), *Sybil* (Schreiber, 1973), and *The Minds of Billy Milligan* (Keyes, 1981) reintroduced the concept to the public. The deliberate exclusion of Dr. Schreiber's eloquent case presentation of Sybil's treatment, delivered at a professional symposium, from publication in the proceedings of that symposium indicates the prevailing attitude (Putnam, 1986, P. 179).

Because the professional journals refused articles on MPD, the modern pioneers in the treatment of the disorder began to disseminate information through workshops, courses and newsletters as the oral literature grew. The oral tradition was formalized in 1984 by Dr. Bennett Braun, who organized the first annual Conference on Multiple Personality/Dissociative States, sponsored by Rush-Presbyterian-St. Luke's Medical Center in Chicago. There is a growing literature on the causes, symptoms, diagnosis and treatment of MPD (Kluft, 1985a; Bliss, 1986; Braun, 1986; Putnam, 1989; Ross, 1989).

Early References

In a cave in southern France is found an Old Stone Age painting of the Horned God. This God represented all the unknown forces in the universe— some good, some bad (Baskin, 1974, p. 9). Demons and devils were thought of as commonplace in Babylonia and Assyria. In ancient Egypt, the exorcism was performed by a team: a physician to cure the ailment and by a priest to drive out the demon of disease (Hoyt, 1978, pp. 6-10).

In ancient Persia of the sixth century B.C., the religious leader Zoroaster founded the religion which became known as Zoroastrianism. The God of Light was named Ahura-Mazda, the master of darkness was called Ahriman. Zoroaster, who was considered the first magician, was also an exorcist who used prayer, ritual and the sprinkling of water to drive out the evil spirits (Hoyt, 1978, pp. 11-12).

Scanned images from a collection of African masks, courtesy Mike "Gwydian" Wiseman.

In India, the mother of Buddha was considered a great exorcist. King Solomon was perhaps the most noted of the Jewish exorcists (Hoyt, 1978, p 14).

Tibetan Book of the Dead

This ancient and revered tome outlines the steps of dying, the luminosity and the other states of mind which will await the spirit of those who pass permanently out of the physical body. It is a guidebook which shows the way beyond the earth plane into the Light (Fremantle and Trungpa, 1975).

The Bible

In the New Testament, fully one fourth of the healings attributed to Jesus consisted of casting out unclean spirits. He specified more than one type of spirit. The Old Testament also makes reference to interference by evil spirits.

ONE FOURTH OF THE HEALINGS ATTRIBUTED TO JESUS CONSISTED OF CASTING OUT UNCLEAN SPIRITS.

The Bible includes many references to reincarnation, although some are quite obscure and open to interpretation. The notion of the preexistence of the soul and the basic concept of reincarnation were voted out of the Christian belief system in 553 A.D. at the Second Council of Constantinople (Head & Cranston, 1977, pp. 156-160).

Middle Ages — Demonology and Mental Illness

In the period of the Middle Ages, 500 A.D. to 1500 A.D., there was a revival of the most ancient superstition and demonology, slightly modified to conform to theological demands. Treatment of mental illness was left largely to the clergy in the belief that it was caused by evil spirits. All sorts of physical pain and scourging were used to drive out the devils (Coleman, Butcher, & Carlson, 1980, pp. 30-33).

In 1484, Dominican monks Kramer and Sprenger produced the *Malleus Maleficarum*, also known as the *Witches' Hammer*. This book was used by generations of inquisitors to send thousands of women to be burned at the stake as witches in the belief they had trafficked with the Devil (Ehrenwald, 1976, p. 105).

Developed over a long period of time, the Roman Ritual continues as the model of exorcism in the Catholic Church. This concept of deliverance is based on the explicit command and example of Jesus to "cast out devils," though the Church to this day fails to differentiate between demons, the minions of Lucifer, and the earthbound spirits of deceased humans. Development of the Ritual continued through medieval times and reached its present format in the seventeenth century (Nicola, 1974, pp. 91-104; Martin, 1976, pp. 547-566).

Scanned image of 19th Century woodcut, courtesy of John E. Williamson (Cherry Tree Software)

Eighteenth Century — The Modern Era Begins

Born in Sweden, Emmanuel Swedenborg (1688-1772) was the master scientist of his time. He wrote treatises in 17 sciences, several of which he founded and developed.

He may have been the last man to have encompassed everything that was known at that time. Late in life he went on to study psychology and all that was known of the mind. He studied his dreams and developed a scheme of dream analysis that stands equal to any in use in psychology today. He delved into the inner reaches of his own mind, and found—and described—too much of the spirit world for the comfort of his contemporaries. His explorations led him far beyond the religious teaching of the day (indeed, of today as well), and he was tried as a heretic.

In his inner exploration he discovered many spirit beings, some of higher orders of intelligence, some of a much lower and more vulgar presentation. He described Heaven and Hell and discussed the way in which spirits attach to living persons. He maintained perfect contact with the world of consensus reality and showed no other signs of mental disturbance or illness.

Emmanuel Swedenborg, scanned image from a woodcut, the *Pictorial Bible*, circa 1882

He seemed able to enter the world of spirits, investigate, and return totally safe and protected. He developed considerable clairvoyance during these explorations (Van Dusen, 1974; Swedenborg, 1979).

Nineteenth Century — The Spiritualist View

Modern spiritualism began in America in 1837 in Mount Lebanon, with communications received from spirits. In 1848 two young girls, the Fox sisters, purportedly received spirit communication in the form of knocking sounds. Spiritualism is concerned with two basic premises: the continuity of personality after death and the powers of communication with the spirits of the deceased. It teaches that death works no miracle, that it is a new birth into a spiritual body (the counterpart of the physical) which is gifted with new powers. Neither punishment nor rewards are meted out. Individuality, character and memory undergo no change. Every spirit is left to discover the truth for itself. Evil passions or sinful life may chain a spirit to the earth but the road of endless progress opens up even for these as soon as they discover the Light (Fodor, 1966, pp. 360-366).

The possibility of the survival of the human personality after death has intrigued people throughout history. The SPR, the Society for Psychical Research, was established in England in 1882 to study mesmeric, psychical and spiritualistic phenomena. The early work on spiritualism was conducted with trance mediums, people who seem to have the ability to make contact with the "spirit world" in an attempt to communicate with the spirits of deceased persons. A spirit could apparently incorporate into the medium, taking temporary control or "possession," and would then speak through the medium's voice. Messages and information usually meant for a loved one left behind would come from the "dead" person. This information was often very private, usually something which could only be known by the deceased and the one receiving the message (Myers, 1904; Lodge, 1909).

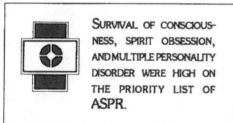

SURVIVAL OF CONSCIOUSNESS, SPIRIT OBSESSION, AND MULTIPLE PERSONALITY DISORDER WERE HIGH ON THE PRIORITY LIST OF ASPR.

Mediumship is defined as the phenomenon in which a non-physical intelligence, usually a discarnate human, assumes some degree of control of a physical body in order to communicate something useful and meaningful. Mediumship is distinguished from the phenomenon of spirit possession in that it occurs only with the deliberate cooperation of the medium and produces a constructive result. The difference is in purpose, duration and effect.

Taken at face value, the initial results seemed to be successful. However an alternative explanation exists which might also account for the apparent contact with the "dead" person. Since clairvoyance (clear seeing), clairaudience (clear hearing), and mental telepathy are all extrasensory perceptions (ESP), these might account for the alleged contact between the medium and the spirits of deceased persons. The SPR and its U.S. counterpart—the American Society for Psychical Research, formed in Boston in 1885—eventually switched their research efforts to the study of ESP (Gauld,1968, pp. 137-149).

Dr. James Hyslop (1854-1920) was professor of Logic and Ethics at Columbia University, New York, from 1889 to 1902. He authored a book on psychology in 1895, and taught the subject at Smith College when the science was in its infancy. The points of connection between psychology and parapsychology were not yet clearly drawn.

Hyslop was elected president of the American Society for Psychical Research in 1906. Explorations of the survival of consciousness, spirit obsession, and multiple personality disorder were high on the Society's priority list under his leadership (Fodor, 1966, pp. 180, 265-266).

As president of ASPR, Hyslop explored the problem of distinguishing obsession from multiple personality. He described his approach:

> I take the patient to a psychic under conditions that exclude from the psychic all normal knowledge of the situation and see what happens. If the same phenomena that occur in the patient are repeated through the medium; if I am able to establish the identity of the personalities affecting the patient; or if I can obtain indubitably supernormal information connecting the patient with the statements made through the psychic, I have reason to regard the mental phenomena observed in the patient as of external origin. In a number of cases, persons whose condition would ordinarily be described as due to hysteria, dual, or multiple personality, dementia praecox, paranoia, or some other form of mental disturbance, showed unmistakable indications of invasion by foreign and discarnate agencies (Hyslop, 1920, p. 387).

More than a theoretician, Dr. Hyslop was an experimentalist and empiricist. After he admitted the credibility of the existence of spirits, it required ten years of investigation to convince himself of the possibility of obsession by discarnate beings as a cause of mental illness. In the years that followed, he accumulated the facts that make it scientifically probable (Hyslop, 1920, p. 385). He is the true pioneer in the systematic investigation of spirit obsession and possession as a cause of mental disorder.

Dr. Carl Wickland was an avowed spiritualist. He was also an exorcist. Wickland graduated from Durham Medical College in 1900, and nine years later became chief psychiatrist at the National Psychopathic Institute in Chicago. In 1918, he moved to Los Angeles and established the National Psychological Institute where he continued the work of healing spirit obsession (Rogo, 1987, pp. 160-163). His seminal work in the treatment of spirit obsession and possession is chronicled in his two books, *Thirty Years Among The Dead* (1924) and *Gateway to Understanding* (1934).

Dr. Wickland first became interested in spirit possession after observing the frequency with which people suffered character changes after engaging in such practices as the ouija board or automatic writing. Many such people required hospitalization for apparent mental illness. Wickland consulted discarnate intelligences through his wife, Anna, who was an excellent and gifted medium. He was told that possession of the living by the "earthbound" spirits of deceased humans was the cause, and that he could alleviate the symptoms of the victims if he followed their instructions. The work was conducted with the help of a "concentration circle," a small group of people assembled to support this rescue work.

Following guidance from the discarnate intelligence, Wickland built a device called a "Wimhurst" machine that generated static electricity. The charges of static electricity from this machine were applied to the head and spine of the afflicted person with a short wand. Simultaneously, in another room, Mrs. Wickland was in trance, surrounded by the members of the concentration circle. Mediumistic ability and the trance state are like open doors to a discarnate spirit.

 HYPNOSIS LOST FAVOR IN PROFESSIONAL CIRCLES, MULTIPLE PERSONALITY DISORDER WAS NO LONGER DIAGNOSED, AND THE PROCESS OF EXORCISM AS A HEALING TECHNIQUE VIRTUALLY DISAPPEARED AMONG THE MEDICAL PRACTITIONERS AND THE CLERGY AS TWENTIETH-CENTURY MATERIALISM FLOURISHED IN AMERICA.

The entity would disengage from the patient, then incorporate into Mrs. Wickland and begin to speak. The voice would often complain about the "fire" running up the back, referring to the static electricity, and would express annoyance at the disturbance.

Dr. Wickland would initiate conversation with the discarnate personality, who would often turn out to be some identifiable deceased person. The first task was to convince the spirit that physical death had occurred and they no longer belonged in the earth plane. Many spirits are oblivious to the fact that they have died, and are extremely confused concerning their whereabouts. Most of the spirits would quickly grasp the nature of their condition, and would willingly go with the guiding spirits who came for them. The guides often turned out to be loved ones who had also died (Wickland, 1924).

Dr. Hyslop was so much impressed with the importance of this type of cure that he established a foundation in his will for the continuance of the work. The James Hyslop Institute was located in New York City, headed by Dr. Titus Bull, a graduate of New York University and Bellevue Medical College. Bull was the first to suggest that one earthbound spirit could have another earthbound spirit attached to it as the result of being a victim of obsession before its passing (Bull, 1932, p. 19). This describes the nested or layered condition of attached entities often discovered in clinical session.

Spiritualism began losing its popularity in 1888 after the public confession by the Fox sisters that they had faked the spirit rappings. Belief in spirit possession became increasingly suspect, and the decline of belief in possession paralleled the decline of interest in multiple personality disorder.

Hypnosis lost favor in professional circles, multiple personality disorder was no longer diagnosed, and the process of exorcism as a healing technique virtually disappeared among the medical practitioners and the clergy as twentieth-century materialism flourished in America.

Twentieth Century—Possession and Exorcism Today
Max Freedom Long was the man who brought "Huna," the ancient psychospiritual system of the Polynesian peoples, into a form that Westerners

could read and understand. In his several books he outlined the secrets of the Kahuna, the priest healer of the Hawaiian Islands. In the belief system of the Hawaiians, much illness—mental, emotional, and physical—was caused by the invasion and possession by spirits. The Kahuna could get rid of these "eating companions" (so called because they used the energy or food of the host) by delivering a large dose of mana, or life energy (Long, 1948, pp. 269-296; 1953, pp. 222-247).

In Japan, a messianic religion was channeled by a man named Mokichi Okada (1882-1955), respectfully and affectionately known as Meishu-sama. He revealed that a major cause of mental and physical illness and human misery was possession by intrusive spirits. If a person's spiritual body became clouded with impurities and toxins, it was easier for an evil spirit to enter (Okada, 1982, pp. 99-103).

The method of healing or dispersing the clouds of impurity is called Johrei. This is a Japanese word which means the act of purifying the spiritual body by focusing the Divine Light of God. It is prayer in action (Okada, 1982, p xvi). Spirits are forced out by the gentle focusing of this energy through the hands, held palm outward toward the receiver of the healing.

Mahikari is another method of healing and releasing attached discarnate spirits. This is based on the teachings of Yoshikazu Okada (1901-1974), also known as Sukuinushisama. The kamikumite, or student of Mahikari, channels True Light through the palms toward the forehead of the client, or to any other area of the body which is diseased. The prime focus is releasing attached spirits which are seen as the cause of most mental and physical ailments (Tebecis, 1982).

Spiritual teacher Paramahansa Yogananda identifies some ghosts as the earthbound spirits of deceased humans which he called tramp spirits. They are troubled for some reason and wander aimlessly. In some cases, they cling to living humans, causing mental and physical problems. Apparently unaware of the extent of the distressing condition of spirit attachment, he makes the statement that God would not allow this interference to be widespread, as living humans have enough problems in the physical world (Yogananda, 1975, p. 270).

Ed and Lorraine Warren have investigated cases of possession for more than 30 years. They have developed a roster of the types of entities which plague mankind, which is quite similar to that of Dr. Ralph Allison. The more ordinary earthbound spirits and haunted houses are quite easily treated.

The Warrens are Catholic and they refer the worst cases involving demonic interference to Church officials. Between 1970 and 1980 in this country, the clergy of the Catholic Church performed over 600 solemn exorcisms (Brittle, 1980, p. 200).

George Ritchie, a psychiatrist in practice in Virginia, was clinically dead for nine minutes as a result of complications of pneumonia. This occurred while he was in Army basic training. During the NDE he was conscious of being out of his body and traveling throughout the universe. Among the experiences he described was an episode in a bar. As an out-of-body discarnate being he could perceive other discarnate spirits as well as the living people who were the patrons. One drunken patron fell to the floor, either dazed or unconscious. Ritchie observed a discarnate spirit rush into his body, apparently through an alcohol-induced weakness in the aura, the protective energy field surrounding the body. He saw the same phenomenon repeated several times during his observation in this location (Ritchie, 1978).

Possession and Exorcism, the work of Traugott K. Oesterreich, first published in German, is considered the definitive volume on possession and exorcism. He suggests that possession is psychological in spite of massive evidence of inexplicable phenomena. He claims that the instance of possession diminishes in a society as the educational level rises. Even in his book, this claim is proven inaccurate. He names William James as the greatest American philosopher and psychologist and acknowledges James' enormous influence on his own thinking. But James' work with mediums provides enough valid evidence of paranormally derived information and temporary possession to shake the foundations of Oesterreich's conventional opinions. In the end of the book, these earlier opinions are in part overcome by later opinions forced upon him by the evidence (Oesterreich, 1974).

For 16 years, Wilson Van Dusen worked as a clinical psychologist at Mendocino State Hospital in California. In an attempt to better understand the mentally ill, Van Dusen sought out those patients who could distinguish between their own thoughts and the things heard and seen. He literally struck up a relationship with both the patient and the persons they saw and heard. The patients resented any reference to hallucinations. To them these voices were real beings of some other world or order of beings.

Van Dusen found consistently that the bulk of the other beings which spoke to the patients were of a lower order—vulgar, threatening, malevolent, persistent, intrusive, boastful, antireligious or nonreligious, deceptive, and not very intelligent.

In direct contrast stand the higher-order hallucinations. These made up perhaps one-fifth or less of the patients' experience. They were considerate, respectful of the freedom of the patients, and genuinely instructive. They claimed power over the lower order and showed it at times. The higher-order beings suggested that the usefulness of the lower beings was to illustrate the weaknesses and faults of the patient. Van Dusen suggests that the higher beings represent what Carl Jung called the Archetypes and the lower order most closely resembles the Id, as described by Freud.

Wilson Van Dusen found that the consistency of the hallucinations, or beings, with whom he communicated through his patients matched almost perfectly with the descriptions of the spirit world and its interaction with humans described by Emanuel Swedenborg nearly 200 years earlier. Swedenborg did not know about psychosis, yet he presented a clear picture of what would now be labeled psychotic. (Van Dusen, 1972, 1974).

Van Dusen (1974, pp. 138-139) makes the guess that the spirit world is the unconscious mind; that most mental experience is participated in by spirits who don't know they are anything other than our feelings; and that the only thing left that is really ours is the struggle to choose. If we are not choosing, then we are going the way the spiritual winds blow, and the pitiful condition of the hallucinating psychotic is just an exaggeration of everyone's situation.

Swiss psychiatrist Hans Naegeli-Osjord, in private practice since 1940, has studied cases of possession and the practice of exorcism extensively. He presents a broad philosophical discussion of the demonic as well as case studies. He also works with earthbound spirit infestation of his clients, and sees mental illness as at least occasionally partially caused by attached spirits. His book was first published in Germany in 1983. He describes his work with exorcism on the mentally ill. In his exploration of the subject, he has discovered the same types of entities which were described by Swedenborg, Van Dusen, and Wickland (Naegeli-Osjord, 1988).

In a landmark case, the application of an exorcism accomplished what was considered impossible. A young man had been under treatment by psychiatrists for several years in preparation for gender-reassignment surgery. Psychotherapy is considered ineffective in reversing the gender dysphoria, the desire for the surgery, the transsexualism. During the young man's visit to a physician who was also a Christian, an exorcism was performed and the young man's desire for the surgery and a female lifestyle disappeared completely (Barlow, Abel, and Blanchard, 1977).

Anabel Chaplin (1977) was a licensed clinical social worker in Los Angeles, California. She practiced visual imagery techniques and meditation as part of her own growth. Her vivid images seemed somehow true to life. One session in particular involved a female friend who had succumbed to a heart attack only months before. She seemed to wrap herself around a man whom Ms. Chaplin also knew. In real life, this male friend had been ill for a time with some indefinable malaise. In the internal imagery Ms. Chaplin directed the form of the deceased friend away from the man and up a stairway into a Light. Several days later Ms. Chaplin had reason to visit the gentleman and his wife, only to find out that his illness had suddenly disappeared at about the same time as Ms. Chaplin's personal visual imagery experience. She was informed that the deceased woman had been somewhat flirtatious with the man prior to her passing. Apparently, this continued after her death.

She continued to do the internal visual imagery work specifically directed toward her clients who came to her for assistance. In her book she recites numerous cases of relief of symptoms typically caused by earthbound spirit interference.

Dr. Edith Fiore (1978) authored one of the first books on past-life therapy, the clinical use of past-life recall. Past-life therapy is a quick and effective approach to many emotional and physical problems. She discovered during the course of her past-life therapy practice that the past lives described often turned out to be the experience of attached earthbound spirits and not at all pertinent to the client. Release of the attached spirits resolved the presenting problems in many cases where past-life therapy proved ineffective, especially in cases which could normally be expected to respond to past-life recall.

Fiore's second book describes the problem and treatment of spirit possession. She estimates that approximately 70% of the population is so afflicted. She is one of the first therapists to deal with the discarnate spirits directly through the voice of the person afflicted with the possession, instead of working through an intermediary, a trance medium (Fiore, 1987a).

Aloa Starr and Eugene Maurey have achieved success in the release of attached discarnates at a distance through the use of the pendulum and prayer. Maurey suggests that the remote work can be attempted on politicians and world leaders for the betterment of the world situation. Of course, the results cannot be known. This is no more an intrusion than a prayer spoken for these people. Ms. Starr requests a photograph or a signature of the afflicted person. The work is done, often without notifying the afflicted person of the time of the procedure. In some cases the afflicted person does not know anything of the procedure. The request is forwarded by concerned and loving family members. The results are often quite dramatic (Finch, 1975; Starr, 1987; Maurey, 1988).

In Brazil, remote spirit releasement is conducted routinely at the healing centers run by the Medical Spiritist Association of Sao Paulo. The work is done without charge. A doctor or a family member can send the name and address of an afflicted person. There is no welfare system in Brazil and these centers serve to fill this need for many people. Spiritual healing is performed in addition to standard health care.

The work of *disobsession*, as it is called, is conducted by a group of six mediums. Four of the people sit in a circle facing a fifth at the center. A sixth person acts as facilitator. The facilitator calls out for the spirit interfering with the

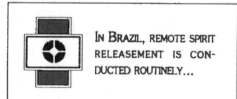

In Brazil, REMOTE SPIRIT RELEASEMENT IS CONDUCTED ROUTINELY...

identified person. That spirit incorporates, or enters into, the medium in the center of the circle. Reminiscent of the work of Mesmer, the facilitator makes magnetic passes with the hand over the person, from the head downward, about six inches to a foot from the body. The spirit is expelled and apparently guided to its appropriate destination (Villoldo and Krippner, 1986, pp. 9-25, 39-54; Rogo, 1987, 219-241).

The Theological View

The religious viewpoint holds that possessing spirits are demons and devils. There is no acknowledgment of earthbound spirits of deceased humans. *The Book of Revelations*, Chapter 12, gives us the story of Lucifer who rebelled against God, thus becoming Satan (which means adversary) and who was cast out of Heaven along with a third of the heavenly host. Satan manifests his hatred for

God, Jesus Christ, and Man (who was created in God's image) by constant attack on human beings, mostly by the fallen angels of various rank, now called demons. Jesus came into this world to destroy the works of Satan (The Bible).

SPIRITS INVADE US THROUGH CHINKS IN OUR NATURAL ARMOR CAUSED BY EMOTIONAL AND PHYSICAL TRAUMA.

Spirits invade us through chinks in our natural armor caused by emotional and physical trauma. If a person gives in to temptation and strongly indulges the carnal appetites or succumbs to the lure of occult or spiritualistic practices, he renders himself vulnerable to infestation by demonic energies (Basham, 1972, p. 127). Without the proper awareness of this condition, continuation of this lifestyle can lead to obsession by demonic influence, which is seen as quite common, and finally to full demonic possession, which some people believe to be rare (Montgomery, 1976).

Dr. Ken McAll is an English psychiatrist and was a medical missionary to China. He used the Eucharist as the vehicle of exorcism and has recorded thousands of cases of healing spirit attachments with individuals and families. He suggests that ancestors may indeed cling to the family and produce a sort of family curse (McAll 1982).

Diabolic possession or possession by the Devil itself is considered rare and is extremely dangerous both for the victim and for the exorcist (Rodewyck, 1975; Martin, 1976; Brittle, 1980, 1983).

Within this century, many people have investigated the phenomenon of spirit possession intelligently and with purpose. A few have sought an alternative approach to healing the condition. In an attempt to be acceptable to the mainstream Western, materialistic, scientifically oriented society, the Catholic Church seeks to diminish the notion of spirit possession, ignoring or denying the possibility, or referring the cases which come their way to a psychiatrist. Except in a relatively few secret instances, the Church fathers have abnegated their responsibility for the spiritual health of the people.

PSYCHOTHERAPY

There are nearly 500 different types of psychotherapy in use today. There are many theories of personality, which lead to numerous approaches to the mental and emotional problems which plague human beings. Each therapist who has developed a different therapeutic approach has perceived his clients through his own emotional filters and his own personal historical biases, both conscious and unconscious. Perhaps he has even used his own approach to pursue his personal self-healing journey.

The purpose of psychotherapy is to promote change in personal traits, attitudes, feelings and behavior. Often, the specific problems or areas of conflict reflect a more extensive pattern of behavior or recurrent tendency. J. D. Frank (1971) has outlined six factors that he sees as common to all forms of treatment:

1. An intense, emotionally charged relationship with the helping person. It is, by the nature of the interaction, emotionally charged, as the client must disclose problems, feelings, and fantasies, and this is typically painful, embarrassing and possibly threatening. The situation must be confidential, as the client must feel secure in confiding in the therapist.
2. A rationale which contains an explanation of the client's problems, and a method of treatment leading to a solution. Important here is the therapist's rational explanation of the client's situation and confidence in the beneficial outcome of the proposed treatment.
3. The provision of new information about the nature and origin of the client's problems and of ways dealing with them. This new information need not be precisely accurate, but must be coherent, logical and illuminating. The information can emerge from the client in a process of self-discovery and insight facilitated by the therapist, or can be taught in a more pedagogic way by a more authoritarian therapist.
4. Hope in the client that help is possible in the form of therapy, and expectation that the therapist is qualified to offer that help. The personal qualities of the therapist are important. If the therapist accepts the client, it indicates that he has confidence that the process will be beneficial. This optimism will usually be transmitted to the client.
5. Opportunity for the experience of success during the course of therapy. This enhances the sense of mastery and instills a growing feeling of self-confidence and capability.
6. The facilitation of emotional arousal. Psychotherapy is most unlikely to prove successful for the client without emotion. A detached, rational view of oneself is rarely followed by substantial change in the therapeutic setting.

Around the turn of the century, Freud maintained that personality congeals in early childhood and is formed, or at least influenced, by traumatic events. Although psychoanalysts disagreed with him on which events were crucial to personality formation, his colleagues unanimously asserted that hardening of the psyche occurs at a young age. Attitudes, impulses and feelings, mostly unconscious, become frozen in the personality formation. In their view, these unconscious forces continue to dictate a person's behavior through a lifetime.

Psychoanalytic theory holds that a person is passive (not consciously taking part) in childhood during the formation of personality, and that behavior is symptomatic of who this passive person is inside. According to this theory, the person is also considered to be passive in treatment, the analyst being responsible for the therapy and the cure. The level of self-responsibility is nil. The analyst delves into the patient's psyche, judges that parts of it are faulty, and attempts to alter it. Toward the end of his life, Freud became extremely pessimistic about the efficacy of psychoanalysis; patients were not being helped as much as he and his contemporaries had hoped. Many psychiatrists continue to use the methods of psychoanalysis.

The second development of psychotherapy is the interpersonal model, developed by psychoanalysts after Freud. This school of therapy argued that the patient is more than a passive being, in that his actions affect others and their reactions, in turn, influence his personality development at every stage. His behavior is more than symptomatic; it affects his own self-image indirectly through the interactions and reactions of other people. This theory was put into practice in the therapy sessions with more vigorous interaction between analyst and patient. An important principle in this model is that a patient's own acts play a part in his condition and cure. The level of self-responsibility for healing is increased.

A third generation of psychotherapy may be called "action therapy." In this school of therapy, there is no belief in the hardening of the personality, at any stage of life. Personality structure is facile and is in the process of rebuilding every day. The role of therapy is to help a person discover new choices which can assist in creating a whole new view, in effect curing himself.

The depth psychology of Carl Jung was a development and departure from Freud's original work. Analytical psychology, as it is also called, extends beyond both the ego and existential levels to include the transpersonal, or numinous dimensions of experience. Jung held that the real therapy is the approach to the numinous, and attainment of such experience will release the pathology. Depth psychology recognizes the capacity of the psyche for self-healing and self-realization, yet is mainly concerned, as was classical psychoanalysis, with the contents of consciousness, and not consciousness itself as the context of all experience (Boorstein, 1980, pp. 23-24).

Behaviorism holds that psychology is the study of observable, measurable behavior, rather than any inner mental life, and rejects any appeal to mental events or processes in the explanation of behavior. The technology of behaviorism has been shown to be effective in a limited range of overt behavioral problems. Subjective experience is ignored in this approach, as well as any notion of consciousness. Classical behaviorism therefore does not and cannot address some of the most central issues of the human condition. Strict behaviorism is being modified as cognition, self-control, and self-efficacy have been recognized and studied as a mediators of behavior. Cognitive behavior modification is becoming a recognized field (Boorstein, 1980, pp. 24-25).

Humanistic psychology addresses the ego and existential levels, aiming toward self-actualization and a balanced integration of the physical, emotional and mental aspects of life. This is the model of a healthy individual. However, it ignores the spiritual dimension. The central concepts are personal growth and human potential; humanistic psychology is strongly directed to practical ends. The object of humanistic psychology is not prediction and control but liberation from the bonds of neurotic control (Boorstein, 1980, pp. 25-26).

Another approach to psychotherapy has grown out of the philosophy of existentialism, the central concern of which is human freedom and the search for meaning and purpose in life. It is especially relevant to the sense of meaninglessness and stress-related disorders. Conscious experience is emphasized over unconscious material such as dreams and buried childhood memories. The client is encouraged and supported in making choices for the future (which may bring anxiety) over choices for the past (which may bring guilt over missed opportunities). The aims of therapy are to increase overall hardiness, which strengthens coping skills, and to encourage future-oriented choices, which lead to growth and an expanding and deepening sense of life's meaningfulness. Emphasis is on the raw experience of being-in-the-world, ego strengthening, and coping in the dualistic level of experience (Boorstein, 1980, p. 26).

Transpersonal psychology has emerged as the fourth force of Western psychology after psychoanalysis, behaviorism, and humanistic psychology. This model draws on both Eastern wisdom and Western science by exploring optimum psychological health and well-being, and emphasizing consciousness as the central focus.

Transpersonal psychotherapy utilizes traditional modalities when appropriate, and differs from earlier approaches to therapy in scope and context rather than in method or technique. Going beyond the false limitations and bounds of earlier schools, the transpersonal work includes peak experiences, self-realization, altered states of consciousness, and consciousness-altering techniques such as meditation and visualization. Many of these altered states of consciousness are considered to be psychotic or at least abnormal and pathological in the first three schools of psychotherapy

In the transpersonal model, the four major dimensions are consciousness, conditioning, personality, and identification. Consciousness is held as the basis of being, the context for all human experience. Mental and emotional content—that is, past and present experience and trauma and its sequela—are held within consciousness; content and process are part of the contents of the consciousness, not consciousness itself. Normal consciousness is considered to be a contracted and reduced state of awareness, perceptually distorted by a continuous blending of inputs, conscious and unconscious, of reality and fantasy conforming with our needs and defenses.

The "normal" person is conditioned to the consensus reality, and tends to be "attached" to the things of this reality. Eastern thought proposes that the stronger this attachment to objects, the more we are possessed, or controlled by them. Desire and attachment are closely linked: Unfulfillment of desire will result in pain and suffering; letting go of attachment is necessary for its cessation. This does not imply the necessity of a life of poverty; abundance is everyone's birthright. A person can own something without being identified with it or attached to it.

The classic example is the man of small stature who purchases a very big automobile to make himself feel larger and more important. If something happens to the automobile, he takes it personally and feels diminished. Perhaps there is a degree of male arrogance and macho attitude connected with the ownership of a shiny, fast sports car. Many such cars are equipped with burglar alarms. The owners spend much energy worrying about the stereo being pilfered or the car being damaged or stolen. This emotional energy directed at the car is an example of the attachment described above.

Personality is seen as central in the model of other schools of psychology. Transpersonal psychology, however, considers the personality as only one aspect of being—an aspect, furthermore, with which a person may choose to identify or not. Health may derive from disidentifying with personality rather than therapeutically modifying it.

As participants in the consensus reality, people identify with many institutions, philosophies and personal objects, and become so enmeshed in these identifications that they are blind to the conditioned tyranny. People identify with being a man or a woman, Democrat or Republican, American, anti-communist, or any one or several of countless other roles in society. On a more personal level, a person might "feel afraid." The identification with emotional content shifts this feeling state to a being state: "I *am* afraid." As a result, a whole series of fearful thoughts is likely to arise. The resulting identification intensifies fear into terror. If such a thought is seen for what it is—as just another thought, as emotional content—then it exerts little effect on the person holding the thought. "I have fear" has less effect on a person than "I am fearful." This is one step toward disidentification.

The goals of transpersonal psychotherapy include symptom relief and behavior change. This model does not exclude the obvious and successful application of more traditional approaches to psychotherapy and the psychodynamic processes. The transpersonal therapist assists the client in disidentifying from these same issues. With this disidentification comes the experience of a larger context. "I am not my anger (fear, sadness, guilt). I *have* angry (fearful, sad, guilty) feelings." Moving to another level in context, the client experiences, "There are feelings of (anger, fear, sadness, guilt)."

In addition, the work is directed to the transpersonal dimensions beyond the dualism of ego functioning in this world. This involves expanding one's awareness of the conceptual framework of transpersonal experience, exploring the existence and potential of altered states of consciousness, learning the importance of assuming the responsibility for one's behavior, and being the source of one's own experience. (Boorstein, 1980, pp. 12-21).

Stanislav Grof, a psychiatrist, performed the first clinical testing of the drug LSD in his native land of Czechoslovakia. After analyzing more than 2,000 controlled LSD sessions, Grof found that the drug did not produce the same result with everyone who ingested it. There was no universal effect of chemical action in the areas studied. Perceptual, emotional ideational and physical phenomena were sensitive to external factors, such as the therapeutic relationship and the setting.

Many of the typical LSD experiences were indistinguishable from phenomena produced by various spiritual practices, hypnosis, sensory deprivation, and other non-drug techniques. He found that administering LSD allowed the deeper levels of the unconscious processes to emerge into the conscious level of mind, where they could be experienced by the client and studied or treated by the therapist.

The various experiences under LSD were recognizably distinct and could be meaningfully categorized. The first level involved perceptual changes. Visual changes included brightness of color and perception of geometric shapes surrounding objects. Sensory stimuli produced responses in inappropriate sensory areas, such as tasting sounds or hearing colors. Such synesthesia and visual changes were probably chemically induced and had no psychodynamic importance.

Memories of childhood and even infancy emerged, as well as other important memories, emotional problems, and unresolved conflicts from various life periods of the individual. In some cases these episodes actually involved reliving of traumatic or positive memories of actual events, while others seemed to be "screen memories" (real memories that block out some related painful memory, fantasy, or combinations of both). Grof suggested that the psychodynamic experiences in the LSD sessions could stand as laboratory proof of the basic premises of psychoanalysis.

The next level of the LSD experience involved the peri-natal memories and included the pre-natal intrauterine existence of the individual before the onset of delivery. Grof refers to this level of the unconscious as Rankian, after Otto Rank, a contemporary of Freud who emphasized the paramount significance of peri-natal experience.

Grof divides the pre- and peri-natal experience into four segments: Basic Peri-natal Matrix, (or BPM) I, II, III and IV. BPM I constitutes the intrauterine existence described as the primal union with mother. BPM II relates to the period of intrauterine contractions. BPM III is related to the second stage of delivery: propulsion through the birth canal. BPM IV is related to the final delivery and dissection of the cord. Grof noted that these segments of the pre- and peri-natal experience are related to certain categories of psychiatric disorder (Grof, 1985, p. 103).

Beyond the peri-natal, Grof's subjects reported experiences involving extension of the time element: fetal and embryonic memories, ancestral memories, human and animal (phylogenetic), and past incarnation memories. Transcending the ego there were experiences of identification with other individuals, groups of people, animals, plants, and planetary consciousness. ESP experiences were also described.

Transpersonal experiences which seem to go beyond generally accepted "objective reality" include: archetypal experiences, encounters with suprahuman entities, deities, demons, and spiritistic and mediumistic phenomena—that is, spirit possession experiences. Grof refers to this level of consciousness as the Jungian stage. Rare occurrences of chakra activation and Kundalini arousal were reported. The ultimate of this experience appears to be the Supracosmic and Metacosmic Void, the primordial emptiness, which is conscious of itself and which contains all existence in germinal form (Grof, 1985, p. 131).

Grof coined the term "COEX system", which stands for *systems of condensed experience*. He describes the COEX as a dynamic constellation of memories which can include fantasy material from several different periods of an individual's present life or past incarnation, with the common denominator of a strong emotional charge, an intense physical sensation, or other important element. He found in his work with clients that these COEX systems are dynamically connected with some facet of the birth experience (Grof, 1985, p. 97). The concept of the COEX is the experiential basis of the bridge inductions in the section Non-hypnotic Inductions (101).

After the drug LSD became illegal, Grof searched for another method of uncovering the same levels of the unconscious mind that were available with the drug. He developed Holotropic Therapy ™, which utilizes deep breathwork and music to alter the consciousness, allowing access to the deeper levels of unconscious mind. In this process a person can uncover biographical data, pre- and peri-natal experience, recall past-life memories, uncover attached entities, and reach the transpersonal experiences.

As Grof discovered, initially the drug did not create the experiences; it simply allowed access to the deeper levels of the mind in a chemically altered state of consciousness. The term "hallucinogen" is not an accurate description of the drug. The memory and the experience is not created by the drug, but has always been present in the mind.

Something important has been left out of contemporary Western psychology and psychotherapy: the transpersonal, or spiritual, dimension of the mind. Some mechanism of repeated embodiment or reincarnation may actually exist. The concept of spirit interference, spirit attachment, or spirit possession may be more than a metaphor which elicits fear in many people and remains veiled in superstition; it may be a very real part of the human condition. The techniques outlined in this manual can be used in clinical situations by anyone willing to accept the premise, even tentatively, and to learn the methods. The modality must be considered a valid approach to a real condition and must not be considered as ritualistic machinations of a deluded or credulous therapist.

From this viewpoint, the entire process takes on a new meaning. It becomes a very necessary part of the training of the therapist dealing with the full spectrum of the human condition. If a discarnate spirit is present and causing a problem, traditional therapy will not change the condition of the client. Spirit Releasement Therapy is the clear, systematically organized, methodical, and consistent process which can and will correct the condition. Success of the approach does not depend on any charisma, intuition, or special gifts of the therapist. It is truly a holistic psychotherapy.

RATIONALE OF REGRESSION THERAPY

People do not live in the past or the future. There is memory of the past and expectation for the future, but the present moment is the only place there is, "the only game in town." The ever-present moment of NOW is all there is. Physical bodies are living in this moment with the present level of chronological age and physical health, the present level of form and function, intestinal content, heart rate, and other physiological states.

Healing in the present moment involves resolving the unfinished business of the past which continues to influence a person in the present moment. It is the residual mental, emotional, physical and spiritual energy of past events which contaminates the present experience. The resolution or removal of these burdensome energies is the goal of any healing approach. As a result, a person can live more fully in the present and fulfill more completely the details of the lifeplan that was arranged prior to the present incarnation.

The five senses perceive the nearby environment and any stimuli present in the moment. The subconscious records all these impressions in keeping with the mind's perceptions and interpretations of these impressions, as it evaluates them for any real or imagined threat to survival. The mind's evaluations are compared with past history of similar circumstances in order to make a judgment regarding present safety and to determine whether any action must be taken. Thus, a present action is often a reaction to an earlier similar circumstance.

This constant perception, interpretation, comparison, judgment, and reaction is going on just below conscious awareness. The mind is always on the lookout. This also means that the past is always present, which is another way of saying that the past is always interfering with the present.

If one examines the physical body, one notices scars—healed places where damage was sustained during some past event. The tissue is distorted and changed somewhat by the trauma and function may be impaired, though there is no longer pain.

The mind also sustains trauma, and there are distortions, changes and scars. The scars of the mind show up as attitudes, behaviors, defenses, phobias, and reactions of anger, fear, and distrust. In short, many of the manifestations of personality are due to the scars of the mind. Psychotherapy attempts to deal with the scars of the mind, though it is often ineffectual because the context is limited to the present lifetime.

The traumatic episode which scars the mind is often deeply buried in the memory, long since forgotten by the conscious mind. This buried material is inaccessible in traditional talk therapy, which is little more than an intellectual discussion of consciously remembered events. Many people have no memory of anything prior to age five or six, while others cannot recall their life before the age of twelve or fourteen.

There is a wealth of buried experience in the memories of those years. What child hasn't felt abused and mistreated, in spite of the best intentions of well-meaning parents? Even before the child learns to speak, there are real or imagined slights or punishments which embedded in the mind without language. This unlanguaged trauma is irretrievable without the use of specific techniques.

Freud and other pioneers in the field of psychology and psychiatry considered the birth experience to be the primary source of anxieties and neuroses in adult life. This has proven both accurate and incomplete. One of Freud's basic tenets was the therapeutic goal of bringing the unconscious into the conscious. Reliving is relieving, recalling a traumatic episode is the first step in healing the pain. He developed several techniques, such as word association and dream analysis, in the attempt to unlock the subconscious mind and locate the cause of emotional problems. Modern hypnotherapy allows access to the deeper levels of the mind—the body mind, conscious, preconscious, subconscious, personal unconscious, transpersonal unconscious, collective unconscious, and the universal unconscious. If Freud had been more proficient in hypnosis, past-life therapy might have been developed a half-century earlier.

Edith Fiore (1978) used hypnoanalysis with some of her clients to help locate the source of their presenting problems. Under hypnosis, the subconscious mind will respond to the suggestions or commands of the therapist. Several people reported events in prior lifetimes as the source of present-life emotional and physical conditions. Fiore did not believe in reincarnation but, as a good therapist, she urged the clients to describe whatever emerged in their exploration. The therapeutic results were so positive that she continued to develop the past-life techniques. With more than 40,000 regressions behind her, she is certainly the doyen of past-life therapy.

Irene Hickman (1983) used non-directive hypnosis for more than 30 years with her patients. Her instruction under hypnosis was to locate a past incident which caused or contributed to the present problem. The result often turned out to be the client's reliving of an incident from a prior incarnation, which would lead to greater self-understanding.

Morris Netherton (1978) directed the client to focus on the sensations in the physical body to uncover the origin of the presenting problem. The somatic bridge past-life induction is described in the section "Non-hypnotic Inductions" (101). The body and mind cannot be separated. For every physical problem there is an emotional component. For every emotional upset there is a physical manifestation. Nearly always, the problem has its roots in a traumatic event in a prior incarnation. The trauma is reactivated during the birth or pre-natal experience and carried forth to manifest sometime during this lifetime. This is what finally motivates a person to seek therapy.

The affect bridge developed by Watkins (1971) was intended to uncover forgotten traumatic events in the present lifetime. The technique is especially effective in eliciting memories of past-life trauma, which can lead to resolution of present life conflicts and problems. The affect bridge is described in the section "Non-hypnotic Inductions" (101).

In trance, Edgar Cayce counseled that scars must be removed from the mental and spiritual self (Woodward, 1985). Many cases of physical disease, disfigurement and accident stem from karmic balancing or perpetuating of the results of traumatic events in prior lives (Netherton, 1978; Woolger, 1987).

The traumatic memories and damaged bodies represent more than scars of the mind or body from events of the present life; they are often scars of the soul as well. The subconscious mind seems to retain the memory of everything that has ever been experienced by the being. This includes the present lifetime, prior lifetimes, potential future lifetimes, the non-physical realms between incarnations, and the entire track of awareness back to and including the experience of separating from Source.

The purpose of regression therapy is to heal the scars of the soul. Nothing is left out, no human experience is denied; the aim is uncovering the truth. No amount of narrowly defined professional training, no restrictive religious training, no arbitrary limits of any kind can be allowed to interfere with the exploration of the spiritual reality. The therapist is the guide across this vastness, the client the trusting companion. Together they seek the truth of any given situation, of the presenting problem, which is found only in the inner wisdom and memory banks of the client. Each session is a spiritual odyssey. The destination is clear, but the path is unknown and unpredictable.

THE CLINICAL FRAMEWORK

The spiritual reality is the clinical framework, the context of regression therapy, from the beginning of creation by Source to the eventual rejoining of all the manifestations of God, Goddess, All That Is in the Oneness, the At-one-ment, the Atonement. This includes the reincarnation cycle and the condition of spirit possession, as described above. This reality includes every vibrational level of physical, mental, emotional and physical manifestation of consciousness.

Some variation of the Big Bang theory may account for the physical universe. Scientists speculate that all the physical particles in the expanding universe originally exploded outward from a small, extremely dense, very hot mass.

Perhaps there is a spiritual equivalent of the Big Bang, parallel in some way to the Big Bang of the universe. The memory of separation from Source as an individual spark of God consciousness is easily accessed in the altered state of consciousness.

The therapist works with the client's subconscious material, whatever form it takes. This may include personal metaphors, dream symbolism, or characters from the movies. The setting may appear to be a past era on earth, in a forest or jungle as an animal, an extraterrestrial space being on a spacecraft or on another planet, or non-physical intelligence in the spirit realm, usually of a much higher consciousness level than human.

The Clinical Framework

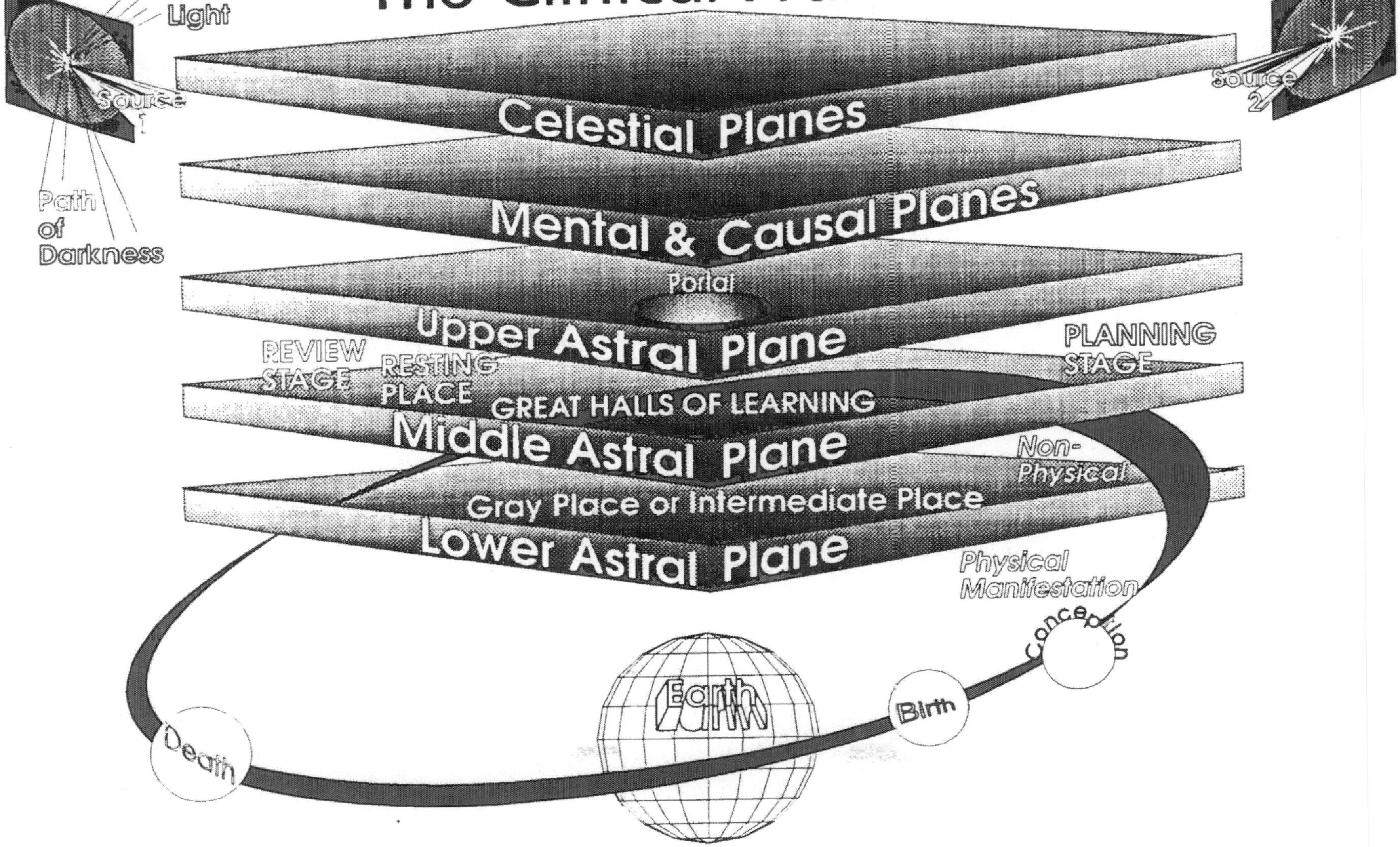

Saucers Over Yosemite

From an original scan, *Saucers Over Yosemite*, by Riverview Memorial Artery

Apparently, there are other planets in other star systems in other galaxies as well as this one which support intelligent life. Past-life memories occasionally take place on these other islands in space. The various physical forms resemble humanoid, lizard, dolphin and other shapes. The intelligence level is often much higher than that of human beings. Some life forms are less dense than human physical bodies. Some seem to be pure intelligent energy from higher dimensions, higher planes of existence. Mental and Causal plane beings can intrude on this reality. Their nature is virtually unknown.

It seems that only a small percentage of God-created sparks choose life on the planet earth. But those who do must come through the portal into this particular system in order to fully engage in the process of human life, the wheel of reincarnation.

Many of the beings from other planets, dimensions, even universes choose to bypass the portal and attempt to latch onto someone else's body. Extraterrestrial beings are occasionally found as attached entities who join humans for various reasons. Regardless of intention, this is not appropriate.

They have other choices available: They can return to their own Light, which may be blue or green or some other color; they can move into the golden white Light of this planet's recycling process and from there come into the earth plane as human in a future time.

When Extraterrestrial beings are associated with a nearby spacecraft, the Commander can usually be called in to speak through the client. In most cases the one in authority will honor the request to withdraw their crew members, exploration teams, and scientific observers or technicians.

Fiore (1989) writes of her clinical sessions with UFO abductees. Under hypnosis, many of these people recalled the experience of being taken aboard alien spacecraft. Several investigators have attempted to document this phenomenon, which is increasing in frequency.

According to the *Book of Revelations* (Chap. 12) in the Bible, Archangel Lucifer and his followers, one-third of the stars of heaven, one-third of the heavenly host, were cast out of heaven by Archangel Michael. Lucifer was cast into the earth and became the prince of the earth. Whether this is reality, myth, or metaphor does not matter in the

THE PARADIGM, THE CLINI-CAL FRAMEWORK OF RE-GRESSION THERAPY IS THE TOTALITY OF CONSCIOUS-NESS.

clinical session. Many clients experience the dark-energy beings, and the descriptions are nearly identical. The effects of the dark-energy infiltration are predictable and the release is usually straightforward. The process is described in the sections on "The Demonic" (272).

Light beings of very high vibration and intelligence also exist, and they are often present during a session. The client will become aware of a pervading loving energy. People with clairvoyant sight can also discern these beautiful beings.

The Akashic Record is the name given to the total account of every thought, intention, motive, behavior, action, and deed of every being here on the planet. This record is available to clients in altered state. It may look like a library, a cave with scrolls packed in rows, a huge book open to the person's own record or some other metaphoric image.

The therapist must work with whatever material emerges, whatever memories and images are presented by the client. The map is not the territory; the description is not the experience. The words describing the event, memory or experience are but inadequate symbols of the feelings and perceptions of a real or imagined experience which had impact on the client. It is the impact which is being uncovered. The residues of that impact are the focus of healing.

The therapist is the facilitator of the process and must participate fully with the material and images described by the client. As the client perceives the therapist as safe and accepting in the face of disclosing such improbable information, deeper subconscious material will surface for processing.

The paradigm, the clinical framework of regression therapy, is the totality of consciousness. This encompasses the entire range of spiritual existence, physical and non-physical. Any approach to therapy is a set of logical constructs, consisting of a reasonable cosmology or model of reality, a model of personality, and an explicit set of guidelines and rules of conduct to assist the therapist and client in achieving the desired therapeutic goals. In this work, the therapist comes from a place of unconditional and nonjudgmental love, holding to the notion of God as Source of all and everything and the final destination for all created beings. The therapist must be prepared for anything in session. It will surely come.

THE THERAPIST

There are a few extra qualifications required by the therapist who chooses to use these modalities. Beyond the established professional standards of propriety, integrity, confidentiality, and personal and professional boundaries, the practitioner must be an unbiased observer and witness of the process as it unfolds in session. The foundation of all such sessions is the awareness that it is a privilege to be allowed into the inner mind of the client. The work must be done with the highest integrity, and with the knowledge that these spaces are sacred.

Hypnosis has been slow to gain acceptance in the professional ranks. Many therapists fear the concept for some reason, and sometimes feel a loss of control when they participate in practice sessions in a training class. Some therapists are so intimidated by the prospect of a client in the altered state that they avoid the process entirely.

It is necessary that any person who utilizes these techniques be comfortable with the altered state of consciousness in their clients and in themselves. The facilitator of past-life, birth regression and spirit releasement sessions also shifts into a level of altered consciousness. Competence through study and training in the techniques of both hypnosis and hypnotherapy is a natural prerequisite to this work.

The therapist is the guide in resolution of the issues, conflicts and traumatic events which are recalled. The client is the leader in the session and provides the information, the setting, the characters and the plot of the stories. Whether they are past lives, psychodrama, active imagination, or pure fabrication is not important. The narrative emanates from the client and must be accepted as real. The most important part of the material is not the actual detail of the encounters but the mental, emotional and physical residues which remain. It is not what happens to a person, it is how they feel emotionally about what happens to them, what decisions and judgments they make as a result, and the physical scars and memories of pain that constitute the residue, the problem, conflict, the areas of discomfort in the present life.

If the client comes out of the altered state while reexperiencing a traumatic memory, the therapist urges the client to go back in and resume the experience. If the client refuses, as is their right, the therapist must not force the issue but attempt to guide the client to some resolution of the emotional upset in present-time consciousness.

Whatever situation emerges in a session, the therapist must carry it through to conclusion and resolution. Rape, murder, wanton killing or any other form of violence in past events must be considered part of the client's drama; the therapist must stay in the process and maintain his or her role. If there is a reaction to any part of the emerging narrative or to the violence being perpetrated, the therapist must note it as something he must resolve for himself at a later time in his own therapy.

In her past-life therapy training class, Dr. Fiore tells of one female client in a session who began to vomit in reaction to the emerging past-life events. Dr. Fiore reacted so strongly, feeling like she also was going to vomit, that she brought the client out of hypnosis. The woman would never again explore that past-life scene. The potential for resolution and healing of the particular issue was lost. Dr. Fiore acknowledges this as a therapeutic error and urges her students to avoid the same error.

It is not for the therapist to deny or qualify any experience which emerges. It must be accepted exactly as expressed by the client. This work will stretch the belief structures and alter the perceptions of reality for most people, client and therapist alike. Without judgment, censorship, or editing of any sort, the therapist must guide the client in finding the truth of any recalled event or expressed feelings. Interpretation has no place in this work.

As in any therapeutic orientation, the therapist needs to experience the work personally in birth regression, past-life therapy and spirit releasement therapy in order to gain an appreciation of what a client is feeling. A study of metaphysics and the spiritual reality is a mandatory prerequisite. The therapist must have some basic working knowledge of the concepts which emerge in altered state session.

Many therapists attempt to conduct past-life therapy and spirit releasement therapy after hearing a lecture or a tape on the subject. This is not sufficient preparation and is potentially damaging for the trusting client. There are basic differences between the contexts of traditional and transpersonal approaches to mental health. There are specific techniques in the modalities presented here which have no analogous form or method in any traditional approach to treatment.

After being introduced to the subject by listening to a tape, some people have found themselves in situations which call for a spirit releasement. This may come as an unwelcome surprise.

A school teacher from Northern California reported that after she listened to a tape on spirit releasement, she proceeded to describe it to a male friend of hers who was a therapist. As she spoke, he doubled over with stomach cramps. Using only the methods briefly described on the tape, she managed to release an attached discarnate entity from him.

A female therapist was conducting a group therapy session. One of the women in the group was also a therapist. As the group therapy leader played a tape on the subject of spirit releasement therapy for her group, the woman complained, criticized, repudiated the information, and denied the validity of the concept. At home later that evening her visiting six-year-old nephew began exhibiting signs and symptoms she had heard described on the tape. Using the basic method demonstrated on the tape, she proceeded to release the attached spirit of her own deceased father from the boy.

The ground of being of the therapist in this work is nonjudgmental and unconditional love. The therapist comes from this place when conducting a session. There is speculation, as so many healers attest, that the healing energy comes from a higher source, and that the healer is only the conduit. So too in past-life and spirit releasement therapies. The therapist may feel baffled by the narrative of the client, and be hesitant to continue, not knowing what questions to pose. If the therapist will stop trying so hard, remain quiet for a few moments and give inspiration a chance, the next question may pop into mind. This is a matter of trust for the therapist.

There can be no trepidation on the therapist's part. For most people, the

THE GROUND FOR THE THERAPIST IN THIS WORK MUST BE NONJUDGMENTAL AND UNCONDITIONAL LOVE.

fear associated with spirit possession is part of the old mental programming instilled by various religions. Movies such as *"The Exorcist"* add to this conditioning and most certainly interfere with the work. Interference by demonic entities is quite prevalent and they can exploit the therapist's fear by causing the client to make intimidating verbal threats or produce growling and hissing sounds.

Faced with the spiritual nature of this work, many people ask about self-protection, especially in the area of spirit releasement and treatment of the demonic. The first line of defense is awareness and understanding. The greater the understanding of these subjects, the less fear and superstition cloud the intelligence. Boundaries are critical. This refers to the normal personal boundaries maintained in any clinical situation, and extends to include any intrusion by discarnates at any time. In many cases an entity will defend its position as an attached spirit by claiming that the host did not say "No" when it first approached. The person did not refuse the entity permission to join.

Tacit permission is given by the act of consuming alcohol or the use of mind-altering drugs for recreation purposes. Occult explorations with the Ouija board, channelling, out-of-the-body experience, or anything similar without the invocation of the Light leaves the door wide open to intrusion by discarnates. Repeated use of the Sealing Light Meditation (361) is recommended to establish and strengthen the invisible mantle of protection. There is great power and protection in invoking the name of Jesus Christ. For those persons who prefer not to use this name, the word Light may be substituted.

A psychotherapist who is well trained in a traditional approach must come to this work with an open mind and a willingness to begin anew. The past training and clinical expertise may establish the proper chairside manner and professional healing attitude, yet the spiritual nature of the uncovered material and the clinical framework flies in the face of traditional psychological theory.

Scanned reproduction of an original woodcut, *"Jacob Wrestles With The Angel,"* (*Genesis 32:24*) from the *Pictorial Bible*, circa 1882

The information which comes either in session with a client or through the therapist's own explorations in the altered state may undermine and destabilize one's perception of reality. Things in this world are not as they seem. Psychic events and so-called paranormal phenomena cannot be explained by nor contained within the materialistic, mechanistic, deterministic, reductionistic Newtonian-Cartesian paradigm of reality. Many people would rather ignore and deny the more expansive reality which challenges the old paradigm, the greater reality within which there is no such thing as paranormal, than to continue to explore the new ground of consciousness.

The therapist must not place the comfort zone of the personal ego before the value of this non-traditional approach. There is no place for denial, rationalization, interpretation or criticism of the images and experiences presented by the client in altered states of consciousness. This material must be honored and accepted just as it comes.

Transpersonal psychology attempts to include those experiences which transcend the usual, normal, safe, and traditional parameters of psychological manifestation. Yet the practitioners of transpersonal psychotherapy and the leaders of the associations which profess transpersonal orientation have ignored any hint of spirit possession and only timidly allow the mention of past-life therapy. Perhaps they have a subconscious need to cling to the illusion of the stability of mainstream thinking, which is stronger than the conscious mind's desire to search the largely uncharted waters of the human unconscious.

This approach to therapy and healing has no limits. The therapist may encounter through the client any of the experiences described by Dr. Stan Grof (1976), who assisted subjects in exploring the farthest reaches of the mind, first with the use of LSD, later through Holotropic Breathwork™, an altered-state experience generated by deep connected breathing.

After attending the Spirit Releasement Therapy Intensive Training, several psychologists have commented that they did not expect to be using the techniques in their practice. At most, they conceded, some new client might request the work. After a few weeks, though, these therapists reported that not only had they used the techniques on new clients, but they had suddenly found some of their regular clients showing signs of spirit attachment. It was as if the clients and entities were waiting for the therapists to learn the techniques.

Old maps of the known world depicted the edge of the waters, beyond which there was nothing but fear and superstition. The inscription on the maps warned, "Beyond here there be dragons." There have been explora-

... THERAPISTS REPORT THAT NOT ONLY HAD THEY USED THE TECHNIQUES ON NEW CLIENTS, BUT THEY HAD FOUND SOME OF THEIR REGULAR CLIENTS SHOWING SIGNS OF SPIRIT ATTACHMENT.

tions beyond the old edge of the world, and into the depths of the human mind, and perhaps some dragons have been discovered and vanquished. Yet fear is the greatest malady and it has yet to be conquered.

The Client

These techniques are most effectively used with reasonably normal people with average and typical problems. They must have the willingness to fully engage in the exploration process and the ability to let go and shift into the altered state of consciousness and report honestly any experience which emerges. The work proceeds smoothly when the client can quickly and easily describe any impressions, images, feelings, impulses, and physical sensations which are stimulated by the therapeutic questioning.

The client must allow other voices to come through the voice mechanism. The other voice may be their own as an embryo or infant, the consciousness of a part of their own body, one of their own subpersonalities, an earthbound discarnate entity, either lost and wandering or attached to the client, a past life personality, another living person, a fragment of the mind of another person, living or deceased, which has attached to the client, a discarnate teacher or master, a guide or the person's own high self.

The client must be able to communicate effectively, converse meaningfully with the therapist, and maintain attention to the process in order to gain most from a session. There must be, at least during the session, a tentative acceptance of the modalities and the underlying philosophy of the clinical framework. Skepticism, criticism, disdain or fear regarding the concepts of reincarnation and spirit possession will interfere with full participation in the process.

The subconscious memories, the so-called right-brain material, will not be accessed through any logical left-brain discussion or reasoned understanding of how and why things happened the way they did. Intellectual explanation or description of the story of some remembered incident will not elicit the emotions associated with the incident. Without uncovering the emotions surrounding a traumatic event, the healing potential of the approach outlined in the manual has little chance of being effectively realized.

For new clients, the best recommendation is a referral from a person who has benefited from such sessions. A person who participates in a session because of the insistence of another person will most likely resent the effort and resist the process. The client must personally desire this kind of treatment and actively seek out a therapist qualified in these methods.

Many good-hearted and well-meaning people attempt to be helpful when they insist on bringing another person to a session. These are the "helpers," the "fixers," often trying to "fix" someone who does not want to be "fixed" in any way. A person who is despondent, unwilling to help him or her self and claims there is nothing to live for is a poor candidate for this approach to therapy. The will to live is necessary for healing to occur (Hutschnecker, 1977). Remote spirit releasement might be a possibility to consider in such a case. This approach is described in the section Remote Releasement (362)

Many people schedule a session without a hint of a goal or an agenda. They profess not to know why they are in the session, only that they have to do it. For these clients, the preferred induction is the Sealing Light Meditation (361). In the space of the surrounding light, they are urged to describe the first thing that comes into their awareness. It may be a deeper or higher aspect of their consciousness which prompts them to schedule a session and it is that aspect which directs the exploration of the session. Occasionally, an attached entity who wants to be released is what prompts the person to schedule an appointment.

The client leads and directs the session with the emerging presentation, and the therapist takes cues and clues from the client's narrative, emotions and body postures in order to guide the session productively to conclusion and resolution.

Some people pause for several minutes before offering a response to almost every processing question. The easy flow of the session is thus interrupted, and valuable time is lost. The therapist can only maintain attention and wait patiently for the replies before going on. In some cases, a long pause might occur in a session which has been moving quickly. The therapist observes the facial expressions and body postures for activity. A great deal of experience may be going on within the mind without any verbal expression, and this often shows in the facial movements. The therapist does not interrupt this inner process. The client will usually resume the description and explanation when ready.

If the obvious facial movement or body posturing ceases and the client does not resume speaking, the therapist can gently ask:

T: "What just happened?"

This might preclude a gentle slide into sleep after the client has silently relived some emotional episode.

A client who is taking prescription medication which dulls the consciousness will not be able to access subconscious material very effectively. Coffee and alcohol or other mind-altering drugs definitely interfere with the process.

The client must be in touch with reality. A person with delusional thinking may not be able to separate reality, physical or non-physical, from active delusions. These therapies are reality based and goal directed toward resolution of traumatic events of the past. Delusions are distinctly different from faulty memories or misinterpretations of traumatic episodes. Delusions, hallucinations and some dreams often have no basis in reality, no relation to a person's behavior and attitudes.

Delusions can be associated with many conditions, including the schizophrenias, paranoia, drug abuse and flashbacks, and some somatic disorders. The person with delusional thinking is not a good candidate for these therapeutic approaches.

The work is not intended for use with the seriously mentally disturbed. The client must be able to communicate, understand and cooperate. Historically, some cases of incorrectly diagnosed mental illness have been successfully treated with remote releasement, conducted through an intermediary person acting as a medium. Remote releasement may also be helpful for the unborn, infants, young children, adolescents, and anyone with attention deficit disorders.

A person who is unable or unwilling to communicate, such as a young child, a rebellious teenager, an alcoholic, a drug abuser, a mentally disturbed person, or someone who is hospitalized, comatose, incarcerated or otherwise unavailable may be helped through remote releasement. Another person can act as the intermediary, the medium, the conduit through which the entity can be contacted. Remote spirit releasement is the classic method of depossession, and is very effective, although it has its limitations and disadvantages.

Following a session, the client may experience a range of emotions, from elation and excitement to sadness and grief, as if a loved one has been lost. Release of the spirit of a loved one is truly a separation and may be experienced as loss. These emotions must be allowed to surface and must be accepted as appropriate after the probing of the deep subconscious memories. A period of introspection is encouraged; a period of quiet time alone without disturbance from the everyday world.

The process of healing continues after the conclusion of the session, and an emotional reaction may develop some days later. Recovery of fragments of soul-mind consciousness can expose the painful memories of the subpersonalities who endured the pain of the traumatic events. It is important to work with these subpersonalities in subsequent sessions.

Physical aftereffects are not unusual. A person may experience fatigue and require bed rest for a day or longer. Some clients have reported a weight loss of several pounds the day following the release of an attached entity. The bloated feeling which resembles the initial stages of pregnancy may disappear following the release of the spirit or spirits of terminated pregnancies. A person may develop a fever and nausea. Diarrhea and vomiting may occur within 24 hours of a session. The body may discharge such residue as a physical parallel to the mental, emotional and spiritual release experienced in a session.

THE SESSION

A session is normally scheduled for a period of two hours. This is flexible and the session is not terminated at a specific time if a person is processing an important issue. It is vital to complete or bring to resolution any conflict which emerges in the session. During a session, many avenues of exploration can open. Such directions can be pursued in later sessions. These other areas might involve earlier lifetimes where a similar situation existed; present life conflicts and interactions with other people often ensue from prior life connections. A client may desire to do remote releasement work on family members in later sessions.

The session is recorded on audio cassette tape. The tape becomes the property of the client. Some people never listen to the session; others replay the tape to learn what transpired during the altered-state work. The session material often begins to fade from conscious memory after a session, much as a dream is forgotten after awakening.

Spirit releasement work is complete and final; successful treatment requires no further effort. The formerly attached entity is on its own path and will not return. Ongoing therapy can focus on healing the vulnerability which first allowed the attachment to prevent future spirit attachments.

The knowledge and awareness gained through past-life regression can continue to expand. As a person replays the past-life portion of a taped session, new insights and understanding can increase the benefits of the past-life session. It is recommended that the client be comfortably relaxed in a quiet place when tape is played, as the altered state will again be induced and the emotions will surface, though probably not as strongly as during the initial experience. The tape should not be replayed while the person is operating a vehicle.

Three to four hours is about the limit of a person's attention and endurance. If necessary, two such sessions can be completed in one day, with a two-hour break between sessions. Some people travel long distances to see a particular therapist, and such intensive work can cover several days or weeks. The work can be tiring for the client if a great deal of emotion is processed. A space of one free day between two days of session work seems to be quite effective for continued internal processing and regaining energy to continue with the intensive work.

During a session, the client is comfortably seated in a reclining chair, a couch or lying on the floor. A light quilt is available for extra warmth if needed. In altered states of consciousness a person often feels a bit too cool. A glass of water is placed near the person. A box of facial tissue is also placed nearby. The therapist hands several tissues to the client at the beginning of the session. A person might laugh and question the need for the tissue. During the emotional release, the need becomes obvious. The act of giving tissue to the client serves two purposes; it suggests that the client can shed tears in the normal course of a session, it also gives the person permission to cry.

The first minutes of the session offer a time to get acquainted, to establish rapport, to ease any discomfort in the situation. A client new to the idea of past-life exploration or spirit interference may have some fear of the unknown and a hesitation to place full trust in the therapist or therapists, if a team approach is used. The therapist can ask simple opening questions:

T: "How did you find out about us?"
    "What led you to choose this kind of approach?"
    "Have you ever experienced a past-life recall?"
    "Have you ever been aware of a spirit near you?"
    "Do you have any questions you would like to ask about us or about the session?"

The therapist offers a brief description of the process:

T: "I am really led by you. As you describe situations, I will ask questions which will bring up memories, thoughts, words, phrases, feelings and emotions about that situation. I would like you to answer with the first thing that comes to mind. It might seem silly or trivial or meaningless to you at the moment. Please feel free to say it right out loud, even if it is foul language or anything else. It comes from your subconscious mind so it is important in the process."

The client might need encouraging on this important point. Some people hesitate to express foul or vulgar language. It might be vitally important in the session to assist the therapist in determining the nature of the problem and the appropriate approach to resolution. Once this is accepted by the client, the therapist continues:

T: "What would you like to explore?"

This leads into the initial interview questions and the session is well underway.

Gentle, non-intrusive, non-directive, non-hypnotic inductions are utilized to gain access to the unconscious memories. The client usually closes the eyes without suggestion from the therapist. This eliminates the added visual input of the office surroundings. Occasionally a client will keep the eyes open during a session, maintaining conscious contact with the therapist. This does not interfere as long as the seeing/watching does not interfere with the flow of the narration.

The eyes may turn upward and scan right and left as the mind searches for visual clues. For most people, the eyes turn upward and to the left for the recall of a visual memory.

The direction of the gaze may drop downward to the left, which indicates an internal dialogue, some introspective discussion. The therapist does not interrupt while the client is in this mode, as it would be an intrusion on a very private conversation. The gaze may drop downward to the right. This is the eye-scanning pattern which stimulates memories of feelings and stored kinesthetic memories (Lewis and Pucelik, 1982, pp. 113-134).

If there is discontinuity and conscious interruption in the narrative of uncovered information because of the open eyes and left-brain consciousness, the therapist gently suggests that it might be easier if the client close the eyes.

The most effective work of the two-hour therapeutic session is accomplished while the client is in altered states of consciousness. Memories and the attendant emotions are accessed through right-brain activation. Alter personalities and subpersonalities emerge from the subconscious levels. Attached entities of various types speak from the level of the subconscious mind.

On the note pad, the therapist sketches two stick figures representing the front and back sides of the client. As the person describes physical sensations or symptoms, these are noted on the sketches, along with any descriptive words or phrases. Any of the phrases, descriptions or body locations can be used as inductions or entry points for the session.

If an entity is discovered, the appropriate questions are posed. The answers are jotted down. When the entity moves into the Light, an arrow is drawn upward through the name to indicate releasement. In the case of numerous attachments, this becomes quite important.

A client may want to tell the story of spirit interference or a house haunting. The therapist familiar with this field might be the first person to listen without interrupting or ridiculing the person. The story might be interesting and the details quite startling, yet this is not conducive to any healing or resolution in altered-state work. The outward appearances of the manifestations might make a good story for some magazine. The client is encouraged to cease repeating the story in favor of exploring the situation in altered state. Only then is it possible to contact the intrusive entities and effect the release and healing.

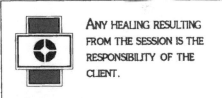

ANY HEALING RESULTING FROM THE SESSION IS THE RESPONSIBILITY OF THE CLIENT.

Even though they schedule a session, some people refuse to fully engage in the painful emotions which emerge. This is not particularly easy work for the client. Uncovered memories can prove quite painful and might reveal unpleasant truths about themselves or loved ones. The client may end the altered-state work and just want to talk. This may be helpful and calming for the person and may prove most beneficial.

At the end of the altered-state work, it takes 20 to 30 minutes for the person to come fully into their regular state of consciousness. This time is taken up with questions and suggestions for work in possible future sessions. The client is cautioned to refrain from alcohol or drugs for at least one day. It is recommended that a great deal of water be consumed. Except for a quiet walk, physical activity should be restricted for several hours. Interaction with other people should be limited to loving companionship.

Driving an automobile immediately after a session is discouraged. If a person travels a long distance for a single session, it is recommended that a friend accompany them to assume the burden of driving home.

A session can be tiring. There is considerable emotional material to think about and mentally process after deep altered-state work. The client is encouraged to honor and respect their part in the process, to acknowledge themselves as the source of the material. For some strongly left-brained people, there is a denial of the material expressed and the process itself after a session, even though the material was profound and accurate in its relevance to their lives.

The healing may be effective even in the face of this denial. The conscious mind has little to do with the process of healing specifically, indeed with the process of illness and wellness in general. In effect, the resolution of the conflict was already accomplished in the altered-state work. Repeated and continued denial might, however, reprogram the subconscious mind and undermine the benefits gained.

Whatever healing results from the session is the responsibility of the client. The therapist is the guide and cannot take credit for the success. It is the ego that wants credit and takes pride in a job well done. This also means that the therapist cannot be blamed for any apparent failure. The actual eventual results of the work of the altered-state session cannot be known at the time. Any expectation or attachment to the results of a session is a sign of ego involvement and will often be met with disappointment. This is the nature of the altered-state session work.

Cat of the Cosmos

From the color original, "*Cat of the Cosmos*," ©1992 by Mike "Gwydian" Wiseman. "If you have ever had a cat," the artist says, "...you must have noticed how it will stand or sit rigidly still and stare at one point on the ceiling...you look, but there is nothing there. From a metaphysical point of view, what if the cat...actually exists on different planes of reality at the same time and is able to see in all dimensions?"

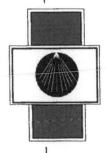

Regression
Therapy

Notes

Quick Guide to Section II

From, *The Sacred Tree,*
©1988 Four Worlds Development
Project. Illustration by Patricia Morris.

Regression Therapy

Regression therapy deals with biographical material, including every experience prior to the present moment. This therapy consists of several parts.

1. Present-life recall deals with present-life trauma.
2. Birth regression treats pre- and peri-natal experience.
3. Past-life therapy seeks to heal present-life conflicts which stem from traumatic events in prior lifetimes, utilizing reincarnation memories.

Several other modalities are necessary in the altered state work along with regression therapy. These techniques extend beyond the biographical level to the transpersonal level of experience.

4. Soul-mind recovery focuses on collecting and reintegrating the fragmented and separated parts of the personality.
5. Spirit releasement therapy aims at releasing and sending to the Light any and all attached discarnate entities, intruders, aliens, implants, thought forms and anything else which does not belong with the client.

Within all these areas, sound psychotherapeutic methods are applied to problem and conflict resolution.

During the exploration of memories through emotional channels rather than ideas and mental process, the client accesses the subconscious mind, or so called right-brain material. Physical and emotional feelings and sensations associated with past incidents are felt, not thought. The left-brain function, the judgmental ego, may attempt to block or interfere with the elicited experience and its associated pain. Survival and blocking of pain are part of the function of the ego mind. The conscious mind often judges the subconscious material as unbelievable and censors the narrative. This interferes with the therapeutic process.

Denial, rationalization and excuses are used by the ego partly to

THE THERAPIST AVOIDS THE USE OF "WHY?" AND "HOW?" QUESTIONS. THE LEFT BRAIN ANSWERS THESE QUESTIONS.

disavow responsibility. For this reason the therapist should avoid the use of "Why?" and "How?" questions. These questions will invite the conscious ego mind to make up reasons, to invent a story regarding the circumstances of any recalled situation. The ego mind does not easily accept anything other than the consensus reality, which does not include the spiritual world or birth and pre-natal memories.

Pre- and peri-natal therapy involves the recall and resolution of perceived traumatic events during this initial period of life, ranging from the experiences prior to conception to the first experiences of the newborn infant. The increasing acceptance of the validity of pre- and peri-natal memory has led to the development of the techniques briefly described below. There is an expanding professional literature on the subject. A professional organization called the Pre- and Peri-natal Psychology Association of North America has been established to advance the field.

The literature on the use of past-life regression as psychotherapy is growing, as is the number of therapists who are willing to reach beyond traditional and arbitrary limits to use this alternative method where other therapies have failed. The Association for Past-Life Research and Therapies was founded in 1981 to promote the growth of this work.

In the clinical framework of reincarnation, the being, or spirit, is eternal. As part of the spiritual journey, many beings choose to incarnate in the earth plane; that is, to take on the form of a physical human body. In the course of lifetimes of human interaction, the being accumulates mental, emotional and physical residue, which is carried from lifetime to lifetime.

The subconscious mind contains the memory of everything a person has ever perceived. Every experience is recorded in the memory, including biographical material from this life, the birth and pre-natal period, other lifetimes, and the non-physical experience between lives. The memory bank includes the perceptions of every past event; the surrounding circumstances and conditions; all physical and sensory input, including subliminally received data; and the thoughts, emotions, feelings and perceptions associated with the event. There also seems to be awareness of the thoughts of other people involved in these past incidents, perhaps transmitted telepathically.

The mind, while receiving the present and immediate perceptions of the senses, is alert to real or imagined threats to survival, based on and compared with past experience. The mind, in other words, is living in the past. This means that every adult interaction, every childhood event, every prenatal experience is recorded at the subconscious level. This can be validated through the use of regressive hypnosis; memories of early events can be retrieved and verified.

Unfortunately, it seems that the more unpleasant the experience or painful the emotion, the stronger the memory trace. Fortunately, the stronger the memory trace, the more accessible it is for therapeutic resolution.

A brief hypothetical example of distorted perception, misinterpretation and confabulation of memory may clarify the operation of the mind. Suppose that a single car accident occurs on a busy highway and ten people witness the accident, five men and five women. The lone driver is a man. He is killed. Each of the witnesses will be focusing at a different part of the accident scene. The center of visual focus is that portion of any scene which will register most clearly in the memory. Each will perceive a small portion of the event and yet believe that he or she has seen the entire accident. The incomplete perception becomes a misperception of the entire accident. Personal judgments such as prejudice against men drivers will further distort each person's account of the accident.

As the investigating police officer questions the witnesses, each will furnish a slightly different version of the accident, including the speed of the car, who was at fault, what the preceding circumstances were, etc., believing it to be the truth.

Several years later, at the court hearing, these same witnesses will relate a different version of the accident. Memory alters the scene even further from the actual event. They will relate their accounts, believing they are telling the truth. This is termed "confabulation of memory."

The police officer determined from what he perceived and from what the witnesses reported that it indeed was an accident and he filed the appropriate reports. The man had a life insurance policy with a large death benefit. The life insurance company accepted the report as filed and paid the claim for the man's death, a substantial amount, to the son who was the beneficiary.

The sudden windfall drastically changed the course of the life of the young man. He made choices in his life path which had far-reaching effects for himself as well as others with whom he interacted. Because of the money, he became less motivated in life, less responsible for producing anything of value to himself or society. He achieved less of his potential than if he had had to earn the money himself.

A deeper investigation into the motives of the man who died in the car might have revealed that he was depressed and that, after long deliberation, he decided to take his own life in a way that would seem accidental. Feeling guilty over the way he had treated his son, he made sure the young man would have a substantial financial cushion.

Did it serve the son to be given a life of such ease? There are many possible paths in life, determined by choices made by an individual. Each path offers learning and spiritual growth, though some choices lead to paths of greater learning than others. These notions are among the intangible and intriguing aspects of the spiritual reality. Some people speculate that alternate realities exist parallel to the apparent consensus reality of this world, and that all possible paths are chosen. Each choice, each path of each living individual, may exist in some sort of holographic projection. Countless parallel universes thus may exist simultaneously.

The police officer misperceived the situation and misinterpreted what he misperceived, and his official report, which included the misperceptions of the witnesses, was therefore a distortion of the truth. This distortion affected the profits of the insurance company, the life of the young man, and everyone with whom the young man came into contact. The ripple effect continues to move outward as the result of such a misperception and misinterpretation.

The events which seem to have the greatest and longest-lasting impact are the traumatic episodes in one's life. Any experienced traumatic event triggers the reaction termed the Traumatic Event Sequence. Perceptions of each succeeding moment of any event are registered in the conscious mind and recorded in the memory banks. These perceptions are usually misperceptions

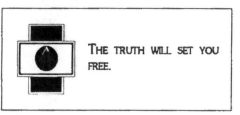

THE TRUTH WILL SET YOU FREE.

due to a number of factors. There is a distorted perception of the reality of a situation. It is this distortion which becomes embedded in the subconscious and colors future similar experiences. It is never what happens to a person that remains in the memory banks and has the lasting effect, but what that person thinks, feels, decides and remembers about the event.

Therapy seeks to unravel the distortions, guiding the client seeking help to a clear perception and experiential understanding of the truth of what actually happened in past traumas. This leads to the healing of the residues. The truth leads to freedom.

In the traumatic event sequence, the perceptions of the traumatic event are usually misperceptions, as in the accident scene described above. One function of the mind is to interpret incoming data. Since what it interprets is a misperception, such data is also distorted. The interpretations of the misperceptions become misinterpretations of the misperceptions.

The mind reacts to these misinterpretations of the misperceptions by assessing the situation for potential danger, or a threat to its survival. It compares this distorted view of the present situation with any earlier similar situation which contained a real or imagined threat to survival. Often the inappropriate reactions to the misinterpretations of the misperceptions lead to false decisions, assumptions, conclusions, and judgments; impossible vows and promises; even threats relating to the event and the persons involved.

The traumatic event sequence consists of these elements:

1. Perception/misperception of a present traumatic event.
2. Interpretation/misinterpretation of the misperception.
3. Comparison with earlier similar events to evaluate any threat to survival in the present situation. This almost invariably leads to an erroneous assessment of the present situation.
4. Judgements based on the erroneous assessment of possible threats to survival made as the result of the comparison of the misinterpretations of the misperceptions with earlier similar events.

5. Reaction which is often inappropriate to the present situation.

The often inappropriate reactions to the misinterpretations and misperceptions lead to impossible vows and promises; even threats relating to the event and the persons involved; false assumptions, erroneous conclusions, faulty judgments, and survival-based decisions such as:

"I will never trust men."
"I will never be beautiful again."
"I will never be rich again."
"I am not good enough."
"I don't deserve...."

These decisions are made during emotionally and/or physically traumatic episodes in this and prior lifetimes, episodes which include a real or imagined threat to survival. Decisions become beliefs, and beliefs are embedded within the subconscious mind. These beliefs color perception and distort interpretation of situations and interactions. Decisions are the basis of prejudice. These decisions, assumptions, conclusions and judgements form the *mental residue*, accumulating as part of the soul consciousness, which can be carried for lifetimes, cluttering the mind and interfering with any present life event which restimulates any aspect of the earlier event.

The problems associated with past-life events which are most often seen in therapy sessions involve residues of the fear-based emotions such as anger, resentment, revenge, fear, guilt, remorse, and distortions of love manifesting as jealousy, possessiveness, even violence.

These emotions may seem to have no basis in present life, yet are carried into many situations and projected onto other people involved in contemporary events. Phobias, existential fear and anger, intractable guilt, even depression and suicidal urges may fall into this category. The resulting emotional responses to present-time events are therefore unnecessarily and inappropriately contaminated by the *emotional residue* retained from traumatic past-life events.

Projection is the process of casting onto another person the ideas or impulses which belong to oneself. It means giving objective reality to a subjective experience. A person who blames someone else for his own mistakes or feelings is scapegoating or using the psychological defense mechanism of projection (Campbell, 1981, p. 486).

Physical residue builds up as the result of injuries, accidents, surgeries, any physically invasive trauma, especially anything which led to a death in another lifetime. It can take the form of birthmarks, physical symptoms with no organic cause, actual illness manifesting in the physical body, even death. The location of some birthmarks seem to be coincident with a mortal wound in a previous lifetime (Stevenson, 1974a). The pattern of the fatal injury often follows the being into a subsequent embodiment as an illness. Medical intervention may be able to alleviate or eliminate the symptoms, yet the pattern of mental energy which created the condition may still be present and may bring about the same condition again or it may erupt in some other form.

Spiritual residue is also locked in the subconscious mind. Soul-mind fragmentation can be carried from one lifetime to another as spiritual residue. Defiance and denial of God and professed atheism may carry forward as a spiritual residue. Violation of another person's free will may incur a so-called karmic debt, which carries a spiritual residue. Karmic debt is the concept behind the admonition, "As you sow, so shall you reap." Karmic debt is part of the spiritual residue. Many people have knowingly participated with the dark forces in prior lifetimes. Many have made pacts with the devil for their own self-serving purposes. This is a particularly damaging spiritual residue which can affect a person in the present time.

The residues can be associated with unlanguaged (nonverbal) interaction. A stern look from a parent can have an enormous impact on a child. Although this may help the parent control the child in a social situation, the effect may go far beyond any discipline intended. The nonverbal communication is interpreted by the receiver, not the sender. This inference will invariably be a misinterpretation of the meaning of the sender. A disapproving look can be devastating to a timid child. Each succeeding instance of the stern look will compound the original unlanguaged impact and the child may never know what the look really means. The effect is a feeling of disapproval and rejection.

The entertainment value of fear is exploited by designers of amusement park rides. Scary masks with fierce expressions are installed in the dark tunnels, and these are suddenly illuminated and thrust out at the riders immobilized in the

THE MENTAL, EMOTIONAL, PHYSICAL AND SPIRITUAL RESIDUES PRECIPITATE THE REPEATED EMBODIMENT IN THE EARTH PLANE.

little cars. The mask might be nothing more than a piece of plastic and rubber, yet it serves to restimulate something from an earlier experience which carried a real or imagined threat to survival. As this earlier fear is restimulated, the rider feels the rush of adrenaline in the body even though he is perfectly safe. This is considered "entertainment". This phenomenon also operates in a happy manner with children's Halloween costumes.

The distortions of the traumatic event sequence and these residues-emotional, mental, physical and spiritual; languaged and unlanguaged-precipitate the repeated embodiment in the earth plane. Situations which are similar in some way to the original traumatic event will arise for the purpose of resolving the conflicts which originally produced the residues. During the planning stage in the interim between lives, opportunities and situations similar in emotional pattern to the original episode are intentionally developed so that these persistent residues may be resolved, eliminated and healed.

Even though memory may prove to be faulty or colored with imagination, the impact of the physical, mental and emotional residue of every perceived and remembered event remains embedded in the subconscious mind. Past-life therapy is a method of retrieving the memory of the original experience, uncovering the residues, bringing the unconscious material into consciousness, and correcting the errors of perception and interpretation. Using the methods outlined in the following sections, the material can be processed, explored, clarified, reframed and eventually healed.

Soul-mind fragmentation is the term given to the condition of the mind which is split or fragmented due to mental, emotional, or physical trauma. When the mind is fragmented the consequences can be far-reaching, as in cases of multiple personality disorder, or less impactful, as in the formation of subpersonalities. MPD is the classic example of fragmentation as the result of childhood sexual abuse.

So-called normal people develop subpersonalities as the result of an unmet emotional need, a real or imagined minor trauma. In some cases the fragment of consciousness, or soul-mind, separates from the confines of the body and brain and the integrity of this personality is impaired. The fragment maintains a connection with the body by a silver thread, part of the silver cord. Recovery of the fragments is possible by way of this silver thread. The fragment is located and treated as a subpersonality. The therapeutic goal is integration of this subpersonality.

Exorcism is an ancient and timeless healing skill formerly practiced by a priest or shaman. Fully one-fourth of the healings attributed to Jesus consisted of casting out of unclean spirits. After Jesus' time, the Church assumed the work of exorcism, considering all the possessing spirits to be demons, minions of Lucifer, the fallen Archangel.

The theory and the process of exorcism were modified during the Spiritualist era, beginning in the mid-nineteenth century. The spiritualist doctrine denied the possibility of demonic beings; a demonic or evil spirit was believed to be the spirit of a mean or evil deceased human. Spiritualist doctrine also denied the possibility of reincarnation.

In contemporary practice, spirit releasement therapy can be learned and applied by any compassionate and open-minded therapist working not through a medium but directly with the afflicted person. The condition seems to be very widespread among our population and the need for this service is great.

PRESENT-LIFE RECALL

An emotional upset in the present moment most often stems from an earlier experience of a similar nature in the present lifetime or an earlier lifetime. In any conflict or upset, three elements are present in varying degrees and combinations.

The first is *unfulfilled expectation*. If one's expectations are not fully met, an upset can ensue. For example, the biggest shopping day is not the day after Thanksgiving but the day after Christmas, when people exchange their unwanted gifts. The gift giver may have spent a great deal of time and money on just the right gift; the present really represents a gift of love. The receiver's negative reaction is unexpected, which therefore upsets the giver; and the receiver too is upset, having wanted or expected a different gift. So both experience upset as the result of unfulfilled expectation.

A second element of upset is *thwarted intention*. Being blocked from a desired object or reward, whether it be a job, a material object, or the love of other person, is cause for upset.

The third and perhaps most significant aspect of upset is *undelivered communication* between people. This includes communication which is not delivered, as well as communication which is not received when expected. The pain resulting from failure to communicate love is the most severe and enduring. Love which is not received, experienced, and reciprocated, and love for another which is not given, expressed, or extended, can create pain which lasts for lifetimes.

The affect bridge age regression, described in the section Non-hypnotic Inductions (101), is used to guide a client back into earlier experiences of trauma, however slight, whether real or imagined, physical or emotional. When the memory is retrieved it is processed, or worked, in the manner described in the section Processing the Conflict (114). In some cases of earlier trauma, recalling and revivifying the event under hypnotic induction and regression with the ensuing abreaction and catharsis brings partial or total relief.

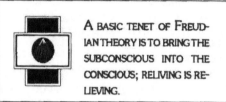

A BASIC TENET OF FREUD- IAN THEORY IS TO BRING THE SUBCONSCIOUS INTO THE CONSCIOUS; RELIVING IS RE- LIEVING.

This was effectively used with combat veterans of World War II and the Vietnam War who suffered from the condition known as "shell shock," "combat neurosis," or post traumatic stress disorder (PTSD) (Silver & Kelly, 1985). Many of these men had amnesia about the actual event, yet experienced the residual fear and anxiety. Under hypnosis the men could recall and relive the events of the traumatic episode, sometimes abreacting quite dramatically. This would often bring relief of the symptoms of anxiety, depression and dysfunction in life.

A basic tenet of Freudian theory is that reliving is relieving; bringing the subconscious material into the conscious mind will lead to resolution of the conflict. Abreaction and catharsis in a safe clinical setting is sometimes an effective way for a client to uncover and release an earlier traumatic memory. It is uncomfortable for many therapists to work with the intense emotional expression of the client. This offers the therapist a clue to his or her own sensitive areas, which could be cleared through therapy.

BIRTH REGRESSION

Birth may be the most traumatic and dangerous experience one can undergo in life. Freud saw the birth as the first trauma and the origin of all anxieties at the root of later psychic problems. He claimed that the experience was too deeply buried in the unconscious to be retrieved. Especially since it happened in the preverbal consciousness, the trauma was not open to analysis.

Otto Rank, who broke with Freud over this point, insisted that the biological birth trauma must be confronted and relived for resolution. Rank treated the entire analytic procedure as a rebirth. Human behavior tends to reenact birth: emotional, sexual, psychosomatic and cognitive patterns seem to be in some sense duplications of an intensified momentary experience during the birth. It seems that most people are fixated or stuck in the birth trauma (Grof, 1985).

Netherton (1978) suggests that the past-life patterns which plague a person throughout the present life are restimulated sometime during the pre-natal period, or during the birth and peri-natal experience. Recall of a past-life situation can be triggered in the mind of the unborn or neonate by a sound or smell, the position of the body during birth, the attitude of mother, or the absence of mother's consciousness caused by anesthesia administered during the last minutes of labor and delivery. The stimulus may be a word or a phrase spoken, especially with strong emotion by the mother or father anytime during the pregnancy, or the attending physician or nurses during delivery.

The major aspect of the consciousness, or the soul, fully connects with the body of the infant at or near the first breath of air. However, part of the consciousness seems to be connected with the body from the moment of conception, receiving and recording all experiences in the forming body, including the thoughts and feelings of the mother. This information is unfiltered, unprocessed, and accepted without judgment or discrimination. The impact of this information can have devastating effects on the mind and life of the person in childhood, adolescence, and adulthood. These distorted memories can be corrected through pre- and peri-natal therapy and birth regression. (Findeisen, 1988)

There are many indications for the birth regression. A woman may describe trouble with her menstrual periods, conflict about an imminent marriage, confusion surrounding pregnancy, indecision about having children, and the emotions associated with motherhood. Birth regression might uncover the source of these situations and bring resolution.

Very often a woman can incorporate the fears of her own mother regarding these areas during her own pre-natal period. These attitudes can follow from one lifetime to another.

One female client experienced being essentially ignored by her mother during the pre-natal period. Wanting to "do it right," the mother read many books on the subjects of pre-natal care, birth and child psychology. During the regression the woman screamed out to her mother to look at her, recognize her, connect with her, to remember that they agreed to do this together and do it right, without all the books. The woman cried out to her mother, angry at being ignored. As an adult, this woman is an obstetrician and gynecologist. At the end of the birth regression she suddenly had the sense that she had gone into the field at least partly because of her mother's preoccupation with doing the birth "right." She had absorbed the intensity of her mother's concern and had made it her own.

Crippled bonding is the term used to describe the interference in the immediate connection between mother and newborn. For men, this can lead to relationship problems with women, a continuous seeking for nurturance, stroking and holding. This can manifest in apparent promiscuity and an inability to connect with a woman in a mature relationship.

One client described his relationship history as a series of weekend affairs. After his birth he was separated from his mother, who was very tired after a long and difficult labor and delivery. He bonded with a nurse, large, soft and nurturing who apparently held him a great deal during the first two days of his life before his mother took him home. This two-day love affair with the nurse translated into a pattern of relationship in his adult life. This became very clear to him during the birth regression.

There are two approaches to the pre-natal and birth experience. During past-life exploration, the natural progression leads from the past life into the Light just prior to the present lifetime. From the planning stage in the Light just before the present life begins, a being can move into the earth plane and locate the woman who will be the mother in the lifetime to come. Women often report sensing the presence of a spirit being for several years prior to pregnancy. After the birth of the child there is no longer any sense of the presence of a discarnate being. During birth regression people often describe being close to the intended parents for a number of months, even years, prior to conception.

The following is a sample dialogue between therapist and client in a birth regression.

> T: "Locate that female who will become your birth mother.
> Where is she when you first locate her before she joins with
> the man who will become your father? What is your thought,
> what is your feeling, do you recognize this woman?"

Because the memory of the greater reality begins to fade at this point when the being leaves the planning stage and comes into the physical, connections with other lifetimes are still present yet beginning to dim.

> C: "Oh yes. She's supposed to be my mother."

> T: "Have you known her in other times?"

C: "Yes, yes I have."

T: "What is your feeling about her? What do you feel about her as you come closer to her?"

C: "Oh God, I don't want to be her kid!" (or) "I love her so much, I can't wait to be with her again."

The feelings about connecting with this person prior to birth can set the tone for the relationship throughout life.

T: "What happens next?"

C: "Well, I follow her for awhile."

T: "Locate the man that she seems to be interested in." (In other words, "Find your father.") "Follow her to an experience when she is with the man that she is interested in."

They may be high school lovers. Perhaps they're very sophisticated and having an affair. Or perhaps he's drunk, even violent.

T: "What do you feel about this guy?"

C: "He seems nice," (or) "Oh it's him again," (or) "God, he scares me."

The reactions can vary widely. Here is some indication of the impending relationship:

T: "Locate the moment when they do get together sexually. Find yourself in that ambience, in that situation. What is happening? How are they interacting with each other?"

This interaction can be loving, with candlelight and music and champagne and flowers. Or it can be rape, incest, a drunken brawl between a husband and a wife. Anything can happen at this point between a man and a woman. The emotions and sensations involved in the interaction between mother and father are fully registered on the consciousness of the incoming being.

T: "How do you feel about coming into this union? How do you feel about this? What are your thoughts about the man, what are your thoughts about the woman? Look and see. Have you known them before? Has this happened before? What are your thoughts and feelings as this is going on right now?"

The therapist may ask for physical sensations at this point, if it seems appropriate. The moment of conception occurs when the sperm meets and breaks though into the egg.

    T: "How does this feel? Experience the connection to the physi-
        cal reality."

The therapist allows the client time to experience this silently, as it is usually indescribable in words. A person may get a sense of electric shock beginning at the top of their head and moving entirely down the length of their body. The response may be from the feminine aspect:

    C: "Oh I don't want them around me, I don't want them to touch
        me, there are millions of them! Oh here they come, push
        them away, push 'em away."

The male aspect may emerge:

    C: "I got to get in there, there are so many others, get out of my
        way, I gotta get her."

The aspects of male and female seem to be present at that time. This also may set the tone for the life to come.

    T: "What does it feel like in the physical?"

Part of the consciousness is present and the client will describe the physical sensations.

    T: "Where are you? Are you in the body or out of the body?"

Most of the time clients will say they are not in the body.

    T: "What do you sense, what are you experiencing out of that
        body? Get a sense of how it is to be there. Of whether or not
        they want you to be there. Whether or not you want to check
        out."

The pregnancy can terminate if the desire to leave is strong enough-that is, by miscarriage. The parent's thoughts of abortion are also registered by the consciousness at the time. A client can react strongly to these thoughts. There can also be some indications of the cause of early crib death.

C: "I don't want this, I'm here and I don't like being here."
"I really want to be with this person."
"This is going to be a really hard life."
"If they don't want me then I'm going to leave."

A being knows everything that is going on at that point, and reacts as a personality.

The therapist guides the client in a thorough exploration of these responses from the parents. If there is a strong or painful reaction, especially if the reaction still affects the present-day relationships, it can be used to bridge to a traumatic episode in a prior lifetime that leads into the pre-natal situation. This will often uncover an instance of role reversal between parent and child in the prior lifetime. There might have been similar thoughts, feelings and attitudes of the parent toward the child in that time. As this earlier interaction is explored, the animosity, anger, resentment, even the resistance to the present-life circumstances often seem to dissolve. As the conflict is resolved or partially resolved, the therapist guides the client forward in the experience.

T: "Good. Skip forward now. Locate something important that happens.... Locate some feeling, sensation, some significant event."

The client may report a time when mom and dad are making love or fighting. The moment when momma discovers she's pregnant is usually registered clearly; dad's reaction when she tells him she's pregnant may be even more significant. He may say: "Oh no, not another kid," or something similar. This is a possible emotional setup for the life to come. If there is a lapse of several months between conception and the discovery of pregnancy the being may feel invisible, unacknowledged, denied. This also foretells an attitude in the family.

T: "Let's move forward now to another significant moment. Locate a significant moment while you're still inside.... Describe something that happens."

This is non-directive and ambiguous enough to allow the emergence of any impinging event, along with the attendant emotional residue. This continues until the client feels that the time of delivery is near. There may be a desire to get out of there. There might be a resistance, an aversion to leaving the security of the womb. Despite this desire, the physiology proceeds to the inevitable conclusion. This reluctance to leave the womb can manifest as a breech presentation at birth.

T: "It's comfortable inside but it's squeezing, getting tighter. It's warm and comfortable and yet it is getting tighter, it's squeezing. There starts to be a squeezing. What happens next?"

C: "There is pressure on my head, incredible pressure on the head, there's no place to go and things are squeezing, squeezing and there's pressure on my head."

The client will usually describe it in that way. And finally, when it feels hopeless, like they're going to be crushed from top to bottom, head to toe, there is an easing of the pressure against the top of the head as the cervix begins to dilate. In the birth canal, they are squeezed. They feel a combination of pleasure and pain and fear and resistance to coming out. They don't want to come out but are being squeezed, knowing they can't go back in, knowing that something is happening that they don't understand. It's happening and there's not much they can do about it. And as the baby emerges, there is usually the bright light, the unfamiliar sound in the delivery room and separation from mother.

If there is anesthesia which dulls mother's consciousness, the infant experiences that momma goes away. There's a separation mentally as well as physically. The child may feel abandoned and rejected. It simply does not understand what is happening. This perceived separation can develop into a fear of separation which may pervade an entire lifetime.

C: "Where did she go? I want my momma. Momma, I want you here! I came to be with you and you left!"

There is often enormous anger at that point.

The therapist encourages the client to cry and express the anger. The newborn has the feelings and cannot express them. The feelings about the birth experience can be expressed in the language of the adult.

T: "Use your ability to speak for the child. Let the infant speak with your words. Take your words back and let the infant say now what it could not say then."

The therapist can use many questions to prompt the client at this time. Here are a few. Pausing briefly after the questions allows the client to access the information. There is no hurry.

T: "What happened?"
"What was your mother thinking?"
"What was your connection with her?"
"Were you in communication before that?"
"Yes, and when did the communication stop?"

C: "Sometime during when the squeezing started."

T: "What was the doctor thinking?"
    "What was the doctor's attitude?"
    "What was the doctor's attitude toward you?"
    "What was your attitude toward him?"
    "What happened as you were being born?"
    "What was your impression as you first emerged and you first came out?"
    "What were the other people thinking?"

C: "It's cold. It's bright and noisy."

The typical delivery room will be described.

T: "Listen for the words of the other people."

C: "'God, what an ugly little thing.'"
    "'Oh, she's so blue, she's not going to make it.'"

The infant picks up the thoughts of the people in the area-the doctor, the nurses, the mother, the father, and after the birth sometimes the thoughts of a nearby entity. An attaching entity will not join during labor or birth, as it is too unpleasant. However, in some cases an entity will attach in utero, little knowing what is in store, and come through the birth experience with the body.

The therapist can probe to determine what the anger is about and also what expectations there were before coming in.

T: "What did happen?"
    "What didn't happen at the time of the birth?"
    "At the time of the conception, what agreements were broken?"

The anger is often about broken agreements. These things can be uncovered and relived, and the attendant emotions expressed.

The second approach to the birth experience is a gentle regression from the present moment backward in time. The intention is established to explore the birth, pre-natal period, and conception. With the client in a comfortable position, the therapist guides softly.

T: "Breathe in deeply, breathe in light as you breathe in and breathe out, relaxing more and more with each breath you take. A little deeper relaxed with each breath that you take. Breathe in the most beautiful color, the most beautiful color that you can imagine, and as that color fills you, let yourself move back. Back in time, back through the years. Back to before you were a child and you were inside your mother. Let

the color carry you back, let the color carry you back to
before you were inside. Before your physical body was conceived. Before the physical experience began. Find yourself
now as a point of consciousness close to the woman that you
seem to be drawn to, attracted to. Close to the woman who
will become your mother. Describe your first reaction, your
response as you locate the woman.

It usually doesn't take much longer than this for the client to access the
memories.

C: "Oh, she's standing at a hall locker, she's a high school
student. Oh she's not married to this guy. But she really likes
him and he's standing there. He's cute."

This is a typical memory.

The therapist continues the probing and processing as described above.
Birth regression is a stimulating process and is a rich source of material, which
can be used therapeutically for the healing of the client.

Another approach to uncovering a precipitating event in utero is the
locater instruction. As the client is describing and expressing the emotion of a
present-life traumatic episode, the therapist can give this suggestion:

T: "Let those feelings take you back. Locate the source of these
feelings while you are still inside mother. In the nine months
before you are born, what month are you in? Say the first
number that comes up."

The client will often state a number immediately.

T: "What are the words? What is the first thing you hear? First
thing that comes to mind."

The client may repeat words or phrases similar to the description and
emotional expression of the traumatic episode.

T: "If these words were coming from the outside, what direction
would they be coming from?"

This often surprises the client. Somehow they know the words are
coming from behind them, in front or to the side.

T: "If you knew who was saying this things, who would that be?"

Suddenly the truth of the situation comes clear. It is mother, father, a visitor, the physician or a nurse in the delivery room. The words may refer to something totally unrelated to the fetus.

A colleague related this brief example: A middle-aged woman suffered alcoholism. She declared a strong desire to quit drinking and had been in residential treatment centers several times. She described walking out of the center directly into the nearest bar for a drink. She felt like she needed a drink and just had to have one.

> T: "Let those feelings take you right back before you were born. What are the first words you hear?"

> C: "You just have to have that drink. You just have to have that drink, don't you?"

> T: "If someone else were saying these words, who would that be?"

> C: "It's my mother. She's yelling at my dad."

Mother was in the very late stages of pregnancy, uncomfortable and lonely. Father came in from a hard day at work. He did not want to have to face his wife in her needy and irritable condition. He walked in, saw the angry expression on her face and went to his liquor cabinet. She yelled at him, unable to control her emotions, "You just have to have that drink...."

This was the source of the inner command to have that drink. This sort of discovery can release the hold of such deeply embedded subconscious programming.

If the therapist begins to suspect or feel intuitively that the events described by the client may be related to pre-birth experience, body memory can be invoked.

> T: "As this is happening, notice what position your body is in. What is your position?"

If the event is occurring during this period, the client will describe the fetal position with knees drawn up, arms across the body.

Human birth is a miracle of existence. A mother's womb is an intricate and delicate mechanism which furnishes the portal or passageway for a non-physical being, a soul, to manifest in the physical world in a human form. This transition is fraught with sometimes painful interference. There is also the fiercely protective force and healing balm of the mother's love. Conversely, there is the devastation when this love is missing.

Ted was about 45 years old. He had given up sugar, alcohol, smoking and red meat, but could not break his hunger for coffee. Ted described releasing a "demon snake" from within himself with the help of some friends. This occurred at the home of an acquaintance. After that event he was free of the thirst for coffee for nearly a year.

Ted made a visit to the same house at a later date. The host offered him some coffee. Without thinking he accepted. From that moment on he was again addicted. As he described the memory of that night he began to experience a tight sensation in his legs. As he focused on the sensation he described what appeared to be the big front blade of a bulldozer. The feelings were about abandonment, his words described being alone.

After the bulldozer image, Ted described being on some sort of conveyer belt, then being dumped out into an alley totally alone. It was also quite clear to him that this was New York City. He did not experience being in a body. There was no memory of having been born, yet the personality definitely seemed like a lost soul, an earthbound spirit. It described joining Ted when he was young, liking him, and enjoying coffee through him. During the release of the demon snake at the house this spirit also left Ted but it stayed in the house. When Ted visited there it came in again when Ted was offered the coffee and he took it.

The entity was asked its name. It did not know. It was urged to locate a time when it was in its own body. It could not recall a body. It did locate an episode which led to the image of the bulldozer blade. The physical body, such as it was, was thrown into a trash can. This was dumped into the rear of a garbage truck. It was the sweeping pusher in the garbage truck which had the appearance of a bulldozer blade.

This was the spirit of a terminated pregnancy, unceremoniously dumped in the garbage. There was no experience of birth. The conscious spirit joins the body at or near the first breath. This was either a stillbirth, a premature birth which did not live, or an aborted fetus. This was not determined. The overwhelming feeling was of abandonment and being alone, and the pleading and unanswerable question, "Why?"

This answered the question of the bulldozer but not the conveyer belt or being dumped in the alley. The initial addiction to coffee was also unanswered. The speculation was that the mother was an addict. She miscarried and disposed of the fetus, dead or almost so, in the garbage can.

There could be no resolution, no answers. Forgiveness finally allowed the spirit to move into the Light. Comfortable and safe after all the years together, the spirit was reluctant to leave Ted. After a loving interchange with him it was persuaded to leave in the company of guiding spirits.

Ted immediately felt better.

PAST-LIFE THERAPY

When past-life therapy is discussed, many people reject the idea of looking into a past lifetime for problems, as they claim to have enough troubles in the present life. This consideration seems valid enough at first; however, when explored in past-life therapy practice, present-life conflicts and problem areas nearly always stem from traumatic events in earlier lives. It is the emotional, mental, physical and spiritual residues retained from traumatic episodes in past incarnations which influence and contaminate present-life experience. This is the excess and unnecessary baggage that people carry, and it interferes with the full expression and experience of love in the present life journey.

Past-life patterns can influence a person's behavior, attitudes, likes and dislikes, relationships, phobias and virtually every aspect of life. Past-life therapy techniques can uncover the events in past lives which cause the dystonic or abnormal behaviors and chronic problems and recurrent conflicts in this life. Resolution of the past-life trauma and its residue can ease or eliminate the present-life conflict. The therapeutic value of past life therapy is to eliminate the residue, or energy patterns, retained from prior lifetime experience. This opens the way for a fuller experience of the present moment, the current lifetime.

Conflict can arise from frustration with an outside source which blocks the completion of a response, or from an intrapsychic conflict in the form of an incompatible response tendency. It is the intrapsychic conflict which often proves to be carried over from a past life. Conflict resolution can lead to the healing of unreasonable anger and resentment, fear and terror, sadness and loss, intractable guilt and remorse, victimization, upsets with undelivered communication, unfulfilled expectations, thwarted intentions, misapprehension and misunderstanding of the motives, attitudes and behaviors of others and irreconcilable differences of all sorts.

The mind is more comfortable if a story, event, even a trauma has a beginning, middle, and ending or completion. Soap operas keep millions of people coming back for more because there is never an ending to the story. In the early days of Hollywood, movie serials such as "*The Perils of Pauline*" were popular for the same reason. A story without an end, an event without a conclusion, a trauma without healing, in fact any incompletion, represents unfinished business. The mind seeks to complete or draw to a closure any unfinished situation. Failure to do so causes anxiety. Inability to do so causes greater anxiety. Gestalt therapy holds that any incomplete Gestalt represents an unfinished situation that clamors for attention. Instead of growth and development, there is stagnation and regression (Perls, Hefferline, and Goodman, 1951, p. xvi).

In Freudian terms, an instinct is said to be an inborn condition which imparts direction to psychological processes. There are two primal instincts: life or Eros, the constructive or generative principle; and Thanatos, the destructive principle or death instinct. The final aim of an instinct is the

THE OBJECT OF PAST-LIVES THERAPY IS TO ENHANCE HARMONY IN THE PRESENT LIFE BY ELIMINATING THE RESIDUES FROM PAST LIVES.

removal of a bodily need. An instinct is said to be conservative, as its goal is to return a person to the quiescent state which existed prior to arousal or disturbance by an excitatory process. An instinct seeks to bring about a regression to the earlier state of repose. This tendency to repeat the cycle from excitation to quiescence is termed the "repetition compulsion" (Hall, 1979, pp. 37-38).

In his later years, Freud recognized the death instinct—Thanatos, or destrudo—as a separate drive. The death instinct tends to return the organism to the earliest state, namely inanimate existence. The death instinct is averse to new experiences, seeks to return to the past, and strives for a state of complete and eternal rest. (Campbell, 1981, pp. 325-327). This clearly resembles the inner peace which is the goal of the spiritual seeker.

Freud seems to have discovered a basic spiritual principle without knowing it. The spiritual being seeks eventually to rejoin the Source whence it emerged. The word religion means "to rejoin". There are so many religions yet there is only one final destination, the one Source to which all will finally return home.

In terms of past-life therapy, the pain of unfinished business in one life can initiate a rebirth into another lifetime. One motive for reincarnation is the repetition compulsion, with the goal of reducing the emotional pain of unfinished business such as undelivered communication and unfulfilled expectation.

The object of past-lives therapy is to enhance harmony in the present life by locating and resolving these past-life traumas, unfinished situations, and incompletions, and to eliminate the residues. The present life can be lived more fully and freely without interference from the memories of past experience contaminating and distorting present experience.

The final result of past-lives therapy is to uncover and resolve all remaining issues, to eliminate the unwanted and unneeded residues, and to achieve and restore perfect peace of body, mind and spirit.

During a past-life exploration, the past-life character is urged to describe everything that happens following the death. Only when the being is free of the residues, leaves the earth plane and is fully in the Light, is the past-life therapy on that lifetime complete.

The Meaning of Past-Life Recall

There are a least four levels of meaning of the past-life regression experience. At the most superficial level, it is fun and interesting to explore one's past, to see oneself as the various characters in earlier dramas. It is simply an excursion through time.

The second level is the therapeutic experience. Many emotional problems and conflicts are quickly and effectively solved through past-life regression therapy, usually in far fewer sessions than with conventional

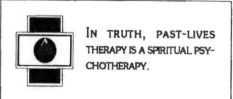

IN TRUTH, PAST-LIVES THERAPY IS A SPIRITUAL PSYCHOTHERAPY.

therapy. Many physical ailments are considered to be psychosomatic, and these conditions may begin to ease with past-life regression therapy.

The third level is an educational journey into the spiritual reality, the so-called inner planes of consciousness. The subject can experience the greater reality of spirit, past, present, and, in some cases, future. There is a deeper realization of purpose in life (or lives), a clearer sense of the meaning of relationships and the transpersonal aspects of existence.

The fourth level of the altered-state regression experience is the ineffable feeling of Oneness, of being connected to all and everything in the Universe, being part of God, Goddess, All That Is.

In truth, past-lives therapy is a spiritual psychotherapy.

The Initial Interview

The therapist needs to approach the initial interview without judgment, with total acceptance of whatever might be expressed, even if the client reveals paranormal experiences. The client's narrative must be accepted without any judgments about reality or unreality, as if it were absolutely true. In the experience of the person relating the experience, it is absolutely true. Within the framework of this therapeutic approach, the therapist has two specific aims in the initial interview:

1. To recognize clues to past-life traumatic events which affect this life.
2. To discover instances of possible vulnerability to spirit attachment.

Healing in the present comes as a result of healing the residue of the past through past-life therapy only if the residue stems from the past experience of the client. If that residue affects the life of the client, yet belongs to an attached discarnate entity, the therapy consists of releasing that entity into the Light and its next step of evolution, and healing the vulnerability in the client which allowed the attachment.

During the initial interview, the therapist must listen between the lines, hear what is not being said, discern the non-verbal communication, and notice the patterns. Repeated patterns of behavior, similar emotional reactions to various life situations, body language, repetitive phraseology when describing the problem areas may indicate a recurring theme of ineffective and inappropriate response to a traumatic event in a prior lifetime. The metaphoric phrases used in describing reactions and interactions in the present life

THE CLIENT'S OWN WORDS AND DESCRIPTIONS ARE USED VERBATIM IN THE PROCESSING.

may be veridical accounts of traumatic situations and interactions in other lives.

The therapist should write these phrases verbatim in his or her notes, and can use them for past-life induction. This cannot be emphasized enough: The client's own words and descriptions are used. The client's metaphor is an emotional word picture of the actual event. This emotional word picture engages right and left brain and offers almost direct access to the traumatic memory.

Once a therapist is knowledgeable about the condition of spirit interference and attachment, it becomes obvious that most people are vulnerable many times during the normal activities of life. These situations are noted as they are described: hospitalization; illness; accidents; deaths in the family; history of familial trauma; drug and alcohol use; combat experience; emotional or physical trauma of any sort, particularly sexual; severe emotional experiences, such as rage, hatred, desire for revenge, depression, and self-destructive feelings; dreams and nightmares, especially of death or being chased; psychic experience; feelings of aversion to Jesus Christ and any church activity. Other vulnerabilities are described in various parts of this Manual.

The therapist notes the body language such as posture and positions, closed or open, muscle tension, movement in the chair, twitches, jerks, tics, and movements and position of the hands. The facial expressions and contortions offer much information. The coloration of the skin and the emotion expressed on the face, the furrowing of the brow, the too-quick smile, the fear around the eyes or the genuine smile, the honest laughter and joy, the love that's expressed, the voice tone, volume and timbre, breathing and heart rate are all clues to the non-verbal communication. These physical indicators are reactions to earlier material emerging to the surface of consciousness. Headache, churning gut, light-headedness or physical pain may develop during this interview process. The pain may be the residue of a fatal past-life injury of the client or the restimulated memory of pain of death of an attached entity.

The empathetic therapist may feel some visceral reactions to the words of the client as the interview progresses. This may be an indication of the therapist's own unresolved issues and it may be an intuitive interaction with the psyche of the client. This psychic connection can be used effectively as a guide for the therapist. The intuitive connection must not be dismissed or ignored.

The health history includes information about normal childhood illness, hospitalizations for any reason, surgeries with anesthesia, organ transplant, either receipt or donation, accidents, or falls with a blow to the head, recall of a near-death experience or NDE, any of which can cause a vulnerability to spirit attachment.

Mental illness or imbalance and any prior psychotherapy must be noted. Any substance use or abuse is important. Any mind-altering experience can open a person to a spirit attachment, whether such alteration is chemically induced or emotionally caused, as in uncontrolled rage, terror, grief, or intractable guilt or anger, hypnosis, out-of-body experience or NDE. Any symptoms of burnout are important to note. The burden of several attached spirits can hasten the course of mental and emotional burnout in a job situation.

An alteration of consciousness can be physically produced by a jarring accident, meditation, or listening to hypnotically rhythmic music, such as shamanic drumming. Modern rock music, with the hard rhythmic sound and lyrics advocating drugs, crime, suicide and Satan worship, are especially damaging to the psyche and open the way for spirit attachment.

Anesthetics are mind-altering drugs. The confused spirits of many people who have died in hospitals remain there, often retaining the drugged state induced by prescribed medication. There is a non-physical emanation from the drugs administered to patients, especially the anesthetics and mind-altering substances such as tranquilizers and sleeping pills. This emanation affects the non-physical beings, the spirits of people who succumb in the hospital wards and surgeries. The spirits wander the hallways and wards in a stupor, just as heavily sedated living persons would, hardly knowing where they are. These entities can easily attach to visitors who are vulnerable due to a state of anxiety over visiting hospitalized friends and relatives.

Many spirit attachments are formed during the recovery stages after surgery. People suffering accident and illness are in a particularly weakened condition. Any emotional trauma or intense emotional feelings can attract like a magnet an entity who died during a similar emotional experience. A physical condition in a living person can draw in the spirit of a person who died as a result of a condition which is similar in any way.

One 62-year-old male client discovered an attached female entity who died of an abdominal infection. She joined him in the hospital after his appendectomy at age six. The story within the family was that he never smiled after his surgery. The woman seemed to be quite grouchy and that characteristic affected the man's personality from that time forward.

The pre-natal and birth history of the client is important, and this includes any of the mother's terminated pregnancies prior to conception. For male and female alike, any terminated pregnancy prior to their conception is a potential source of an attached spirit. The spirit of a terminated fetus (and this may be the spirit of a deceased twin) may be present with the mother or attached to the new fetus and may continue to be attached into adulthood. For a female client, any terminated pregnancy is a source of spirit attachment.

Lowered immune system function causes greater susceptibility to spirit attachment. Any chronic or recurrent physical ailment is noted. Many conditions seem to be mysterious in origin, elusive and undiagnosable. The symptoms are definitely present, yet no cause can be determined by medical examination. These conditions are often relieved after the release of an attached entity who suffered or died of such an ailment.

Dan was a 38-year-old client with symptoms of heart trouble who had suffered with this condition for some years. Numerous medical examinations revealed no physical cause for the symptoms. During the session, he began to clutch his chest and left arm. Tears streamed from his eyes. He appeared to be suffering a heart attack. However, in moments the pain ceased and his expression became calm.

The questions were then directed to the one who had just felt the heart pain. This was an assumption by the therapist, which proved to be accurate. The one who responded was an older man who had died of a heart attack. When the client was about six years old he was standing waiting for a school bus. The entity had died some time earlier in the same area. For some reason he was drawn to the child and simply attached. The entity was stuck in the death experience, repeatedly imposing on the host the painful signs of heart attack which were part of his own body memory of dying. The symptoms manifested in the younger man without any organic cause. The entity was released into the Light. The client was examined the next day by a physician. Blood pressure and lung volume were normal for the first time since the physician had begun his tests and examinations of the man.

Attached discarnate beings may be the cause of many cases of mental disorder misdiagnosed as schizophrenia, bipolar disorder, depression, MPD, suicidal tendency and conditions such as Alzheimer's. Many ailments, physical

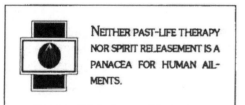

NEITHER PAST-LIFE THERAPY NOR SPIRIT RELEASEMENT IS A PANACEA FOR HUMAN AIL-MENTS.

and psychological, are diagnosed from the symptomatology rather than through discovering the cause. The symptoms of an actual condition may be quite similar to the signs of spirit attachment. Without discovering the actual cause of a physical or mental condition, a diagnosis must be suspect.

All too often, a health practitioner treats the symptoms and not the cause of the problem. The range of diagnostic categories must be broadened to include the spiritual dimension of the human being. Neither past-life therapy nor spirit releasement is a panacea for human ailments. Physical and psychological examinations are necessary in order to rule out organic cause for pathological physical conditions and actual mental disorders.

A history of the family tree may offer clues to past-life connections and unfinished business and a source of spirit attachments. Family history includes substance abuse, insanity, any mental illness, physical ailments which could be hereditary, inappropriate behavior in the family, patterns of trauma, suicide and tragedy. Criminal behavior, sexual abuse, drug and alcohol abuse, or insanity among several extended family members may indicate demonic interference, particularly if it follows only one side of the family, maternal or paternal.

In a family there may be a pattern of the first-born son or daughter dying at an early age or becoming insane. This may seem like a family curse; however, this sort of pattern does not mean there is anything magical operating. The consciousness of the forming fetus remembers everything spoken in its vicinity. It may turn out that in past generations, some jealous husband discovered his wife's pregnancy was the result of an infidelity and cursed the wife and her child, and her child's child, etc. This angry threat is retained in the memory of the fetus. If this one is female, when she grows into adulthood and conceives a child the information can be passed on to the next generation during the pre-natal period.

The client is asked about the earliest memories. Some people don't remember anything before age 12 or 14. This is a good indication of repressed memories of sexual abuse. Some people can remember events which occurred at age two or three, some even earlier. The therapist asks the client about the childhood in general:

> T: "Were you nurtured?"
> "Did you have imaginary playmates?"

These might not have been imaginary at all.

> T: "Were you treated with love?"
> "Were you ignored?"
> "How was your relationship with your parents?"

In many cases of child abuse, the parents themselves are discovered to have carried attached entities, often demonic in nature.

The client is queried about suicides, recent deaths, deaths of anyone close.

> T: "Did you feel the presence of the deceased one after the death?"
> "Have you ever seen them in dreams or received any messages in dreams?"
> "Have you felt their presence in the therapy room?"

In two separate studies conducted in rest homes, it was found that two-thirds of the widows saw, sensed, heard or felt the presence of their deceased husband after the death. They were given anti-hallucinogenic drugs. Two-thirds of them still saw, sensed, felt or heard their deceased husbands. The women weren't hallucinating.

The following questions can uncover a wealth of information from the client regarding past-life residues and spirit attachment opportunities.

> T: "What are the presenting problems?"
> "What are the areas of discomfort?"
> "Why were you referred?"
> "What led you to schedule an appointment?"

"How have you felt since making the appointment?"
"Have you had dreams since making the appointment?"
"Have you heard voices?"
"Have there been illnesses?"
"Was there any disturbance that came up just before the appointment?"
"Did you have an urge to cancel the appointment?"
"Were there signs of any illness on the morning of the appointment day?"
"Were you sleepy on the way to the appointment?"
"Was there any other interference in getting to the appointment?"

An entity can interfere with the normal thought processes of a person. The entity knows that the appointment is made for the purpose of exploring for the presence of attached discarnates, and it will resist any such attempts at being dislodged.

The client is asked to describe the present-life circumstances.

T: "Do you have satisfying relationships with friends of both genders?"
"Is there a primary love relationship?"
"How do you sleep?"
"Are you rested?"
"How is the physical energy level?"
"Does food satisfy your hunger?"
"What about eating and drinking patterns and habits?"
"Do you have compulsions, obsessions, or addictions of any kind?"

The sudden onset of any aberrant behavior may well indicate a recent attachment. The therapist asks about dreams:

T: "Do you dream?"
"Do you remember your dreams?"
"Are there repeating patterns in your dreams?"
"Do you have repeating dreams?"

Certain dreams seem to indicate past-life memories, especially traumatic incidents, often the death in the prior lifetime. Recurring dreams which awaken the client because of emotional turmoil may indicate unfinished business, undelivered communication.

In a session using a dream as the entry point, the client is guided into the dream, then directed to recall events prior to the beginning of the dream. The client is directed to carry the narrative beyond the usual end of the dream. This will often uncover the past-life that is surfacing in the dream. Processing the emotional residue of the events to completion, as described below, will usually eliminate the recurring dream.

The dream might also be the memory of the death of an attached entity recalling its own final trauma. If the determination is made that this is an entity, the releasement procedures are followed as described in the section Spirit Releasement Therapy (199).

Psychic ability is often an open door to spirit attachment. Precognition is an ability which many people have. Undiscovered mediumistic ability can be a wide-open doorway to spirits.

T: "Do you know who's on the phone when it rings?"
"Do you know before you pick it up?"
"Do you think of somebody and soon get a letter from that person?"
"Do you find lost things?"
"Do you have premonitions which come true?"
"Do you hear voices?"
"What is your opinion of your psychic ability?"

By this time the client should be comfortable enough to acknowledge these abilities with the therapist.

T: "Do you see auras?"
"Do you see spirits?"
"Do you feel other people's emotions?"
"Are you uncomfortable with the emotional atmosphere where groups of people gather, such as shopping malls?"
"How empathetic are you?"

Empathy may border on psychic connection. This empathy is a clear pathway, almost an inducement to a lost spirit.

Many people can recall a near-death experience. This out-of-the-body state can be an invitation to an attached entity.

Three categories of client-furnished elements are:

1. Somatics (gestures, facial expressions and color, shifts in body position, muscle tension, jerking, shaking, position of arms and hands, etc.).
2. Language style (the use of one representational system or inner sense namely, visual, auditory, or kinesthetic-more frequently than others).
3. Important or significant statements usually spoken with visible emotion.

The therapist observes the client carefully and respectfully, utilizing these three elements and any other information and spontaneous behavior to assist the client in his own self-induction into the altered state. This means switching from ordinary mental activity, or left-hemispheric functioning, into right-hemispheric experiencing of the inner, subconscious mind. Memories of one's entire life experiences, including birth and the pre-natal period, are available in this altered state of consciousness. This is also the level of mind at which the disembodied consciousness of a deceased person seems to attach.

Hypnotic Inductions

Hypnosis is the classic approach to retrieving past-life experience. The first book about the recall of past-life memories through the use of hypnosis was written by Col. Albert de Rochas, and published in France in 1911 (Rogo, 1985, pp. 16-17).

An amateur hypnotist named Morey Bernstein (1956) described the reincarnation memories of a Colorado housewife while under hypnosis. His book, *The Search for Bridey Murphy*, became a best seller at the time. It was made into a movie and caused a great deal of controversy.

The World Within

Computer art from the color original, *The World Within*, ©1992 by David Palermo.

Dick Sutphen (1976, 1978, 1987) has done extensive research in the field of reincarnation. He was a practicing hypnotherapist and regression therapist for many years. He worked with many couples in romantic relationship, gathering information which indicated that lovers return time and time again to find each other and marry.

Most modern past-life therapists and researchers utilize hypnosis to induce the altered state of consciousness which allows access to memories of prior lifetimes (Fiore, 1978; Wambach, 1978; Snow, 1989).

A major and valid objection to the use of hypnosis in past-life recall is the fact that a person is more open to suggestion during hypnotic trance. It is suspected that a person in induced trance is more likely to attempt to please the therapist by offering answers even when there are none. In other words, the answers are likely to be fabricated.

In tests of memory retrieval under hypnosis, this was found to be so. If a witness at the scene of a crime gets a good look at a license number it can be recalled under hypnosis. If the witness only glances at the license plate, he might recall the number under hypnosis. When the actual vehicle is found, the memory of the number might be accurate for three or four out of six numbers. The gaps were filled in by the mind.

In one experiment, adults were hypnotically regressed to childhood and asked to recite poems memorized at the younger age. The subjects recited the poetry far more clearly than during awake recall. When the hypnotically recalled verses were compared with the actual verses, it was found that many of the phrases of the recalled verse were improvised, even though they were accurate in rhyme and meter (Zilbergeld, Edelstien and Araoz, 1986, pp. 53-55).

Incremental Regression

The hypnotic state can be induced by various methods. It is the alpha level of brain activity which is the desired level of trance. When a person is in this level, the eyelids will display the characteristic flickering movement associated with dream sleep-that is, rapid eye movement, or REM. With the client in this state the suggestion is given to move back to an earlier experience in the present life.

T: "Think of something that happened to you last week."

The client describes briefly some event.

T: "Recall a happy event from your teen years."

The instruction to recall a happy event will engender less resistance in the client. Again, the client will easily relate some memory.

T: "Recall something in your life before you started grammar school."

This memory will come more slowly; the client will doubt his memory.

T: "Move back farther now, recall a time before you could walk."

This frequently elicits a scene of a child standing in a crib, frustrated at the limitation imposed by the crib's bars. Strong emotions will begin to emerge.

T: "Recall hearing something before you were born. Recall something while you are still inside your mother."

At this point the therapist shifts the languaging to present tense. For the person in altered state, the time frame of the memory is the present moment. The client may describe hearing something spoken by mother.

T: "Where are you as you hear these words?"

The listening point may be inside the warm, dark womb; it may be outside, observing mother in her pregnant condition. The words may be totally innocuous; they may be emotionally charged and connect with some present-life problem. This is processed to completion, as described in the section Processing The Conflict (114).

T: "Move back even farther now, before you were with this little body inside mother. Move back even farther. (brief pause) What comes?"

This will elicit a memory of a past life, usually a placid scene, as there was no emotional or physical stimulus connecting present-life problems with the past life.

The incremental method can be used to examine a specific item. For example, a person may want to explore her fear of medical doctors. The therapist gently guides her into her memory banks.

T: "Think of a time when you were in a doctor's office."

The client may remember a recent visit. This is a non-emotional memory, a left-brain function recalling a date and time.

T: "Recall and describe what happened there."

As the client begins to describe the visit, the therapist shifts into present tense.

T: "What is the doctor doing?"

"What is he doing to you?"
"How do you feel when he does that? What happens inside you?"

These questions will usually elicit emotions. The feeling aspects, emotional and physical, are stored in the memory associated with the right brain. The client will describe the events with feeling and rising emotions. If the narrative is delivered without emotion or affect, the therapist can direct the person deeper into the feelings.

T: "Focus on the scene, focus on the feelings, move right into your body. What are you feeling, sitting right in front of the doctor?"

As this experience is revealed, the therapist responds appropriately. When the episode is finished, the therapist moves the client to an earlier similar incident.

T: "Recall another time when you felt the same way. Let those sensations in your body carry you right back to another time when you felt the same sensations."

This usually uncovers an earlier event. This is the affect bridge and somatic bridge in action. What began as an incremental induction through mental recall becomes an emotional linking with earlier events through emotions and physical or somatic linking through visceral sensations. This will usually lead to a past-life traumatic event.

Contrived

A hypnotic induction can include contrived devices to locate present-life memories as well as past-life situations. The therapist can suggest the image of an escalator moving downward to another level and time. An elevator can take a person down or back to an age which corresponds to the floor number indicated over the door of the elevator. If the client is claustrophobic, however, this elevator image might stimulate some discomfort.

The clients have enough problems of their own and the therapist does a disservice by using a contrived and unnatural imagery as an induction. It simply isn't necessary and can add to the burden of traumatic memories. As the next example shows, this can be overt and immediate. It can also register at a deeper level of the unconscious mind without the awareness of the client or therapist.

One therapist used the image of a time machine for a female subject as a demonstration of a past-life induction. The woman imagined getting into the machine and starting it up.

As he guided her back into earlier incarnations, she suddenly jumped in her chair. In her imagery she had just crashed into a mountain. The trauma was thus compounded and the therapist had to assist her out of this unnecessary burden.

Guided Imagery

The client is guided in visualizations of various familiar places. He can be guided to cross a bridge connecting this lifetime and a past life. He can be guided into the foyer of a large building which contains many doorways leading into other times and places. A long, well-lighted hallway with many doors can be suggested. It may seem as if one doorway appears to be brighter than the others. That doorway will open onto a past-life scene. A special room can be suggested in which each wall is a huge video screen on which are playing scenes from past lives. The client can step right into the one which seems to draw his attention.

A lush garden scene is particularly non-threatening. The client is guided past beds of flowers the colors of the rainbow. The first color is red, then orange, yellow, green, blue and violet. These are the colors of the chakras and the visualizations tend to balance and soothe the energy of the client. Just past the beds of flowers there are tall trees with roots that go deep into the earth and branches that reach skyward. This suggests security and grounding and also gives permission to reach for something higher.

Beyond the trees there is a clearing bathed in sunlight. The client is directed to be seated on a small bench in the clearing and feel the warmth of the sunlight. This is the invocation of the protection of the Light. It is also a safe sanctuary the client can return to in case of a traumatic surprise during the regression. The client is directed to walk to the gate at the end of the garden and to describe the gate. He is then directed to step through the gate into the experience of another lifetime, another lifetime which is important to him. He is directed to close the gate firmly behind himself.

The exit at the end of the garden is often the rusty iron gate or heavy wooden door of some structure in the setting of the past life. It becomes the first glimpse of the lifetime to be explored.

This guided imagery induction is presented in expanded form in the sections Dual Regression (149) and Group Regression (158).

Direct Suggestion

In the discussion preceding the induction, the therapist and client decide on the subject to be explored. It might be an emotional problem, physical condition or present-life situation needing clarification. Once the client is successfully shifted into the alpha state by any standard hypnotic induction, the direct suggestion can be given to locate a past life that holds the source of the item decided upon. This can be quite successful. The scenes which emerge can be processed as described in the section The Sequence of a Past-life Regression (112).

Non-hypnotic Inductions

Alterations of awareness and consciousness are normal and continuous. People shift daily from deepest sleep to the highest levels of the fully conscious awake state. A person might be so intensely concentrating on either work or play that peripheral details go unnoticed. Focusing on a good theater performance, movie or an important lecture can produce the same results, and a person may require some moments of reorientation at the conclusion of the event to be fully present in real time and present location. Daydreaming can take the person away from a boring situation. Meditation is a departure from full waking awareness (Spiegel & Spiegel, 1978).

The hypnotic state is a focused awareness brought about by direct suggestions made by the therapist. This shift in conscious is real for the client, yet artificially induced. In the therapeutic setting, exploration of a person's emotions will focus the consciousness of the origin or cause of a present-life problem. This is the indirect approach, the non-hypnotic induction. It is a process of utilizing the client's own inner conflict to direct the session. There is much less chance of contaminating the client's experience with the attitudes and emotional residue of the therapist. The suggestion to the client to focus on the emotions or sensations is a direct and powerful induction which can immediately shift the consciousness into the altered state. The session can proceed without any further imposed induction technique.

Traditional authoritarian hypnotic induction techniques are unnecessary for most people in this therapeutic approach. The consciousness of the client is altered as he or she focuses on the inner feelings. Personal feelings and emotions are the key to past experience. Heightened emotion can shift the conscious focus from the present moment to an earlier instance of similar feeling.

The client answers the questions posed by the therapist as openly and honestly as possible. Without hypnosis, the client is usually able to observe and recall most, if not all, of what transpires in a session. For some people who go into deep altered state, the memory of the session fades after returning to normal consciousness. This is one reason for taping the session.

State-Bound Memory

Memory is mutable and changes with age. The "good old days" may not have been as good as they are remembered. Traumatic memories can be repressed even though earlier memories are accessible. Whole tracts of one's life can be removed from conscious access by this mechanism. Confabulation of memory occurs when memory is interspersed with fantasy or when elements of the memories of several related events blend into one another. The memory will be related as if it were true and the client will believe it to be true.

Memories may be altered by adding material from questions or statements as from a therapist. This is termed "suggestive confabulation". For this reason, extreme care must be taken by the therapist when a client is in altered states of consciousness. Biographical data from this or another lifetime can be distorted by multiple choice questions or descriptive statements offered by the therapist.

Memory, learning and behavior can be bound to a state of mind induced by any stimulus. The stimulus can be mind-altering drugs, any strong emotion, sensory stimuli of taste, sound, smell, visual image of a color, shape, movement, a tactile sensation or sense of feel. Memory can also be stimulated by bodily sensations such as pain, pressure, temperature, or position. Anything which can be perceived in any manner, physically, mentally, or emotionally can elicit memories of earlier experience.

A rebirthing client caught the fragrance of freshly cut pine wafting up from the garage workshop below the treatment room. He did not realize the scent was actually in the room in that moment. It instantly restimulated a childhood memory of being in his grandfather's carpenter shop. This began a string of experiences which were meaningful for the therapy.

A woman client described an evening when her grown children were visiting. Her 21-year-old son sat close to her and she ran her fingers through his hair in a motherly caress. She was instantly transported in her mind to an event more than 20 years earlier. It was the memory of holding her infant son and caressing the same silky hair which she so loved.

A female client described the sudden onset of the physical sensation of nausea whenever she heard any version of the song, "What's new Pussycat?" When this song was popular she was pregnant with her now-grown daughter.

A male client described how a taste of a tangy raspberry mousse stimulated a mental image of Sedona, Arizona. Another taste of the raspberry mousse stimulated the imagery of a favorite restaurant in that town. The third taste brought back the happy memory of a dinner several years earlier which had ended with a delicious and tangy raspberry mousse.

After watching a frightening movie at night, a person is more likely to react fearfully to unidentified sounds. A poignant movie may remind a sentimental person of other episodes of sadness and loss. A person in a happy mood may laugh at simple things which would not ordinarily cause laughter. An angry person will find little humor in the funniest of jokes.

The process of past-life therapy utilizes certain states of mind to access earlier traumatic incidents by following the track of emotion from the present time into the past event which holds the origin of the experiential residue. Once a certain emotional feeling tone is elicited in a session, earlier incidents which involved the same feeling tone are easily accessible. The track of similar emotion will lead directly to the original episode. Since therapy revolves about present-life problems and conflict resolution, the original episode will inevitably prove to be a traumatic event.

Edith Fiore (1987b) suggests that 98% of her client's presenting problems stem from prior-lifetime traumas. If the subconscious material is retained from other-lifetime experience, then past-life regression therapy may be the most efficacious route to resolution of the pain and conflicts of the present lifetime.

Non-hypnotic inductions draw on the state-bound memory to induce an altered state of consciousness in the client. The following techniques are designed to elicit the specific past lives which hold the traumatic event, the engram of the experience. The *engram* is defined as the persisting psychical trace (usually in the form of an unconscious or latent memory) of an experience (Campbell, 1981, p. 219).

The Metaphoric Induction

Metaphor is the symbol system of the subconscious mind. Word pictures and visual descriptions often clarify a concept more fully than an intricate discussion. This is exemplified by the saying, "A picture is worth a thousand words." In the next section Recovery of Soul-Mind Fragmentation (167), physical and emotional trauma often lead to a fragmentation of the personality or soul-mind. Recovery of the separated fragments is necessary for healing. The fragments of consciousness are still

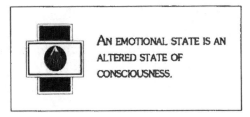

AN EMOTIONAL STATE IS AN ALTERED STATE OF CONSCIOUSNESS.

connected to the being, that is, the client. The client is directed to locate that connection through the metaphor of the silver thread, a part of the silver cord which connects the soul with the body.

> T: "Follow the silver thread you see coming out of the hole in your heart. Where does it take you?"

Most clients can sense this cord or visualize it. This leads the person into the traumatic incident which caused the fragmentation. The visual metaphor can be used in many situations.

The Affect Bridge

The affect bridge was developed by John G. Watkins, Ph.D. (1971). It is described as a method of experientially moving a client from a present to a past incident over an affect, that is, an emotion or feeling, which is common to both events rather than through an overlapping idea or mental concept in the manner of psychoanalytic association.

An overreaction—the intense and often inappropriate emotion which is experienced in a present-time conflict—is often a carryover from an earlier time. It is the residue of a traumatic past-life event which was never resolved. Separate events which are similarly characterized by highly charged emotional states are connected or linked by those particular emotions. Specific past events can be elicited by recalling and linking with recent events. This is the basis of the affect bridge as a past-life induction technique.

As a client describes a present-life problem or conflict, the associated and often denied or repressed emotion will begin to emerge. This is encouraged by the therapist. As the story unfolds, the therapist asks how the client feels about the situations involved. The details of the story are not as important as the emotional reaction to the events. It is these emotional feelings which are carried as residue. A verbal description of the feelings is not the affect; the client is urged to continue to describe the conflict and to feel those feelings, to really get into the feelings.

There is no need for a formal hypnotic induction to guide the client into a relaxed and altered state of mind in an attempt to access the past-life memory of a traumatic event. An emotional state *is* an altered state of consciousness. The upsurge of emotion is the link; the memory is already accessed. Once the link with a traumatic past-life event is established, the past-life experience is available in its entirety. The affect bridge is, in effect, an instant induction. REM is detectable almost immediately.

The therapist aids the expression of the feelings by pacing the client in voice and emotional tone. This will usually lead to an upwelling of the emotion or emotions and a cessation of the narrative. The therapist waits at least 10 to 30 seconds as the client immerses more deeply into these strong feelings. It is imperative that the therapist not interrupt by reacting to his/her own anxiety regarding this period without words, and the emotions expressed out loud by the client such as cries, moans, sobs, gasping, choking, gagging, foaming at the mouth, retching, vomiting, or bodily movements such as shaking, kicking, stiffening, or clenching of the hands.

As the client's emotion begins to subside, the moment will come when it feels appropriate for the therapist to continue. Recognition of this moment becomes easier with experience and trusting of one's own intuition.

The suggestion is given very gently because it is so powerful.

T: "Recall another time when you felt this same way. (pause) Let these feelings take you back to another time when you felt the same feelings. (pause) Allow yourself to remember another time when you were feeling these same feelings."

This is the affect bridge. The suggestion can take many forms, as these three indicate. Often this suggestion is a sufficient catalyst for the client to access the traumatic event in a prior lifetime, along with the attendant emotions. This often proves to be the event responsible for the present life problem.

The Somatic Bridge

For every physical condition, there is a psychological component. For every emotional problem, there is a physical manifestation, a somatization of the emotion, a bodily sensation. The client is invited to focus on the body and notice any physical sensation which begins to come into awareness. This is an effective beginning with a person who shows low affect or expresses little emotional feeling (Araoz, 1985, pp. 36-39).

As a client describes the problem, the emotion usually builds. The emotion may cause some physical sensation which the client may describe as a tightening of the muscles of some part of the body, increased heart rate, rapid or constricted breathing, head pounding or hurting, tingling sensation in the hands or feet, or some other sensation somewhere in the body. This is the physical residue of past-life trauma still carried in the subtle body which affects the physical body (Woolger, 1987, pp. 161-188).

To initiate the somatic bridge, the following questions are asked using the client's exact description of the physical sensation. The client's description of the sensation must not be rephrased by the therapist. The words used by the client in describing the sensation become the symbol for the sensation, not the sensation itself, and the therapist must use the identical symbols to elicit the same sensation or reaction from the prior event.

The therapist directs the client to give words to the physical sensation:

> T: "If that _____(sensation) could speak, what is the first thing it would say?"
> "If it could speak, what is the first thing it would say right now?"
> "If that _____(sensation) had words to say what would that be?" The therapist must use the client's exact words to describe the sensation.

This will elicit words which may have been spoken by someone else at the time of the physical trauma. The words can also be the words or thoughts of the client in the past-life personality at the time of the trauma. It must be noted that the words may also be those of an attached earthbound spirit, a possessing entity. Specific techniques are described in the section Differential Diagnosis (237).

If there is hesitation in response to these questions, the therapist asks the client to focus on the physical sensation.

> T: "If it had a size, shape, color, or movement, what would that be?"
> "If there were a scene or an image associated with the sensation, what would that be?"

This is a more general guidance into the traumatic past-life event and may be more effective in some cases.

Another aspect of the physical residue in the body memory is posture and position. A client may be describing a present-life situation, problem or conflict. In searching for words to describe the problem, the posture may straighten, the head may tilt backward, the arms and hands may reach out positioned as if holding something.

A young woman was describing her anguish over her feelings of helplessness in caring for her newborn child. Her arms extended in front of her, palms upward. The therapist directed her to focus on the emotion and the position of her hands and arms.

T: "As you focus on your hands what comes to mind? Feel your hands out in front of you, what image comes?"

C: "I'm holding a baby! It's dead. My baby is dead!"

She immediately went into the anguish of the past life and the actual physical position of holding her infant in her outstretched hands. She blamed herself for the death. Working through this mental, emotional and physical residue helped resolve her anguish in the present-life situation as a new mother.

A certain physical activity can trigger memories of prior lifetimes. This is often described as *déjà vu*. Walking through a street, alley or building in a country never before visited in this life can stimulate the recall of the neighborhood.

One client described having such an experience when he entered a 200 year old building in France while vacationing there. He suddenly felt that he knew the entire floor plan of every story of the building. A tour of the structure proved his fantasy inaccurate. The layout of the building was nothing like his "vision." Further investigation revealed that there had been extensive renovation some years previously. The drawings of the original floor plan completely validated his first vivid impressions.

Dr. Helen Wambach (1978, pp. 1-2) described an upsetting experience. She was visiting a Quaker memorial as a "Sunday tourist." She entered a small upstairs library room, went automatically to a shelf of books and took one down. She somehow knew it had been her book. As she looked at its pages a scene came before her inner eyes. She was male, riding a mule across a stubbled field. The sun was hot and his clothes felt scratchy. The man was deeply absorbed in the book which was propped in front of him as he rode. It was a minister's account of the between-life state while he was in coma. Dr. Wambach seemed to know the contents of the book even before she turned its pages.
As she emerged from the spontaneous trance, she had many unanswered questions. She became deeply involved with hypnotic regression work. She

conducted past-life regression workshops with thousands of subjects across the country. Her research on past lives is presented in her two books (Wambach, 1978, 1979). Her work on future-life progressions was published posthumously, included with work of co-researchers Dr. Leo Sprinkle and Dr. Chet Snow (Snow, 1989).

The Linguistic Bridge

Language is a symbol system which is used to indicate thoughts and ideas, to communicate desires and intentions and to describe experience. The words are not the experience. As a client describes the problem areas, phrases will be used which represent the emotions, feelings and physical sensation. These words and phrases become the specific symbol and must be used verbatim to elicit those same feelings again in the therapy session.

The therapist must not rephrase or paraphrase the client's description of the feelings. Although the words may not be accurate or elegant, they are the key to the inner experience of the client and must be used exactly as uttered. The clients have their own answers and solutions to the problems; it is the work of the therapist to guide them to those solutions. The client will provide the clues; the therapist must be astute, aware, and attentive to these clues.

As the client describes the problem areas, the therapist listens for the key descriptive phrases. These may be highly emotionally charged phrases and indicate some of the emotional residue carried from other lives. Although it may seem unimportant to the therapist, the residue is whatever judgment the person made of it.

Anger, rage:

C: "I'll get even with that S.O.B."
   "He isn't going to stop me this time, he will not get in my way."
   "I'm never going to say anything again."
   "You'll see."

Fear, terror:

C: "God, I'll never come back again, I never want to get into that situation again."
   "I feel like I can't breathe, I just want to get out of here."
   "They can't leave me alone with it."
   "Don't hurt me anymore."

Sadness, depression:

C: "I want her so, I want to come back, I'll miss her."

"I feel like I don't deserve _____."

"Oh, I wish I had it to do over again, I'm going to have to come back."

"Those who know get in trouble. I can never let them know."

Guilt, anxiety:

C: "I know I was responsible for _____, and if I had to live the rest of my life with this pain I'd rather die."

"I'll have to make up for that."

"Oh God, I never should have _____." The blank can be anything.

The residue of any past trauma becomes part of the language system. A phrase can indicate retained birth trauma.

C: "I feel blocked in life."

"I feel like I'm up against a solid wall."

"I just can't seem to get started in life."

"Everything seems to be closing in on me."

"I feel like nobody wants me."

The phrase can be a metaphoric description of a past-life trauma. These phrases suggest the source of retained physical residue:

C: "I feel like I'm a prisoner in my own house."

"When I'm around her/him, I feel like I can't talk, I feel dumb."

"It felt like a spear in my heart."

"If she leaves me I know I'll die."

"I have to have my back toward the wall. If my back is to the crowd every sound is like a knife in my back."

The phrases often indicate soul-mind fragmentation even when the subject has not been mentioned in the session.

C: "Part of me just wants to go away."

"Part of me just curled up and died when he did that."

"I just died inside."

"I just went numb inside."

"I'm leaving, I'm out of here, I'm gone."

"I'll never show them that side of me again."

"Part of me just went inside and hid."

"The soft part was afraid to come out again."

The phrases often describe the condition of spirit attachment. At the subconscious level, a person is aware of the presence of others.

C: "My grandfather is still in me."
"I can still hear my grandmother's voice telling me how to make piecrust."
"There is always that little voice inside saying 'Let's have just one little drink.'"
"I felt like a different person after the accident."
"It feels like there's someone else in my body. It feels like I'm not alone."
"It doesn't feel like my anger. It's like someone just lashes out. I'm always surprised when it happens."
"People tell me that when I drink, I become another person."

More insidious is the infinite phrase, open ended, without temporal or quantitative limit. This is the mental residue, the leftover decisions, assumptions, conclusions and judgments made during the trauma and pain in the earlier event. When they indicate self-judgments, these self-directed commands can wreak particular havoc for many lifetimes with self-esteem and self-confidence.

C: "I'm scared I might have to do that again."
"I just need to do more."
"I'm not doing enough. I can't do enough. I can never do enough."
"I'm not enough."
"I'll never be beautiful again."
"I'll never be rich again."
"I would never want to be rich."
"I can never trust men."
"I can never trust women."
"I won't go through this again."
"I will never leave him."
"It's better to be seen than to see."
"Nobody is ever going to hurt me like that again."

These infinite phrases often contain such words as "ever," "never," "always," and "forever," which might be meaningful to the ego which recognizes nothing beyond its present life. The spirit being, however, seems to honor this proclamation of the ego and attempts to implement the declared behavior.

Phrases containing the words "better than," "more like ___," and "not enough," always imply comparison and can be particularly destructive. The standard of comparison is always arbitrary and therefore false. Though the original standard is long gone and forgotten, it is somehow glorified, enlarged, even more unattainable in the forgetting, and the striving to attain it is even more ardent.

With attentiveness and experience, the therapist becomes more adept at recognizing these signal phrases. As the phrases come up during the initial interview or during any discussion, they are written down word for word. Any one of them can be used as a linguistic bridge, the entry point into the past life which holds the source of the problem. If they are expressed during the past-life exploration, the client is asked to repeat the words. Repetition of the phrases reinforces and emphasizes the statement, compounds the feelings, and intensifies the emotion.

As the client's voice grows louder and more emotional with the repetition, the therapist keeps pace, urging the repetition more firmly.

T: "Say it again," or, "Say that again," or "Repeat."

Three repetitions are usually enough to get the client into a sufficient level of emotion to access the appropriate past life. If the phrase is an incomplete sentence, does not uncover strong emotion, or does not uncover the past memories, the client is asked to articulate the next words that come.

T: "Finish that sentence."
"What are the next words?"
"What words come after that?"
"What comes next?"

This is continued until the thought is complete and the link is established and the past life has been accessed. The use of the client's descriptive phrases is a major aspect of the Netherton method of Past Lives Therapy (Netherton, 1978).

Past-Life Induction
Any of the above three bridge inductions used alone can elicit a past-life memory. The emotion is the link. Using the three together almost always brings up the traumatic event in another lifetime. As the client is repeating the phrase, experiencing the emotions (perhaps several at the same time) and feeling the physical sensations in one or more parts of the body, the therapist gently and firmly suggests:

T: "Let those feelings, let those sensations in your body, let those words take you back to another time, another place when you felt the same things. (pause) Say it again."

The client's ability and willingness to allow emotion to surface are essential to the success of this method of past-life induction. Some clients are very intellectual, extremely guarded against their emotions, well defended against revealing inner feelings. Therefore, this approach may not be effective at first with some people, such as police officers, physicians, lawyers, the macho man, women in depression or fear, people who are separated from their feelings as a result of early abuse, or anyone resistant to the expressions of feeling and emotion.

Connected Breathing

If the client cannot or will not allow expression of feelings and emotions after the therapist has used these three approaches, another type of induction-involuntary shifting of consciousness-may be more effective. The therapist instructs the client to breathe deeply for several breaths, then to breathe deeply and a bit faster than normal. After several minutes of this deeper, more rapid breathing, the consciousness begins to alter, as the increased ventilation causes a change in the blood chemistry. After 5 to 7 minutes, the client is asked to repeat the phrases again. These techniques work with most resistant clients.

Mike was a police captain nearing retirement. After many active years in the field, he had a desk job. He was well defended emotionally and hardened from his years of dealing with people in the way a police officer must. Despite this facade, Mike was a deeply sensitive man and longed for a meaningful relationship with a woman. His emotional defenses were so well established that intimacy seemed impossible. Most women were put off by his apparent coldness, aloofness, and emotional distancing. Because of this, he felt it would be unfair to a woman to establish a relationship leading to marriage. He wanted to explore past lives with the hope of being able to open himself to a loving interaction.

None of the direct access inductions worked. Hypnosis had no effect. Therefore the therapist guided Mike into connected breathing. He cooperated fully and breathed deeply and rapidly, without hesitation between breaths. Within about two minutes he began to tear slightly.

Another minute of connected breathing brought him to sobbing, deep mournful sobs. He was open. He discovered several lives of solitude and separation, lives as warrior, as soldier, as one who has no family because of dedication to the protection of the people. These were lives of selfless dedication which eliminated the possibility of a normal interaction with a woman, offering no hope of future years together to produce offspring and nurture a family. Mike had discovered his dharmic path as warrior (Sutphen, 1987).

However, the breathing technique may not work with a person who is aware of hyperventilation and hypoxia, the lack of oxygen. Jim was a 42-year-old obstetrician. He was also a well-trained private pilot. Well grounded in the medical model, he wanted to explore past lives with Val, his fiancée, as well as to explore the process of spirit releasement, which had seemed to benefit her so much. His childhood was emotionally traumatic: His father was alcoholic, his mother religious and strict. His feelings had effectively been suppressed since his early years. The bridging techniques were ineffective.

He breathed as he was instructed, yet blocked any emergence of feelings. His overriding concern as the breathing continued was the onset of symptoms of hypoxia: light-headedness, tingling of the muscles around the mouth, tingling and minor tetany in the muscles of the hands. He recognized this as a lack of oxygen stemming from hyperventilation. As a pilot, he had been trained to immediately dive to lower altitudes when he experienced these signs of hypoxia. He couldn't sufficiently overcome this urge to uncover his emotional feelings. However, as he relaxed and breathed normally, he felt safer and responded to suggestions to recall another time when he and Val were together. The altered state was sufficient to allow the memory of a prior lifetime to emerge.

In a group session of connected breathing, participants pair up for the exercise. One partner lies on pillows on the floor; the other sits beside him, maintaining connection and acting as a non-judgmental guide. Jack was one of 30 participants in a group session of connected breathing. About five minutes into the breathing, Jack began to moan. The moans grew in intensity, a loud wailing moan with each outbreath. After about 30 minutes of this wailing, it began to subside. After the exercise, Jack remembered the sounds as his mother's moaning during the labor of his delivery. The recording mind of the infant had absorbed the mother's emotion, sensation and vocal expression as his own. It was released in the connected breathing exercise.

The Sequence of a Past-Life Regression
The non-hypnotic inductions described will usually elicit a traumatic scene in a past incarnation. The therapist guides the client in exploring the details of the scene through the eyes of the character, the past-life personality. The present tense is used in the languaging of the questions. This is the process of identification with the past-life character. The client's name is not used, and there is no mention of any details from the present life. For a person recalling and reliving a prior lifetime, that life *is* the present moment. The therapist orients his viewpoint and verbal interaction to the present tense in that time.

In the lifetime being explored, the first traumatic event which is discovered often ends in death. The client is guided back through the entire traumatic event several times and directed to notice more details each time. The next step is the exploration of the precipitating events and circumstances that occurred just prior to the traumatic event that led to the death scene. The attendant emotional residue is reexperienced and resolved.

The assumptions, decisions, conclusions and judgments surrounding the event, the other persons involved, and the death itself are explored, as this mental residue can form the basis of beliefs which contaminate subsequent lifetimes, including the current life.

Physical trauma and its remaining energy patterns are probed to determine what physical residue remains in the present physical body. Exploring and processing the residue is the resolution-phase of the past-life regression therapy session.

As long as a client is fully identified with the character of a past life, the therapist continues to work in that past-life setting with the client. No mention is made of prior or future lives, including the present life. Occasionally, a client will mention some recognition of a person or similar situation in the present life and the therapist acknowledges and perhaps briefly explores the connection, then gently urges the client back into the lifetime being processed.

The client is guided through the death experience. Any remaining emotional, mental, or physical residue is resolved and the being moves into the Light. This is the disidentification phase of the regression, the separation from the character and its problems. Only when the being is fully in the Light is that past life complete. From the review stage in the Light, connecting lifetimes can be explored and processed.

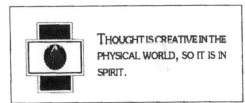

THOUGHT IS CREATIVE IN THE PHYSICAL WORLD, SO IT IS IN SPIRIT.

In the non-physical dimension or spirit space, situations may be described metaphorically. There is no physical matter, no solid furniture, no buildings as they are known in the physical-level energy vibration of earth. There are no solid bodies. A spirit being can change form. The true form is the spark of light with a specific recognizable energy vibration, a point of conscious energy.

A being can take the form of a familiar loved one when making an appearance to a living person to bring a message. This seems to be for the purpose of not frightening the person. One or more loved ones may greet and guide a newly deceased spirit into the Light. In the death scene in a past-life regression, the newly deceased spirit will often recognize a friend or loved one coming from the Light to assist.

This familiarity establishes the contact, and the spirit will willingly accompany the guiding one. When asked to look again and describe the guide, the response may indicate that the identity is the same But the form is now a bright point of light. As the newly deceased spirit looks at its own form again, it also sees a spark of light, though not as bright as the guiding one.

As thought is creative in the physical world, so it is in spirit. It simply manifests more quickly in spirit. As a being thinks of his surroundings, so they will appear to that being. This may be confusing to the therapist.

Tom and Sandy were guided in a dual regression. From the planning stage, she wanted to hasten into life and she wanted him to accompany her. He was hesitant, though he knew he would lose contact with her if she went in and he remained behind in the Light.

Sandy described a theatrical stage. She was on the stage prior to the curtain going up. Tom was hesitating in the wings, hiding among the layers of hanging curtain.

Tom described a long, gently sloping chute heading downward toward the physical dimension. Sandy was partly within the chute, ready to descend into earth reality, and he was standing outside refusing to enter the chute with her.

The therapist must be alert to such metaphors presented by clients who are describing non-physical experience. Tom and Sandy were in the same place. The important aspect of their interaction was not the surroundings, which seemed to be totally different for each of them, but the emotional interplay between them. In the process of questioning, the therapist assumes that the two are involved in the same event. If this is not so, the clients will make it known immediately.

In many cases, the death scene is described by a spirit who will not move toward the Light after leaving the body. Many will describe moving toward a living person and attaching to or merging with them. This is an attached spirit speaking through the client. In such a case the past life explored was that of an attached entity, not the client. This condition of spirit interference or spirit attachment is addressed in the section Spirit Possession (12) in the Introduction. Treatment for the condition is described in the section Spirit Releasement Therapy (199).

Identification into the Character

These induction methods will nearly always elicit traumatic events in other lifetimes because of the link between similar affect in the current-life problem and conflict areas, and the originating episode in the prior lifetime which led to the retained emotional, mental, and physical residues. The client may react strongly to the memory which emerges. The therapist paces the client by at least partially matching the emotional tone in the guiding questions.

The therapist uses present tense when questioning the client about the past-life experience. The client is urged to experience as directly as possible whatever develops in the scene that emerges. The therapist asks for and uses the name of the past-life personality. This is the process of identification into the character, which is the first step in working or processing the past life.

The more direct the experience, the more healing potential is realized. Dissociation from the event will significantly reduce the possibility of resolution of the conflict in the past and the present. Dissociation of feelings from traumatic events in the present time is considered to be a pathological coping mechanism, as in the case of MPD.

Processing the Conflict

Processing any conflicts to resolution is the second step of the therapy. The client is guided through the uncovered traumatic event to its conclusion, which is often death. The client will describe floating, the cessation of pain, often viewing the body from above. This is the death experience.

The therapist guides the client back into the body to a time before the traumatic event began.

T: "Move right back into the lifetime, skip back to a time before
this thing began. (pause) What is happening?"

Going through the event the second time, the client is urged to notice and
describe more details of the event.

T: "As you go through the event again, notice what is happen-
ing. How are you interacting with other people?"
"What is happening to your body?"
"What are people doing to you?"
"What are you doing to others?"
"What are other people doing to each other, in the vicinity?"
"What words are other people saying?"

These words from other people can be directed toward the character in
the past life or they may be directed to someone else in the vicinity. In the
traumatized altered state of consciousness, the subconscious mind perceives any
words as being focused on itself. This is similar to the pre- and peri-natal recording
mind accepting everything spoken as being directed toward itself.
As the being leaves the body, the assessment continues.

T: "As you come out of the body, this time notice even more
details of what is happening in the area. What are other
people doing?"
"What emotions and sensations do you take with you into
spirit? What feelings and sensations?"

Once again, the client is directed back into the lifetime to explore the
circumstances leading up to the traumatic event, to determine what part his
character played in the incident, and the extent of his responsibility in the
circumstances of the event. Once again, as he moves through the death into the
spirit space, the client is directed to notice the emotions, physical sensations, and
assumptions and decisions made regarding the situation. These are the residues:
emotional, physical and mental.
As the residual emotions are revealed and sensations described, the
therapist directs the client to locate the source of each one. Then it is worked to
completion. Each residual emotion and sensation is worked to the point that the
emotion is no longer triggered and physical sensation is resolved or disappeared.

T: "What emotions and feelings do you carry from the lifetime as
you separate from the body?"
"Let that _____(feeling, sensation) take you right back
into the life you are exploring, or another lifetime. Locate the
first moment you felt that way."

This often reveals an earlier event or situation, sometimes a traumatic event in another lifetime. This event is worked to completion like any traumatic event sequence.

The client is urged to notice what decisions and assumptions he is making, what conclusions and judgments are being drawn as a result of the experience. This is the mental residue of a lifetime which develops into belief systems in future lives.

After the client describes separating from the physical body in the death, the therapist continues:

T: "Let that _____(thought, decision, assumption, judgment) take you right back into the life, or another lifetime. Locate the first moment you had that thought."

The episodes uncovered in this manner are worked to completion, often through abreaction and catharsis. The source of these thoughts and feelings may be located in another lifetime; the conflict may span several lifetimes. These connecting lifetimes are accessible, if necessary, by this process. As the client reexperiences in this way, the misperceptions and misinterpretations will begin to clear. As this residue is processed, the traumatic event is reframed. From a more realistic viewpoint, without emotional and judgmental distortion, accurate perceptions allow for the truth to be known. The truth eases the pain. The truth will lead to freedom. This is the releasing and healing of the residues.

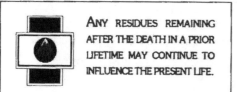

ANY RESIDUES REMAINING AFTER THE DEATH IN A PRIOR LIFETIME MAY CONTINUE TO INFLUENCE THE PRESENT LIFE.

The process is repeated with any mental, emotional, or physical residue which remains after the death and carried to complete resolution. This means that the client will feel no emotion or physical sensation after going through the death once again. The limiting and restrictive assumptions, decisions and conclusions that were made during times of stress will be seen as false and inappropriate for the current life circumstances. Any of these residues remaining after the death in a prior lifetime will continue to influence the present life.

The After-Death Experience

The spirit lifts from the physical body, usually with a great sense of relief. Pain is diminished or absent. Emotions which, such a short time before, were so painfully important quickly dim in significance. Some clients burst into laughter at this point. Conflict and turmoil are often dissipated and replaced with calm acceptance. The concerns and problems which constricted and interfered with one's progress in life seem ridiculous. The entire drama of the life is left behind. The petty squabbles and egocentric strivings take on a cartoon-like appearance.

The scope of awareness and understanding expands. What becomes clear is the importance of the power of love in human interactions, and the sadness over the missed opportunities of expressing and experiencing love.

The spirit often remains close to the grieving loved ones in a futile desire to comfort them. When this proves impossible, the spirit may begin to drift upward toward the Light. A newly deceased spirit may remain in the area of its death for many earth years, confused and bewildered at the changes in the loved ones left behind. The living people seem to age quickly, as if they were characters on a video run at high speed. A lost spirit may finally move toward the Light on its own. It may be helped along toward the Light by living people performing rescue work. The Light is an ineffable brightness which always comes at the time of death. The death experience is nearly identical with reports of the near-death experience (Moody, 1975; Ring, 1980; Sabom, 1982).

The following case is typical of such a confused spirit.

Charles was an engineering professor in his late 60s. Though he believed in reincarnation, his strong analytical mind had never been able to shut down enough to allow past-life impressions to emerge. He had attempted past-life regression several times, without success. This therapist used a guided body relaxation for the induction. Charles was instructed to move into the experience of another lifetime.

> T: "What is the first thing you experience? What are you aware of right now?"

The therapist waited for the response. Time stretched out. After about three minutes Charles responded. Each answer was presented slowly and deliberately. The responses were coherent; the images or impressions simply took longer than average to form. With each question, there was a one- to two-minute wait for each response.

> T: "Look down and describe what you're wearing."

Charles paused as the image formed.

> C: "Cowboy boots, jeans, a plaid shirt, and a cowboy hat."

"Curly" was the name of the past-life character. He was a cowboy working near the mountains, possibly in Colorado. He described walking around the ranch near the big house, by the corrals and bunkhouse. Though he could see people in the big house, they seemed not to take notice of him. This is an indication to the therapist that the character is in spirit and no longer embodied.

> T: "Curly, as you walk about the ranch, are your feet touching the ground?"

C: "About every ten feet."

He still did not realized he was no longer alive in his body.

T: "Locate your physical body."

C: "I feel like I'm being pulled backward. I'm traveling along a dry creek bed. Even though I'm going backward, I can see full view where I'm headed. There is a bridge over the creek bed."

The command to locate the body drew him backward in time, back along the path he traveled after he died and separated from his body.

C: "There is a pile of clothes or something at one end of the bridge. (pause) Oh, it's about the size of a man's body. (pause) It looks like the clothes I was wearing. My God, I believe I died. It seems like my horse threw me by this bridge."

Curly simply was not aware that he had made the transition. With this realization, he began to lift upward. He watched his body and other details on the ground disappear as he rose.

C: "There is a light over by the mountain. I seem to be heading toward it."

T: "What do you look like now?"

C: "I still have my jeans, plaid shirt and cowboy hat. The Light is closer now. It is like a funnel coming toward me."

T: "What are you wearing now?"

Charles was continuing to approach the Light.

C: "The funnel is closer and brighter. I just have my plaid shirt and cowboy hat now."

T: "What happens next?"

C: "I'm at the end of the funnel. I just have my hat now. I'm getting lighter."

T: "All right, what's happening now?"

C: "I'm all light now. Hat's gone. I'm going up into the Light."

That was the completion of the lifetime. Often, the spirit does not realize what has happened. When led to discover the truth, it may readily move to the brightness. In one sense, Charles performed rescue work on his own lost spirit in another lifetime.

This case gives rise to speculations about the nature of time. The spirit was wandering about the ranch which had been his workplace, apparently remaining on the earth plane. Was he earthbound at the time? Would he have become earthbound if the session had not taken place? If Charles was a reincarnation of Curly, then Curly had to go to the Light in order to return to earth as Charles. Yet the rescue of this confused spirit apparently took place during his future incarnation as Charles. Is the imagery nothing but imagination? Or is it possible to reach across time and space in the non-physical space of the altered state of consciousness? The answers to these speculations are not available to the logical conscious mind.

In the case of strong emotional ties to the survivors, or of fear of many kinds (anger and feelings of vengeance, guilt, addictions or compulsions), a being may either remain in the surrounding area or attach to another person. If the being does manage to break away from the earth plane and move into the Light, these mental, emotional and physical residues may manifest in future lifetimes as problems and conflicts. This is the focus of the next section, "Clearing the Death."

Clearing the Death

The consciousness often separates when death is obviously imminent. Many people report dreams in which they fall from a cliff and never hit the bottom. Similarly, many clients report death scenes in prior lifetimes in which they emerge from the body just before the moment of pain and death, then observe the fatal incident from a vantage point just above. The memories of the trauma are thus buried in the body and suppressed, yet the effects continue.

The client is directed to move through the death once again, remaining in the body to fully experience every sensation and feeling in every part of the physical form. The client is urged to relate this experience in detail. This includes describing what part of the body hits first, the sounds of the impact, the position of the body parts as they are damaged, and any words associated with the event. These words can belong to the dying person or they can be uttered by other people nearby. This is especially important if the words are spoken by an assailant who causes the death. Every detail is retained in memory and can affect the physical body in the present manifestation.

Even though the consciousness may separate from the body, every bit of the sustained trauma is registered in the recording mind, much as every pre-natal experience is retained. These memories must be uncovered and expressed, along with the attendant, emotions in order to release the present-life effects of that denied and buried physical trauma.

This is part of the physical residue which is retained through lifetimes. If there is still physical sensation after processing in this manner, the client is directed to disengage from the sensation, to disidentify from the body and its pain.

> T: "Leave that body behind. Leave every sensation and every symptom of illness in that body. Leave it behind you."
> "That is no longer your body. Leave the pain of death in that body where it belongs. Leave the sensations of every condition in that body as you separate from it. That is no longer your body."
> "Leave the pain of that body with the body where it belongs. That pain does not belong to you any longer. Let that pain remain with that body."

Use of the article "that" further disengages, linguistically, the item to which "that" refers.

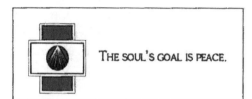

THE SOUL'S GOAL IS PEACE.

As a client relives and describes a death scene, it may actually be an attached entity who is recalling the pain of its death and imposing that memory on the host. These commands can also work on the entity. However, the preferred treatment for the attached and interfering entity is releasement into the Light. This normally relieves the sensations of pain experienced by the host, at least the layer generated by the entity.

Resolution of the mental, emotional and physical residue within the lifetime is beneficial to the well being of the person in this lifetime. It also precludes the necessity of another lifetime of facing the same issues. Beyond that, the soul's goal is peace. When perfect peace is finally realized, the being will be free to leave the wheel of rebirth.

Disidentification from the Character

After resolution of the residue and separation from the lifetime, the being moves toward the Light. The client will often describe lifting up and away from the physical surroundings, through the roof of the building, up toward the clouds. There are many variations, but there is an identifiable similarity. As the physical scene fades below; deceased loved ones may greet the newly deceased spirit; sometimes the greeters or guides appear as bright sparks of Light. That particular lifetime is complete only when the being is fully in the Light. Variations from this path are discussed in the sections Spirit Possession (12) and Spirit Releasement Therapy (199).

As the newly deceased spirit moves toward the Light, the form changes. The clothing fades away, the body dissolves into wispiness, the personality submerges, and it becomes also a spark of Light, only dimmer than the guides who come. There is usually enormous joy.

Once in the Light, the being encounters the review stage (Whitton and Fisher, 1986). There are usually from three to seven counselors or advisors in this place. Other lives are accessible from this stage, past and future, which bear upon the lifetime just explored. The characters in the lifetime can be located in other times and places, including the present life. Current lifetime conflicts and personal interactions with these others can be examined. Conflicts which span several lifetimes can be explored and evaluated with regard to the present-life circumstances. It becomes clear to the client that the lifetime just recalled is part of a larger picture, a greater plan. The character and personality manifested by the being in the life just passed is seen as only temporary, and confined to the lifetime just explored. This disidentification from the character is the third step of the sequence of a past-life regression.

Connecting Lifetimes

Some interactions between people are linked by strong emotional and mental residue through several lifetimes. Once out of the body and disidentified from the character of the past life, the being can be in touch with the review stage in the Light. From that place, connecting lifetimes can be easily accessed.

> T: "Is there another lifetime involved with the events in the lifetime you have just explored? (pause for answer) Locate that lifetime."
> "Locate the event in another lifetime which set the forces in motion that led to the situation in the lifetime just explored."
> "Locate the karmic event which led to the present-life conflict."

The locator command can be asked in any of several ways. The recall usually comes quickly. With the therapist's guidance, the client is able to work related events in the connecting lifetime and to explore interactions with other people. Beings can incarnate together repeatedly, often in different relationships, yet the client recognizes the characters quite well. The normal purpose for repeating incarnations together is for karmic balancing and to give the beings involved the opportunity to resolve a karmic debt. The original situation which engendered the karmic debt is termed the karmic event.

The karmic event is the original episode which set the forces in motion that led to the trauma in a past or present lifetime. It is the force that continues to bring up problems and conflicts, and will continue to bring up similar conflict until it is resolved by the being.

A simple example of a problem stemming from a karmic event and its outcome is a phobia of heights. A client with this phobia may recall, under hypnosis, another lifetime where he fell to his death from a high cliff. Logically this should alleviate his phobia; yet he finds he still suffers from the irrational fear, though it is somewhat diminished. In a subsequent session he is directed to locate the karmic event associated with his fear of heights. He recalls an earlier lifetime when he pushed someone off a cliff. His later fall to the death was the karmic balancing of the earlier crime. His phobia in the present life is the emotional residue.

Additional Techniques

Techniques of past-life therapy vary considerably. There are as many styles of PLT as there are past-life therapists, many of whom have written fine books on the subject. There are as many uses of the method as there are clients who seek relief of pain or solutions to problems. Every person is unique and every problem is individual. However, a number of techniques are almost universal in application. A few of these are described here.

Firm Guidance

If a client does not move into a past-life experience immediately with the affect or somatic bridge and repetition of phrases, firm guidance may be indicated. Several commands may be used in a firm yet gentle voice.

T: "Let those feelings take you right back into another time, another place when you felt the same way."
"Let that _____(emotion) take you right back into another lifetime."
"Locate those feelings in another lifetime."
"Locate the source or cause of the feelings in another time, another place. (pause) Repeat the words again."

Specific Commands

Specific commands can guide the client into other areas of the lifetime being explored or into other connecting lifetimes. Using the analogy of a video tape, the therapist can guide the client backward or forward along the track into earlier or later scenes. The therapist can use these suggestions quite gently:

T: "Skip forward to the time when...."
"Skip back to...."
"Locate...."
"Recall...."

If a client has difficulty moving backward or forward within the lifetime being explored, the therapist can be a bit more firm with these suggestions.

T: "Locate the source or cause of the condition."
"Let that scene fade now, and locate...."
"Start again at the beginning of the event. Notice what decisions you are making. Look and see, get a sense. What is your feeling of what is going on? What exactly is happening to you?"
"Go to the very last day of your life."

When the client is moving freely through the events of a lifetime, the therapist can use more gentle instructions to prompt:

T: "Explore and describe your feelings."
"Look around. Is there anything nearby that would make you have the feelings of _____ (emotion)?"

As the client becomes well involved in the lifetime, non-leading guidance will assist the impressions of seeing and feeling more and expanding the experience. These directions are delivered quietly and without emotion.

T: "What are you experiencing now?"
"What are you aware of right now?"
"What's happening? What happens next?"
"Go on, what next?"
"Describe."
"Explain."

Look at the Feet

As the details of a past-life memory begin to emerge, they may be sporadic, interrupted, fleeting and fragmented. The conscious mind may discount any images or feelings. The therapist can direct the client into the experience by focusing on something quite innocuous.

T: "Look down at your feet. What are you wearing on your feet? What are you wearing on your body?"

This direction bypasses the conscious interference by offering curiosity as the impetus instead of fear of discovery of a trauma. Later in the regression, a client may wander from the traumatic events into another lifetime, evidenced by totally different surroundings, different circumstances, perhaps as the opposite gender. The therapist can return the client to the target lifetime by directing the attention back to the feet and shoes described earlier. The feet become the anchor for the lifetime. The work of resolution can continue in the specific lifetime where the trauma was first discovered. Connecting lifetimes are explored later.

The Assumptive Question

The therapist first assumes the affirmative answer to ambiguous and speculative questions, then asks the next question. This approach bypasses the defensiveness which would often interfere with the truth.

Example: In a case of suspected history of sexual molestation, the therapist does not ask:

> T: "Were you molested?"
>   "Did someone touch you?"
>   "Did someone do something bad to you?"

These questions restimulate the guilt, shame, and humiliation of the incident and may lead to denial. Instead, the question is:

> T: "What happened to you as a child?"
>   "What happened to you?"
>   "Recall something that happened to you when you were young."
>   "What do you remember?"
>   "Think back to when you were a child. Way back, before you were ___ (six, five, four, three, etc.). What happens to you?"

In the case of a suspected entity attachment, the therapist asks:

> T: "How old was she when you attached like this?"

Caught off guard by the question, the entity will usually answer immediately. The age given will be important later in ongoing therapy as this will indicate a vulnerability which must be healed.

An attached entity may deny interfering with the host if asked directly. Example: There is always some consequence of a spirit attachment, even if it is just a drain of energy. The question is:

> T: "How have you affected _____(client)? How have you affected her physically?"
>   "How have you affected her emotionally?"
>   "How have you interfered with her relationship with her____?" (parent, husband, boyfriend, children)

Example: In the case of a possible suspect in a crime, the therapist does not ask:

T: "Were you there at the crime? Did you do it?"

Instead, the question is:

T: "What happened at the scene? What part did you play?"

The Speculative Question

A therapist must be cautious and aware of the state of mind of the client and knowledgeable about hypnosis and altered states in general. In the altered state a person can be highly suggestible. The subject material of the question can be embellished by the subconscious mind, then accepted and included as part of its own memory. This is one source of confabulation of memory. Critics of hypnosis and hypnotically derived past-life memories point to this mental capability as a flaw in this approach to therapy.

Multiple-choice questions are definitely leading questions and must be avoided. Questions that begin with "why" and "how" call on the reasonableness of the ego mind, the same faculty which manufactures excuses and lies. (Ask why, get a lie.)

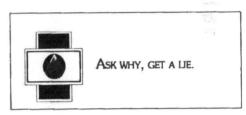

ASK WHY, GET A LIE.

While the speculative question borders on being a leading question, it is a bit less directed. It is softened by a preface such as, "Can you recall...?" or, "Did you ever...?"

T: "Can you recall feeling...?"
    "Can you recall doing...?"
    "Can you recall being...?"
    "Did you ever think about...?"
    "Did you ever feel like...?"
    "Did you ever want to...?"
    "Can you recall wanting to be a boy?"
    "Did you ever just want to give up?"
    "Did you ever get really angry?"

The Open Question

The open question is one without end, without limit on the subject matter, time, age of the client, without condition of any kind. This sort of question touches the raw, unhealed places, the unspoken thoughts, the unfulfilled desires and expectations. These questions open the closed door of childhood hurts, denials and invalidations.

T: "What happened?"
    "What didn't happen?"

"What do you remember?"
"What would you like to say?"
"What happened to you when you were a child?"

The personal traumatic memory can include the pain inflicted on someone else. If a violent scene was witnessed or overheard, the perceptions and interpretations can be internalized. Fear and guilt contaminate these memories.

T: "What happened to someone else?
"What happened to her?"
"What happened to him?"
"What did you try to do?"

The Conditional Question
Often there is resistance to exploring fully some painful or frightening aspect of a traumatic event. Calling on the imagination—which comes from within the subconscious of the client and is part of memory—the therapist asks this question:

T: "If you did know what was happening, what would that be?"
"If you did know what was being said, what would that be?"
"If you did know who it was, who would it be?"
"If you did know what you did, what would that be?"
"If you did know what was in the room, what would it be?"
"If you did know what was at the top of the stairs, what would that be?"
"If you did know who was standing in the dark room, who would that be?"

The information may seem like imagination as it begins to unfold, yet the emotional content is certainly not imagined and the client soon realizes that she really did know the answers.

Mind Merge
In a traumatic interaction with other people, a person is often left with intractable anger and resentment, guilt and remorse, feelings of abandonment and rejection, and a total lack of understanding of the thoughts and behaviors of the others involved in the interaction. The agonizing and unanswerable question, "Why?" continues to stab deeply, perhaps for lifetimes.

The mind attempts to rationalize, to explain, to develop excuses for the behavior and outcome. This results in confusion without resolution. This residue cannot be resolved, as there is no truth in the misperceptions and misunderstandings of the viewpoints, motives, intentions and behavior of the offenders. There is no logical basis for the actions and no unraveling of the situation without some understanding of the thinking of the other people involved in the trauma.

An effective technique for reaching an understanding of the thinking of another person is based on the possibility that all minds are connected

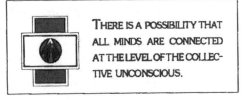

THERE IS A POSSIBILITY THAT ALL MINDS ARE CONNECTED AT THE LEVEL OF THE COLLECTIVE UNCONSCIOUS.

at the level of the collective unconscious. It also calls for the use of a little fantasy. The therapist directs the client back to the scene of the trauma, to a position close to the other person.

> T: "Now imagine stepping out of your body. Cross the space between you and the _____(client's descriptor of the other person) and step into his body. Come up into his head, turn and look out his eyes, merge with his mind and think his thoughts."

The therapist addresses the other using the descriptor.

> T: "Hey you, _____, (descriptor) what are you doing here? What's happening. What are you doing to _____?" (the past-life character of the client)

The client will respond as the other person. The probing continues until the picture is clear from the viewpoint of the other person. The information garnered in this manner will present a surprisingly different viewpoint regarding the traumatic incident. With this information and viewpoint, the situation can be more easily resolved, reframed, and the residue healed.

It is possible to gain even more insight and information by regressing the other person while the fantasy connection is intact. The precipitating events and prior connections with the client can be viewed. The regression can move into a prior life and connecting lifetimes, through the death experience, into the spirit space, into virtually any location which can be explored in any past-life regression. The client will experience both their own and the assumed viewpoints simultaneously. This experience often has a remarkable effect on the client regarding the intractable anger and lack of understanding for the behavior of the abuser.

There is a further step in this process which can bring even more understanding. If the other person locates the original traumatic event in this or a previous lifetime, interacts with the other persons involved, yet fails to gain clarity on the issue, the other person can be directed to step into the body and merge with the mind of one of those persons. The questioning then shifts to this third person.

This is especially helpful in a case of childhood abuse. A female client may gain some understanding of the behavior of the abusive parent or other perpetrator by connecting with him/her in this manner. The therapist guides the perpetrator to an earlier circumstance which contributes to the abusive behavior. The perpetrator in this process will often recall a childhood incident when they were abused, and the decisions that were made at that time. Child abuse often passes from parent to child in generation after generation within a family. This process can assist the client to locate the original cause of this devastating behavior.

As the client assumes the identity of the other persons involved in the emotional trauma, the new viewpoint offers totally different perceptions of the event. This can lead to clearer interpretations and final judgments of the outcome. False perceptions and beliefs regarding any situation can be cleared and dissolved in a brief time. This allows for new attitudes and behaviors in the present-life situation. This process can lead to forgiveness and healing of extremely painful memories.

Brenda was 28 and had a poor relationship with her parents. She recalled from her childhood an emotionally traumatic instance with her father. As the child she was, she felt ignored and unloved. The therapist guided her to step into her father's body and merge with the mind and view the situation from his perspective. Father was directed back to the time when he learned that particular way of behaving with a child. He recalled a childhood incident with his mother where she seemed too busy to pay attention to him.

The therapist directed him to step into the body and merge with the mind of his mother to find out where she learned the behavior. She recalled a childhood incident where she felt abused and ignored by her father. Mother was directed to step into her father's body and merge with the mind to continue this process of discovery.

The client, Brenda, was sequenced back to her thrice-great-grandmother. As she was moving toward this woman she suddenly sensed a recognition.

C: "She looks so familiar.... She looks sooo familiar.... She looks like me somehow. She is me! That's who I am! THAT'S ME!"

Brenda had discovered that she was a reincarnation of her great, great, great grandmother and it had an enormous impact.

Over a year later, she reported wonderful changes in her life as the result of this experience.

Brad had trouble with relationships. His difficulty stemmed from his lack of trust and fear of abandonment. Nothing in this life could account for his attitude toward women. The feelings took him into an ancient lifetime. In the religion of the time, priests and priestesses were housed in sacred temples of healing. One of the functions of the temple priesthood was healing through sexual interaction with those who came to be healed. Contemporary sex therapy and the function of sex surrogates seeks to produce a similar outcome.

In that lifetime, Brad fell deeply in love with one of the temple priestesses. She returned his love, deeply and sincerely. For him it was total human fulfillment. Of course this was expressly forbidden within the religious structure, and she was subject to punishment if they were found out. Suddenly she ended their liaison with no explanation or further contact of any kind. She did not seek to communicate with him, nor attempt to escape from the temple to be with him as they had planned. He was barred from seeing her in the temple. She simply ceased to exist as part of his life. He was devastated.

He would sometimes see her from a distance but she would never respond to his calls. He lived out the lifetime without companionship and in total despair over her incomprehensible behavior.

The therapist instructed him to recall an instance of seeing her within the confines of the temple. The feelings of love and abandonment welled up. He was directed to step out of his body, to move across the space between them and into her body, merge with her mind, then to turn and look out her eyes and think her thoughts.

He was amazed to discover that she loved him as deeply as ever she had, and also felt her devastation at the loss of their love. There was little chance of escape, and she had discarded all thoughts of that avenue. What had precipitated the severing of their connection was not the fear of punishment for herself but the threat to his life if they continued to see each other. The temple priest in charge had forbidden her to see him again on threat of death to him. The land was not so vast nor the population so great that they could have evaded the authorities. He would have been hunted and killed without recourse or mercy. It was because of her great love for him that she abruptly and permanently ended their connection. This knowledge eased his pain considerably.

Further probing revealed the corruption within the temple. She had come to the healing temple with high ideals and compassion for the people needing solace. She felt it to be a high calling, which indeed it was, at first. Over the years, however, the priests who controlled the religion fell prey to the lure of riches offered by some of the citizens. The fairest of the temple priestesses became no more than temple prostitutes, saved for the decadent pleasure of the jaded rich of the population. The temples devolved into covert houses of prostitution. Her high ideals and precious faith were demolished by the corruption and it nearly destroyed her, yet there was no hope of escape from the temple which had become her prison.

After the interaction with the other or others is complete, the client must be disconnected from each of the other persons contacted in this process. It is a fragment of soul-mind consciousness which links and merges with the others. Without disconnecting, the client would remain fragmented and literally attached to the other being.

T: (to the other) "We thank you _____, (descriptor) for your
assistance this day."

(to the client) "Separate and come out of (his/her) mind, step
out of (his/her) body, come totally back into your own body
and mind. Disconnect completely from (his/her) energy.
Come fully back into your own energy space."

Achieving balanced thinking requires more than one point of view.
Under-standing the thoughts and reasoning, motives, desires, intentions, and
emotions of the other person or persons involved in a situation clears the
distorted thinking of one-dimensionality. This can erase the intractable anger and
confusion which can last lifetimes.

As a person realizes and acknowledges responsibility for his life events,
there is less blaming of others. This is part of the healing process and a restoration
of personal power in the course of one's own destiny. Blaming other people for
one's misfortune is always false. That lie can cause a trauma to repeat through
lifetimes, until the "victim" realizes the falsehood of the beliefs which hold the
pattern in place. The same holds true for assuming guilt about causing another
person's misfortune. Guilt is always false.

Resolving the Unknown

So much pain is caused by the broken promise. If a promise is broken
purposely, the pain is multiplied. If the promise is unfulfilled because of conditions
beyond the control of the one who promised, then the pain is eased or erased.
There is no vow more fervently sworn to a woman than the impossible promise
of the warrior to return from battle, or
the sailor to return from the sea.

THERE IS NO VOW MORE FER-
VENTLY SWORN TO A WOMAN
THAN THE WARRIOR'S IMPOS-
SIBLE PROMISE TO RETURN
FROM BATTLE.

Usually it is the sweetheart or
wife who is left behind, and perhaps
children. Without knowing what has
happened to her lover, the sweetheart,
fiancé or wife is left in emotional limbo.
She has little choice but to wait, re-
maining faithful for years, leading an unfulfilled, lonely, wasted life. The added
factor of the unknown fate of the beloved increases the fear of separation and
makes the abandonment especially poignant.

This past-life trauma can trigger fear of abandonment and annoying
clinginess in present-life relationships. The same fear of abandonment can
surface with very little provocation.

Many women in therapy recall such past lives in which they died after
perhaps years alone, never knowing what had happened to their men. As the
death scene is recalled, the therapist can assist in resolving the mystery. In the

non-physical spirit space, there are no barriers of time or distance. This means the spirit can return to any moment in the lifetime just ended and observe the events as they transpire from any viewpoint.

Anne was a former nurse who had been promoted into a management position in the large hospital where she worked. She was a strong, vital woman, small of stature and exquisitely feminine and loving with her husband Jeremy. He was a dynamic, outgoing businessman who was not always in tune with Anne's sensitivities.

Occasionally, Jeremy would spend a Saturday or Sunday at his business office, catching up on paper work. As he would leave for the day, Anne would feel the pain of separation, even though she knew he would be only a few miles distant and a phone call away. In her distress, she would ask when he planned to return home. Because he did not know, he would respond vaguely. She would insist on knowing his return time. It was not manipulative, but her soft and gentle insistence irritated Jeremy. It was much more than a question about when he would be home for dinner. This annoying clinginess bothered both of them, but for different reasons. Anne wanted to break this behavior pattern.

As she followed the feelings back, she quickly discovered another lifetime when she knew Jeremy. He was a crewman on a square-rigged merchant sailing ship nearly two centuries earlier. She was a librarian in a small town in Scotland. The instruction was to locate the last time they were together. She described walking with him to the pier where the ship was in the final loading stages prior to departure on the outgoing tide. It was a tearful farewell; she loved him deeply. This was to be an extended trading voyage. He promised to come back to her. They were to be married on his return.

Months passed and the ship did not return. The months became years. There was no word. Neither the ship nor any of its crew ever returned. She never completely lost hope; she clung to his last loving promise that he would return and marry her. She died in middle age, empty in her heart, her impossible and irrational hope blinding her to the truth of what must have happened.

As she emerged from the body at death, her spirit was directed to again find the last time they were together in life and to follow and observe what happened. She described the departure of the ship. She was directed to skip forward to some significant event aboard ship.

Within weeks of leaving port, the ship encountered a vicious storm at sea. Though it was a well-constructed vessel, there was little chance of surviving the tempest. The ship foundered in the storm and everyone was lost.

Viewing this, knowing he could not return, knowing that he had not broken his loving but impossible promise, and that there was nothing he could have done, she was able to bring closure to the emptiness she had endured for the years of her life after his departure.

Within a month Anne joined a medical tour to China and several other Asian countries. It was the first time in nearly 30 years of marriage that she had been separated from Jeremy for any length of time. There was no fear of separation and abandonment, no clinginess. The anxiety was gone.

Forgiveness

The act of forgiveness is enormously powerful. The word forgive means to give away, to pardon, without any residual burden of guilt or blame. After processing to resolution the conflicts with other persons in past-life events, whatever residue remains may be released by forgiving, or at least being willing to forgive the other person or persons for their motivations, intentions and behaviors. This process calls on imagination.

> T: "Bring into your awareness the other person involved. Look
> directly into the eyes of this other one. Can you see them?"

If there is hesitation on the part of the client, the therapist urges this direct interaction. If the client displays anger, fear, sadness or guilt, the therapist gently urges the client to contact the other, to look into the eyes, even if it is painful.

If the other person hesitates, the client asks (and if necessary, insists) that the character in the imagery of the client look toward the client. The therapist assures the other that this pain can cease, that peace is available. Once they are facing each other, the questions are directed to the client.

> T: "Can you forgive the other for what has happened?"

If there is hesitation, the question is altered.

> T: "Can you be willing to forgive the other? Willingness is the
> first step to forgiveness. That is all that is necessary right now.
> Are you willing to forgive?"

The answer is usually affirmative. If not, more processing of the past-life events and the connecting lifetimes may be necessary.

Willingness to forgive is all that is really necessary. It is not the ego but the Higher Power who forgives through a person. Willingness opens the door for this action.

Forgiveness, even the willingness to forgive, signals the end of the unfinished business of the past. When forgiveness is fully experienced and realized, it becomes clear to a person that there really never was anything to forgive. The misperception and misinterpretation of the behavior of the partner is what caused the pain. It is not the partner who brings the feelings of disappointment but rather the impossible expectations which lead to disappointment. Relationships end, but love is eternal and love never dies. It is lonely after a partner dies, but it is not a betrayal. There may be a broken promise, but the promise may prove to be an impossible promise, spoken in the heat of love or passion.

Blaming the other is false. Each being is responsible for his or her own life. Anger and blame are always false. Forgiveness releases the other person from the focus of the baseless and unwarranted emotion. Forgiveness also releases the angry person from the chains of anger and blame.

Self Forgiveness

The final forgiveness is self-forgiveness. The client must be willing to forgive himself or herself for their part in the traumatic event of the past. It is the unresolved guilt and remorse which so often holds an emotional pattern in place through lifetimes. The result is continued self-punishment in the attempt to atone for the perceived wrongs.

THE FINAL FORGIVENESS IS SELF-FORGIVENESS.

These emotions are always false; therefore this considerable suffering is unnecessary.

> T: "Can you forgive yourself for the part you played in this event? Can you forgive yourself for whatever you did in that time?"

The case of Sandy and the attached entity Amandahjah, in the section Couples Counseling (392) is a good example of the healing power of self forgiveness. False guilt kept the entity earthbound, self-forgiveness was the final key to his release to the Light, even after he had received Sandy's forgiveness and God's forgiveness.

The one to be forgiven may be deceased. In the case of loving couples, they must face the fact that one partner will leave. Relationships always end, either by choice or by death of one of the partners. This can be extremely painful. A normal reaction of the survivor is anger at the one who has died. Because of this anger, the survivor may feel guilty at having unloving thoughts and feelings toward the deceased, such as this anger and resentment. Forgiveness is necessary for the deceased mate and for one's self.

> T: "Can you forgive your partner for leaving?"

If there is hesitation the question is altered.

> T: "Can you be willing to forgive the other for leaving? Willingness is the first step to forgiveness. That is all that is necessary right now. Are you willing to forgive?"

When the pain is too great or if there is a total lack of understanding, the process of Resolving the Unknown, as described above, can ease the pain. The technique of Assuming Another's Viewpoint can be used to first resolve the intractable emotion then to alleviate the pain and allow for the forgiveness. The beings in such relationships will often return to be together in future lifetimes. The decisions made in anger and grief at the loss of a mate will interfere with full expression of love in future lifetimes. Caution and lack of trust can interfere with the full and delicious experience of intimacy until there is fuller knowledge and forgiveness.

> T: "Now that you understand more clearly what really happened, can you forgive your partner for leaving in that way?"
> "Can you be willing to forgive yourself for the way you behaved?"
> "Can you forgive yourself for the things you said about your partner, the things you thought about _____(him/her)?"

Self forgiveness can free the person from the chains of self imposed guilt, remorse, regret, and self blame. These emotions and self judgements are also false.

Healing the Residue

Moving forward in the Light to the planning stage for the present life, the client can examine the purpose for the life to come. Interactions with others can be surveyed. This allows the client to see what reciprocal teaching was set up between themselves and any other persons in their life. When one takes responsibility for one's own part in any situation, blaming ceases, anger and resentment disappear, guilt and remorse are relieved. Forgiveness and love are the result.

WORKING THROUGH THE FEAR-BASED EMOTIONS TO COMPLETE FORGIVENESS CAN OPEN THE PATH TO THE FULL EXPRESSION AND EXPERIENCE OF LOVE, WHICH IS THE FINAL HEALING.

Healing the residue in the setting in which it first developed is a major aspect of past-life therapy. This healing often manifests immediately in the present-life circumstance. Another result of this therapy is the effect on people other than the client. Often, the conflict in a past life involves the same dynamic that exists within present-life conflicts, and the protagonists in the past-life situation are identifiable as persons involved in the present-life situations. The present conflicts and interpersonal tensions are frequently recognized and interpreted as issuing directly from the destructive patterns in earlier lifetimes. Resolution of the conflicts in the past lifetime often brings astonishing results in the form of change within the other person, the identified protagonist in the earlier lifetime, who might be hundreds or thousands of miles away at the time. Often within minutes of the session and without any form of communication, there will be changes which parallel the events described in the session (Grof, 1985, pp. 47, 48).

Almost any problem or conflict in the present life can be traced to a past-life trauma. The problem can be explored and resolved using this approach to therapy in the outlined sequence of a past life regression. The therapist allows the client to explore as much as necessary. Connections and interactions with other people may be important antecedents to present-life conflicts. Nothing which comes up can be considered trivial. The process of the inductions and questioning uncovers the engram and leads the client into the original source or cause of the presenting problems and conflicts. The original trauma can be resolved with these techniques. The process works.

The therapist guides the exploration from the initial opening experience into an expansion of the awareness of the event, finally to a logical closure. The object is to eliminate the residues of the past which interfere with the present-life situation. The emotions of anger, fear, sadness and guilt seem to leave the greatest residue. Working through these fear-based emotions to the point of complete forgiveness can open the path to the full expression and experience of love, which is the final healing.

Further Applications of PLT

Past-life therapy is unlimited in its application to the problems of the human condition. There is no end to the number of avenues of discovery through PLT. Physical, mental and emotional problems can be explored. Talents and skills can be enhanced. Relationships can be traced through the ages. Some people find that their beloved pets have been with them before. Virtually anything can be traced to a past-life connection, either here on this planet, on some other physical world, or in the non-physical realm. However, the client must have the mental capability to communicate meaningfully and be cooperative.

Phobia, Fear, Suspicion, Depression

It is possible to explore and resolve phobias, the irrational, persistent fears which plague so many people. Phobia is often caused by the memory of death in another lifetime. The circumstances of the death become the specifics of the phobia in this lifetime. A common phobia is the fear of water. As people describe their phobia of water it becomes much more specific in detail. Such details include deep water, rushing water, muddy water, dark water which prevents visibility, water over the knees, water up to the chest, water in the face, crashing surf, even large bodies of still water such as a lake. The past-life inductions often take a victim of such a phobia right back into the death trauma and the details of the death are identical with the specific description of the phobia. It is usually relieved or eliminated in one session.

The illogical and unreasonable beliefs which control one's thinking can be probed and dissolved. Paranoia, undue suspicions, fears and prejudiced thinking can be uncovered in past lives and resolved through this therapy. Depression can sometimes be viewed as frozen anger. Past-life exploration can assist in the alleviation of this debilitating condition. A client can be regressed to the cause of any mental or emotional condition.

Marion, the woman whose NDE was described in the Introduction, wanted to explore past-life therapy. In session she disclosed a lifelong phobia. She had always had a morbid, baseless fear of losing a leg in an accident. She described the motor scooter accident in which her phobia was violently realized. Her companion was driving; she was riding on the rear seat and had no control.

Just before the accident occurred, she cautioned her companion to slow down. He passed a slow-moving truck, swerved to miss an oncoming vehicle, lost control of the motor scooter and slid under the truck. A huge tire crushed her thigh. As she lay motionless on the ground, bleeding profusely, she suddenly was aware of a great and unexpected peace. Her phobia—or perhaps her premonition—had materialized. In some strange way which she could not understand, this put her mind at rest.

In several past lives she found the same leg damaged or lost. In the connecting or karmic lifetime, she discovered that she had caused a similar wound to another person. One possible method of erasing karma is retribution. An eye for an eye and a tooth for a tooth is a rather brutal way of balancing the karmic debt. A less painful way of balancing such a burden is to save another person from a similar calamity.

If she had engaged in past-life therapy for her phobia prior to the accident, would she have circumvented the accident? This can never be known.

The following case is typical of the shift between past-life regression and spirit releasement, which is often necessary during a session. One purpose of this session was to explore for the cause of a phobia of cars.

Eighteen-year-old Dierdre wanted to explore her love of reggae music, Black night clubs, her relationship with her boyfriend, and her fear of crossing the street. She was deathly afraid of being run down by a car.

Her relationship was used as the entry point in the session. As she thought of her boyfriend, her emotional response bridged her into a former lifetime. She described herself as an old Black woman dying in her bed. Her grandson was visiting her and comforting her. This was the boyfriend. The old woman died. Instead of going to the Light she sat on a hill and waited for another body. This was the first indication of a possible entity attachment. This earthbound spirit attached to a series of people. The last person she attached to before Dierdre was an infant girl.

When the girl was about five or six years old, she ran out into a street from between two parked cars. An oncoming car hit her going full speed. The child died instantly. The entity emerged from the child's body, fearful and eager to move on.

T: "Wait a moment before you leave. Look back at the little body."

C: "Oh, there's someone else coming out of the body too. Wow, she's walking toward a door over there. It's real bright in that doorway. Wow, that's interesting. I wanna see what that is. Oh-oh, the door just closed."

And off she went in a different direction. Dierdre was about 12 when the entity joined her. She brought a memory of Dierdre's present boyfriend, her affinity for Black people and their music, and the fear of automobiles which she had suddenly acquired when the person she was attached to was killed by a speeding car. This phobia was not the result of any of Dierdre's past lives, nor the death trauma of the entity, but the experience of a little girl who died with an attached spirit. The entity acquired the fear through the death of the host body, and imposed it on Dierdre.

The entity was confused about her next step of spiritual evolution. Dierdre realized the truth of the situation about halfway through the session. She had grown quite fond of the Black lady without even knowing she was present. The therapist explained the situation and the consequences of spirit attachment. Dierdre decided to release the old woman. The two had a silent, internal conversation for some minutes and then Dierdre, in tears, signaled she was ready. The releasement procedures were completed quickly.

Eating Disorders

Dieting has become a national obsession in America. The language is sprinkled with such phrases as, "Thin is in," "You can't be too rich or too thin," and "Think thin." Fat people have publicly protested against the prejudiced attitudes against them and the preferential treatment given to people of normal weight. The conditions of anorexia and bulimia are being diagnosed more frequently than ever before.

The appearance of a young woman suffering with anorexia is disturbingly reminiscent of the photographs of the inmates of the German concentration camps of World War II. Past-life regression with the anorexic woman may reveal such a life-and-death experience.

The last ten pounds is the hardest to lose, as many dieters will attest. In past-life regression, many people will recall death by starvation. When they lost the last ten pounds in that lifetime, they died. Thus the goal weight loss of "just ten more pounds" is equivalent to death. The instinct for survival may thwart this goal. Millions of people die of starvation each year, even in today's world.

Past-life therapy is an important adjunct to any weight-control program. The emotional factors are widely recognized in the problem of overweight. What is not recognized is the past-life source of the emotional factors.

Recovering Lost Talents

Some clients have the desire to express themselves artistically. Past-life regression can assist in the recovery or recall of forgotten skills, such as painting, sculpting and writing, enhancing the present-life abilities of a person. It is possible to recover lost techniques such as clay formulation and pottery-making skills, and systems of healing.

Writer's block can be explored for another lifetime cause. One client recalled a lifetime in which he was a scribe who kept track of those who paid their rent on time. Those who did not remain current were evicted by the landlord. This scribe was conscience stricken and vowed never to write again. Such a writing block can be eased or eliminated through past-life therapy.

Historical Exploration

Direct observation of historical periods is available for writers and others interested in such exploration. Successful experiments were conducted at Stanford Research Institute on the phenomena and process of distant or remote viewing-that is, perception of a target location or structure distant in time or geographical location (Targ & Puthoff, 1977). Former Dean of Science and Engineering at Princeton University Robert Jahn (1987) presents convincing data on the accuracy of distant viewing or distant perception. He also set up experiments which examined the effect of consciousness on physical events at a distance. The results of his work suggest the need for a new look at the physical reality.

Tracing Relationships

Almost any relationship can be traced into past lives. This can be an interaction with a business associate, a family member, or romantic partner. Married couples have almost certainly been together before (Sutphen, 1976, 1978, 1988). The client is requested to bring her partner into her awareness as if he were standing directly in front of her. The feelings generated by this awareness are encouraged. The affect bridge and somatic bridge are used to prompt the client to recall another time when she knew this person, another time when she felt similar feelings and sensations.

The scene that emerges might be emotionally charged or quite benign. Directing the client to skip backward to the first meeting in the lifetime being explored will open the dialogue nicely. Skipping forward to several important events will bring into view the emotional issues they may still be working on in the present incarnation. The event of the death of the first one to die may uncover promises and vows which may still be drawing them together in this lifetime.

REGRESSION TO THE OPPO-SITE GENDER CAN BRING A NEW UNDERSTANDING BE-TWEEN THE SEXES.

The earlier relationship can be similar to the present-life interaction or it may be totally different, yet include similar emotions. A love relationship can exist by choice. A relationship clouded by fear-based emotions can offer the opportunity for resolution and forgiveness of earlier conflicts.

There is a difference in the way men and women think and process information. Communication is inadequate and difficult for many couples. Lack of understanding and appreciation of the viewpoint of the marriage partner can be painful for both partners. Regression to a lifetime as the opposite gender can bring surprising clarity and empathy for each other.

Most women cannot understand the warrior mentality, the urge for competition, or the attraction of battle and death. Many women can recall lives as men, often in the role of soldier or warrior. This will bring an understanding of the male mind, though most women cannot condone the aggressive attitudes and behavior shown by some men.

The most sympathetic husband cannot comprehend the physical sensations and experience of his wife's pregnancy. Recalling a past life as a pregnant woman can immediately shift the man's understanding of his wife's discomfort.

Many marriage partners, male and female alike, resist full commitment to the other partner. This hesitation may originate in a prior lifetime when the other partner died first. The partner who remains in a physical body on the earth plane can suffer the greater agony. The wife who loses her husband to war can harbor the most bitter resentment. The husband whose wife dies in childbirth feels helpless in the face of such a loss and can grow to hate the child if he or she survives.

In these situations, it is natural for the partner left behind to make fear-based decisions regarding marriage, relationship, that particular partner, and love in general. These decisions can interfere with future incarnations when these two again have the opportunity to grow together through a loving, committed partnership. Exploration of several lifetimes in sequence can uncover these circumstances and decisions. What partners often discover is that they actually took turns leaving first. They both made similar decisions. One of the opportunities available in returning together is to forgive the partner for leaving, and to forgive themselves for being angry, unloving and unwilling to commit.

Incest

There is absolutely no justification for incest. It is a terrible violation for the victim and indicates serious mental disturbance in the perpetrator. Some writers have described incest as the most extreme form of deviant behavior, the universal crime. Incest has been described in mythology and literature throughout human history. Grave consequences follow the discovery of incest, even if the perpetrator is for some reason unaware of the blood relationship (Renshaw, 1982). This is exemplified in the story of Oedipus who killed his father and married his mother. When he discovered the truth of what he had done, he plucked out his own eyes and was finally destroyed by the gods.

However, in a very few cultures today, certain incestuous relationships are allowed. In the past some royal families, such as the Incas of Peru, the Pharoahs of Egypt, and Hawaiian royalty, practiced incestuous marriage relationships to maintain purity of the blood line (Kempe & Kempe, 1984, pp. 4-5).

The adult who initiates and perpetrates the incest is the one who crosses the boundaries and violates the innocent child. In some cases, the child or adolescent may enjoy the attention and even the physical sensation, but the emotional damage can be devastating. In civilized society, it is assumed that the adult is aware of the appropriate and responsible behavior toward children which is demanded by law and morality. Unfortunately, this is often a false assumption. Reports of incest and child molestation are increasing terribly. Many of the perpetrators were themselves molested as children. This may explain the deviance, but it cannot justify this totally inappropriate and irresponsible behavior.

In some cases of incest, the perpetrators have been treated through past life therapy. It is sometimes discovered that the parent and child in the present life were in fact lovers or mates in a former lifetime. This cannot justify the behavior in the present time, but may shed some light on the adult's motivation and perhaps compulsion to connect in this way. This discovery can lead to communication and possibly forgiveness between the people involved in this damaging interaction.

Past-life therapy can help to assuage the emotional pain of childhood sexual abuse. The following case involves incestuous molestation, past-life connection, and spirit attachment by the perpetrator, who joined her after his death.

Diana was 36 years old, intelligent, attractive and had been involved in a lesbian relationship for some years. This behavior had always caused her some confusion. She tried to explain that she wasn't actively lesbian, she just seemed to be avoiding men. Her menstrual period had ceased for about five months earlier in the year. It had started again spontaneously with no further signs of irregularity. There was no apparent physical cause which could be determined through medical examination.

She wanted to explore three areas of concern in her life: her lesbian behavior, the interruption of her menstrual period, and a recurring irritation and tightness in her throat coupled with an irrational fear of unknown but terrible consequences if she dared to speak out the truth. The portion of the session which covered the past-life cause of the throat irritation is described in the next section Physical Ailments.

Diana's sexual preference for women was apparently influenced by a strong male entity who called himself George. George expressed hostility, defiance and a refusal to cooperate with the therapist. He was determined to stay and remain in control. He enjoyed the sexual interaction with other women. This defiance is a reliable indicator of demonic influence. Further exploration established that this was the case and the dark one was released by the methods described in the section Treatment of the Demonic (323). Free from the influence of the dark one, George was cooperative, apologetic and helpful. Before he was released into the Light, he agreed to erase whatever mental programming regarding sexuality that he had imposed on Diana.

Diana's grandfather was the next to emerge. He had joined her after his death, though they were not particularly close while he was alive. Grandfather claimed to be quite concerned with Diana and the course of her life. She acknowledged that he had molested her when she was a child. She felt resentment and sadness over that violation. She did not describe the extent of the incest with grandfather, though she did indicate there were instances of molestation by others as well.

He felt some guilt and remorse over the molestation, but his main concern was her lesbian lifestyle. He admitted that he caused the interruption in her menstrual cycle. He wanted to get her attention in a way which would focus her awareness on her femininity and sexuality. He thought she would then be able to resume a more natural sexual orientation and lifepath. Intuitively, the therapist felt that this seemed to indicate some genuine caring and unfinished business from an earlier time.

Diana was directed to locate another time and place when she knew the one who had been her grandfather. She was sweetly surprised as the memory surfaced. She was his older sister. As young children, they were very close and she was old enough to protect and care for him. There was a deep love between them. As her sexuality began to develop, she found herself regarding her brother differently. Her love for him expanded to include physical curiosity and sexual exploration. Eventually she seduced him into sexual intercourse. She claimed it happened only once, and it left her with terrible guilt and remorse.

Again, the therapist felt intuitively that this deep love and urge to connect sexually seemed to indicate more than aberrant exploitative behavior. Diana was gently directed to recall another time when she knew this person who had been her grandfather and brother. Suddenly she smiled warmly. She described a lifetime when she and her young sweetheart were very much in love and planning to be married.

The experience of this deep and passionate love was immensely healing to Diana in those moments. She was directed to bring the knowledge of the rightness of their connection forward to their lifetime as brother and sister. Though distorted in its manifestation, the love had continued. She was able to forgive herself for seducing him. The guilt and remorse eased. She brought that healing energy into the present life and viewed her childhood sexual abuse in a new light. Her pain and resentment toward grandfather and the other perpetrators began to dissipate.

Past-life regression for either the host or the attached entity is, in effect a dual regression, as they both fully experience the recall. Grandfather also felt the emotional burden lift. He agreed to remove any remnants of physical distress that he had caused. Forgiveness of each other and self-forgiveness cleared the way for the expression of love. Diana released him with love, and Grandfather willingly moved into the Light with his wife, who came to guide him home.

Past-life therapy served both the client and the attached entity in the healing of the unfinished business, the anger and resentment, and the guilt and remorse stemming from inappropriate and irresponsible behavior in the distorted expression of love.

Physical Ailments

In an unpublished study, researchers called for subjects with terminal illness who had been dismissed by their physicians as untreatable. Several hundred people responded. Under hypnosis, each was directed to locate the cause of the condition. The majority of them located a past-life event which contributed to the illness. In over 70% of these subjects, the life-threatening condition went into remission (Denning, 1988).

The mind-body connection cannot be denied. The interaction between mental and emotional function and physical health is well established. What is evidenced in the clinical application of past-lives therapy is the connection between prior-life trauma and present-life ailments. Spirit releasement therapy expands the evidence even farther. An attaching spirit can impose its own residue on a living person, causing mental, emotional and physical problems. It is still a mind-body connection but the mind and body belong to different people.

Diana went on to describe a previous therapy session in which she had explored a past life in Egypt as a male stone carver, working inside a pyramid which was to be the tomb of a Pharoah. Extensive stone carvings were placed in the burial chamber.

On the day the carvings were finished, the stone carvers were ushered into a small room by three guards. One by one, the stone carvers were forcibly shoved against the wall and their throats were cut. This action was taken to prevent them from revealing the nature of the carvings and the secret truths they depicted.

This was the source of Diana's fear of the consequences of telling the truth and the tightness and irritation in her throat. However, there was no relief from the condition after that past-life therapy session. This might suggest that there are traumatic events from other lifetimes contributing to the symptoms; it might also indicate an attached earthbound spirit imposing the condition.

Diana was invited to focus her awareness on the physical sensation of the irritation in the throat, and to go fully into the emotional feelings. The somatic bridge, affect bridge and linguistic bridge used together are extremely effective for past-life induction.

T: "If that irritation in your throat could speak, what would it say? If the feelings could talk, what would they say?"

C: "'I can't speak. I can't speak.'"

The response was immediate and highly emotional.

T: "Say it again. Let the feelings come. Say it again."

As she repeated the phrases, she accessed the past life instantly. This opened up the entire past-life memory which she had described earlier. The story continued. The stone carver lamented over the lack of time to meditate and prepare for death. As spirit, he lifted from the body but perceived no Light. This is an indication of the possibility of spirit attachment. The lifetime is not over until the newly deceased spirit moves completely into the Light. The therapist must not use leading questions at this time. Instead, the questions should prompt the narrative without suggesting a direction or agenda.

T: "What happens next?"
The stone carver was alone in the room; the guards had removed the bodies, the other spirits had moved on.

T: "What happens next?" The question is repeated gently whenever the unfolding account slows or stops.

The spirit finally moved out of the room, wandered about the town, observed people in the streets, occasionally tampering or interfering with their energy. He was feeling a bit angry. He really did not know what to do nor where to go next.

T: "Skip forward to the next thing that happens."

This instruction often leads to the memory of the actual attachment of a spirit. Certain events seem to be more easily recalled. The more emotional energy involved, the more easily the memory is triggered. Diana jerked in the recliner and began to cry softly.

T: "What just happened?"

C: "He just came in to me."

T: "How old are you?"

C: "About 13."

T: "Stone carver, what happened to you? Do you know this
woman? Who is she to you?"

C: "She wouldn't have anything to do with me. She was married and wouldn't even talk to me. I wanted her."

This was in the Egyptian lifetime. They were both incarnated at the time. The stone carver was not a past incarnation of Diana. After his death, he wandered about the area, but did not find her there. He attached to many people before he found Diana in her budding femininity in the present lifetime.

He was able to express his anger and resentment at her rejection of him in that lifetime. Beneath that was the love he felt for her. He soon realized that he could not be with her in the way he wanted as long as he remained connected in this way. He eagerly moved into the Light.

Pete, a 35-year-old male client, suffered from diabetes. He was taking 12 units of insulin per day. A regression to the source of the condition uncovered a lifetime as an American Indian. On a hunt he was attacked by a bear; his body was clawed back and front. The abdomen was torn open, the internal organs severely damaged. The client was asked to describe what happened next. Perceiving the Light coming for him as he rose out of his physical body, he detected the identical damage in the subtle or supraphysical body.

He was directed to hesitate before going into the Light, and to visualize a tendril of that Light extending directly into the damaged areas filling the subtle body. After about 10 minutes, with very little prompting, he reported that the area was filled with Light, and he was feeling comfortably warm. He moved into the Light and the regression was over. Within 20 minutes Pete felt the need for food, his body was beginning to produce insulin. Three months later, his intake of insulin had been reduced to one-fourth of the former amount. One year later, it had been further reduced to one-tenth of the original dosage. His physician had no explanation, yet did not criticize the procedure. He acknowledged that the mind was very powerful. Pete was delighted.

Guided imagery is a recognized therapeutic adjunct. Careful use of this healing technique can enhance the results of the sessions and assist in reframing faulty memories, rescripting the past, correcting the persistent residues, and easing the pain associated with trauma (Simonton, Simonton & Creighton, 1978; Achterberg, 1985).

Animal Lifetimes
Many traditional theories and philosophies of reincarnation reject the notion of transmigration of souls, that is, animal existence as part of spiritual evolution of a human soul. Regardless of this, many people recall the experience of being an animal. Eagles revere their mates and offspring and unselfishly gather food for these others. Tigers roar at the intended prey, not out of anger but to cause fear and with it a temporary paralysis. After the kill the tiger may set aside the uneaten remains of the carcass, knowing he will want to eat again, not out of any concept of storage for a future time. There is no conception of time.

Land of the Sacred Cow

Computer art from the color original, *Land of the Sacred Cow*, ©1992 by Mike "Gwydian" Wiseman

Dolphins live in marvelously cooperative community with each other. They communicate telepathically in total thought-gestalts. Every aspect of a situation is included in the instantaneous communication.

There is a low level of consciousness in most animals, not including the whales and dolphins. There is little or no consciousness of being conscious. Animal thought processes are developed enough for decision making and these decisions are largely focused on survival in the animal habitats of forest and jungle. These survival-based decisions can affect human behavior many lifetimes later.

Many people have recalled what seem to be animal lifetimes. Whether this is an actual physical incarnation in animal form in the spiritual path of exploration, or a brief attachment of consciousness to a living animal cannot always be determined. After the death of the animal, the consciousness rises to join a group soul of dogness, tigerness or whatever animal it was.

Finding Purpose in Life

Many people complain about losing their purpose, their drive, their direction in life, their very reason to live. Depression can be the cause or result of this attitude. A specific and a bit fanciful guided regression may help alleviate this complaint. The garden meditation, described in the section Group Regression (158) is used for the induction. From there, the client is directed to the experience of choosing to come to the planet earth the very first time. In group regressions, over 70% of the participants recall that choice; in private sessions, a higher percentage can remember the event.

People recognize themselves—either in the non-physical, spiritual realm, or as physical non-human beings—choosing to come to earth on a voluntary (in most cases) mission of mercy. They come to bring help, education, healing, art, music and poetry. They come to rescue the beings who arrived earlier and became mired in the heaviness of earth, the gravity and low vibration of the energy, the competitive attitude of the ego as manifested on this planet. They come with the intention of awakening those who have lost the awareness of their true being and identity. Invariably the ultimate purpose is to bring love.

Unfortunately, many who came on these rescue missions also became mired in the low consciousness of this place and forgot their spiritual identity and why they had come. Slowly through eons of time and countless incarnations here, the spark of God consciousness continued to expand and grow. The vibrational frequencies of this area of the universe are increasing.

Many people are awakening to their spiritual heritage and birthright. It is almost time to graduate from this level of reality.

Exploring the Spiritual Reality

The spiritual reality can be explored in the altered state of consciousness. There are many levels of awareness and states of consciousness available for investigation. The spiritual realm is more vast than anyone can imagine (Monroe, 1971, 1985). Regression therapy deals with resolution of issues anywhere and any time prior to the present moment.

The interim between lives is accessible in deep altered states of consciousness (Wambach, 1979; Whitton and Fisher, 1986). The client can be moved forward and backward in the interim stage by sequence, by succeeding events, by accomplishment, by duration of activity, but not by time. Time does not exist in the non-physical realms.

> T: "Skip forward to the next significant event, to your next activity. What is happening?"
> "Move back to the beginning of this activity. What are the circumstances, what are you aware of in your vicinity?"
> "What activities do you engage in where you are?"
> "Do you participate with others? How do they appear to you? Describe."
> "How do you communicate with each other?"
> "Describe the halls of learning."
> "Locate your first meeting with the counselors in the review stage."

"What do you know of human life?"
"Skip forward to the planning stage just prior to the lifetime when you will be called _____ (client's name)."

Much information can be garnered from this experience.

Hidden Standard of Perfection

The memory of existence as a geometric shape may emerge in a session. The first experimental creation of the individual spark after separation from Source is the thought form of a clear sphere. The clear sphere is displayed as a sort of identification badge. Each spark created a slightly different sphere for easy identity. The sparks, having no form, identified themselves with their clear sphere identification badge. They

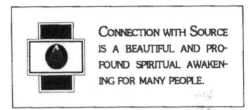

CONNECTION WITH SOURCE IS A BEAUTIFUL AND PROFOUND SPIRITUAL AWAKENING FOR MANY PEOPLE.

began to think that was who they were. Shapes other than spheres and colors instead of clear and colorless came much further down the time track of the spirit beings.

Since there was no individual creation prior to the clear sphere it became the *de facto* standard of perfection for all future individual creations. Everything which came after was compared with the first. There was always some difference and simply because they were not like the first they were judged as inferior. This is the hidden standard of perfection which can affect personal self-worth and self-esteem in the present life in the present creation, the physical body and personality.

Separation from Source

A person can recall the original separation from Source as an individual spark of consciousness. This exploration is most accessible after the being emerges from death experience and moves into the review stage in the Light.

T: "From where you are in the Light, begin to move back. Move back, back, before you were ever in human body, (pause) back across the dark fabric of time and space. (pause) Move back before the Universe. (pause) As you move back, faster and faster now, open your awareness to your destination. (pause) Moving back toward your first experience of being. (pause) Back into the experience of Oneness, (pause) back into contact with the Source, (pause) before you ever became a separate spark (pause) of consciousness. (pause) Back (pause) into the Brightness, (pause) the Oneness, (pause) the Source. The experience of being together with everything. How does that feel?"

It may be difficult for a person to describe the ineffable experience of being One with God. The experience is what's important, not the description for the therapist.

> T: "In the Light, notice that something is about to occur. There is going to be a rearranging, a division within the Light. Individual sparks of Light are forming. Still all together, each spark has its own vibration now, just slightly different from all the others so each one can be identified. Individuation has just happened. Notice how that feels." (pause) "Now something else is about to happen. The outside layer of sparks is going to separate from the Source. They are going to leave. How does that feel? (pause) And now another layer, and another, and now your layer, and you explode from the surface, hurtling away from Source. As you go, notice that many others are hurtling outward also, many in your same direction, others going in different directions. Separating from Source now. Exploded from Source. What decisions are you making about being sent out? (pause) Leaving home now. (pause) And there was nothing you could do about it. Notice how that feels."

This is often the original cause of feelings of rejection, abandonment and separation in the present lifetime. The feeling is reactivated during the birth process into the present incarnation. A client in a birth regression may spontaneously skip to the original separation from Source. The therapist must follow such a switch and stay in whatever paradigm or framework the client describes.

> T: "Streaking outward from Source now slow down your movement. By an act of will slow your movement. Now stop, change direction, turn back toward the Brightness, begin to move back toward Source. (pause) Faster now, move right back towards the surface of that brightness." (pause) "Slowing down now, merge right into the surface. Merge again with Source. What decisions are you making about this experience? (pause) Retain your individual vibration, and merge with the Oneness. How does that feel? (pause) "Now once again, the separation comes. You move outward from the Source. Not so fast this time. How does that feel? Moving away this time, what decisions are you making?"

The therapist can repeat the directions to return and separate several times, until the client is free of the anxiety of separation. Usually it takes no more than four or five returns.

> T: "Moving now back into the review stage in the Light. Recall everything you just experienced with Source. (pause) Describe."

The client should be able to describe the sensations of the Source experience, the original separation, and the feeling of being able to return. This may ease any pain of rejection and abandonment in the present lifetime.

It is a beautiful and profound spiritual awakening experience for many people.

Dual Regression

Tracing a relationship together can be a romantic excursion in time for two people. Dual regression can be a wonderful addition to couples counseling, though it is not limited to romantic relationships. The induction consists of a chakra linkage through visualization of light color energy. The two people lie side by side on a bed, on the floor, or in adjacent reclining chairs. Questions are directed at each of the participants

THE INVOCATION OF LIGHT IS IMPORTANT IN ANY ALTERED-STATE EXPERIENCE.

separately. Each person remains in his or her own experience and answers appropriately, even though each can hear the other's answers.

Once the two people are comfortable, side by side but not touching, the therapist guides the induction.

> T: "Close your eyes and focus inward. Focus deep inside to the very center of your being. Find your own spark of Light there, your own Light, deep inside. Feel it, see it, sense it there, imagine it there, deep inside you. (pause) Imagine that the spark of Light glows warmly and expands in every direction, upward and downward. The Light expands clear into the tips of your toes to the top of your head, from fingertip to fingertip, filling every cell of your body. (pause) Imagine the Light expanding outward, beyond the boundaries of your body about an arm's length in every direction, a shimmering bubble of golden white Light all around you."
>
> "Imagine now at the base of your spine, the location of the first chakra, the color of red. Bright, clear, apple red. The base chakra, the energy of survival. Sense that color red flowing upward and outward, arching across toward your partner, connecting with the first chakra of your partner.

Visualize an arch of red connecting your base chakra to the base chakra of your partner. (pause)

"Imagine now at the level of your genitals, the second chakra, the color orange. Bright, clear, tangerine orange. The energy of generativity and sexuality. Sense that color orange arching across toward your partner, connecting with the second chakra. An arch of orange and an arch of red, connecting the two of you now . (pause)

"Imagine now at your solar plexus the color yellow. Bright, clear, lemon yellow. The third chakra, the energy of intellect, power, control. Sense that color yellow arching across toward your partner, connecting with the third chakra. An arch of orange, an arch of red and an arch of yellow, connecting the two of you now." (pause)

"Imagine now at the level of your heart the color green. Bright, clear, emerald green. The heart chakra, the energy of unconditional love. Sense that color green arching across toward your partner, connecting with the heart chakra, the fourth chakra. An arch of orange, an arch of red, an arch of yellow and an arch of green connecting the two of you now. (pause)

"Imagine now at the level of your throat the color blue. Deep, clear, tranquil blue. The throat chakra, the energy of creativity and communication. Sense that color blue arching across toward your partner, connecting with the throat chakra, the fifth chakra. An arch of red, an arch of orange, an arch of yellow, an arch of green and an arch of blue connecting the two of you now." (pause)

"Imagine now at the level of your brow the color violet. Deep, clear, soothing violet. The brow chakra, the seat of intuition, the third eye. Sense that violet color arching across toward your partner, connecting with the sixth chakra, the brow chakra. An arch of red, an arch of orange, an arch of yellow, an arch of green, an arch of blue and an arch of violet connecting the two of you now." (pause)

"Imagine now at the top of your head the white light. Bright, clear, white light, the combination of all colors. The crown chakra, the energy of the highest consciousness. Sense that white light flowing from you, surrounding you and your partner. The arches of red, orange, yellow, green, blue, and violet connecting the two of you now and engulfed in white light." (pause)

"Imagine yourself lifting out of your body, out through the white light, together in spirit with your partner. Back now, back in time now, back together to another time and place when you knew each other. Allow the light to carry you back into the experience of another lifetime when you knew each other. Locate another lifetime when you knew each other and you interacted together. Find yourself in the experience of another lifetime. (pause.) What is the first thing you experience? What is the first thing you are aware of in this place?"

These instructions are given slowly and clearly in a soft voice. Whichever person speaks first, the therapist responds and pursues the conversation for a few minutes. At a logical stopping place, the therapist switches to the other partner.

T: "As she is experiencing _____, what are you experiencing?"

The other partner may be in the same moment, at an earlier time or later time in the same lifetime, or in another lifetime. The conversation is pursued briefly, then the focus switches to the first partner.

T: "As he is experiencing _____, what is happening to you? What are you aware of?"

If the partners are involved in the same experience, it is easier to continue the exploration and discussion. If they are clearly not connecting yet, then at an appropriate time (not in the midst of a trauma but in a more neutral scene) the therapist urges them to locate a mutual experience.

T: "Move forward or backward in time in the lifetime you are experiencing. Locate the very first time you are together. Locate the first time you recognize each other. Locate the very first experience together. (pause) What are you experiencing?"

This may lead them to their first meeting, however unusual it may be.

In a class setting, two therapists, Al and Bill, who were also good friends, decided to take the roles of client for the purpose of exploring what past connections they might share. The student acting in the role of their therapist was nervous about the process, doubting her ability. The induction went well. Al described living alone in a small hut far from the town. He was a soldier and received an urgent summons. The town was under siege.

Bill was a scholar in a cloistered setting, living a sheltered life behind the walls of the sanctuary. The soldier was part of a group sent to protect the sanctuary, an important part of this town. The attackers were turned away but the soldier was mortally wounded.

After the battle had subsided, several of the scholars went out of the building to where the wounded soldiers lay. One of the scholars (Bill) carried the dying soldier (Al) into the walled enclosure where the wounded could be tended. The soldier died in the arms of the scholar before anything could be done. He had literally given his life in defense of the scholars and their sanctuary.

The student therapist could not make sense of the experiences being related until about halfway through the session, when the soldier described the sanctuary walls from the outside. It seemed to be the outside of the same building the scholar described from the inside. The first connection between these two friends came with the death of the soldier.

They both understood the profound nature of the unconditional love expressed in the scene. For the soldier doing his duty, it was the giving of his life for unknown persons inside. For the cloistered scholar who dedicated his life to education of his students, it was the realization that someone had died to protect the sanctuary and preserve his life and purpose.

It is a serious decision to join with another person in a marriage contract. Two married people may hesitate to separate as quickly as two people in casual relationship. For this reason, marriage offers a great opportunity for two people to balance karmic residue from earlier times. In a way they are literally forced together. If they face the problems together without separating and without destroying each other, they may well heal ancient conflicts. What is also available is the possibility of the deep and fulfilling expression of love and experience of love.

Married couples and couples considering marriage almost always discover prior lifetimes together in loving relationship. These may be preceded in

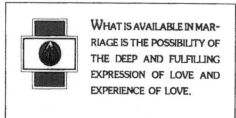

WHAT IS AVAILABLE IN MARRIAGE IS THE POSSIBILITY OF THE DEEP AND FULFILLING EXPRESSION OF LOVE AND EXPERIENCE OF LOVE.

turn by lifetimes as brother and sister, parent and child, cousins, good friends, fellow warriors, even brief acquaintances. Even farther back they might discover violent interaction in the time of the cave dweller. Many people locate their first earth incarnation in that primitive time.

Occasionally two people will recall separating from Source as a single spark of Light. The later separation into twin flames can bring sadness to the human heart, yet they see that they are together again with love. They also have the burden of whatever residues they have accumulated, and the problems of ego contamination in the present relationship.

Many people feel a longing during these times, a longing not for a romantic partner so much as for their "other half". It is difficult for many to put words to this longing. It is beyond loneliness, beyond the ego, beyond the body, beyond the heart, it seems to be a soul longing. Perhaps there is some spiritual truth in the concept of twin flames and soul mates.

Many people consider themselves to be soul mates. During past-life therapy, they may discover that they simply have karma to balance. Their mutual attraction is the soul's way of bringing them together in an attempt to balance the past conflicts.

Gail and Stan seemed very much in love. Stan had experienced a past-life regression several months before he met Gail. He recalled a life in a small town in Idaho in the 1800s. The session was quite meaningful to him. In that life, he was married and felt a deeply loving connection with his wife. Though she died at a fairly young age, he raised the children and attained some political prominence in the town. It was a good life.

When they met in this life, they felt a strong mutual attraction. In an intimate moment Stan described to her his past-life regression in Idaho. He turned to look at her and was stunned as he suddenly recognized Gail as his beloved wife in the earlier lifetime. They wanted to be regressed together.

When the induction was complete, Gail was the first to respond.

G: "There is a wavy motion. We're moving."

S: "You're scared."

G: "I'm not scared. We're on a sailing ship. We're going somewhere."

T: "Where are you coming from?"

A gentle probing often focuses the recall into more specific details.

G: "England. We're going to the new world for some reason. Where is our luggage? Where are the children? I am scared."

S: "We've been accused of doing something. We're going to the prison colonies. The children were left with your sister in London."

Their names were Henry and Angela. They had been accused of some minor crime and were being exiled to the prison colonies in the new world, which was America. He promised her he would take her back to see the children sometime. It was a promise he was never to keep.

In the new land, they were boarded with an old Black lady. She took good care of them until they were able to build their own place. They were very much in love. A short number of months later, in their own simple home, she became ill. Henry reminded her of his promise to reunite her with her children, but she could not hold on. Angela cried with deep sobs, knowing she would not be able to see them again. As she died quietly, he was also sobbing; he was heartbroken.

T: "Are there any promises you make to each other before you leave the body?"

G: "I'll always love you, Henry."

S: "I'll always love you. I can never give you children."

T: "Come to the very moment you leave the body, Angela. What happens?"

G: "I'm out of the body, I'm up above it."

T: "How does it feel. What emotion do you feel floating above your body?"

G: "I'm free."

Stan was still crying. Gail's voice became peaceful and soft. She was concerned about Henry and the Black woman who had come to help. They were grieving and crying. She could not help them. She began to cry.

G: "I feel so bad that he is grieving. I left him down there all alone. I wish he could be here. It's so much better here."

T: "He can't know that. And there is nothing you can do. What do you do next, Angela?"

G: "Floating, higher and higher, becoming smaller, like a point. It was like one little problem out of so many all around. There were problems all around the world. So many."

T: "Look around. Can you see anyone else? Can you see your children?"

Gail burst out crying and laughing at the same time. She recognized her children in spirit. They had died in England. Henry and Angela never knew. Now she was with them and there was joy.

T: "Henry, what are you experiencing, what are you doing?"

S: "Just holding her, stroking her hair. She has such beautiful hair, beautiful eyes." He was totally unaware of Angela's experience in the Light with her children. "I feel so alone, all alone. We had a good life together. I have so many regrets. I could not give her the seed to have a child. I promised I'd find her children."

Several years later, Henry returned to London to seek their two children. He was wary and very careful in the streets of London. He was still considered a criminal. He went to the sister's house only to learn that the children, Michael and Christina, had died. He felt that he had let Angela down again. His silent vow to her at her deathbed was that he would see her again.

Stan jerked in the chair.

T: " What happened, what just happened?"

S: "It's finished. I'm ready to go. It's over."

In his depressed state he wandered the back streets of London. A group of young toughs attacked Henry, beating him unmercifully.

S: "Oooh! Ow! That did it."

T: "What happened?"

S: "Someone clobbered me right on the head."

T: "What happens next?"

S: "My body relaxes. They got the wrong man. But it doesn't matter."

T: "Remember your thoughts about being finished, ready to go? For your purposes, did they get the wrong man?"

S: (laughing) "No. I don't think so. I'm done. I'm up out of my body."

T: (more softly, to Gail) "Dear one, as this is happening to him, can you see him from where you are?"

G: "Oh yeah." (joyful laughter)

T: "He doesn't see you yet, does he?"

G: "No."

T: (more firmly, to Stan) "What happens to you?"

S: "I hang around watching them beating my body. It is absurd. I'm just loving them. There is so much more to do or to complete. It's time to rest now for me."

T: "Keep looking around. What do you experience?"

S: "Well, there are the heavens, the stars. I never pictured anything like this. There is a lot of swirling. A lot of stars rushing by, and they got thicker and thicker. There's a lot of white. A lot of white light all around. And it's like I see Angela's eyes looking through. (laughter) I know she doesn't need to have a form, but I still need her to have a form."

T: "Yes, the eyes are the windows of the soul. It's how we recognize each other. She would give you that form so you could recognize her. Later you will recognize her by her vibration."

S: "Yeah."

T: "How is it now, being together in that space?"

G: "Ecstasy."

S: (laughing with her) "Wow. It's like there is no separation. Wispy...."

Both their voices trailed off, their expressions were joyful.

T: "Exactly so. There is no separation. In the inner being. There is only ONE. There is only the blending and connecting of consciousness. In human form, this is what we seek without knowing what it is that we long for.

S: "It's like one long orgasm. There is no beginning, no ending."

They laughed together.

T: "This is what it is like to communicate, to blend in spirit. It is
what we know deep within ourselves. It is what we remember.
And it is the ego that holds to the illusion of separation. In
spirit we are all one. This is the experience."

They enjoyed the bliss for a few minutes and were ready to move further.
They explored the life in Idaho which Stan had previously recalled. In the third
lifetime they discovered, Gail found herself as a male Brazilian attorney, single
and very active in amorous pursuits, and Stan experienced being an older married
Chinese peasant woman. They were surprised by this switch. They never
connected in the lifetime.

The therapist guided them to a moment of intimacy with their partner.
The Chinese woman was with her husband in their little hut, the attorney was on
a picnic in the country with a young lady friend. They were directed to express
love for their partners. As the lovemaking proceeded they discovered some
differences in the experience of being the opposite gender.

At the point of mutual pleasure with their partners they joyously realized
that there was no difference in being a man or woman at that moment. It was
very much like the blending they had felt when they were both in spirit without
gender. The most important interac-
tion is the sharing, the giving and receiving of love. The petty ego-oriented
problems that seem so predominant in
people's lives just seem to fade in the
vastness of love.

THE PETTY EGO-ORIENTED
PROBLEMS THAT SEEM SO
PREDOMINANT IN PEOPLE'S
LIVES JUST SEEM TO FADE IN
THE VASTNESS OF LOVE.

A few months after this dual
regression, Gail and Stan dissolved their relationship, without rancor, blame, guilt
or negative feelings. They parted in peace and love. They were not soul-mates
but they did have that lifetime of pain and regret to heal and forgive.

A nice variation on this dual induction is the garden meditation which is
given in the next section Group Regression. After the instruction is given for the
invocation of light in the clearing, the partner is invited into the visualization.

T: "Notice that your partner is walking across the clearing in your
direction. Invite that one to sit with you on the bench. Notice
how you feel being this close to your partner. Now stand up
from the bench and begin to move across the clearing, hand
in hand, toward the gate or doorway at the end of the garden.
On the other side of gate is the experience of a lifetime when

the two of you knew each other. You may be alone or together after you step through to the other side. Take whatever comes. Trust your impressions. Trust whatever experience comes to you. Now step through the gate and close it
firmly behind you. What are you aware of now? What are you
experiencing?"

The dialogue can begin.

Group Regression

There are many workshops and seminars which include group past-life
regressions as the main focus. This can be helpful for participants in exploring
issues in a general manner. Some people report major changes and healings as
a result of this experience. The seminar leader is usually skilled at individual past-
life therapy, and there are usually several assistants at the seminars who are also
competent as past-life therapists.

In many instances, however, some very troubled people attend these
seminars with the hope of resolving some major issue in their lives. It is not
intended to be therapy or a substitute for therapy. For some people the brief
regressions designed for exploration can exacerbate the emotional problems
which brought them to the seminar. If they do not make this known in the
seminar, it cannot be processed.

For these people, the seminar might seem like a negative experience. If
they are fortunate enough to have a therapist trained in past-life therapy
techniques practicing in their vicinity, that person can assist them in resolving the
issues which were stirred up in the seminar.

Attendance at a past-life regression seminar or any other experiential
growth seminar should be approached with cautious awareness and discernment.

For the therapist who wants to facilitate small group past-life regressions,
there are several important points to consider. Everyone in the audience needs
a tissue or handkerchief. There is often a great deal of crying, usually silent. A
good target destination to suggest for most people in a small or large group
regression is the experience of a happy or pleasant lifetime. Many people will
describe a happy event in a pleasant lifetime which may become unpleasant or
quite unhappy.

Participants may want to explore some specific issue in their lives. It can
be anything emotional, such as a phobia or hot temper; mental, such as a
prejudiced attitude, indecisiveness, or procrastination; or physical, such as a
chronic or incurable illness. Relationship is always a popular issue in past life
regression seminars.

The facilitator guides the participants in choosing an item, some aspect
of their present life, which causes a conflict or problem. This item includes the
emotional issues involved, the circumstances in which this item occurs, the
feelings caused by the item, and anything else associated with the item. Once

these details are considered, the participant is guided to choose some symbol which stands for this item, some symbol which can be used in the regression. It can be a face, a word, a single scene from memory, anything which can metaphorically stand for the item.

Most participants in small groups follow the instructions quietly, and everyone returns when the awakening suggestion is given. Occasionally one person will uncover some painful memory and will cry aloud. As the regression begins, the suggestion is given to stay focused on one's own experience.

> T: "Remain focused on your own inner experience. If someone cries or laughs you can ignore it and focus even deeper into your own feelings.

For any person who does not want to continue in a painful memory, the safety release suggestion is necessary.

> T: "During the regression if you want to stop the experience for any reason, you may take a deep breath and open your eyes. You will be able to do this if you choose to. You are in complete control of the depth of the experience, you are in control of your own mind."

If one or several people in a group regression choose to come out of the experience, they may need some brief guidance to help them release the emotional memories. For this reason it is wise for two skilled past-life therapists to be present for a small group regression. For a group of 20 or more, the presence of an additional therapist is recommended.

The garden meditation is often used for the group induction.

> T: "Take a good deep breath. As you relax more comfortably right where you are sitting or lying, take another deep breath. Begin to imagine standing in the warm sunshine, feel the grass beneath your feet, the breeze blowing by your cheek."

This calls on the kinesthetic sense to reinforce the experience. Next the visual track is engaged.

> T: "Imagine, begin to visualize in front of you, a green hedge surrounding a large beautiful garden. There is an opening in the hedge just in front of you. As you walk through the opening, notice the large flower beds. There is an area of red flowers closest to you. Gaze at the red flowers. Feel the color red. Bright, clear apple red. Feel the energy of red in your body." (pause)

"Next, there is an area of orange flowers, bright, clear, vibrant tangerine orange flowers. Feel the energy of orange." (pause)

"There is an area of yellow flowers, bright lemon yellow flowers. Feel the energy of yellow. Different from the energy of red and orange. Feel the colors in your body." (pause)

"Feel the rich green of the grass under your feet. Notice the green of the leaves on the flowers, the green of the tall hedge around the garden. Feel the healing energy of the green color." (pause)

"Next there is an area of blue flowers, deep tranquil blue. Feel the soothing energy of blue in your body." (pause)

"An area of violet flowers, a deep, rich royal purple. Reach out and touch one of the velvet smooth petals. Feel the deep rich energy of the violet color all through your body."

The visualization of colors is aimed at balancing and energizing the chakras or energy centers of the body.

T: "Beyond the flowers now, there is an area of trees. Tall, strong trees. As you walk among the trees, be aware of their roots, which grow deep into the ground, firmly anchoring them to the earth. Notice the branches and leaves, which reach upward, reach skyward toward the sun."

The purpose of this imagery is to establish a firm sense of grounding before reaching into the unknown territory of a past-life memory.

T: "As you emerge from the trees into the clearing, notice the bright sun above. Notice there is a bench in the center of the clearing. As you walk toward the bench, notice the size, shape and color of your bench. What kind of material it made of? As you seat yourself comfortably on the bench, run your fingers over the surface. Notice the temperature and texture of the surface of the seat. Feel the sunlight warm you. Feel sunlight bathe you in warmth and light. Feel the life-giving warmth penetrate and permeate your body, every cell of your body. This is a safe place, a safe sanctuary, and you can return here anytime you wish."

This is the invocation of Light for safety and protection. It is comforting and it establishes a safe sanctuary. People can escape some disturbing experience by either opening their eyes or retreating into this safe sanctuary.

Depending on the focus of the regression, the facilitator phrases the instruction appropriately, utilizing and initiating the mechanism of the affect bridge or somatic bridge.

> T: "As you are safely and comfortably seated on the bench, recall a time in your present life when you felt _____. (happy, angry, sad, guilty, jealous, abandoned, etc., or physical sensations of pain, tingling, cramping, itching, swelling, nausea, etc.) Let the emotions rise, feel the physical sensations in your body."

If the participants have chosen their item without discussion, the instruction should be general.

> T: "As you are safely and comfortably seated on the bench, recall an event in your present life which involved your item. Bring into your awareness the symbol of your item. Allow the feelings to rise. Feel the emotions as you face your item. Feel the physical sensations in your body. (pause)
>
> "Rise from your bench now, walk toward the gate or doorway across the clearing at the end of the garden."

The facilitator assumes a more commanding voice:

> T: "Now, in a state of expectant curiosity, open the gate or door and step through. Step cleanly through and close the gate or door firmly behind you. Completely into the experience, fully into the experience of another lifetime. Another lifetime which holds the answer, the source, the cause of your item."

There is no more mention of the present lifetime. All questions are addressed to the past lifetime in the present tense as if it were the only experience. A person in that altered-state experience in a past life is just as unaware of the present-day lifetime as a person in normal waking consciousness is unaware of past lives. It is important to pause for 30 seconds to a minute between questions which are meant to elicit images. For some people, the pauses are too short, and for others too long. There is no solution to this.

> T: "Now look down at your feet. Notice what you are wearing, if anything, on your feet." (pause.)

"Notice what you are wearing on your body." (pause)

"Notice if you are wearing anything on your head." (pause)
"Expand your awareness. Notice your surroundings. Is it
daytime or nighttime? (pause) Are you indoors or outdoors?
(pause) Are you in a populated area, a town or city, or in a
country location? (pause) Just notice your surroundings."
(pause)

Because of the use of the affect bridge or somatic bridge mechanism, the
participants will quite likely find themselves in a traumatic event.

T: "Where are you? (pause) Allow yourself to have clear impres-
    sions. What is happening to you right now? (pause) Notice
    what are you experiencing. (pause) What exactly is happening
    to you? (pause) What are they doing to you?" (pause)

If no one is doing anything to the participant, there will be no image or
answer to the last query. The meaningless questions will be ignored.

T: "Notice your circumstances. Are there other people near you?
    (pause) Is anyone with you? (pause) Are you alone?" (pause)

    "Move to the end of this event. Notice exactly what has
    happened to you." (pause)

If the bridging mechanisms have taken the participant into a traumatic
event, it may well end in death.

T: "If you leave your body at this time, notice what that feels like.
    (pause) Explore the experience of leaving your body in death.
    (pause) Don't leave the area, just notice what it feels like in
    spirit." (pause)

    "Now move back before the event began, come back into
    your body before the event began, skip back to the minutes
    before the event started. Before the event began, what are
    your circumstances? (pause) What are you doing? (pause) How
    are you interacting with other people? What happens that
    leads to this event?" (pause)

    "What is your part in this event? (pause) How do you partici-
    pate in the event? (pause) Notice more details this time as you
    move through the event. Exactly what happens to you?

(pause) How is this connected with your item?" (pause)

"Once again, come to the end of the event. What assumptions and decisions have you made regarding your item? (pause) What judgments have you made?" (pause)

"Let that go, now. Skip back to an earlier moment in the lifetime you are exploring. Locate the place where you live. (pause) Find yourself standing in front of the place where you live. Notice the size, shape, the architecture, the construction. (pause) Does it stand alone, or are there other similar structures nearby?" (pause)

"Find yourself inside this place where you live. Notice the furnishings, the decorations. (pause) Are there other people living there? (pause) How do you interact with others there?" (pause)

"Let that scene go. (pause) Skip forward or back, and locate another event which has to do with your item. (pause) Find yourself at the beginning of the event now. What are the circumstances? (pause) Where are you? (pause) What is happening?" (pause)

"Moving through this event, notice the details, notice what is happening to you. (pause) Notice how you are interacting with others. (pause) At the end of the event, what assumptions and decisions do you make regarding your item?" (pause)

"Skip forward, now, to the last day of the lifetime you are exploring. Find yourself in the last moments. (pause) What are your last thoughts about the lifetime? (pause) What are your last thoughts about your item? (pause) As you separate from the body, notice what thoughts, decisions, and judgments you carry with you. Notice what emotions you take with you. Notice what physical sensations you bring with you." (pause)

This is the mental, emotional and physical residue from that lifetime.

T: "As you rise, notice the brightness, the Light which comes. (pause) Notice if there is anyone you recognize in the Light. (pause) Move fully into the Light now." (pause)

"Skip forward now in the Light to the planning stage just

prior to the lifetime you will be living in _____. (present
year) (pause) In the planning stage, all the beings who will
interact with you are present. Think of some significant being
in your life and call that one out from the others. (pause)
When the being is face to face with you, you can communicate freely. What roles will you play together in the coming
lifetime? (pause) How do you agree to serve each other in
your spiritual progress and learning? (pause) Is there any other
communication between you?"

This is the planning stage where the agreements are formed for the
coming lifetime. Choices are made regarding gender, health, wealth, geographic
location, parents, mates, children and other aspects of the coming earth sojourn.

T: "Call out to your primary spirit guide in that place. When that
one is close to you, ask for any information or advice which
would be important for you to hear at this time. Listen carefully." (pause)

"Let that go for now. You can recall this planning stage in the
Light at any time. You can call to your own primary spirit
guide in that place for advice and counsel. You can do this
any time you choose." (pause)

"Take a deep breath and come back into your body right
here, right now. Focus on this moment in time, this location
in space. Come fully back into your body now. Reconnect
your consciousness with every cell of your physical body. Take
control again, take charge of your body and mind, right here,
right now. Take another deep breath. Get ready to open your
eyes into your regular state of consciousness. Another deep
breath and open your eyes. Wiggle your toes and fingers.
Stretch your arms when you want to. Another deep breath.
Welcome back."

Participants may want to share their experience. In a small group, it
works for each person to share with the entire group. In larger groups, it works
better for the participants to form into groups of three to five persons and share
within the small groups. Everyone who wants to should be able to express
themselves.

The questions can be focused on any aspect of life, such as relationship,
childhood, parents, occupation, travel, illness, or anything else. This regression
offer a simple format for this exploration.

The optimal time for a group regression varies from 20 to 40 minutes.

Most people will continue to follow the instructions for 25 or 30 minutes. Beyond that, some people will begin to fall asleep. Those who choose to lie down may begin to snore after 20 minutes. The leader must judge the appropriate time limit. Usually between 60% and 80% of the people in such a session will experience feelings, images, meaningful scenes, and some emotion. A few may describe vivid impressions and sweeping emotions.

Often, in a group regression there will be some people who will recognize others in the group who were involved in their past life.

Future-Life Progression

Future-life experience is nearly as accessible as past lives.

In his past-life therapy practice, Dr. Bruce Goldberg (1982) directed clients to locate the cause of present-life problems. Many of them described lifetimes in the chronological future, locating traumatic events which were the root of the present-life problem. His findings indicated that the clients found resolution of present-life problems with the future-lives progression as easily as with past-lives regression

In the non-physical realm, time is not linear and there is no sequence of events as there is in the physical space-time continuum. Time is said to be non-existent; all events occur simultaneously. The past-life therapist must work within this paradigm which contains time and no-time, without attempting to explain the unknown and unknowable. The important focus is the impact on the client of any real or perceived event or trauma, regardless of the origin, and resolution of the residue of that impact.

Dr. Helen Wambach progressed several thousand people into future time periods, namely 2100 and 2300 A.D. Only 7% to 9% of her subjects experienced physical existence in 2100, and 10% to 14% experienced physical existence in 2300. In further analysis of the information, there was a surprising correlation between the ratio of males to females in past lives, future lifetimes and the present-day ratio, which is about 49.5 female to 50.5 male.

These figures emerged regardless of the ratio of males to females in the participating groups. Perhaps the results of future-life progressions can be taken seriously because of the statistical accuracy of this and other factors described in Wambach's books. Dr. Chet Snow carried on Dr. Wambach's work after her death, in the U. S. and in France. His accounts of future time periods are detailed in his book, *Mass Dreams of the Future* (1989).

The garden meditation can be used for progressions. Only the destination instruction is different.

> T: "On the other side of the gate or door is the experience of a future life in the time period _____. (2100 A.D. to 2150 A.D., 2300 A.D. to 2400 A.D., 2500 A.D., or any other suggested period) Take whatever comes. Now, in a state of expectant curiosity, step firmly through the doorway into that

time period. You can experience the lifetime directly in your own body or through the eyes of another person if you do not have your own body."

Meaningful questions involve living conditions, type of habitat, eating utensils and type of food, type of clothing, interaction with alien beings from other planets, solar systems or galaxies, type or work or occupation, length of life and attitude toward death. Another interesting avenue of questioning is the exploration of the events of earth history during the last decade of the twentieth century and the first decades of the twenty-first.

Future Quest

While the true purpose of Stonehenge eludes modern attempts to divine its secrets, its timelessness evokes a synchronistic—if mysterious—link between the past and the future. Computer scanned image from the color original, *Stonehenge*, artist unknown, courtesy Mike "Gwydian" Wiseman and America Online

Recovery of
Soul-Mind
Fragmentation

Notes

Recovery of
Soul-Mind Fragmentation

Soul retrieval is a shamanic approach to healing. In the native tradition of shamanism, illness was an indication that the soul had vacated the body. The shaman journeyed into the underworld to retrieve the soul and return it to the sick person, restoring wholeness and health (Ingerman, 1989, 1991). The technique can be modified and utilized in the clinical setting.

In the process of treating people for the symptoms of spirit possession or spirit attachment, it is not unusual to find a fragment of the mind of a living person as an attached entity. This condition invites speculation about the other person whose mind fragmented and from whom the fragment separated. As part of the exploration within a session, the therapist can be alert for signs of the condition of soul-mind fragmentation in the client. Fragmentation seems to be a common condition stemming from the many perceived traumatic situations in life, ranging from minor to major, real or imagined.

Soul-mind is a term coined by June Bletzer (1986, p. 575), and for convenience the concept will be used here. Soul-mind is defined as the mechanism which records the sum total of a being's experiences through incarnations, forming the physical bodies and life-styles from these recordings. It is also called the *memory bank*. It is a permanent intellect or consciousness that composes a person's character or individuality and never dies. It may be synonymous with the subconscious mind, a sort of ethereal biocomputer incapable of discernment or decision making, a recording device which accepts the concepts, suggestions, ideas, and emotional evaluations of the conscious mind as these are dropped into it, and neatly organizes this material in compartments.

Colorful metaphors and colloquialisms in the language often cloak an underlying truth about the human condition. The title of the song, "I Left My Heart in San Francisco," may be literal and not simply a romantic lament. There are many such phrasings in the language, such as: "nobody

COLLOQUIAL PHRASES SUCH AS "NOBODY HOME" AND "EMPTY HEADED" ARE MORE THAN JUST METAPHORIC; THEY ACCURATELY DESCRIBE THE CONDITION OF FRAGMENTATION.

home," "he's not playing with a full deck," "she's out to lunch," "empty headed," and "he's out of his mind." These terms are more than just metaphoric; they accurately describe the condition of fragmentation.

Much Afraid

THE EMOTIONAL
TRAUMA CAUSED BY
...PHYSICAL VIOLATIONS
CAN INITIATE DISSOCIA-
TION AND SPLITTING OF
THE CONSCIOUSNESS AS
A COPING MECHANISM.

"Much-Afraid," scanned from *Pilgrim's Progress: Peerless Edition*, circa 1890.

Life in human form can be considered a physical experience for a spirit being. In this human experience, many people suffer traumas, primarily physical and emotional. Physical traumas which lead to soul-mind fragmentation can be any bodily intrusion, with a real or imagined threat to survival such as surgeries, organ donation and transplants, amputations of limbs, beatings or damage to any part of the physical body. Military combat situations, battlefield wounds during conditions of war where emotions run high, shattering of bodies by explosion, decapitation, atrocities such as severing of the genitals—all these cause severe fragmentation with intense emotional residue. Any sexual abuse, such as rape or incest, usually causes fragmentation of the personality or soul-mind.

The emotional trauma caused by these physical violations can initiate dissociation and splitting of the consciousness as a coping mechanism. Emotional trauma following loss of a loved one, or the sight of a loved one being seriously harmed, can lead to personality fragmentation. The experience of the trauma is literally stored in a fragment of the consciousness, a subpersonality which becomes separated and isolated from the main consciousness.

The percentage of fragmentation can range from minor to total. There can be any number of separate fragments. Each fragment maintains a connection with the main consciousness by a thread, a fiber of the silver cord which attaches the soul, the contracted spirit, to the body. The body can function as long as the silver cord maintains its connection, even if there is total evacuation of the fragments. Once a person passes through death and the silver cord of the contracted spirit is disconnected, a discarnate earthbound spirit that attempts to attach to a newly deceased body cannot maintain life in that body.

When the silver cord has been disconnected, the fragments continue to be connected to each other by the silver threads, even after the being leaves the physical body in death. The fragment of the soul-mind associated with a severed body part remains with the body part, yet is still connected by a thread to the main consciousness, wherever it is.

A fragment can become partially dislodged and still remain connected to the body. A fragment can follow the person like a balloon on a string. It can remain at some distant location or structure. It can also attach to another living person. A fragment can actually go to the Light. In all such cases of separation, the silver thread connection remains, and it is this link that makes the recovery process possible. It seems that a fragment can reincarnate as a separate living human. There are cases on record of two separate people recalling the same past life. Fragmentation is just one explanation.

A young woman recalled a love affair in the present life. She had vacationed in France a decade before. She fell in love, only to be hurt, as the affair could never be fulfilled. A fragment of her "heart" remained in the romanticized setting and sadness was the emotional energy maintaining the fragmentation. Many clients have described unfulfilled love affairs in prior lifetimes. Deeper investigation has revealed fragmentation resulting from the emotional pain, and the fragment remained lost in the setting of that lifetime. The person was born into this life in a fragmented condition. These past life fragments can be recovered and reintegrated in session.

One person angrily scolding another is sometimes referred to as "giving someone a piece of his mind." A sympathetic friend can lovingly offer to "shoulder" some of the emotional or physical burden of another person.

Thirty-five-year-old Tina described a serious automobile accident involving her friend Annie. Annie sustained massive damage and was not expected to live following the accident. Suffering terrible pain, she continued to hang onto life. Tina visited her friend in the hospital and in her love and compassion for her friend, expressed her desire to help: "Oh, I wish I could take some of your pain!"

After that visit, Tina began to experience pain which seemed to relate to Annie's wounds. In the altered state during a session, Tina discovered that a fragment of Annie's consciousness, which she assessed as about 30%, had joined her. Annie had apparently fragmented severely in the accident and that fragment had accepted Tina's invitation.

Diagnosis of fragmentation is fairly straightforward. Nearly everyone who has suffered trauma has some form and degree of the condition. No one symptom is diagnostic, though a combination of symptoms may be indicative.

The language of the client will describe the condition of fragmentation. A person may describe the experience of feeling dissociated, ungrounded, disconnected, of feeling like they are not in the body. The eyes may appear vacant or lackluster. The senses may seem muffled, a person may sleep a lot, and feel apathetic toward life. They may feel like they are "not all there," "not at home," as if something is "missing." There is a feeling of emptiness, of having no heart, of having an empty tube inside.

A client may describe a feeling of "numbness" in emotional or romantic situations. This can result from a painful loss of a loved one in this or another lifetime or a sexual violation which involved pain, anger, guilt or any other unacceptable emotion. The feeling part may have submerged or separated at the time of the loss or violation.

Dissociation and spontaneous out-of-body experiences may be reported as routine in a client's life. Depression, reticence in social situations, or a fear of commitment to relationship, job, or life in general may be signs of fragmentation. In the therapeutic session a client may seem to drift away, may tend to emotionally disappear or display totally flat affect as the therapist is talking.

Treatment begins with a scan of the body by the client in altered state which may disclose dark or shadowy spots, voids, holes, and empty places. These are the symbolic spaces left by the fragmentation. The client is directed to look for the threads that lead out from the holes. When these threads are found, some will appear darker, some lighter. Joyful or happy episodes can cause a fragmentation almost as easily as unhappy occurrences, and the threads to these fragments may appear light, even silvery.

The client is directed to choose the thread which seems to be most prominent-brightest, darkest, thickest, in some way standing out-and to pursue this one first. The thread will lead to a scene, an event, a trauma in this or another lifetime. The client will recall the event, and observe and describe the fragmentation and the separation of the fragment. Some people in session do not perceive the silver thread which connects the fragment. Even so, the connection remains intact and the separated fragment can be recovered.

The trauma is processed for the mental, emotional and physical residues, as for any traumatic event. These residues are retained by the fragment, the subpersonality formed by fragmenting. The exploration uncovers the circumstances leading to the event, the event itself, and the misperceptions and misinterpretations of the event.

This leads to the discovery of mental residue: the thoughts, assumptions, conclusions, decisions, and judgments. The emotional residue consists of feelings of anger, fear, sadness, and guilt. The physical residue is pain or other physical sensations associated with the event. The distorted perceptions and false beliefs held by the fragmented subpersonality are cleared in the processing. The residues are cleared as the truth is discovered.

When the conflict resolution is complete, the fragment is invited back into the body in the present moment. It is welcomed into the body wherever it belongs-sometimes into the empty hole or tube inside, into the head, more often into the heart. The traumatic event is then reviewed as a whole consciousness, reframed in whatever manner is necessary. Since the fragment will usually be a young child subpersonality who must be shown that it did not and will not die, it is imperative to prove that it survived the trauma, and this adult—the client—is who it became. The primary fear of the child during the trauma is that it will not survive.

As a client describes a traumatic memory, the therapist can ask questions such as the following:

> T: "What happens to your essence, your spirit, as your body is being touched like that?"
> "Where do you go when that happens?"
> "Where are you as you watch?"
> "What happens to you deep inside?"

Some clients can recall and describe incidents of childhood molestation, during which they stood across the room watching the molester fondling their little body. One client reported leaving her body lying in bed while father was touching her. She just went outside and sat on the roof until he went away. Many victims of molestation report floating near the ceiling during the periods of molestation. In many cases, the fragment which separates does rejoin the consciousness, forming a sub or alter personality that is the age of the child at the time of the molestation.

It is helpful to know the percentage of fragmentation. "Percentage" is a linear, mathematical term, and math is a left-brain function. "Portion" is the word used in the therapeutic questioning, as the right brain can sense a portion and describe it. However, the description is often given in percentage.

> T: "What portion of your essence is standing in the corner watching?"
> "What portion of you leaves your body when he touches you like that?"

The answer can be a fraction, such as one-half or one-fourth. It is more often described in terms of percentage, such as 30%, or 60%, even 90%. The fragmentation can be 100%, or total evacuation, which opens the way for total possession by a spirit, earthbound or demonic.

In many cases of fragment attachment the fragment proves to be a close family member, most often a possessive and protective parent in this or a prior life, in particular the loving, overprotective, overbearing, and possessive mother (McAll, 1982; Crabtree, 1985, pp. 160-165). In other cases, strong emotional feelings such as anger, rage and hatred, lust, vengeance, jealousy, and possessiveness can cause fragmentation in a person and subsequent attachment to the object of these powerful emotions. The purpose of this type of fragment attachment is revenge, conscious interference, or control of the host. This fragment is often accompanied by an attached demonic entity.

One female client was in love with her minister. Fortunately and wisely, he maintained appropriate distance and behavior. During the session she discovered that, indeed, in her longing she had fragmented and that fragment was attached to him. She also discovered a demonic entity with her. It stated that it had previously attempted to intrude on the man in order to interfere with his ministry, as he was a fine and powerful teacher of the Light. The attempt to attach to the minister was unsuccessful, and the dark entity subsequently located this woman who loved the man. It was easy to attach to her. It was preparing to move into the minister by way of the silver thread connecting the fragment of her mind with him.

The traumatic incident which originally caused fragmentation can sometimes be located in another lifetime. The fragment can literally be floating free or clinging to a location or structure on earth in the present time, even though the event occurred in another era. A child can be born with the condition of fragmentation. The recovery for a young child must be done remotely.

Witchcraft and black magic, spells, hexes and curses can cause a fragmentation of the practitioner, witch or sorcerer. The fragment of consciousness gives power to the curse. This fragment remains with the victim of the magic or curse. There is always dark energy involved in this sort of intrusive activity. The demonic entities are released appropriately and the fragment is sent to the Light. If the practitioner is still living, the attached dark ones are released to their Light through a remote releasement described in the section Remote Releasement (362), and the fragment is sent back to the person.

Fragments of the mind of a living person can be attached to one or more other living persons. The condition of fragmentation is not healed by death of the fragmented person. This means that the newly deceased spirit, the discarnate entity, remains fragmented. This fragmented entity can then attach to still another living person. Thus, an entity can be attached to two or more living individuals.

A session with a young woman revealed an interesting situation. Gwen, the subject, was well aware of the presence of Richie, her brother who had died in an automobile accident some months earlier. The single car accident often proves to be a suicide (MacDonald, 1964). She loved him so deeply that she welcomed him to join her after his death. A scan of past lives suggested that they had been lovers in other times.

With very little explanation of his situation and the effects he had on his beloved sister, Richie expressed his love for Gwen and was ready to separate from her and move into the Light, but it appeared to be too far away. Since there was no resistance on the part of either of them to the release, this was an indication of interference. It turned out to be another entity attached to him. As he explored within his own being, he discovered the nested entity, but could not identify it.

The questions were addressed to this nested entity.

T: "You, the one inside Richie, inside Gwen, step forward and speak. You the one interfering with these people, speak up."

C: "Yes, what do you want?"

T: "Who are you and what are you doing here?"

C: "I'm their mother."

She revealed that she was indeed their mother and she had attached when Richie was about two years old. As mother was still living, this proved to be a separated fragment of her consciousness. Her possessive and overpowering love, along with her fear of inadequacy for the job of raising a child, had caused her to fragment and attach to her tiny son.

This situation provides an interesting twist to the classic concept of spirit possession, in which a living person is considered to be influenced by the spirit of a deceased person. If the living mind-fragment remains connected to the spirit of the newly deceased person, then a deceased spirit is being possessed by a living person.

Fragmentation gives rise to every combination and variation of spirit attachment with the living and deceased. Fragments of deceased spirits can be attached to other deceased spirits and/or living humans. Fragments of living humans can be attached to other living humans and/or deceased spirits.

FRAGMENTATION CATEGORIES

The degree of fragmentation and separation that results from trauma ranges across a spectrum of severity from minor to total. For the sake of clarity, the following categories are defined. Any category is arbitrary and imposed and cannot cover all cases; however, this system renders the concept a little more manageable within the clinical paradigm.

Fragmentation can occur at any age; trauma is not confined to children and young people. A woman who loses her husband can suffer such grief that she feels "dead" inside. This may be a case of submerging, or it may be evacuation. An unborn child can fragment in utero as a result of a family upset or a discussion of abortion.

As a result of being overwhelmed by fear in a battle situation, a combat soldier can fragment severely. The fragment can separate and remain nearby or it may evacuate. Many Vietnam veterans suffered the condition termed Post-Traumatic Stress Disorder. Fragmentation and separation may play a large part in this condition.

Severe trauma or depression can lead to total separation and evacuation. This can lead to coma. It can also allow total possession of the body as the consciousness follows, still connected by the silver cord.

Subpersonality and Alter Personality

These are the classic fragments; they remain within the framework of the person's mind at the level of the subconscious mind. The *subpersonality* is described as a structured constellation or agglomerate of attitudes, drives, habit patterns, and belief systems, organized in adaptation to forces in the internal and external environment. It is considered to be crystallized energy that is "split off" from the whole of the personality, usually at a young age, as a result of some unmet basic need or drive or emotional trauma (Crampton, p. 712). It remains intact at that same age, diligently attempting to meet the original unmet need, even though many years pass.

Multiple personality disorder is the result of severe emotional and physical trauma. In most cases of such trauma, extensive fragmentation is inevitable. Further study of MPD patients reveals that some of the fragments have indeed separated. These fragments can follow nearby, attach to another living person, or move into the Light.

In MPD, there are many degrees of severity of dissociation. There can be several to several dozen alter personalities, each complete and functional by itself. The super multiple may evidence several hundred alters. There may be severe fragmentation with special-purpose fragments limited to specific functions, or shattering, where several thousand fragments may be present and yet the parts may remain together.

During a particularly hideous Satanic ritual, which can include extreme sexual violation, human sacrifice, even cannibalism, a child forced to watch or participate may cope with the terror by splitting at each new moment of perception of the scene. The memory of each fragment is thus likened to a photographic slide. The therapist must piece together the ritual by eliciting each fragment and the memory of its moment of perception.

There is a growing literature on the causes, signs and symptoms, diagnosis and treatment of multiple-personality disorder (Kluft, 1985; Bliss, 1986; Braun, 1986; Putnam, 1989; Ross, 1989).

Treatment of the subpersonality is similar to healing the inner child. The steps in this approach include:

1. Identification, recognition and acceptance of the subpersonality.
2. Determination of what it wants and needs.
3. Regression to the real or perceived traumatic event which precipitated the split.
4. Therapeutic resolution of the mental, emotional and physical residue.

FRAGMENTATION CATEGORIES

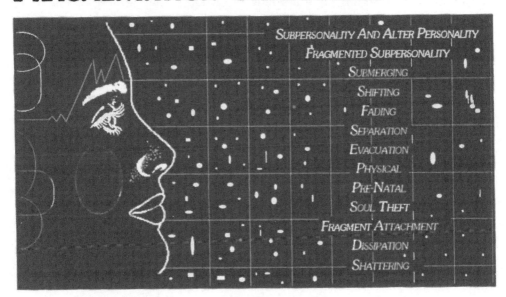

5. Disidentification from the subpersonality.
6. Communication and cooperation between client and
   subpersonalities, which leads to:
7. Integration.

As the client describes a past event and the emotion begins to bring tears or anger, the therapist can further encourage the subpersonality.

T: "How old do you feel right now? How old do you feel as you
   describe that memory?"

This will bring a response of an age, such as "10," "7," "3." The therapist uses this number as the designator of that subpersonality and speaks in a voice tone appropriate to a client of that age, encouraging the subpersonality to speak through the voice of the client.

T: "What happens next, 3? What happens to you next?"

As a client describes with emotion a traumatic childhood situation, the voice might take on the tone of a child's voice. This will be the subpersonality emerging and speaking. The narrative may shift to present tense. This is certainly the young child personality reliving the episode. The subpersonality is frozen in time, fixated in the event, and always on the lookout for signs of repetition or continuation of the trauma.

In a gentle voice, the therapist encourages the narrative in the present tense without judgment or comment on what is happening and without expressing sympathy.

    T: "What happens next?"
       "What are they doing now?"
       "How does that make you feel?"

Nobody has ever listened or paid attention to the pain and pleas of the child. The story will usually emerge easily. The therapist listens with interest and acceptance, yet without sympathy or judgement.

    T: "Are there others there with you, 3? Are there others older or
       younger than you?"

Often, the subpersonality will be aware of others. If not, the questions are aimed at any others who might be present.

    T: "Is there someone else who feels the same way? Is there
       someone else who does not like what happened to 3?"

Other subpersonalities may respond to this.

    T: "Is there 6, or 7, or 8?"

At this point, another subpersonality might answer and claim to be 9. If the question even gets close to the age of another subpersonality, it may respond. Most likely there are dozens, even hundreds of tiny splits, most of whom are not sufficiently formed to respond intelligently.

The therapist offers these subpersonalities the assurance that the one who hurt them is no longer here. They cannot be hurt now. The grown-up part can protect them from mother or father now. It isn't the same any more. The subpersonality is frozen in time, the time period of the trauma. The grown-up client may be able to reassure the little one of the safety. The young subpersonality may not trust the grown-up, but may trust the 12- or 14-year-old. It may trust the 18-year-old but not the 16, who was too rebellious and got into trouble.

The subpersonalities are introduced to each other. A sort of family therapy may be needed to get them to communicate with each other, trust each other, and begin to work together. Integration can proceed out of this mutual cooperation.

The subpersonality can be identified by its emotional reactions to life situations. It has a situation-specific response to any event, which is similar in any way to the original precipitating trauma. This is often a regressive behavior, easily identified by the client. As the client recalls, identifies, and observes the behavior, she can figuratively stand back in the observer position. The behavior can become quite humorous to the client at this time. When a certain experience is recognized and "owned," or acknowledged as her own, it is not so threatening. Paradoxically, the client can feel the feelings more strongly and explore them more fully when she is not identified with them. This is the process of *disidentification*, which is vital in the treatment of subpersonalities.

If the precipitating event was emotionally traumatic, therapy may require abreaction and ventilation of the originally suppressed and unexpressed emotions. The "child" wants to be recognized, heard and validated. Just as with a real child, after the tantrum there follows more harmonious, even tranquil, behavior.

Guided imagery can be an important part of the healing of subpersonalities. As the client recalls the traumatic event in childhood, she perceives and describes the child at that age. The client is urged to visualize herself kneeling down and reaching to the child with open arms. In the imagery, the child almost always runs into her arms to be hugged.

The child and client are asked to dialogue and make agreements about spending time together-for example, five minutes a day for three days a week. In the inner silence, or meditation, time can be distorted; five minutes of real clock time can be experienced as all day. In this way, the child can receive nurturing for a whole day in each of three five-minute periods a week, if the client agrees to give that much. The adult must keep the promise to spend the time with the inner child. If this promise is not kept, the inner child once again feels betrayed and the connection between them is damaged and could be broken. The subpersonality must be considered as a whole complete person within the framework of this therapy.

As this communication and cooperation proceeds, the barriers between the person and the subpersonality cease to exist. The subpersonalities naturally fuse.

Voice dialogue is an effective approach to working with subpersonalities and the inner child (Stone and Winkelman, 1985 and 1990). Psychosynthesis is the method developed by Roberto Assagioli, a contemporary of Freud (Assagioli, 1965; Vargiu, 1974; Crampton, 1981; Brown, 1983). Healing the inner child is becoming recognized as an essential part of psychotherapy (Federn, 1952; Berne, 1961; Whitfield, 1987; Grove, 1988; Abrams, 1990; Bradshaw, 1990).

Fragmented Subpersonality

A subpersonality can be fragmented. The fragmentation of the subpersonality can occur after the original splitting away of the subpersonality from the main personality. A subpersonality can manifest as an urge, a habit, a repeated reaction to similar situations. It can emerge as a playful part of a person when allowed to come out. It does not take over completely as an alter personality in MPD; the person is usually totally aware of the emotional behavior, whether joyful, fearful or sad. A real or imagined threat or trauma can elicit the behavior of the subpersonality, often to the embarrassment of the person. This subpersonality can respond to a perceived traumatic situation and can fragment just as any personality. These fragments must be recovered and reintegrated with this subpersonality before the subpersonality can be integrated with the main personality.

Submerging

This subpersonality is often discovered as the severely damaged inner child. Almost universally disowned in our civilized world, it nearly disappears inside, as if in a deep sleep. It is the one who is capable of total trust and intimacy with other people. Because of this, it has been hurt repeatedly. This subpersonality needs a strong protector/controller subpersonality. A strong protector/controller cannot tolerate the vulnerable child and so disowns it, often so completely that the protector/controller no longer worries about it (Stone and Winkelman, 1990).

In a classic case of MPD (Keyes, 1981), the main personality, Billy Milligan, submerged at about age 16. He was suicidal and the prominent alters took over. He reemerged during therapeutic sessions six years later.

Careful and sensitive work is required with the damaged and vulnerable inner child which has submerged. Trust is a major issue with this little one. The adult client may deny the existence of this subpersonality. Its very existence is at first rejected by the only one who can really understand the pain of that inner child. The initial stage of therapy involves the adult and is aimed at recognition and acknowledgment of the dysfunctional family, especially the abusing parents. Failure to recognize and treat this submerged inner child may result in physical illness. The child is the foundation for the life of the person.

The submerged part may not be a child. Fragmentation can also occur in the adult, due to serious trauma, whether mental, emotional or physical. Candace was a highly intelligent, efficient, well-grounded, no-nonsense business-woman. She had engaged in a few romantic affairs in her 38 years but had never committed to a serious relationship. Then she met Rick, an affable, open-hearted Italian, and things quickly changed for her. Passion became part of her life and she was seriously contemplating marriage. Her mother adored Rick.

Candace was troubled; in intimate moments with Rick she found herself becoming numb to him and his affections, almost mechanical. She was planning their life together, turning her affections and attention toward him exclusively; and yet faced with a full life ahead, she was puzzled by this numbness. She felt vaguely angry at some of his behavior and his inability to make sound judgments.

In past-life exploration for the source of the anger and numbness, she discovered a scene in which she saw herself holding his body and wailing loudly. He had lost his life in a futile and senseless battle. She felt like part of her died in that moment. For the remainder of her life she was mechanical and lifeless, devoid of emotion. It was safer; feeling was too painful.

Guided back to the circumstances leading up to the trauma, she saw that they had had a terrible argument the night before. The argument centered around his decision to engage in this battle. She did not share his loyalty to the leader. He had pledged himself in military duty to the unscrupulous leader of their people, and he thought that was more important than staying with his family. In her heart, she knew the danger of this conflict. Although she knew he would not survive, she could not put this into words.

Candace did not go into a deep altered state of consciousness. She often opened her eyes during sessions. Even then she could vividly track the past-life experiences, but with little emotional involvement. Still in the altered state, Candace scanned her present-life body. There was an emptiness and a huge hole in her heart, yet no thread extended from it. There was buried anger, deep sadness and the familiar numbness.

She was guided to the last day of the lifetime she was exploring. Emotionally, she was still numb; even the anger within her was dead. After the death of the physical body she maintained this frame of mind, the decisions regarding the safety of the numbness, and the anger about Rick's judgments and actions.

As a spirit, Candace was guided back to the night of argument, and directed to step into her husband's body and merge with his mind so she could think his thoughts and speak his words. Without the barriers of time and space, she moved quickly into that space. The therapist directed the questions to the husband.

T: "You, soldier, what do you think of your wife? What's going on with this argument?"

C: "She's just a woman. They don't understand. I'm a soldier, it's my life. I have a duty."

T: "What about your duty to your family?"

C: "I pledged my duty to the leader. It's my career. I'm a soldier."

T: "And your father before you, is this a family thing?"

C: "No, his fealty was pledged to another. He didn't follow our leader as I do."

What Candace realized, by thinking his thoughts, was that all this loyalty and duty to the leader and commitment to the cause was purely mental, and involved with ego and maleness. He could do nothing else and still maintain his male pride. What he could not say was that he saw the futility of the cause and the upcoming battle. He felt stupid putting his commitment to the leader and military duty above family. It was just not voiced. It was unspeakable within the current small-minded cultural mentality.

Bound by the same mentality, she could not voice her real fear that he would not return alive to her and their two children. It was not financial insecurity she feared; that security was already assured. It was the deep love connection she felt between them that she dreaded losing.

They did not tell the truth to each other because of this limiting mental attitude of their time. Love was not communicated between them, nor expressed and acknowledged. This was the lie: the unexpressed truth of their love.

She remained merged with his mind watching the battle, and felt the thrust of the spear which pierced his body. He hovered over the body after his death, observed his wife as she found his inert form. Listening to her wailing cries, he realized with deep sadness what he had lost. He knew beyond any doubt how futile and stupid this battle had been and how meaningless his commitment. He loved her deeply and he decided to stay with her. He tried to help her, to comfort her, and could not. He stayed by her side until her death.

In his death, he fully understood the lesson. He realized that love is the most important experience, but it was too late for that lifetime. He wanted another opportunity to love. As she emerged from her body in death she saw him, but she still was distant, too numb to join with him in spirit. They moved into the Light separately.

Disconnecting from his mind, Candace softened toward him. Her anger diminished. His deep sadness and his suffering allowed her to see that he had loved her, had realized his misdirected loyalty and duty. It was time for healing.

T: "I call out to the female who left. I call out to that damaged part of the woman who held her dead husband on the battle-field. The woman who died inside. Wherever that fragment is. The opportunity is back. He learned his lesson. The opportunity for love is back. It is your lesson now. He learned his."

C: "She's rising up. She didn't go anywhere. She's standing up inside me. It's like she's crippled."

There was no silver thread, because the fragment had not vacated; it had submerged deep inside, becoming dormant, comatose, numb and almost dead.

T: "Help her up. Help her like an old woman. Help her gently. Has she seen all this? Does she understand?"

C: "I think so."

There was wonder and surprise on Candace's face.

T: "What does she want from you?"

C: "She wants me to voice the feelings. The things she couldn't say then."

T: "What will she give you in return?"

C: "Joy."

With a smile beginning to form, Candace felt deeply the transformation of the sadness, the anger, and the feelings of numbness.

This was the beginning of major change for Candace. As she later described "the walls came tumbling down."

All there is is love, and the barriers to expressing love to others and experiencing it as others extend love. The emotional barriers are anger, fear, sadness, guilt. The mental barriers are judgments and beliefs which stem from false decisions, assumptions, con-

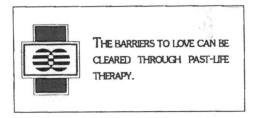

THE BARRIERS TO LOVE CAN BE CLEARED THROUGH PAST-LIFE THERAPY.

clusions and judgements made during traumatic events in this life and prior lifetimes. These are the emotional and mental residues which can be cleared through past-life therapy.

Shifting
A state of being partially out of the body is common among traumatized people. They feel like they are not quite in all the way. The client may feel "spacey" much of the time. In session, they may seem to drift away. Attention span may fluctuate.

Chandra, a 40-year-old female client, talked about herself in this way. She described floating up so that her feet were just about chest level. She had endured numerous surgeries in her life. She was allergic to many things, including many medications. Her father began molesting her when she was 18 months old. It started as fondling. At age 13 he actually penetrated her in sexual intercourse. This continued until she left home at 18 to get married. She had not developed MPD as a coping mechanism; she had used the out-of-body escape from the abuse.

The category of *shifting* includes the partial out-of-body state in which the fragment floats from its moorings, so to speak, yet overlaps the physical form, as described in the case of Chandra. Treatment begins with the recognition by the therapist and the client that this condition exists. The client is guided to the awareness and acknowledgment of the causes of the condition, the traumatic event or events. The residues are resolved as well as possible. Forgiveness of the perpetrator can bring the final healing of the memories. Growth and change can follow this healing.

There is the condition of an overlapping fragment, slightly ajar in some direction, stuck there because of anger, fear, guilt or some other painful emotion, such as the next case.

Sandy was 27. As a result of a strict religious upbringing, she was unaccustomed to complaining and always placed others before herself. She had worn dental braces for ten years and was faced with the possibility of replacement of both of the temporo-mandibular joints, the hinge joints in her jaw. At age 17 she was a passenger in an automobile driven by her boyfriend on a Friday-night date. They had crashed into a vehicle parked at the side of a narrow road. Sandy slammed forward, her face impacting on the dashboard. Still conscious, she emerged from the car and made her way to the other car to check on injured people. The car was empty.

The ambulance transported her to the emergency room at the hospital where her mother worked as a nurse. Her first thought was to locate her mother to assure her that she was fine, which she certainly was not. Sandy ran out of the emergency room before the attending personnel could stop her. Nurses caught up with her in the hallway before she found her mother and returned her to her bed in the ER. As she lay awaiting treatment, she felt the need to use the restroom. Facing the mirror she saw for the first time her bloodied and distorted face as well as her blood-stained clothing. The appearance of the damage was enough to put her even deeper into shock. She felt a stabbing pain in her left side.

An unidentified pain in her left side about the middle of the ribs turned out to be a fragment of consciousness, a dissociated part which did not separate, did not reintegrate, did not manifest as an alter, but did interfere with healing. She was almost literally scared to death by the sight of her own blood. Such a scene almost always looks worse than it is, especially to the untrained eye, and this fragment believed she had nearly died. This fragment remained connected at the left side of Sandy's rib cage, angled up at about 45 degrees, as though trying to pull itself out, yet being stuck at about the waist.

At church on the Sunday morning following the accident, people asked how she was feeling. Her reply was the automatic "Fine", although a part of her was screaming out for attention, wanting someone to recognize and acknowledge that she was badly damaged, that her survival was threatened. She could not say it for herself. Her resentment grew enormously.

That angry, resentful part kept the pain in place year after year. After the years in braces and several surgeries on her jaws, she was still in extreme discomfort and severely depressed. The physicians, dentists, and oral surgeons assured her that it was only psychosomatic, which further infuriated her. The subpersonality could only use the pain as its communication device to the outside world and to Sandy herself. No one had ever discovered her presence

She had married, three years prior to the session, a sympathetic and loving husband who could do nothing to alleviate the suffering. During the session the subpersonality was recognized and acknowledged for the first time. It expressed anger toward the therapist as just another doctor telling her it was going to be all right.

This case called for extensive therapy on the fragmented part. Sandy also needed some restructuring of her sense of self-worth, which had been severely distorted by her religious upbringing.

Fading

This is a typical behavior of the child in alcoholic or other dysfunctional families. They describe wanting to fade into the woodwork, to vanish into the furniture. They literally try to disappear; they do not engage in life. It is a behavior which continues into adulthood. This person can be very quiet in a group. They may dress quite plainly; women may use little or no makeup. Other people have difficulty recalling their presence in any group. They just seem to fade.

Andrea described herself as sitting "sort of beside" her body. She had never quite fully entered the body at birth. Never having made the decision to commit to the present lifetime, she incarnated this time with a mother who gave her up for adoption at birth. Her adoptive family was emotionally dysfunctional, though not physically abusive. Her lack of commitment to her life affected many areas of her experience. She was socially reticent, dressed plainly, and had refused to commit to marriage with the man she had lived with for 11 years.

In session, she was guided to the birth experience in her current life, when she had seriously considered not joining the body. Her resistance to the connection with her own body was traced to a trauma in a prior lifetime. The trauma was processed to completion. Returning to the moment of connection in the present life, she was able to make a new choice to come fully into the body, to engage in life.

Fortunately, the factor of alcohol was not part of Andrea's dysfunctional family life. In the barren emotional climate of her home environment, she just never developed any sense of belonging. This exacerbated her original lack of commitment to life. *Codependency* is the description of the behavior arising within the dysfunctional family. Alcoholism or any other compulsive disorder can be the predisposing factor in such a system (Beattie, 1987). It is estimated that 96% of all families are to some degree emotionally impaired (Bradshaw, 1988).

Group therapy in the 12-Step Program of Adult Children of Alcoholics is generally effective for survivors of dysfunctional families. The deeper issues involved with fragmentation and fading can best be treated through this individual therapy. The client is guided back to the actual trauma when the personality fragmented and separated. That fragment literally faded in and out of the personality, subsequently blending and leaving, but never completely returning to fully integrate.

Fear contains two elements: the memory of past pain, and the anticipation of future pain. The greatest fear of the subpersonality which separated at the time of the trauma is death. The continued assurance from the therapist will assist this one in realizing that it did not die, it survived the original trauma, whatever it was, and all the succeeding episodes of similar trauma.

Another fear is the anticipation of continued pain at the hands of the perpetrator, whoever that was. The fragment is directed to see the client, now an adult, in their present-life situation. The fragment is asked to notice that the perpetrator or perpetrators are no longer present in that role, even if they are still living. The subpersonality is directed to view life in the present moment.

As the truth of the present situation is slowly accepted, the fear begins to disappear, and the fragment is finally willing to merge with the full consciousness. Guided visualization of golden light surrounding the client at this point builds up the strength of the essence of the fragment for the literal rematerialization and resolidifying of itself. This leads to the final integration.

Separation

Severe trauma may result in a significant percentage of the soul-mind escaping and following at a safe distance, still connected by the silver thread. A person with any degree of separation fragmentation is seriously vulnerable to entity attachment and possession. Separation leaves an open door through which any passing entity can enter and attach. Without the complete soul-mind intact and in attendance it is relatively easy for another consciousness to enter and take complete control. A person in coma may be suffering severe fragmentation and separation.

Separation fragmentation may be encountered following emotional trauma such as a broken heart, depression and suicidal urges, explosive anger, and violent argument, or physical trauma such as wartime combat, amputation, accidents, surgeries, severe beating, incest or rape. Such a trauma can often be located in a prior lifetime of the client. If the separated fragment remains attached to a past-life location, the condition is considered to be evacuation.

An entity may experience separation fragmentation following organ donation, decapitation, loss of limbs, or disintegration of body parts in an explosion. This fragmentation may continue after death. The fragments may remain on the battlefield, at the hospital, or with the organ-transplant recipient.

One client, who will be called Laura, proved to be very proficient in remote spirit releasement. It seemed as if her High Self could come through and see the target situation very clearly. Laura described Lise, her niece, as a baby with nearly vacant eyes, who seemed to be "not at home." . She was six months old and not responding at all normally. The family was understandably concerned.

Laura had asked a psychic for a reading on the child and the information had come through automatic writing that only a small portion of the child's soul was attached to the body. The rest was some distance away. Laura seemed quite concerned, and this was her stated reason for the session.

She went into altered state easily. Her head dropped forward, she slumped over, arms and shoulders hanging limp. Twenty or thirty seconds passed and she straightened up, eyes closed, and her voice asked what was happening, curious about the purpose of the meeting. This voice identified itself, after some questioning and testing of the spirit as a being from the Light, as her High Self in training, new at the job, practicing to become a true High Self. This was a new experience for the therapist, who wisely withheld judgment as it seemed to be truly a being from the Light, not a deceiver, not an earthbound.

The therapist asked this being if it could connect them with the spirit of the child. It agreed to try. Laura described a brief visual image of a ball of light falling into a pit of blackness, seeming to connect to nothing at all. After a few more seconds, a being emerged calling itself Alan, and acknowledged his rightful place as the soul of the female child, Lise. However, he carried such a burden of guilt over failing in his last lifetime that he could not fully engage in this lifetime. He knew that a life experience was designed to allow the opportunity for resolving old conflicts, yet he still labored with the turmoil of the failure.

From the point of view of the planning stage in the Light, he described his lifeplan as Alan. His main purpose was to bring light to the being who was to be his mother. She had lost sight of her own path somehow. He was to make his transition at age 21, his purpose fulfilled. But his mother never found the light, lived a debased life, showed no love for him, and he gave up; he threw himself in front of a trolley at the preordained age of 21, feeling as if he had failed. In spirit the feeling of failure was even stronger, yet it did not hold him earthbound as might be expected. He went into the Light and prepared to be born as Lise. The plan did not call for his return to the same mother, though she is part of the family again.

Guilt can be alleviated in several ways through past-life therapy. Reviewing or reliving the original events can bring a fresh viewpoint. Seeing the circumstances through another person's eyes can alter the burden of feelings by bringing a truer perspective, eliminating false assumptions, judgments and decisions. Exploring the situation with the purpose of discovering the being truly responsible for the outcome can bring the insight which will dissolve the false guilt feelings instantly.

With this in mind, the therapist asked Alan to recall his first experience as Alan entering into the physical plane from that planning stage. The brief imagery that Laura had described earlier now came back with meaning. Suddenly Alan described himself as a ball of light hurtling into a pit of blackness. It turned out to be the moment of his conception. There was an enormous dark energy already there, a demonic being he could not overcome. Nor could his mother, as she was not even aware of it. Even after his birth and years into his life, the intrusive, parasitic dark energy interfered with his purpose of bringing his mother into an awareness of the light. Calling on the Mighty Rescue Spirits of Light to bind the dark being in a capsule of light, the therapist assisted in its release to its appropriate destination in the Light. Alan now realized that he was not at fault for the "failure" of his mission and purpose in that lifetime. The realization erased his guilt.

The therapist next guided him to the moment of conception in the present-life experience as Lise. He immediately perceived that there was another being, an earthbound spirit, not dark, who was interfering with his birth mother. This attached entity quickly agreed to go on to the Light. Alan had performed double duty in just a few minutes. He assisted in the release of the demonic entity from his mother in the former lifetime, clearing her path to choose for the light, and also in locating and releasing an attachment interfering with Lise's mother.

Alan felt the effects of this work immediately. He described moving close to Lise. Seeing her, he wanted to incorporate into the little body, the body that was rightfully his. As he did he described being part of her. He declared that he was no longer Alan. That personality disappeared as suddenly as the false guilt which had kept it in place.

Laura and her husband saw an immediate change in the child. She seemed to be more "at home" in her body, more responsive. A year later she was quite responsive and seemed normal. Of course, there is a natural developmental process as a child matures from six months to a year and a half of age. However, they both agreed that there were immediate changes resulting from the session.

Evacuation

Terror can lead to fragmentation and evacuation, a more distant separation, though the silver thread remains connected. A significant percentage of the soul-mind can abandon the physical body and attach to another living person. Severe depression can cause a fragment to actually move into the Light; it is a kind of little death. Death of a loved one can bring about this condition.

People in relationship are often found to exchange fragments. This can happen in a love relationship, parent and child, or any other close interaction. When one of the partners in such a relationship dies and the newly deceased spirit moves into the Light, the fragments are also transported there. If the newly deceased spirit remains earthbound, it may still be burdened with the mind fragment of a living person.

The session with Laura and her High Self working with her niece was very clear. Laura wanted to continue using this gift of spiritual healing for the benefit of others. She mentioned her brother-in-law, Len, who had come home from the Vietnam war diagnosed with undifferentiated schizophrenia. He was on medication which allowed him to hold a menial job and function at a minimal level. He lived with his father. Laura's husband, Fred, a gentle, loving man, had been close to his younger brother before the conflict. Since the war there had been little communication between them.

Fred visited his brother regularly and described him as hiding somewhere inside, feeling that perhaps only 20% of him was really present. Laura had not met Len until his return from Vietnam. He had not spoken more than a dozen words to her in that 15 years. Because of prior success of the releasement techniques with other Vietnam veterans, the therapist suggested to Laura that she and her husband might want to do a session with the intention of helping Len.

Late that night after her initial session, she told her husband the story of the child, Lise. In the middle of her narrative her head dropped and High Self came through. Fred had no prior knowledge or experience with this phenomenon. It came as a total surprise to him. Within moments he began suffering severe diarrhea and vomiting. When she took him to the emergency hospital in the early morning hours, the medical personnel could find no cause for his condition. Later in the day she took him to a larger hospital, where more extensive tests showed no organic cause for the problems he was suffering. This condition persisted over the next two days.

Several days later, they had a session together agreeing to attempt a distant healing, a remote spirit releasement, for his brother, Len. They talked with the therapist about what had happened in the first session and about Fred's brother. Len's story was gruesome and not totally clear. He and five of his buddies were in a hotel room in Saigon, where they normally slept. Enemy soldiers burst through the door, firing automatic weapons. Len dove beneath the bed; the others were shot, some falling to the floor, others onto the bed. The bed crashed through the floor, down to the lobby level. This was as much as Len would tell about what happened. Soon after that episode he was sent home.

As the three were talking, Laura's head suddenly dropped, her arms and shoulders went limp, and High Self came through again. She apologized for surprising Fred by coming through as she had done that first night without warning or preparation. She explained she was new at this and was working very hard at her practice to become a true High Self. She agreed to be more careful with Fred. She also announced that there were two little black spots of energy inside him and that it was these dark ones which had made him ill a few nights before. He reported feeling nothing as the remote releasement of these dark-energy beings proceeded to completion.

After the dark ones were gone from Fred, High-Self-through-Laura shifted her focus to his brother, Len. She located the traumatic event which triggered the fragmentation: a moment of great fear in the jungles of Vietnam many years before. She assumed his identity and began to relate the story from his viewpoint. What emerged was quite different from the version Fred had put together from Len's meager account.

On patrol with his buddies, Len had lost contact with them. He could not call out because there were enemy troops nearby. In his terror and aloneness he silently called to his brother for help. He recalled some of their fun times together as kids; he felt very close to Fred. And according to High Self, his soul-mind essence fragmented at that point and separated, leaving only about 20% there to keep the body going. Len waited until dark, found his way out of the jungle and back to the hotel in Saigon. When he opened the door he found the bodies of his buddies, lying dead in the room. They joined him in spirit, and this was his present condition.

The therapist began working remotely with Len through Laura's High Self. Bob, an attached spirit and a spokesperson for the group, assisted all the others as the Light came. Each of the attached spirits came forward and recognized the spirit of a loved one in the Light and joined them for the journey home. It was mutually agreed that Bob should stay to help Len in the process of healing. He was first strengthened by stepping into the Light and then stepping back into Len. The motivation for leaving Bob attached temporarily was the hope that he might cause a brief lapse of memory at the right moment, causing Len to begin skipping his medication. It was expected that the physicians in charge would notice the changes and perhaps alter the diagnosis of schizophrenia. This was a brave hope.

The other 80% of Len's soul-mind essence was located. It had attached to a Vietnamese soldier after it had separated from Len. This distant separation and attachment constituted an evacuation. The fragment expressed the terror of being separated from his buddies in the jungles of Vietnam. The fragment was assured that Len had survived, the body was alive and well, and it was needed at home. It was carefully guided back to integration by High Self and other spirit guides.

A few weeks later, the therapist received a letter from Laura, stating that her husband was feeling fine. When he visited his brother Len, he seemed to detect a spark in his eyes that had not been there before. She also reported that Len had conversed in a meaningful way with her for the first time ever. A year later, both Laura and Fred saw a considerable change in Len. He was still far from being totally functional, yet he was more of a person than he had ever been since returning from Vietnam. In this case of evacuation, a large fragment separated, remained in the earth plane, and found an attachment site in another living person.

Sadness and depression can lead to fragmentation. Eleven-year-old Danny was in the throes of depression and apathy. After his parents divorced he remained with his father, who was unhappy, depressed, and very low-key in his energy level. Danny was doing poorly in school and was generally unsociable. He was interested only in sports. In session, Danny discovered an attached spirit, a young Black kid named Andy. The boy was from New York and had died in the streets. He liked basketball and this is what had attracted him to Danny.

Andy was soon ready to go to the Light. He perceived it as a basketball court. The floor was white, the walls were white, the backstops were white, the ball was white, the coach was dressed in white, the bleachers were white. When asked if anyone was sitting in the bleachers, Andy replied that Danny was there. It turned out to be a fragment of Danny estimated at about 20% of his soul-mind.

This was the source of the apathy in Danny's attitude to life. Danny wanted the part back. At first it was reluctant to return, though finally it did so. Andy eagerly went into the Light and the fragment was reintegrated.

Danny was like a new person. He was happy, laughing, more sociable, and he began to perform better at school work. The father refused to have a session. Within a few months, Danny had reverted to his former state of depression. He did not have another session but it seemed most likely that the return of the depression indicated that fragmentation had occurred again. In the unchanged environment with his depressed father, Danny succumbed again to the low energy. This was a case of evacuation, where the fragment was not just floating somewhere but had gone to a specific location, the Light. Danny literally had one foot in the grave.

This points up the need to work on the whole system, the total environment, the entire family, not just one member who has the desire to change and the courage to work in a session. This also makes obvious the wisdom and need for remote spirit releasement work on the other members of a family.

Physical

Decapitation as punishment for crime has a long history. In earlier times, battles were fought between warriors armed with swords, and many heads rolled on these battlefields. Serious accidents often result in decapitation. Surgical removal of body parts, whether something as small as a tooth or an appendix, or as large as an arm or leg can lead to fragmentation and separation of the fragment of consciousness associated with the part.

There is a commonly held misperception in the male mind that the genitals make the man. Throughout the history of war, casualties on the battlefield have been mutilated by the opposing soldiers. The genitals are cut off and stuffed in the mouth of the victim. This was repeatedly seen during the Vietnam War. Many American dead were discovered in this condition (Hendin & Haas, 1984, p. 5). It is a supreme insult, meant to discourage and intimidate the troops. It works.

An entity who suffered physical dismemberment, either accidentally or purposefully, even if the dismemberment occurred after death, will remain fragmented following the death. This condition must be healed. The etheric form of the separated member must be recovered and replaced before the entity returns to the Light.

For the client who has lost a body part, there needs to be exploration, discovery and expression of the emotions associated with the loss. For the surgery patient, there may be fear and anger. For the combat soldier, there is anger, defensiveness and vengefulness. The accident victim feels anger, resentment, and feelings of injustice.

An organ might be donated by one family member for transplant into another as a life-saving gift. This is motivated by love. Past-life exploration might reveal other motivating factors and karmic balancing in this altruistic act. The life energy of the organ remains with the organ but the fragment of soul-mind must be recovered. If the organ donor dies before the recipient, this connection may lead to spirit attachment.

A variety of guiding suggestions and questions can assist the client in locating the fragment.

> T: "Find the silver thread between your body and your _____."
> (part)
> "Locate the connector between you and your organ."
> "Reach out and locate that part you left behind, wherever it is."
> "Locate your _____." (physical body, head, genitals)

An entity who suffered any form of dismemberment while alive may not want to go anywhere without his parts. There may be an element of shame at being seen in an incomplete state. Decapitation is a condition commonly found in an entity who is reluctant to go to the Light. The entity might blame the host for inflicting the injury in the present or a prior lifetime. It is often easier for an attached entity to recall the surgery, accident, or battle which led to the fragmentation than for the living person in altered state to remember the incident.

> T: "Recall that moment when you were hurt. Recall the event
> when you lost your _____. (part) What happened?"
> "Locate the missing parts you left behind. What happened to
> you?"

With the recall of the original event, the trauma can be processed to completion. The therapist then directs the entity in healing itself.

> T: "Pick up your head. Place it right on your shoulders. Does it
> fit? Brush it off, clean it and try again. How's that? How does
> that feel?"

Simple and direct, this often works. If there was a shattering, as in a mine or bomb explosion, the soul-mind essence might be scattered like dust, flower petals, or pieces of a jigsaw puzzle. This may require a bit more guided imagery.

> T: "Reach out, gather the little pieces, scattered like flower petals
> in the wind."

This is a more gentle imagery than recalling bloody bits of flesh scattered on the ground.

T: "Gather the pieces to you, gather them and begin to fit them together like pieces of a puzzle."

Metaphors can be very effective in healing imagery.

T: "Bring it all in. Is there anything still missing? Reach out, pick it all up. Are there other pieces left in other times and other places? Reach back, locate all your missing pieces. Recover everything that is you. You deserve to be whole and complete. You have a right to claim all your parts. You need to have all your parts and pieces when you return to the Light. You will need everything intact for your next lifetime."

Certain birth defects may be the result of fragments left behind. Accidents resulting in lost body parts might be the manifestation of past-life fragmentation and incomplete recovery.

Pre-Natal Fragmentation

The soul or spirit being does not fully join the physical body until the first breath or shortly afterward. A portion of the consciousness is with the forming embryo from conception and records everything without discrimination or filter of any kind. Well before birth, the incoming soul can assess the family situation and future options, and may attempt to reject the coming life journey. This can result in spontaneous termination of the pregnancy or sudden infant death syndrome (SIDS).

If the choice for death in utero is not fully realized for some reason, the next attempt to leave may result in a severe fragmentation. The fragment, usually more than 50%, may be the sensitive, feeling part of the being. This leaves the tough, resilient, defiant, aggressive part to brave the infancy and childhood. There seems to be a better chance for survival if this stronger part is in charge.

The adult client be painfully aware of the lack of the sensitive feeling nature. He or she may immediately recognize the other part as something which was conspicuously absent, something dimly remembered, and welcome the sensitive part back in. The adult is often ready and eager to fully engage in life as a complete human being.

Soul Theft

In Shamanic literature, the condition of soul theft is described (Ingerman, 1991, pp. 98-119). Soul theft usually occurs because one person desires power over another person. This often results from sexual molestation. The survivor often describes feeling as if the perpetrator (father, stepfather, uncle) stole her soul.

The soul theft may be the result of a curse, hex or spell cast by a black magician or sorcerer. This type of curse and fragmentation is sometimes discovered in past lives, and the curse may still be affecting the client in the present life. Past life therapy techniques can assist in uncovering and resolving the prior lifetime event. Remote Releasement (362) and Treatment of the Demonic (323) are almost always necessary to completely heal this condition.

In the present time, this condition is likely to be the result of Satanic cult ritual activity. This is in the nature of a curse, and the power behind this hideous activity is the same universal demonic energy described in the section The Demonic (273). The connection and the vulnerability often come through sexual activity, either forced or consensual. The clearing of this energy is done through remote releasement focused on the one who sent the curse, and the process of treatment of the demonic. After this releasement, the fragments can be successfully recovered and reintegrated in most cases.

Many women report love affairs with men who were possessive, even violent. These affairs often end with bitterness and anger, and the women describe feeling as if the men still held their heart. In some cases, the men have vowed to possess their heart, to keep the women under their control, even after the termination of the relationship. In session, fragmentation is usually discovered. The fragment is held by the lover and the motivation behind this violation is the dark energy. The men, of course, are found to be partially or totally controlled by the demonic or dark-energy beings.

Additional Examples

In clinical practice many cases of fragmentation are found which do not correspond to these arbitrary categories. One woman discovered a sort of armoring across the back of her head, shoulders and arms. This was a defensive thought form developed in childhood. Beneath the armor, she seemed to be missing the back of her head and the back of her upper arms. Recalling her childhood, she described how her mother had jerked her around by grabbing the hair on the back of her head. Mother also grabbed her by the back of her upper arms. There was so much unlanguaged pain, anguish and anger in these areas that they had fragmented away and attached to mother.

The severe emotional toll of a lost love affair can initiate a fragmentation which may not be recoverable. Such a fragment may evacuate so far away it seems to be in another universe or dimension. It may just dissipate into nothingness. This will become clear to the client after searching with no results.

Fragmentation can take the form of shattering, also seen in MPD. The shattered fragments can scatter far and wide.

This requires some assistance from the rescue teams of Light. The therapist can call out for help.

> T: "I call on the rescue teams of Light. We need help in gather-
> ing these scattered fragments of _____ (client's name),

wherever they might be."

The client will be able to describe the activities of these helpers. The client may be able to recall a traumatic event or series of events which led to the shattering and scattering.

The categories only cover a few of the variations of fragmentation which a therapist can encounter in practice. It is the concept of fragmentation which is important. With the knowledge of this condition the therapist can remain alert to signs of fragmentation, which, like dissociation, may be a useful coping mechanism during a traumatic moment. However, the lasting effects of fragmentation can be extremely debilitating for the person. Recovery of the fragmented soul-mind can bring a profound healing for the client.

FRAGMENTATION AND HOLISTIC HEALING

For the most part contemporary traditional psychotherapy fails to recognize the spiritual reality, and the possibility of soul loss. The ancient native traditional healers accepted it as commonplace and knew how to journey into the non-physical space to recover the lost fragments. The condition is also commonplace in the modern world, and it still causes much sickness. It is a condition which must be healed back into wholeness.

The term *holistic* stems from the word "wholeness," meaning completeness, totality of body, mind, and spirit. Fragmentation as the source of illness is an important concept in the native healing traditions. Soul retrieval, the shaman's approach to healing soul-mind fragmentation, has been considered by present-day mental health practitioners to be nothing more than magic and superstition.

Clinical psychotherapy is derived from empirical observation, and methods developed by trial and error from these observations. Unfortunately, in present theories and approaches to therapy, this concept has not found its way into accepted practice. From a wider perspective—the spiritual reality—it is obvious and quite effective. It may prove to be an important contribution to the concept of holistic healing.

Adoration

"Adoration," from an ancient drawing scanned from the *Pictorial Bible*, circa 1882.

Spirit
Releasement
Therapy

Notes

——— Quick Guide to Section IV ———

From, *The Sacred Tree*
©1988 Four Worlds Development Project, Illustration by Patricia Morris.

— Spirit Releasement Therapy —

Many traditional therapists reject the notion of past life therapy, partly because it is based on the questionable philosophy of reincarnation. Many traditional therapists and past life therapists reject the notion of Spirit Releasement Therapy because it is based on the objectionable and, to many people, frightening possibility of spirit possession. Spirit possession is an age old condition, a notion at least as old as written history. Reincarnation is ancient belief prevalent among most people on the earth. Healing therapies based on these concepts are new within this century. In clinical practice, the open minded therapist with a working knowledge of these modalities will find evidence of both conditions; past life trauma and spirit attachment.

Historically, the treatment of spirit possession has been primarily in the hands of the shaman, medicine man, or clergy. Rituals of many sorts have been

Sending forth the twelve apostles (Matthew 10: 5-7), scanned from the *Pictorial Bible*, circa 1882.

used, from verbal incantations and incense to beating with sticks. Baptism and christening of infants is a form of exorcism. The Finnish sauna and the attendant beating with branches is another form of exorcism. The Native American sweat lodge is a means to the same ends. Jesus commissioned the twelve disciples to heal the sick and cast out unclean spirits (The Bible, Luke: 9). After them He also commissioned 70 more disciples (The Bible, Luke: 10). Ministers today perform "deliverance" on those afflicted with "demons." They employ much exhortation and prayer.

Spirit Releasement Therapy and Past Life Therapy (PLT) are closely linked in clinical application. The interaction which led to the spirit attachment is often discovered in a past life of the client. This must be explored through the techniques of past life therapy. The past life events described and experienced by a client may not be part of the soul memory of that client, but that of an attached entity. PLT with an attached entity will not benefit the client if the entity is not released. Even the best therapy will produce no change in the presenting problem if an entity is the cause of the problem.

A very important aspect of past-life therapy is the exploration of the death scene, the circumstances leading to it, any emotional, mental or physical residue carried from the lifetime, and the events after the death. The therapist continues to probe for a description of what happens after separation from the body, the next awareness of anything other than the gray place. The newly deceased being may describe a brief period of wandering before moving into the Light.

Prompting the being in this manner may also reveal the moment of attachment to the host in the present life. This is often a surprise to the client. Most attached spirits do not make their presence known to the host. Most people are not aware of these undesirable parasitic attachments.

The earthbound spirit does not move on to the next step of spiritual evolution, does not go to the Light, does not participate in the Review Stage, the Resting Stage, the Halls of Learning, or the Planning Stage. Spirit attachment or possession is not part of the Life Plan developed by the being in the planning stage. However, there are rare exceptions in which the attachment is actually planned by both beings involved as part of the karmic balancing. In these cases, the roles of host and attached spirit may have been reversed in an earlier lifetime.

In one case, the attached entity claimed that the plan for attachment was mutually developed by three beings: itself, the person who was the host, and the therapist who released the attached spirit. The karmic ties between them went back many lifetimes.

If the client describes rising from the body after death of the physical body, viewing the scene from above, rising toward the sky, finally moving into a brilliant Light, with no residual emotional, mental, or physical connections to anything or anyone in that lifetime, then the regression therapy work on that life is complete. There is usually a healing of the concomitant problem in the present lifetime as a result of this approach to therapy.

Even though past-life therapy has proven effective for many of the problems which motivate people to seek psychotherapy, spirit attachment has also been discovered at the root of the same range of conditions. Dr. Edith Fiore (1987b) speculates that nearly everyone at some time in their lives is plagued by some degree of spirit interference. She finds that the typical presenting problems of her clients may stem from either past life trauma or an attached discarnate entity.

THE OBJECTIVE OF THE SESSION IS TO RELEASE ANY AND ALL INTERFERING ENTITIES FROM THE CLIENT AND TO SEND THEM INTO THE LIGHT, WHICH IS THEIR NEXT STEP OF SPIRITUAL PROGRESSION.

Since the earthbound spirit is often locked into its own personal conflicts and traumatic death experience, and since that emotional disruption is imposed on the host, the most effective method of treatment of these problems is to release the entity from the host. Past-life therapy will not eliminate a condition if it is imposed by a discarnate spirit.

This therapeutic method is best used on an individual basis. It is not a group therapy. The therapist offers a brief explanation of the concept of attached discarnate consciousness, or spirit possession, and the process of Spirit Releasement Therapy. The objective of the session is to release any and all interfering entities from the client and to send them into the Light, which is their next step of spiritual progression.

As the questions begin to focus on the presenting problem, the entity involved may be provoked to speak. It is the client's voice mechanism but the tone and timbre may change. Occasionally there is an accent or foreign language totally unknown to the client (Stevenson, 1974a, 1984). The client may experience a mild dissociation as the entity begins to speak.

As with past-life therapy, the client must be willing to work and have the mental capability to communicate meaningfully. The attached entity must be able to converse through the voice mechanism of the client. Success depends on meaningful dialogue between the therapist and the entity or entities. Without conversation with the entity, through the voice of the client, there is little possibility of resolution of the conflicts of the earthbounds or transformation of the dark-energy beings, the demonic entities. Growling, yelling or moaning cannot produce meaningful interchange.

In some cases, the spirit who attaches can separate itself from the living host. Apparently some are able to move in and out freely. The reasons for this ability are unknown. It seems that some cases of spirit interference last only a few hours, days, months, or years. However, most attached entities don't seem to be able to leave on their own.

Some entities will identify two or more separate instances of attachment to the same person within one lifetime. During the narration they will describe their separation from the client and their subsequent return. Allison (1980) describes one case of a female multiple who had two attached entities, one male and one female, who loved each other. The male entity would move from the woman into her various lovers in order to be able to experience sexual intercourse with the female spirit whom he loved.

May, a female therapist, attended an intensive training session covering these techniques. She became enraged while observing a demonstration of a spirit releasement on a Vietnam veteran. Several of the attached spirits were casualties of the war. Her feelings of rage bordered on violence toward the trainer. This was totally irrational, even to her. During the demonstration she felt a searing pain in the side of her abdomen. When she shared these feelings with some of her friends in the class they encouraged her to remain and complete the training. She did not feel the same anger during the rest of the demonstration sessions.

In a subsequent private session, several attached earthbound spirits were discovered. They revealed the source of May's anger and the pain in her abdomen during the demonstration. It was George, the spirit of a deceased Vietnam war combat soldier, who was incensed at what he perceived to be a violation of the rights of the attached spirits during the demonstration in the training. In his anger he left, bursting out of her side and causing the pain. It was a safe assumption that he did not go to the Light still carrying that anger.

The therapist used her exact verbatim description.

> T: "I call out to the angry one who burst out of May's side during the demonstration."

That identifier was enough to summon the spirit. He was still angry. The anger involved the disturbance of the attached spirits in the demonstration subject. More explicitly, it also involved the war itself, the attitude of the American people toward the war and the young soldiers, the treatment of the veterans when they returned, and the plain fact that he had died. With brief therapy, his anger was eased and he was willing to move into the peace of the Light.

Cheryl volunteered as a demonstration subject at a lecture on Spirit Releasement Therapy. After the lecture, she approached the presenter and asked a question.

> C: "Can an attached entity leave?"

> T: "Yes, sometimes they can leave the host. Why do you ask?"

> C: "I know my grandmother was with me after her death a few years ago. I could hear her voice. She even told me how to make pie crust. But she hasn't been talking to me for the last month."

> T: "Grandmother, are you here with Cheryl? Are you here right now?"

Abruptly, Cheryl began to cry and her body began to shake. In a soft voice she said, "Yes."

> T: (gently) "You haven't spoken with Cheryl for the last month, Grandmother. What happened?"

> C: "I knew she was coming here. I didn't want her to volunteer. I don't want to leave."

Cheryl had learned of the lecture only days before. Her grandmother knew more than a month in advance. After brief therapy on her grandmother, which included the resolution of a past-life trauma which involved her marriage with grandfather in the current incarnation, she and Cheryl bid a tearful farewell to each other. She went into the Light.

SPIRIT RELEASEMENT THERAPY—THE NAME

The process of developing a name for this approach to therapy was intriguing and frustrating. The entire concept of spirit interference or attachment met with superstitious resistance to the ominous specter of demonic possession and exorcism, as depicted in the movie, *The Exorcist*. Specific and literal descriptions such as minor exorcism and clinical depossession aroused irrational fear and even anger in many people. The title or designation for the work needed to be descriptive, inclusive and accurate, yet distinctly different from and not suggestive of demonic spirit possession or the stylized religious rituals of classic exorcism.

The word Spirit had to be included; this is the simplest label for a disembodied consciousness of any sort. Such words as "separation," "detachment," and "release" were considered for the process, the minor exorcism itself. "Separate" means to set apart, to disconnect; but the process is so much more than just a disconnection of a spirit from a person. "Detach" means to separate or unhook. "Detachment" describes the process of detaching, a part so dispatched, and indicates aloofness. Use of the word detachment as part of the description and title of this work seemed incomplete, cold, unfeeling, and woefully inadequate.

The word "release" is defined as a verb. It means to set free from restraint, confinement or servitude, as with hostages or pent-up emotion; to relieve from something that confines, burdens, or oppresses. Release is also defined as a noun. It signifies the relief or deliverance from sorrow, suffering, or trouble; discharge from obligation or responsibility; relinquishment of a right or claim; the act of liberating or freeing, as from restraint. This one word carries so much of the essence of the therapeutic work. Adding the suffix "ment" indicates the process of releasing.

The designation Spirit Releasement Therapy, therefore, most accurately expresses the compassionate nature of the therapeutic work, which can bring enormously beneficial results to both the person needing help, the client, and the often numerous disembodied beings or spirits which are attached and interfering with the living person. It is far more than simply unhooking the spirit from the client. It is a very personal release and healing of the deep pain of perhaps lifetimes of crippling emotional burden and residue for everyone concerned.

THE SEQUENCE OF A SPIRIT RELEASEMENT

The process of Spirit Releasement Therapy consists of six distinct phases or steps. In most cases, all six steps are necessary. In some cases, however, the process moves swiftly in a session, and the lines between the steps seem to blur.

The first step is to *discover and identify any attached discarnate spirits or entities*. Seldom is there only one entity attached to a person. There are numerous clues that guide the therapist in discovering an attached entity. During the therapeutic questioning, the client will repeat the words of an entity as they seem to pop up into the conscious mind from the subconscious. The attached spirit seems to function at the level of the subconscious.

The second step is *differential diagnosis*. The earthbound spirit of a deceased human is the most common attachment, yet there are also many other types of non-physical beings that interfere with living people. The different types require specific treatment. For some, there is no known treatment. The steps in this section are used for dealing with the attached earthbound spirit of a deceased human being.

The third step is to *dialogue with the spirit*. This is done for four specific purposes:

1. To resolve the emotional conflicts or physical needs that have kept the earthbound spirit on the earth plane.
2. To determine the specific circumstances that led to the attachment to the client.
3. To discover the client's vulnerability or susceptibility that first allowed the attachment.
4. To assess the effects of the spirit attachment on the client.

At this point, the discarnate entity is treated like any other client with an emotional problem. The therapist assists the entity in resolving these issues for one purpose: to release it from the client. It is necessary for ongoing therapy with the client to discover the circumstances that led to the attachment, the vulnerability that allowed the attachment to this person and to identify and assess the effects of the attachment.

The fourth step is *release of the spirit into the Light*. The entity is usually greeted by the spirits of family or friends who have already passed on. This is a phenomenon similar to that described in the NDE. There is often a tearful reunion as the spirits of the deceased loved ones come to welcome the earthbound spirit home.

The fifth step is the *Sealing Light Meditation*. It is very important and necessary to fill, metaphorically, the space left by the departing being or beings. The client is directed to imagine a brilliant spark of Light deep in the center of the body. It glows and expands to fill the body, then expands outward about an arm's length all around, forcing out anything unlike itself. It forms a shimmering protective bubble of Light surrounding the person. The client is urged to repeat this visualization of the Sealing Light Meditation several times each day.

The sixth step is *ongoing therapy*. Other entities, or layers of entities, are often discovered during subsequent sessions. After the release of the attached entities, the therapeutic goals include healing of the specific conflict or susceptibility of the client that initially allowed the attachment. It is essential to resolve the conflict and to heal the emotional vulnerability to prevent new attachments. Inner child healing and treatment of subpersonalities is an important aspect of ongoing work.

Though an entity may have engendered a condition, the impress of the habit or behavior sometimes remains—a sort of groove worn in the psyche—even after the release. This remnant of behavior is more easily treated through traditional psychotherapy, once the attached discarnates are gone.

An attachment can cause arrested emotional development of a person. The emotional age of a person after the release of a strong-willed entity may be very nearly the age at which the attachment occurred. A client may need assistance in literally growing up, or maturing emotionally.

A subpersonality that split off as a result of an earlier emotional trauma can influence the behavior of the client. Much of the continuing therapy is focused on healing the inner children and adolescents and integrating the various subpersonalities involved.

Any approach to ego strengthening and enhancement of self-image is important. Therapy is directed toward consolidating the gains made and establishing comfort with a new way of being in the world. For many people, there is very slight, if any, noticeably different way of being, while others report major changes in some or many areas of their lives.

The experience is profound for the client, and very satisfying for the therapist.

The Six Phases of Spirit Releasement Therapy

1. Discovery and identification of any attached discarnate spirits or entities.

2. Differential diagnosis.

3. Dialogue with the spirit.

4. Release of the spirit into the Light.

5. Sealing Light Meditation.

6. Ongoing therapy.

Discovery of an Attached Entity

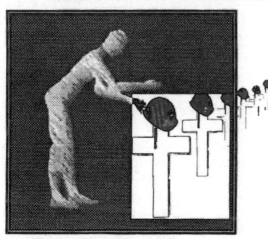

"Reaching Through Time," by BT.

Alva, a nurse working in a Veteran's Administration hospital, described an experience with a Vietnam veteran. Richard was a Black man from Virginia who was raised as a Catholic. The attending psychiatrists conducted a sodium pentothal interview, during which two other personalities spontaneously emerged and spoke through Richard's voice. One of the voices called himself Alfred; the other was Tom. They both claimed that they had died in Vietnam just prior to joining their buddy. The psychiatrists ignored this information and Richard was diagnosed as having a dissociative disorder, not serious enough to warrant hospitalization. The doctors were ready to release him from the hospital. Because of Richard's strict Catholic background, he thought the voices were "demons" and he was terrified.

A psychiatrist worked with Richard on an outpatient basis, attempting to raise his self-esteem, improve ego strength, and generally to enhance his ability to cope. This had no effect whatsoever on the attached entities and the voices Richard heard.

A therapist who was familiar with spirit releasement also worked with Richard, releasing the two earthbound spirits and a number of dark-energy beings. After the release Richard was as frightened as ever, unable to understand what had happened, and confused about his life.

The past-life work and spirit releasement work must be done in conjunction with traditional therapy. These two approaches do not offer a miracle cure. They are specific techniques for specific problems. The major changes made possible with these techniques must be integrated and assimilated carefully, with a knowledgeable therapist as facilitator.

Most attached entities will not be as obvious as those that were with Richard. Some clients who are familiar with the condition, and who suspect that their own symptoms may indicate an attached entity, may ask for a session to investigate specifically the possibility of spirit interference. The direct approach is quite effective. The scanning exploration and mirror technique can be very helpful in discovering the unwanted intruders. A reluctant entity may be compelled to demonstrate its presence as the client engages in the process of connected breathing.

A therapist may utilize past-life therapy with a client to locate the source of the presenting problem. Although a lifetime may emerge and the details appear to be related to the problem, the symptoms may not diminish after completion of the regression. Further exploration may reveal that the lifetime was that of an attached entity. The therapist must be well versed in the techniques of Spirit Releasement Therapy and the differential diagnosis

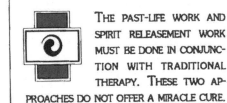

THE PAST-LIFE WORK AND SPIRIT RELEASEMENT WORK MUST BE DONE IN CONJUNCTION WITH TRADITIONAL THERAPY. THESE TWO APPROACHES DO NOT OFFER A MIRACLE CURE.

guidelines, and have a general knowledge of metaphysics and the non-physical spiritual reality.

In a past-life session, the after death behavior of the being is a major factor in differentiating between a past life of the client and an attached entity. In the ideal sequence at the conclusion of a lifetime, the newly deceased spirit rises from the body, moves higher above the death scene, perceives the Light and goes into that peaceful vibration. This is almost certainly a past life of the client.

Ethan described his five year marriage to Glenda. There was very little sexual interchange between them and this bothered Ethan. There were obvious factors in the present life which contributed to this situation, but Ethan wanted to explore the past life influences. As Ethan followed the energy of the relationship back, he discovered a lifetime in which he, his parents, and his beloved younger sister were traveling toward the West in a covered wagon. The trip was hard on this small family. Along the way, his sister grew weak and died at about age 9. He was 13 or 14 at the time, and he blamed himself for not taking care of her. He felt responsible and suffered guilt over her death. He vowed to take better care of her next time.

Moving back again, Ethan discovered an earlier lifetime when the two were again brother and sister, devoted to each other. He died first, well advanced in age. As spirit, he waited for her to make her transition, which came several years after his death. The Light was apparent to them and they moved toward it, hand in hand. At that point, he suddenly developed a fear of losing contact with her in the Light, which is faulty thinking, and expressed the desire to "get back on the ride again." He so enjoyed life and his association with his sister, that he wanted to go right back in, find bodies to take over, and live again. She resisted, he insisted, and she gave in. They attached to the children who eventually went out West in the covered wagon. That was a memory of spirit attachment, not a past life experience.

The boy was five when the spirit (Ethan) joined him. The little girl was just a few months old when the spirit of the reluctant sister (Glenda) joined her. The burden of the attached spirit weakened the girl so that her health failed. This is what led to her death on the trail. Ethan was dismayed by his discovery of the added karmic debt produced by his insistence on attaching to living people, just to "get back on the ride again."

The newly deceased spirit may hover or float near the scene of death, the hospital, the battlefield, the accident site. It may describe rushing to its home to be near the family. It may describe floating in the gray place, the intermediate place. The therapist prompts it to skip forward to the next thing that happens. This may eventually lead to joining the Light without any description of attachment to a person or place. This tends to indicate a past life memory in which there was a little delay before moving on.

The narration may reveal the passing of a considerable length of time between the moment of death and the connection with another body. The most effective question which prompts without leading is the following:

T: "What happens next?"

The one narrating the past life memory may describe joining or coming into the client in the present or a prior lifetime, which defines it as an attached spirit. However, there are variations which must be further explored before the present-life condition of spirit attachment can be confirmed.

The past-life character may describe leaving the body at death and immediately going into another person. At first it may seem obvious that this is an entity attached to the client. As the therapist continues to probe for information, however, the one speaking may describe the death of the person it joined. After separating from that one the spirit may then attach to someone else or move into the Light at that time. It may attach to a series of people, leaving some at death and leaving others while they are still living. It may describe finally going into the Light, in which case it is a past life of the client and the client may have discovered that she was an attached or possessing spirit in another time.

To explore the possibility of a present-life attachment, the therapist directs the questions to the one speaking:

T: "Recall the very last time you attached to a living person."

If that connection occurred in the present lifetime of the client, then an attached entity has been discovered.

A spirit can remain in a location or building, such as a battlefield or the house where it lived and died. The spirit may eventually become disenchanted with its situation and choose to find the Light by itself. There are people who specialize in dehaunting houses or buildings and locations known to have "ghosts" such as cemeteries, battlefields, and stretches of highway where many unexplained accidents occur. This is termed "rescue work," and is a compassionate and largely thankless endeavor. A client may recall being a haunting spirit which was finally rescued by such Light workers.

THE CLIENTS HAVE WITHIN THEMSELVES THE SOLUTIONS TO ANY PROBLEMS WHICH EXIST IN THEIR LIFE.

The therapist continues to probe for the description of either joining the Light or joining another living person. The discovery questions must continue until one of these two events is uncovered to establish the certainty of the condition of spirit attachment.

Past-Life Therapy Techniques

The attached entity may be discovered during the induction phase of past-life therapy. A basic tenet of these modalities is that the clients have within themselves the solutions to any problem which exists in their life. The inductions described above are directed toward the most prominent manifestations, emotional and physical, of the presenting problem.

Through specific questioning, the therapist directs the client to explore the immediate emotional feelings and physical sensations associated with a problem. This may elicit an attached entity which turns out to be the cause of the problem. Personifying a physical sensation and asking it to speak can lead to a conversation with the attached being. It will be the client's voice mechanism, yet the personality is often recognizably different. The process is comparable to the phenomenon of switching between alters in a person with MPD.

The voice and words spoken may surprise the client. An emerging visual image or a sudden physical sensation or involuntary movement of some part of the body may be quite distressing. These responses are encouraged by the therapist as part of the uncovering and discovery process which can lead to resolution of the problem, whatever and whenever its source. Without the use of authoritarian hypnotic inductions, the critical faculty is still operating and the client is likely to question the subconscious material which emerges. There is often disbelief regarding the uncovered information. The client's reaction may be skeptical:

C: "I don't know where this is coming from."
"I don't believe this stuff."
"I can't say that."
"This is crazy!"
"I don't believe in the devil."

The therapist urges the client to trust whatever comes into emotional, physical or mental awareness, in the form of visual images, thoughts, feelings or words, and to just describe any scene or express any words as they come to mind. The therapist should encourage this trust on the part of the

THE EARTHBOUND SPIRIT IS FIXATED IN THE DEATH TRAUMA, MANY PEOPLE ARE STUCK IN THE BIRTH TRAUMA.

client to accept the emerging information throughout the session. This is the subconscious material which must be processed in resolving the problem areas.

After sufficient information is presented, it is possible to make a safe and accurate differential diagnosis between a past life of the client and any one of several types of discarnate beings. The appropriate therapeutic approach can then be implemented.

The verbal response may depict a traumatic scene in what appears to be another lifetime. While it may appear to be a past life of the client, the facts become evident after the death in the lifetime being explored. If the being does not move toward and into the Light but remains on the earth plane, immediately or eventually seeking connection with the host, this is an attached earthbound spirit. The discarnate entity is physically and emotionally fixated in the death trauma, and the symptoms experienced and expressed by the client may be the entity's memory of its death throes.

The experienced past-life therapist may have an intuitive sense that the lifetime and death being described are not appropriate to the client. The time setting may be after the birth of the client. The description may include an interaction between the one speaking and the client. The following question may clear up the suspicion immediately without interfering with the past-life recall.

T: "How old was _____ (client's name) when you joined her in the present lifetime?"

The contracted spirit, that is, the rightful owner of the body, will describe conception and birth and be aware of the planning stage prior to coming onto the earth plane. It will not be aware of any difference or separation between itself and the client speaking. This question will not interrupt the flow of the past-life regression.

Conversely, an attached entity does not participate in the planning stage. It was not in the Light prior to this attachment. It will know the age of the host at the time of attachment and the details surrounding the situation when the attachment occurred. In response to the therapist's questions, the entity will provide information regarding the vulnerability or susceptibility which allowed the attachment, the details of its location prior to coming in, and its motivation for joining.

It is unusual to find a spirit that attached prior to the birth of the infant. Discarnate spirits do not want to experience the birth trauma. If the attachment was formed at or before the birth of the client, the therapist asks:

T: "Look and see as you join this tiny infant. Is there already someone there? Is there already someone in the body?"

This refers to the contracted spirit, the being who planned this lifetime in this particular body with this particular family.

The contracted spirit may not join the body completely until after the birth, sometimes several weeks after the birth. However, the body consciousness, a portion of the total consciousness, is connected with the body from the moment of conception. The entity who attaches at birth or in utero is aware of the presence of the contracted spirit. It is also aware of its own location prior to the attachment. The question will usu-

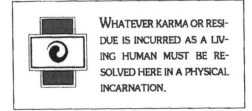

WHATEVER KARMA OR RESIDUE IS INCURRED AS A LIVING HUMAN MUST BE RESOLVED HERE IN A PHYSICAL INCARNATION.

ally catch the entity off guard. It knows at this point that it has been discovered. It might even ask the therapist how he/she knew and might even comment on the cleverness of this discovery.

As the client describes this attachment process, the therapist shifts from past-life therapy to the spirit releasement procedures. The purpose of Spirit Releasement Therapy is to separate the parasitic attachment from the client, not to resolve the issues of the entity. The only aim of therapy on the entity is to bring resolution of the issue or issues which maintain the attachment to the client. The end result of the process for the client is freedom from the attachment, and for the entity to move into its next step of spiritual progression (that is, the Light).

Whatever mental, emotional, or physical trauma is incurred by a being in a lifetime as a living human in his or her own physical body must be resolved here in a physical incarnation before death, not by attaching to another human and acting out the issues. Past-life therapy is only minimally effective on a discarnate being. It is inappropriate to do extensive therapy on the entities through the mental apparatus and sensorium of the client, imposing the mental, emotional and even physical pain of another being onto the host.

An attached entity may be discovered during a past-life regression, with the entity attached to the past-life character. The releasement is facilitated in the setting of the past life.

In a training demonstration of a past-life regression, an entity was discovered. It was attached to the person in another lifetime, the past-life personality of the subject. As the release was accomplished and the being was moving with the guides toward the Light, the therapist asked the entity:

T: "Were you attached to this woman in her present incarnation?" (referring to present life of the client)

The entity answered, apparently confused by the absurdity of the question, as if the questioner did not understand the spiritual reality:

C: "Of course not, I'm being released here. You are releasing me now." (referring to its time setting, the past life of the client)

The contemporary event experienced by the entity transpired in the life perceived by the subject and therapist as a past life. To the entity, it was a current-time experience and was complete without "future" consequences or connections.

This situation raises speculation about the metaphysical concept of simultaneous time, the apparent illusion of sequential events and lifetimes, and the notion of time as the context, the fabric of physical existence. People in altered state have described lifetimes as "bubbles of time," discrete segments of distorted continuity of the greater context of the timeless spiritual realm.

The altered state of consciousness is one avenue into the greater timeless reality. Through this woman, the therapist reached from the present bubble of time into another bubble of time to release that attached entity. Was it necessary at that precise moment of this reality? Was the script already written? Did these two people somehow agree earlier, perhaps in the planning stage, to accomplish this particular healing at this particular time? What if she had decided not to attend this class? Are other bubbles of time, that is other lifetimes, always accessible? Could this releasement have been completed at another session in this life or from another bubble of time, a future lifetime? These are some of the unanswered questions generated by this work.

Fragmentation

Any trauma or shock can lower the resistance to spirit attachment. The resulting fragmentation can open a pathway for spirit attachment by earthbound or demonic entities. When fragmentation is discovered, further probing will nearly always reveal attached entities.

Kevin, a 20 year old boy still lived with his divorced mother, Jeanne. He was emotionally immature and did not cope well with life. When Kevin was about six years old, there was severe emotional upheaval in the home. Father left soon afterward. A major fragment of Kevin was the six year old, very angry and appearing to be still running away from the situation. This anger seemed to be a distortion of Kevin's will to live, much of which left with six.

Another major fragment was the sixteen-year-old who fragmented as a result of a broken love affair. So-called puppy love can be very powerful and the effects of a lost love at that age can be as devastating as any breakup in adult relationships. Sixteen just did not want to hang around. He was the deep, feeling part of Kevin. The loss of the feeling part left Kevin rather listless, uninterested and uninteresting.

These fragments had to be convinced that Kevin needed them more than they needed him. He really needed them in order to keep on living. They finally agreed to reconnect and give their energy to the whole of Kevin. It was their body that would die if they refused.

Without the recovery and reconnection of the fragments, the client often does not have the will or personal power to resist the dark entities. These fragments carried a surprisingly large amount of Kevin's will to live. As they returned, Kevin gained the inner strength to shield himself from the continued assault.

The major demonic entity with Kevin was part of a dark network which targeted school age children of all grades. It first appeared as a slick, arrogant, hoodlum type who pandered to the desires and emotional needs of children and teenagers wanting to be part of a group or clique. It joined Kevin when the fragmentation occurred at age six. It was also involved with drug use and sexual deviation. The dark network exploited the inevitable rebellious nature of older teens. It also worked through the girl Kevin loved when he was sixteen. She was wholly controlled by the dark forces.

This demonic entity was surprised at the capsule of light in which it was so quickly and easily subdued. The network was extensive, insidious and effective, attempting to subvert young minds on a planet-wide scale. The effects of this network cannot be known for certain in the world. Such youthful rebellion has long been accepted as a natural part of maturation and there seems to be more experimentation with sex and drugs in recent years. The results of the release of such a dark network cannot be measured. Because of the obvious and immediate success of the releasement work, both on the human spirits and the non-human spirits, this work is done largely on faith. This work is described in the section Release of the Dark Entity (325).

The Direct Approach
The phrases and descriptions a client uses to describe the presenting problems or conflicts can offer a clue to a spirit attachment. Such statements as the following suggest the presence of another being:

C: "I was different after _____."
"Other people tell me I changed after _____."

This can refer to an illness or surgery, accidents, vacations, moving into a new dwelling, any sort of change or significant event. As the client recounts a present-life event, the pronoun "we" may be used when the event was a solo experience. There is a subconscious awareness of an entity, and this languaging—which comes from the subconscious or preconscious—suggests the presence of another.

A person may describe an awareness of other "people" living inside. Feelings of an internal battle of some sort or a sense of being taken over by something may prompt the words such as the following:

C: "Something just comes over me."
"I watched myself doing _____."
"Part of me wants to do one thing, and part of me wants to do something else."

During a session, the sudden onset of inappropriate, unexpected, or unfamiliar emotional expression or outburst may indicate a switch from the client's personality to that of the entity, much like a switch between alters of a person with MPD. The unexpected reactions may be coming from an attached entity.

A client may describe internal dialogue or conflict over some issue. A simultaneous duality of feeling or attitude can signal the presence of an active entity. This is not a case of simply weighing the alternatives before making a decision about something. This may be described as a confusing dichotomy of intention and desire, even behavior. A person might abhor the use of drugs and at the same time seek a source of supply for the substances. It seems as if two tracks of emotion or thought are running at the same time. This can be enormously confusing.

Hostility and defensiveness toward the therapist and emphatic refusal to leave are definite indications of an attached entity. If the one speaking gives an account of its own death and subsequent attachment to the client, this is a typical memory of a separate, attached earthbound spirit. The therapist encourages conversation with the personality speaking. An earthbound spirit has lost only its physical body and often doesn't know it is dead.

A client may suspect the presence of an attached spirit after reading or attending a lecture on the subject of spirit possession and Spirit Releasement Therapy. People who learn for the first time about the concept often have an intense physical or emotional reaction to the information. This is usually the reaction of the entity. Many clients are referred by other people who have enjoyed positive results from Spirit Releasement Therapy. Some clients will request the assistance of the therapist in exploring for any attached entities.

From the description of presenting problems, a therapist may suspect the presence of an attached entity. If there is another consciousness present it will quickly become evident to the trained therapist.

When there is sufficient indication of a spirit attachment, the therapist can proceed directly.

The client is guided in the following relaxation. It is the invocation of Light both for protection and guidance.

The Dove and the Olive Branch, symbolic of "The Rescue" in Greek culture.

T: "Close your eyes and focus inside. Focus deep inside to the very center. Find your own spark of Light there, your own Light, deep inside. Feel it, see it, sense it there, imagine it there, deep inside you. Imagine that the spark of Light glows warmly and expands in every direction, upward and downward. The Light expands all the way into the tips of your toes up to the top of your head, from fingertip to fingertip, filling every cell of your body. Imagine the

Light expanding outward beyond the boundaries of your body
about an arm's length in every direction, a shimmering bubble
of golden white Light all around you."

The subconscious mind is a stimulus-response mechanism. Whether in
words, images, emotional reaction or overt behavior, the subconscious mind
can't fail to respond to incoming stimuli. This function is similar to the automatic
survival mechanism, though with less critical input and outcome. Responses are
established through past experience, purposeful training and education, or
mental programming, both voluntary and involuntary. Commercial advertising,
especially through the use of subliminal messages, takes advantage of this faculty
of the mind.

The attached entity is functioning within the level of the subconscious
mind of the host. The urges, attitudes, likes and dislikes, appetites and behaviors
of the entity seem to blend with the client's own. Responses to stimuli which at
first seem to be normal to the person may indeed originate from the entity, a
being with its own separate history and burden of emotional residue.

Such a response may not be appropriate in the life of the unsuspecting
host of a spirit attachment. Without the knowledge of the condition and the
effects of spirit attachment, a person can be confused indeed by conflicting urges,
strange thoughts, sudden and unexpected emotional responses and unacceptable behavior. Such unbidden thoughts and emotions often seem to pop up into
a person's awareness.

It is this function of the subconscious mind which is called into operation
in this process. The client is urged to state any "pop-up" answer, to repeat the
very first thing that comes to mind in response to the following questions:

T: "Is there another person here, is there someone else inside
this body? Is there another here besides _____?" (client's name)

The answer is often a surprise to the client. These are typical responses.

C: "No. Stop."
"Help me."
"Let me out."
"I want to get out of here."
"Yes."

Any of these responses will open the way to a dialogue with the being
trapped inside.

The question can be repeated several ways. If the client shakes the head
no, or says "No" immediately, it can be considered a reply from the conscious
mind. An entity will answer from the subconscious level; it will be a "pop-up"
response, and usually slightly delayed. If he says "No," the next question is:

T: "Who said no?"

This will open the dialogue with the entity. It is almost impossible for the object of this questioning to refrain from responding.

Some frightened or less cooperative entities may present a more negative response.

C: "Go away."
    "Leave me alone."
    "I'm not leaving her."
    "You can't make me leave."
    "I'm staying right here."
    "I don't want to talk to you."

There may be rough or foul language used. This is not a personal affront from the client. It is an attempt at intimidation by the entity. The therapist must ignore this tactic.

These replies immediately open the dialogue with the discarnate. The first words uttered are used as the identifier until a name is disclosed. The therapist continues with questions such as these:

T: "You, 'help me,' how old are you?"
    "You, the one who is 'staying right here,' how old was _____
    (client's name) when you joined her?"
    "You, the one who 'doesn't want to talk to me,' what is the
    first thing you would say to me if you did want to talk to me?"

The therapist can ask for that part which feels or behaves in the manner described by the phrases during the initial interview. Using the descriptor expressed by the client will often elicit an entity responsible for the behavior. The therapist can use an approach such as the following:

T: "I want to talk to the part that uses drugs."
    "I want to talk to the part that says 'we.'"
    "I want to talk to the one who felt different after surgery."
    "You, the angry one, what's your name?"

These probing questions will initiate the dialogue with the attached entity responsible for the particular behavior or attitude. Information from this dialogue will assist in determining what type of entity it is and what treatment approach must be followed.

The response from the entity may be a physical sensation anywhere in the body. There may tingling, a sudden tightness of some area of the muscles, pain, heat or cold, electric shock, gurgling or churning in the gut. The somatic bridge questions are utilized.

> T: "If that _____ (sensation) could speak, what is the first thing it would say?"
> "If it could speak, what is the first thing it would say, right now?"
> "If that _____ (sensation) had words to say, what would that be?"

The therapist must use the client's exact words These questions will often elicit a verbal response from the entity.

The sensation may become more intense as the questioning continues. The sensation may change or move in the body. This is a sure sign of an attached entity who is attempting to evade the therapist.

In a class on the subject of discovery of attached discarnates, a young woman in the first row suddenly felt a gurgling in her intestines. She was startled by the sensation and described it as it moved upward in her body. It was not confined to her intestines. It moved up through her chest, throat and into her head. She was quite distressed by this, yet continued to articulate the sensations. As suddenly as it had begun, the disturbance seemed to pop out the top of her head. It was completely gone. The woman was quite shaken. It did not speak. It did not express emotion in any manner. It was a purely physical manifestation of an entity release.

During the initial interview in a clinical session, 35-year-old Louella described her lonely life. She could not seem to maintain a relationship with a man for more than about three months. As she settled back in the recliner, she offered one more piece of information.

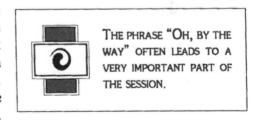

THE PHRASE "OH, BY THE WAY" OFTEN LEADS TO A VERY IMPORTANT PART OF THE SESSION.

> C: "Oh by the way, I had polio when I was two. Sometimes my right leg bothers me."

> T: "All right, take a deep breath and focus inside. Locate that spark of Light at your very center...."

> C: "OOH! My head. It hurts!"

She grimaced and grabbed her head with both hands. She sat upright in the recliner.

T: "Come out of her head! Stop hurting her! Come out of her head! We know you are here, stop hurting her!"

She took her hands from her head in relief and lay back in the recliner. A moment later, her right leg lifted off the chair, her foot about eighteen inches above the ottoman.

C: "This is what happens when I'm in bed with a boyfriend. My leg spasms. It always happens after we make love. It's that polio!"

The sensation had shifted from pain in the head to muscle spasm in the leg. This proved to be the activity of an entity. It was her husband from a lifetime in Egypt, around 550 A.D. He had gone to war across the Mediterranean Sea. He promised to return to her. He kept his promise, but only after he was killed in battle. He had found her in successive incarnations and had attached 42 times.

C: "She's my wife. She's mine. I don't want her to be with any other men."

These were his words. He was literally trying to kick the other men out of bed by causing spasms in the leg.

When an earthbound spirit is found, it is often not alone, and it can be the spokesbeing for a group of attached entities. It may be part of a group, or it might be aware of groups of entities elsewhere within the client. The questions are aimed at uncovering other groups.

T: "Are you aware of any other groups of entities with _____?" (the client)

C: "Yes, there is a group down in her right leg."

T: "You, the ones down in the right leg, is there a spokesperson for your group?"

One will speak. It will assist in getting the others to move out. Before they all go to the Light, the therapist calls on them for help.

T: "Is there anyone else in your group who knows of any other groups attached here?"

Someone may know of other groups, even though there is little or no communication between them. This probing in group after group continues until no one present has any knowledge of any other single entities or groups of entities within, attached to, or surrounding the client.

Some alter personalities in a person with MPD will claim to be separate beings. If the therapist tentatively accepts this information as true and proceeds with the treatment questions described in the section on differential diagnosis of alter personalities, a determination can be made.

Dreams

Apparently, dreams can be influenced by the different types of spirits. Deceased loved ones often appear with messages of comfort or warning. The being who has made the next step in the spiritual progression to the Light can come back to deliver such a message. They will appear peaceful and be surrounded and bathed in light. There will not be human emotionality, only an effusion of peace and love. The eyes are clear and bright. The earthbound spirit may appear with light around and behind yet not be in the light. The expression is often troubled. They may request something for themselves rather than offering some message for the living person. A demonic entity may assume the guise of a loved one, yet be stern and demanding. The eyes will be black or red, sometimes glaring and shiny.

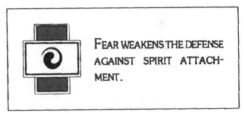

FEAR WEAKENS THE DEFENSE AGAINST SPIRIT ATTACHMENT.

Gargoyle-like faces which come in dreams are often generated by dark entities and are meant to frighten the dreamer. Fear weakens the defense against spirit attachment.

The night before her session, Ann's deceased husband came to her in a dream urging her to cancel her scheduled appointment for a spirit releasement. He claimed the therapist was a fraud. She did not follow his advice but kept the appointment. The first entity discovered was a man from the time of the cave dwellers. Confused and dull witted, this one was released to the Light quickly and easily. The second was her sister, deceased about seven years earlier. This was a shock to Ann.

She was asked to recall her dream. She went into a much deeper altered state as she described the dream image of her husband standing and shaking a finger at her. When asked the color of his eyes in her imagery, she was surprised as she saw that his eyes were very dark; in life his eyes had been a light blue.

The therapist demanded that this one look directly at Ann so that she could look deeper into its eyes. It turned from her and sat down on a bench. As the therapist demanded that it show its true form, she described it as melting down to a little swirling dark blob. It was a small demonic entity which did not want to be discovered, and it had attempted to dissuade her by assuming the guise of her deceased husband. However, the eyes are the windows of the soul, and cannot be disguised. If it had not made itself known in the dream, it might have escaped detection. This is typical of the short sightedness and even the stupidity of the lower demonic beings.

Doris, a 50-year-old attorney, described being awakened from a dream by the impact of a bullet in her chest. She was male in the dream and another man had just shot him/her. The body fell to the floor and the shooter turned and ran. The spirit of the victim stood up out of the dead body and attempted to follow the gunman by running normally, not realizing that a spirit can move instantly to any location.

The gunman escaped and the newly deceased spirit drifted into a cocktail lounge. He described many people (spirits) floating about the room and near the ceiling, standing next to patrons at the bar, and in the mirrors on the walls. This surprised him. He could not get anyone to talk with him so he moved toward the door. Outside in the bright daylight stood a woman talking with someone. This hapless spirit moved toward her and somehow just merged into her body. This woman was the client; the dream character was an earthbound spirit, reliving its death trauma.

Pam was a very troubled young woman of 20. She had recently attacked her estranged husband with a knife, stabbing him several times in the abdomen. He refused to press charges of assault and she was released by the police. At 16 she had attempted suicide. She held an unreasonable hatred for her father. Neither she nor her mother could recall any circumstances which would justify this hatred. She was rough in manner and speech and had been a tomboy since childhood.

She complained of suffering from a repeating dream. The therapist asked her to close her eyes and recall the dream. She described standing in an open field unable to move. She was asked to look down at her feet and describe what she was wearing. At this point Pam shifted or switched into the personality of the entity and she remembered nothing more of the session until she returned to her normal state of consciousness.

C: "I'm wearing combat boots and I can't take another step. There are huge black hands coming up at me from out of the ground. I'm too scared to move."

T: "What's your name?"

C: "Bob."

T: "Look around Bob, can you see anyone else?"

C: "Yeah, there are a bunch of slant eyes running along that road."

T: "Are you on anything? Did you take anything before?"

C: "Yeah, I dropped acid, I took LSD."

T: "Bob, what year is it for you?"

C: "1966."

T: "What happens next?"

C: "I'm falling over backwards, I hit the ground and a mine blows up under me."

T: "What happens next, Bob?"

Bob quickly emerged from his body. He and the men of his patrol had walked into a mine field. After the first explosions, his mind, distorted by the effects of the drug LSD, perceived the mines as huge black hands reaching menacingly toward him. In his fear he reeled backward and fell. His terror instantly came true.

Bob followed the wooden box containing what was left of his body. It was flown home to the States, where he soon lost interest in it. He drifted from place to place. He recalled seeing a little girl being hassled by some boys. It was Pam when she was about six years old. His sense of justice propelled him toward her. He joined her without hesitation and slugged the nearest boy. The bullies scattered when they saw that this little girl was not to be intimidated. Bob stayed on as a sort of protector. He also imposed his emotional pain on little Pam.

Neglected by his parents, Bob had been unhappy in his life. He had grown rebellious and at age 16 he had attempted suicide in a desperate call for attention and love. His father showed no sympathy or concern and told Bob to join the army, that it would "make a man out of him." He hated his father for that.

Bob exerted an enormous influence on the course of Pam's life. The rebelliousness, the rough mannerisms, the suicide attempt, the undeserved hatred toward her father, the violent temper and behavior were all manifestations of *his* maladjustment, not hers. Her life had nearly been destroyed because of it. Her repeating dream was his death experience, which he recalled over and over again, but within her mind.

He refused to leave during the first session and was verbally abusive, even threatening, toward the therapist. His story came out piece by piece, interspersed with periods of defiance, rebellion, and lack of cooperation. He finally lowered his head and refused any further conversation. However, expressing and ventilating his emotions eased his pain and combativeness, and Pam was actually affectionate with her mother after the session.

During the second session, Bob finally agreed to separate from Pam and move into the Light, much to the joy of the spirits of his buddies whom he described as standing nearby, cheering. He recognized the guiding spirit who came for him as his father. Bob was reluctant at first to face him, feeling again the hurt and anger of his youth. With prompting from the therapist, he finally communicated with his father. His father apologized for his lack of concern and love, and acknowledged Bob's viewpoint; he began to listen to his son for the first time. Bob softened at this and reached out to his father with less bitterness. They finally took each other's hand and the separation from Pam was swift.

Pam felt much relieved after the release. She was more affectionate with her family and apparently more comfortable and well adjusted. A number of months later, however, she simulated a holdup in a convenience store. She brandished a hand gun at the clerk. Then, after a few minutes, she laughed and placed the gun on the counter, saying she was just kidding, and walked out of the store. This was the last report received by the therapist.

Perhaps there were dark beings remaining with Pam after her sessions. In her scattered and fragmented condition, other dark ones could have joined her. It would have taken several more sessions to heal the wounds caused by the attached earthbounds. Traditional therapy could have helped heal the emotional scars in the family. It is impossible to determine what effect was imposed by the attached earthbound spirit, Bob. The significance of the rebelliousness, suicide attempt, and hatred for father cannot be dismissed. Was she meant to be a rebellious person from the beginning? Did Bob's emotional pain permanently scar her psyche and direct her behavior? These are the unanswerable questions in a case like this.

Physical and emotional trauma imposed by an external source such as rape, incest, the atmosphere of a dysfunctional family life (especially with an alcoholic member) can impose a clearly discernible and predictable alteration in behavior patterns for the victim. Can the internal trauma of a spirit attachment alter the course of a person's life? Within the clinical framework of this therapy, the answer is a resounding "YES!" The attachment is not part of the planning stage in the Light prior to embodiment. Only half the cases of spirit attachment reveal any connection between the host and the spirit. There is nothing to balance, to avenge, no debts owed, nothing to give to each other, no lessons to learn from the interaction. It is plainly and simply a violation of free will.

Organ transplants

The organs and body fluids carry physical body life energy. They can also carry a fragment of consciousness. Cases of physical fragmentation were described in the section Fragmentation (171). Blood transfusions as well as organ donation can open the way for spirit attachment by mind fragments or newly deceased human spirits.

A male client went through the process of a releasement of a mind fragment of a living person. Near the end of the session, the therapist noticed a neat scar just above the ankle on the inner side of one leg. When questioned about this, the client revealed he had undergone a complete blood replacement shortly after his birth due to an Rh blood factor incompatibility. A fragment of the mind of a blood donor had joined him along with the transfusion.

Sharon wanted to do a remote releasement for Don, her husband, who had just undergone a heart transplant. Their teenage daughter had stayed with him in the recovery room following surgery. As he regained consciousness his first words to her were angry and scolding. It was unlike him to treat her in this manner and her feelings were hurt. He did not seem like himself.

In the session, as Sharon connected with Don she focused on the first thing that came. It was a physical sensation of tightness in the chest. The words associated with it were:

C: "It's too tight in here. It's too tight, I can't breathe."

Questioning revealed that it was Alex, the young man who was the heart donor. Alex and some friends were playing Russian Roulette. Alex lost; he shot himself in the head and he died instantly. His mother was grief stricken; his father was angry at the stupidity of the act. They accompanied the body to the hospital. They gave authority to the doctors to use the organs for transplantation.

Alex was baffled by the entire episode. It happened so fast he did not yet understand. He watched the surgeons removing his organs.

C: "My kidneys went one way, my liver went another way, and my heart went somewhere else. I followed my heart because that's where I live."

His first awareness of the destination of his heart came when he saw Don on the operating table with his chest cut open and his heart missing. Alex was physically larger than Don so there was less space in the chest cavity. This was the cause of the sensation of tightness first expressed in the session.

Alex was eager to leave when he understood the situation. The therapist asked him if there were any other spirits attached. He said he could see the scars where the others had been but they left when the man "died." The entities had interpreted the removal of the heart as the death of the body.

The Near-Death Experience

Many people have had a near-death experience. Some recall the NDE; others are not aware of it or fail to remember it after they regain normal consciousness. (Moody, 1975; Osis & Haraldsson, 1977; Ring, 1980, 1984; Gallup, 1982; Sabom, 1982).

In a session with Katy, a 31-year-old female client, she described her outbursts of temper and surprisingly foul language. The first entity who emerged was a motorcyclist, rough in character, belligerent toward the therapist, and unwilling to leave. Deeper probing uncovered a female entity who was attached to him. A demonic entity had infiltrated her consciousness. It was released to its appropriate place in the Light. The female entity was then eager to leave. The biker apologized to Katy, acknowledged that the therapist was not such a bad guy, and agreed to go to the Light.

Katy recalled that some 20 years earlier, she had stopped at the scene of a motorcycle accident. She had offered her beach towel to the attending police officer to cover the body of the deceased biker. Her natural compassion was the opening for this motorcycle rider who died alone on the highway.

With further probing another spirit emerged. He was a very tired old man, not sure about what he was doing with Katy. He recalled and described his experience of dying in a hospital and moving toward the Light. He perceived a young woman approaching him, not from the Light, but from the direction of the hospital.

She linked her arm with his and he heard her say:

"We'll get through this together."

At this point they moved back into her body together. Again, her natural compassion was the invitation for the attachment. When Katy resumed her normal state of consciousness, she described her very serious gall bladder surgery some years previously. After she recovered, the physicians had told her of the severity of her condition, the complicated surgery and the concern they shared regarding the possibility of her survival and recovery. They had informed her of any cessation of vital signs. This was her first awareness of her NDE connected with the surgery.

While the contracted spirit is out of the body during the period of clinical death, another entity can move in, whether invited or not. During this time the attached entities can also leave like rats leaving a sinking ship.

Another NDE was related by a woman who died during childbirth. It involved not only her but her baby girl, who died during the delivery. After a difficult labor she felt herself lifting from her body, free of pain. The spirit of her deceased infant rose beside her. She appeared to be about three years old. They lifted effortlessly, hand in hand toward the Light. The feeling of love between them was intense. At the entrance to the garden just outside the Light her child, now appearing to be about six years of age, turned to face her. Releasing her mother's hand she held up her own little hand in a gesture meant to block mother's progress into the Light.

In a clear soft voice the child said:

"You go back, Mother, it's not your time yet. I have to go now."

The woman reported that she felt such a complete exchange of love with her child during the experience she never felt the need to grieve. Perhaps the total communication of love between the two left no unfinished business, no motivation for continuing together, and no need for grief.

Out-of-Body Experience

The OOBE can be spontaneous and unplanned or purposely undertaken for various reasons. Involuntary OOBE can occur in drug use, physical trauma and pain, severe emotional arousal, continuing negative circumstances, meditation, hypnosis, even sleep. Voluntary OOBE can occur as the result of meditation and practice, usually with some specific purpose in mind. Spiritual learning can occur, distant places can be explored, lost souls can be assisted in finding their way to the Light by persons who chose this manner of helping. This is termed Out-of-Body Ministry (369).

Robert Monroe (1971, 1985) described his out-of-body journeys in intimate detail. On at least one occasion, he returned to another physical body, not his own. He was able to make the correction and after that experience used his right big toe to identify and return to his own physical form. He claimed that he knew of no instance of another being coming into the body of an astral voyager.

Ed, a 35-year-old man, wanted to explore past-life therapy. In the scene that emerged he was floating in a room with a high ceiling and he recognized Egyptian artifacts. He located his body lying on a stone slab in the center of the room. Further probing led him to the realization that he was not in a crypt, his body was not dead. This was some sort of temple and he was undergoing some sort of initiation. As he was trying to recall more of the circumstances, his attention was diverted to the stone slab and his body. He was sitting up! He was aware of floating in a high corner of the room and his body stood up from the slab and was walking toward the door! He floated toward the doorway and out into the open only to see his body swiftly walking around a corner and down a stairway.

With strong intention he caught up with his physical form and quickly moved in, wresting control from the entity who had taken over in his absence. Ed was quite anxious and the entity was quickly expelled. It was not determined whether the entity had been there before the initiation began and the out-of-body experience occurred or if it had come in during the absence of the consciousness.

The shaman often uses rhythmic drumming as well as certain plant substances to facilitate separation of consciousness from the physical body in order to undertake the healing journey for his or her patient. There are friendly and helpful beings in the astral plane; there are also opportunistic spirits and mischievous beings who will take advantage of the unprotected, unoccupied body.

LEFT: Scanned reproduction, "Demons and Angels Contending for the Soul of a Dying Man," *Ars moriendi* (Augsburg, circa 1471) BELOW: Scanned reproduction, "St. Michael Trampling on the Dragon," Martin Schongauer (1420-88).

Some misguided people have used the powerful plant ayahuasca in a dilettante exploration of the drug-induced altered state trip. They claim to make friends with the astral beings encountered. Without the proper training and preparation, however, this can be spiritual suicide, enormously foolish, and psychologically dangerous.

Anthropologist Michael Harner (1980, pp. 2-8) describes his first exploration of the sacred shaman's drink made from ayahuasca, the "soul vine." He was able to

recall the experiences after the effects of the drug were gone. From the deep recesses of his lower brain he had a dim perception of large reptilian creatures showing him the primordial earth. In this scene, black dragon-like beings fell from the sky, exhausted. They had flown to earth to escape their enemy out in space. These creatures claimed to have orchestrated the proliferation of life forms on the planet in order to produce bodies in which to hide and otherwise disguise their presence. They also claimed to be the true masters of humanity and the entire planet and that humans were but their receptacles and servants.

Harner shared this tale with two young missionaries who worked in a nearby area. In turn they read him a passage from the *Book of Revelations*, Chapter 12, which described how Archangel Michael cast Lucifer, the serpent, the dragon into the earth and his angels with him. This parallel information was met with surprise and wonder by the self-avowed atheist anthropologist.

Later, Harner sought out an old retired shaman, a veteran of many such drug-induced journeys into the astral planes. When the shaman heard the claim of the black creatures who said they were masters of the world, he replied with a grin, "...they're always saying that. But they are only the Masters of Outer Darkness." This so piqued Harner's interest that it was his first step toward becoming a master shaman.

It is interesting to note the similarity between the description of the shaman's journey and classical theological literature. Perhaps the story of Lucifer and his legions of demons plaguing humanity is more than a myth. This is explored in the section The Demonic (273).

Imaginary Playmates

The imaginary playmate of childhood can be nothing more than the invented product of a coping mechanism of the child. Having a pal, even if it is imaginary, is easier than being alone. Children often exhibit visual psychic abilities and describe seeing auras, the colored energy patterns around living people, animals and plants. Haunting spirits in houses are often seen by children.

Many cases of spirit attachment begin in childhood. When queried, the entity will clearly state that it followed the child, sometimes for several years, until there was a moment of vulnerability. Often it was the result of a blow to the head as the child fell. The entity may admit that it somehow caused the fall.

Ginny was a working psychic. In her session, she discovered she had numerous attached earthbound entities. Her psychic ability had acted like a beacon to so many of them and her natural compassion was the open door. Ginny was concerned about her six-year-old son, Grayson.

Grayson was an unusual child, elfin in appearance, with large clear dark eyes and broad smiling face. He was also gifted with his own psychic ability. He could see the lights on the palms of his hands. When his mother was tired he would offer to make her feel better by placing his lighted hands on her back and neck. It worked.

Grayson had an imaginary grown-up friend named Charlie. Ginny wasn't sure that Charlie was imaginary, and she wanted to find out in the session. Charlie came through Ginny quite easily. He died in young adulthood. He had been working on a healing device which would have revolutionized the health professions. It wasn't finished when he died and it was nothing which could be completed by anyone else. The principles were not clearly written anywhere. Charlie found Grayson and wanted to complete the work on his invention through this psychically gifted healer when he grew up. With little explanation of the spiritual reality, Charlie agreed to go on to the Light.

Ginny did not tell her son of the session. Several days later a friend of the family asked Grayson about Charlie. Grayson thought for a moment, then replied that Charlie had gone on vacation.

Connected Breathing Technique

Deep conscious breathing can alter the consciousness. Within a few minutes of connected breathing—that is, breathing with no hesitation after the inhalation or exhalation—a person will begin to feel tingling sensations in the hands, arms, feet and legs. The fingers and hands can become straight and tense in a mild tetany. The mouth becomes pursed and round, as if saying "Ohhhhhh." A person passes beyond the condition of hyperventilation into a state of increased inner awareness. A sense of increased energy accompanies this experience.

In this altered state, the client has less conscious resistance to the answers elicited by the questions of the therapist. The increased energy can dislodge an attached entity. If the entity is not discovered and released into the Light, it will reestablish the attachment after the session as the person returns to normal breathing patterns and energy levels.

Andrea, a 23-year-old female client, wanted to experience a conscious breathing session. Lying on the floor, she began the process of deep connected breathing. Within a few minutes she was experiencing the effects of the breathwork. Suddenly she cried out:

C: "There's something sitting on my face."

T: "Get off her face! Let her breathe!"

In a moment she announced that it was on her chest and it felt like a man sitting on her.

T: "Put light between you and it."

C: "I don't know how."

T: "Glow like a light bulb."

The metaphor worked. She immediately felt the relief.

T: (demanding:) "You, the one sitting on her chest, what is your name?"

This one dutifully answered. It was an attached earthbound spirit which had been loosened by the breathing. He quickly chose to go to the Light.

Body Work

Vigorous massage and deep-tissue body work can stimulate the memory of a past life or rouse an entity lodged in the physical body. There may be a reaction as if an old wound is opened up. The client may report severe pain in an area with no present-life history of trauma. The somatic bridge can be used to uncover the past life or the attached entity.

Deep-muscle manipulation in body work can provoke unexpected emotions. The affect bridge can be used to locate the source of these feelings and reactions. As with any mental, emotional or physical response, the source may be a present life, a pre- or peri-natal experience of the person or of mother, a past life or an entity.

A visual image or scene may suddenly emerge into the consciousness of the client. This may be a past-life scene or it may also be a visual memory of the entity. It may be the past-life incident in which the client and the entity, then embodied, interacted in the traumatic event which continues to bind them together. The entity is often fixated on the death trauma, and the scene will replay with every restimulation of the memory. The deep massage may provide that stimulus.

If the body worker is knowledgeable in these techniques, the entity can be released quite easily. The area of the body where the entity is lodged is often the site of chronic pain or discomfort, undiagnosable and untreatable within the medical model. Relief often comes with the release of this entity.

Mirror and Body-Scan Techniques

The mirror technique works well for highly visual persons. The therapist directs the client to see themselves standing in front of a special mirror.

T: "This mirror allows you to see through your body as if it were translucent. Any imperfections or disruptions of your energy will be visible to you in the mirror. Any discolorations, splotches, shadowy, dark or grey places are quite visible to you. Notice any faces or shapes, not necessarily human. Describe anything you can see on or in your body. You may notice figures or shapes standing close by."

Exploring this visualization brings the client into deeper levels of the subconscious memory. Each shape, shadow or figure described by the client is marked a stick figure sketched on the therapist's note pad. One stick figure is sketched for the front of the body, one for the backside. Each of these spots is explored individually, through the probing questions described in the above sections. As each spot is addressed, the therapist uses the exact words of the client to describe it.

> T: "If that dark circle over the knee could speak, what is the first thing it would say?"
> "If the grey shadow in your gut had a size and shape, what would that be?"
> "If that blurriness over your heart had a color, what would that be? What would it say"
> "As you focus on that moving green blotch, what happens?"
> "Is there a scene or image beginning to form?"
> "If that face had an expression, what would it be? What would it be saying?"

These spots on the mirror image may turn out to be any of a number of things: present-life childhood accidents, such as a scraped knee or broken bone; emotional hurts, such as a scolding by a parent; trauma suffered by either mother or infant during the birth process; thought forms projected from another person; emotional or physical past-life trauma; or attached spirits. Each one is processed in turn, beginning with the darkest one.

The body-scan technique is used for clients who are less visual and more kinesthetic. They are asked to scan their body for feeling clues for the spots described above, and for physical sensations of any kind. The same sort of questions can be asked:

> T: "If that tingling sensation in your legs could talk, what would it say?"
> "If that tightness behind your eyes could speak out, what would it say?"
> "If that pain in your gut had a color, what would it be?"
> "If that snake in your intestine had something to say to you, what would that be?"

These inductions can elicit memories of present- or past-life events or an attached spirit, whichever is the cause of the problem or condition which was discovered as a spot of disrupted energy in the mirror image or body scan.

Exploring the Chakras

The seven major chakras, or centers of consciousness in the body, lie along the spine and are associated with various physical, mental, and emotional aspects of human behavior (Rama, Ballentine, and Ajaya, pp. 216-280). In the course of human interaction, events take place which stimulate the energies associated with the various chakra levels. The emotional or physical trauma endured by a person can render those energy centers vulnerable. They are opened like doors to allow entry and attachment by an entity. This can be discovered in past lives or in the present.

> T: "Look into the level of the fourth chakra, the heart. Is there someone or something there that does not belong?"
> "Explore the second chakra, the level of the sexual energy. Is there someone else influencing that energy?"
> "Focus deep into the seventh chakra, the crown chakra, the spiritual center. Is there someone or something interfering with that center?

The full self-exploration by the scanning or mirror technique must include the chakra exploration.

The Pendulum

The pendulum has long been used as a divining instrument for such projects as mineral exploration, water dowsing, archeological research, locating missing persons, and medical diagnosis (Finch, 1975, pp. 18-23). In the hands of a trained person, it can be used to discover a great deal of information about a person, including health factors, intelligence level, strength of will, and the presence of attached entities (Long, 1959).

Release of attached entities can be accomplished at a distance with the use of the pendulum (Starr, 1987; Maurey, 1988). This release can be achieved with or without the person's knowledge or permission. It is essential that the pendulum operator ask permission of the High Self before proceeding with this remote releasement.

It is possible that the operator of the pendulum must have a degree of psychic ability in order to successfully accomplish the desired results. It is also possible that everyone has some degree of psychic ability and intuition and simply ignores or denies this spiritual gift.

The Ouija Board

People have used instruments of divination similar to the Ouija board for more than 2500 years. In ancient Greece, the philosopher and mathematician Pythagoras encouraged such an instrument. Earlier in ancient China, such instruments were commonplace and were considered a non-threatening way of communicating with the spirits of the dead. In third-century Rome, in thirteenth-century Tartary, in North America prior to the arrival of Columbus, in France of the nineteenth century, such instruments were used to predict, divine, and locate lost articles and missing persons (Hunt 1985, pp. 3-4).

In rare instances, the Ouija has been used to release earthbound spirits. Even so, its use is fervently discouraged for this or any other purpose. Without thorough education and preparation, opening the door to one's psychic ability is unwise. One type of opening question constitutes an open invitation to any spirit:

"Is anyone there?"
"Is there anyone on the board right now?"
"Is there anyone who wants to communicate?"

This open invitation will be accepted, and the spirits who arrive may become permanent residents. Many cases of serious and damaging possession have begun with an evening of innocent "fun" with the Ouija board.

Channelling

Mediumship is considered to be a psychic gift, not a pathological condition. A person with this gift seems to be able to go into a trance or altered state of consciousness and give up conscious control of the mind and body. The "spirit control" enters and speaks, sometimes moving the body as well. Mediumship is, quite literally, spirit possession with a specified purpose and duration.

The purpose of mediumship has classically been the transmission of wisdom from a discarnate teacher or master from another dimension or level of spiritual vibration. In ancient Greece, the term used for the medium was Oracle, and divine wisdom was thought to be transmitted through this person.

MEDIUMSHIP AND CHANNELLING CONSTITUTE SPIRIT POSSESSION BY PERMISSION WITH A SPECIFIED PURPOSE AND DURATION.

Channelling is the term used currently to describe the process of transmission of spiritual wisdom through the mechanism of the person who is the channel. Channelling can be done in deep trance in the same way as earlier mediumship. Some people with this gift prefer to remain conscious, and repeat the message rather than giving up total voice and body control to the spirit being coming through. This is termed *conscious channelling*.

There are classes which purport to teach the process of channelling. If the teachers of such classes are unaware of the spiritual reality and do not teach the normal precautions, there can be very unpleasant results. There are many cases of people in such classes who opened themselves to receive a spirit teacher and were surprised to be contacted instead by a lost earthbound entity. The permission was given in the channelling process. It was not a violation; the door was opened. Many of these entities refuse to leave at the end of the session.

Carol was a 55-year-old therapist who was interested in metaphysics and the spiritual teachings. She attended a course on channelling. The homework after the first class was to meditate. During the meditation she was to open herself up to channel someone who would be for her own highest good. This was the only instruction, the only precaution. A spirit joined her and would not leave. She developed a severe pain in her stomach.

In Carol's session, the questions were focused on the pain in the stomach.

T: "If that pain in the stomach could talk, what is the first thing it would say?"

C: "I'm her mother. Don't send me away."

This was a surprise to Carol. Her mother had died of stomach cancer some years earlier.

T: "What happened?"

C: "I've been wanting to join my daughter ever since I died but she's too strong. When she asked for someone for her own highest good to come in, naturally I came in ."

Mother's good intentions, coupled with Carol's invitation without discernment, had caused this attachment. Mother's presence explained the pain Carol experienced in her stomach.

With very little communication between them, they were ready to separate from one another for this time. Carol discontinued her channelling class. Her stomach pain disappeared.

Unlike true mediumship, in which the controlling spirit leaves after the purpose is fulfilled, the earthbound who attaches at this invitation may not want to leave. This process is similar to using the Ouija board, except the whole body and mind serves as the divining instrument.

Differential Diagnosis

The second step in Spirit Releasement Therapy is differential diagnosis. The earthbound spirit of a deceased human is perhaps the most common attachment. However, there are many other kinds of non-physical beings which interfere with living people. The following guidelines assist the therapist in determining the nature of the attachment and thus the course of treatment. The type of attached entity determines which procedure is followed in the releasement process. There are methods of differentiating between subpersonalities, alter personalities, thought forms, and separate entities of various kinds, human and non-human.

This is the first step in developing a diagnosis. The first question directed toward the attached entity will aid in determining the next steps of the procedure.

T: "Have you ever been alive in your own human physical body?"

If the answer is affirmative, then there is a series of questions which will lead to more precise diagnosis. The responses will assist the therapist in determining which category best fits the attached discarnate entity. If the answer is negative, attention is focused on the categories of non-human entities and energies.

HUMAN ENTITIES

If the discarnate entity has a history of human life, the therapist asks for information in the following order:

T: "Are you male or female?"

Usually, the entity is quite certain of its gender. The terminated pregnancy knows its gender. The mind fragment will insist it is presently alive in its own physical body. It is certain of its gender.

T: "How old are you?"

The spirit of an older female may hedge or hesitate to answer. Discretion and sensitivity must be used in finding the approximate age.

T: "Are you over 10? Are you over 20? Are you over 30? (etc.)"

A pause between each question will assist a confused entity in recalling its age. The terminated pregnancy does not know its age in years. Such a spirit does know how far along in the pregnancy it was.

The subpersonality or alter personality will state the age at which it split off from the main personality. Without therapy, it remains at that age. With therapy and healing, it often seems to grow up and finally merge or integrate with the core personality at the present age. An alter personality may claim an age much older than the person at the time of the dissociation. This alter may turn out to be a past-life personality of the person, or an attached earthbound spirit who died at the declared age.

T: "What year is it for you?"

The earthbound spirit is fixated in the year of its death. The mind fragment of a living person knows the present date. The terminated pregnancy is not aware of the date.

T: "What is your name?"
   "How do people address you?"
   "When someone calls you by name, what name do they use?"

Different forms of this question can help a confused spirit recall its name. The more time that passes after the physical death of the human, the more difficulty the spirit has in recalling its former name. The mind fragment does not hesitate in disclosing its name. The terminated pregnancy has no name. The therapist offers this spirit a chance to take a name for itself.

It is important to know the circumstances leading to the attachment in the current life. Present-life vulnerability can be healed in ongoing therapy. If the circumstances of the attachment represent a continuation of past-life conflict, past-life therapy may assist in bringing about resolution.

T: "How old was _____(client's name) when you joined her
   in this life?"

The earthbound and mind fragment will know the person's age at that time. There might be two ages given, since in some cases an attached spirit can separate and reestablish the attachment at a later time. The spirit of an unborn child usually does not know the age of its mommy. It simply stayed with her after the termination.

The therapist can gain information about the circumstances of the attraction and subsequent attachment through the following questions:

T: "What attracted you to her?"
   "Was it mutual in any way?"
   "Did she invite you to come in?"
   "Did you ask if you could join her like this?"
   "Did she give you permission to join?"
   "What allowed you to attach to her like this?"
   "What was the opening that allowed you to get in?"
   "How was she vulnerable to you?"
   "How was she susceptible to you?"

The answers are often surprisingly honest and clear. This is an important area and becomes the focus of ongoing therapy, as healing this vulnerability may protect from new attachments in the future.

T: "Where were you before you joined her?"

Neither the subpersonality nor the alter personality will have any awareness of its existence during the client's present life prior to splitting. The earthbound will have a clear memory of everything about its own life, its death and the events between that point and the attachment to the host. The mind fragment will know it was with its own body. The terminated pregnancy will usually describe the Light.

On several occasions, this question has brought startling information and disturbing insights into the workings of the spiritual reality. The following is such a case.

Gloria was a 45-year-old bookkeeper. Her deceased grandfather was discovered to be with her. He joined when she was eight years old, shortly after his death. This could have been a typical family setting. It is not at all unusual for a grandparent to attach to the young grandchild. This case was different.

T: "Where were you before you joined her?"

C: "I was in the intermediate place, the gray place."

T: "What were you doing there?"

C: "Just waiting."

T: "Waiting for what?"

C: "Waiting to join someone. I didn't know where to go."

T: "What happened?"

Scanned excerpt from the *Pictorial Bible*.

C: "I was assigned to Gloria."

T: "Did someone send you?"

C: "Yes, Joshua and the elders."

T: "How were they dressed?"

C: "They were in long gray robes and they had long dirty white beards."

This was not any part of the Light or the planning stage. It was not anything from the dark side.

T: "Go on."

C: "They had a big book of information. They assigned me to Gloria. They said I could learn things with her."

T: "Your granddaughter Gloria?"

C: "That had nothing to do with it. I could learn by being with her."

The big book of information was described as tattered. It was reminiscent of last year's telephone book or a well-used Sears catalog.

T: "Can you still contact Joshua? Call him."

Joshua came. He and the elders had appointed themselves as assigners of lost souls. They tried to determine where a lost soul could best learn by attaching. They assigned spirits to attach. They freely acknowledged that they had nothing to do with the Light. They were noble and well intentioned, and this seemed like a good idea at the time. The big book they used for information was identified as last year's discarded akashic record book. It was a moment of fine spiritual humor.

The guiding spirits from the Light were present. The request was made for one of them to talk to Joshua and his group of elders regarding this misdirected effort. Joshua quickly understood and was ready to go on to the Light, accompanied by his group of elders.

T: "Wait Joshua, before you go to the Light. Are there any other groups like yourselves in the intermediate place doing the assigning?"

C: "Oh yes, there are groups all over the intermediate place."

Joshua and several of the guiding spirits were requested to search for the other groups and escort them home to the Light. They agreed.

The information-gathering questions continued:

T: "What was the purpose for attaching, this time?"
"What did you want to accomplish?"
"How do you serve her by being here like this?"

"Like this" refers specifically to the spirit-human connection. The spirit of a husband may have definite reasons for being with his wife. The spirit of a mother may feel she must stay with the child. Whatever the desired effect, it cannot be fulfilled by attaching as a spirit.

T: "How many lifetimes, including the present time, have you
been with her like this?"
"Have you known this one (the client) in another lifetime
when you both lived in your own physical bodies?"

If there was a past life together, the earthbound spirit is encouraged to
recall and describe the shared experience. This is past-life therapy on the entity.
The client will also perceive the lifetime recalled by the entity. In effect, it is a dual
regression, and can bring healing for the client as well as the entity. The
unfinished business which connected the two can be resolved and the entity can
be released.

T: "Recall the last day you were in your own physical body in the
lifetime when you knew each other. What happened?"

Usually, the violence will be recalled along with the anger. The death and
separation of loved ones will be remembered with the sadness and loss of that
separation. The therapist can reassure the client that only the physical body dies.
Love is eternal. The deathbed promises may be affecting the entity.

"I'll always love you"

This is the truth.

"We will be together again"

This is a loving promise.

"I'll never leave you"

This is an unwise and impossible promise and often leads to spirit
attachment.

"I love you. I will return to you. I will come back!"

This is the warrior's timeless vow, the soldier's impossible promise. So
many millions of men have died in futile battles through the eons, leaving beloved
wives and sweethearts back home, alone and desolate. Vast numbers of these
spirits have returned and attached to their loved ones, finding them again in
lifetime after lifetime.
As in all spirit attachment, the effect on the women is not a true
manifestation of the love these men proclaim. When they realize the damage they
have inflicted by fulfilling their erstwhile promise to return, they agree to leave,
reluctantly parting from their beloved.

The warrior's impossible promise:
"I will return to you."

Montage (top, center and bottom left) scanned excerpts, primarily from "The War Against Gibeon," the *Pictorial Bible*, circa 1882.

Definitive answers to these questions will identify the earthbound spirit, terminated pregnancy, or mind fragment of a living person. Sparse or evasive answers will lead the therapist to seek other diagnostic information, as described in the next sections. Firm answers to the appropriate questions tend to indicate the correct diagnosis.

The therapist next gathers data regarding the nature and extent of the interference caused by the attachment.

> T: "How have you affected her physically?"
> "How have you affected her mentally?"
> "How have you affected her emotionally?"
> "What damage have you caused her by being here?"

This information is important in dealing with habits, addictions, and behaviors imposed by the attached entity. These behaviors can disappear completely after the release, or they might continue sporadically with little or no power over the client. Traditional therapy can erase the last traces of such residue imposed by the spirit.

If there was trauma at the age of attachment, the entity may have joined to assist the person. It might have experienced a comparable trauma in its own lifetime, the similarity of the condition acting as the attraction. Conversely, the entity may have caused the trauma in the present lifetime.

If the trauma experienced by the client resulted in the formation of a subpersonality, the subpersonality can be holding onto an earthbound spirit. A subpersonality is a constellation of conscious energy as is the spirit. They are of a similar vibration and can perceive each other and interact fully. Therapy and healing with the inner child or subpersonality can resolve the conflicts and needs which have maintained the connection with the entity.

Earthbound Spirits

The earthbound spirits, that is the spirits of deceased humans, have identifiable characteristics and specific signs of attachment.

They have gender and a name.

They retain the age at which they died.

The present date for them is the date of their death.

They feel and express human emotions and can influence the host's emotions by imposing their own emotional residue.

The opinions, judgments, prejudices, and belief systems of the entity can affect the host's intellectual outlook. This is the mental residue that is imposed by the spirit.

The earthbound spirit is often fixated on the physical and emotional trauma of its death and can impart to the host the physical and emotional symptoms of that trauma. This is part of the emotional and physical residue.

An entity can impose the physical symptoms of any illness it suffered in life, as well as the limitations of any physical impairment. This includes addictions to alcohol, drugs and food.

They know the host's body is not their own.

They may have served a useful purpose at one time.

They don't sleep.

They have no concept of time. They do have memory of events. The following question will usually bring a vague answer:

T: "How long have you been with _____ ?" (client's name)

This question will bring a specific answer.

T: "How old was _____(client's name) when you joined in this lifetime?"

They use the energy of the host, and chronic mild fatigue is sometimes the only symptom.

The host often feels invaded, soiled, violated.

The host experiences no amnesia except in cases of total possession and takeover.

The sudden acquisition of a skill such as diesel-engine repair or facility in a foreign language may indicate a newly formed attachment.

A sudden change in personality, especially after accident, surgery, heart attack, organ transplant, trauma, grief, loss of loved one, combat, or use of mind-altering drugs may signal a newly attached spirit.

If the attachment was established for the first time in the present lifetime of the host, then the entity usually has an awareness of the present-life connection or relationship and can recall the course of its actions from the time of its own death to the experience of attachment. The entity usually has complete memory of its activity and environment prior to locating, following and finally attaching to the host.

The attachment can be reestablished lifetime after lifetime. It knows the reasons for attaching, including past-life connections, and how many lifetimes the attachment has continued.

The entity usually has a memory of the connecting lifetime when it interacted with the host, when each of them lived in his or her own physical body. As the entity describes that lifetime, the client can recall the experience also.

In approximately half of the cases of spirit attachment, there is no apparent connection in this or any other lifetime. The entity comes in randomly, without requesting or receiving permission or invitation from the host. This appears to be a violation of free will.

There is no limit to the number of discarnate entities that can attach to a living person. They may be single, nested or in groups.

An earthbound spirit can have another entity attached to itself. That one can be another earthbound or any other type of entity. There seems to be no limit to this chain of nested or layered attachments.

The entity is aware of its motive for attaching to the person. The aim might have been helpfulness, which is noble but impossible. The newly deceased spirit of the mother of a young child might want to stay to take care of the child in a valiant but fruitless effort to protect and nurture the little one. She only interferes.

The intention can be totally neutral and benign. The attachment can occur just because of physical proximity to the person. People who work with the dead and dying are natural targets. Nurses, police and fire personnel, medics and mortuary staff workers can pick up many stray entities.

Gerry was in his mid forties. In session, he discovered an attached earthbound spirit. It was a man who had drowned and he was angry about losing his life. This information suddenly jarred Gerry's memory. He had been a captain in a city fire department some 12 to 15 years earlier. He did not disclose the reasons for separating from the department. On one particular call, his company was the first to reach the lakeside dock where a drowning victim was laying after being pulled from the water.

Being the first to arrive, Gerry applied mouth-to-mouth resuscitation in a futile effort to revive the drowning victim, a strong young man who had fallen from a speedboat on the lake. He was not wearing a personal floatation device, and apparently lost consciousness when he hit the water at high speed.

An ambulance transported the body to the hospital, and Gerry ordered his engineer to follow the ambulance, certainly not a normal procedure. Gerry walked into the hospital, following the gurney on which the body was being carried, and tried to get through the doors to the emergency treatment room. He felt a powerful compulsion to stay close to the body. He was not allowed to follow the body into the surgery room. This was off limits to emergency personnel and information was only given on a need-to-know basis. Gerry stood at the doors for a considerable time, trying to observe the activities around the body. He finally had to leave. He never understood this behavior, and only during the session did the reason become clear.

His lady friend reminded him that his life had begun to deteriorate after that incident at the lake. He had related the story to her many times, never finding any logical reason for the direction his career and personal affairs had taken. Not until the release of the attached spirit during the session did it come clear to him.

Feelings of anger, revenge, and resentment for past injustices can result in an attachment by an entity bent on exacting retribution. The motive may be vengeance; the intention is to cause harm in any way possible, even death. This is usually seen as the result of murder or battlefield killing, in this or a past life. One or more nested demonic entities will always be found in such a case. Vengeance, hatred and rage are open invitations to the demonic entities.

An entity attachment may be totally self-serving, established for the purpose of satisfying its own needs, appetites, desires for food, drugs, alcohol, sex or even personal power.

Motivated by a distorted love, the spirit of a jealous husband can follow or attach to his widow. He will join her in order to jealously and possessively guard her from the affections of others, forgetting that the marriage vow was "until death do us part." A woman's grief at the loss of her husband can also hold the spirit of her mate from moving on to its progression. The spirit of a loving wife can remain with her widower husband.

The grief of the host over the loss of any loved one may be sufficient to hold the spirit of that loved one in the earth plane. A grieving family can hold the spirit of a recently deceased loved one from moving into the Light.

Guilt and remorse over inflicted pain can lead to an attachment for the purpose of righting the perceived wrong. The conflict can seldom be resolved in this way; the entity is stuck in the emotion. Conflict resolution requires meaningful dialogue between the entity and the host. This is the function of the therapeutic intervention.

A vigorous, goal-directed, success-oriented male who suddenly dies may feel cheated in the fulfillment of his material goals and may seek through another person's body to gain wealth or complete a project.

The spirit of a deceased elderly or mentally disabled person often feels very tired and confused. A person who dies in youth or middle age is usually angry over the death, looking for someone to blame. There is often a need for revenge.

This need can attract the dark energy forms, the demonic beings who seek to exacerbate any situation involving unrest, disruption, hate, rage or revenge. They offer the opportunity for revenge in return for the soul of the angry spirit. At this point the newly deceased spirit is fixated on just one thing: getting even. It does not understand what it means to bargain away the soul, and this contract with the darkness is often struck in the moments following death.

The spirit of a deceased child is most often terrified and confused about everything. Dealing with the lost spirit of a child is a most poignant experience for the client and therapist. The child does not understand why no one pays the slightest bit of attention to its tearful pleas for help. It feels totally ignored, abandoned and unloved. In the clinical setting, a stuffed animal is a great comfort to a child entity, no matter what age the person who carries the spirit of that child.

An earthbound spirit can be fragmented, as can a living person, and the fragments of the entity can be attached to two or more living people simultaneously. A fragment can also be attached to another earthbound spirit.

The client may have a history of good mental, physical, and emotional health, without any history of dissociation as a coping mechanism. This tends to rule out MPD, which typically develops as the result of childhood sexual trauma.

Once the spirit understands its condition (that it is deceased and permanently separated from its body) and its situation as an attached entity, most earthbounds will agree to separate and move into the Light. Some earthbound spirits require assistance in resolving their emotional turmoil.

Past-life therapy may not prove beneficial and may not help in the resolution of the presenting problem of the client. However, it may help in resolving the emotional reasons for the attachment and it may lead to release of the entity. Past-life therapy does not help an entity resolve its problems.

Terminated Pregnancy

Pregnancy may terminate in a number of ways: miscarriage, either natural or as the result of an accident or trauma; intrauterine death; abortion; stillbirth; or the death of the mother. A being may leave the planning stage in the Light and linger in the vicinity of the future mother for a considerable period of time prior to conception, even several years. If the target body is destroyed in any manner, that being must return to the Light through the reincarnation cycle, just as any newly deceased spirit must do. In addition to miscarriages and stillbirths, the increasing number of abortions leads to a large number of earthbound spirits of the unborn.

This spirit has no name and no experience of being born. It is unsure if it had its own body, as it spent little actual time in the forming fetus. It will often describe the body as quitting or stopping. This is a naive way of describing the death or termination by natural miscarriage.

It does know its gender. This is part of the original plan developed in the Light. The spirit will make up a name for itself if the therapist offers it the chance. It may be a descriptive term like Sunshine, Joyful, White Cloud, or a plain human name like Jim or George.

It is often very sad and cannot understand why mother did this. There may be anger over the abortion. The spirit of the terminated pregnancy may attach to the mother because of anger and lack of understanding or the simple need for closeness. It may stay because it agreed to be a friend to the mother and not realize the impossibility of being a friend as an attached spirit. The spirit may attach to the next embryo or fetus as it develops within the mother. Thus a new baby may be born with an attached spirit. Such a person may have symptoms usually associated with memories of an abortion or miscarriage, yet the trauma belongs to the attached being.

The spirit of a terminated twin may attach to the surviving twin and adamantly claim the body as its own. The birth experience would coincide with the live birth of the client. This one will be angry at the host, defiant toward the therapist, and insistent on staying. Further probing will reveal that there were two embryos and two waiting spirits at the beginning of the pregnancy.

The spirit is a complete fully developed being, not at all diminutive in intelligence, language, awareness or understanding. The role of terminated unborn infant is a thin mask. A brief explanation from the therapist is frequently all that is required to resolve the issues. A scan of past-life connections and an exploration of the planning stage will help allay the anger, diminish the pain and bring understanding. These little ones deserve another chance and most often get one very soon.

Janet was accompanied to her session by her regular therapist. The progress of therapy had stopped. This question was asked in the beginning of the session:

T: "Have you ever had any abortions?"

The woman clutched her abdomen, yelled out in pain, and fell from the couch to the floor, where she remained for the rest of the session. She was living with a man she had no intention of marrying and had become pregnant by him seven times in as many years. She had chosen to abort every time. All seven of the entities were with her, causing emotional pain and physical symptoms. They all claimed to love her and had chosen to be born to her in order to be her friend. They were frustrated at the impossibility of the situation. One by one they agreed to leave. By the end of the session, Janet was free of pain. Her therapy progressed well after that session.

The spirit may attach to someone performing or assisting with the abortion. One female client remained with her adult daughter to comfort her during an abortion. The spirit of the terminated being attached to its grandmother. In a scan of past lives it was revealed that she was supposed to be its mother in a former lifetime, and she had aborted it then. It had attempted to return to the family in this manner.

A nurse who assisted a physician in performing abortions discovered that she carried over 200 of these spirits. Her compassion had opened the doors for them. She had to leave the job.

A 42-year-old woman discovered and released the spirit of a terminated pregnancy. She was six years old when it attached. Her father was the abortionist, and his clinic adjoined their house. The spirit, which had been six months along in utero, had a strong desire to live. The little girl next door was the closest living body.

Subpersonality

The subpersonality has a memory of its own body, which is the present body of the client. Subpersonalities often develop in pairs of polar opposites, with the tendencies of one balancing out the tendencies of the other. For example, the good little boy and the rotten kid, the Madonna and the prostitute, the iron maiden and the fairy princess. This concept is similar to the Parent, Adult and Child described in Transactional Analysis, or the "complexes" of psychoanalysis. Each subpersonality has some valuable qualities that are important to preserve in the process of healing and integration (Crampton, 1981).

The subpersonality has no memory prior to splitting off in the present life. However, working with the subpersonality may lead to a past-life memory with unresolved conflict, and death in the past life at the declared age of the subpersonality. The precipitating event in the present life may have emotional components similar to the trauma which led to death in the prior lifetime.

Alter Personality In MPD

There is a growing literature on the causes, symptoms, diagnosis and treatment of MPD (Beahrs, 1982; Kluft, 1985; Bliss, 1986; Braun, 1986; Putnam, 1989; Ross, 1989). The following information is not meant to be complete but relates directly to the problem of differential diagnosis between MPD and spirit attachment.

In the true multiple, there is normally an amnestic barrier between the alter personalities. However, in an altered state of consciousness, sometimes referred to as hypnotic trance, one alter can recall the activities of the other alters when they were "out," that is in charge of the body. It seems that the memory of the alters exists in the subconscious portion of the mind. Hypnosis is the usual method of discovering, diagnosing, and treating the condition of MPD. Hypnosis is the primary therapeutic method for accessing the subconscious portion of the mind.

Within this clinical framework, a disembodied consciousness can separate from a dying person and join a living person, infiltrating and somehow connecting within the subconscious mind. Hypnosis is also one method of probing for any attached consciousness which may be interfering with a client.

Onset of MPD seems to develop over a long period of time, with the precipitating events in early childhood. About half of reported cases have under ten alter personalities; the other half have from ten to over one hundred. Impairment varies from mild to severe, depending primarily on the relationship between the personalities. At least two of the alters recurrently take control of the person's behavior (APA, 1987, pp. 269-272).

Spirit attachment is usually sudden and the accompanying changes are often apparent immediately. Long-standing spirit attachment may be discovered when a person comes into therapy to work on a chronic or continuing problem area. Except in the rare cases of full possession, the entity does not take over completely. The effect of spirit attachment is manifested and experienced in unusual ego dystonic drives, appetites, urges, contradictory thinking, internal voices, arguing, and dialogue.

The person diagnosed with MPD usually has a history of a poor concept of good mental, physical, and emotional health. Spirit attachment is not determined by the health concepts of the host.

The multiple has a history of emotional, physical, and most often sexual abuse in childhood without any sense of control of the circumstances. Spirit attachment is not determined by the childhood sexual history of the host.

Alters usually have a feeling of belonging, being part of or owning the body. Entities are usually aware that they are separate beings. In a futile attempt to remain and not be dislodged from a seemingly comfortable place, they might attempt to persuade the therapist that the body they inhabit is their own. Other alters will refute the entity's claim.

A traditional therapist may not believe an entity when it claims to be a separate consciousness. Should the therapist attempt to integrate such an entity, the attempt will be unsuccessful and the best result possible may be co-consciousness.

Although there are amnestic barriers between most alter personalities, attached entities often know about other entities or groups of entities and certainly know about the host. Entities with a multiple know about the alters, and the alters may recognize the entities as separate beings and not part of the "group."

Alter personalities form, emerge, fragment, and split off at a time of trauma or need. Dissociation is a coping mechanism for a traumatic or stressful situation and almost always begins in childhood.

The alter has no memory of existence in the current lifetime prior to forming and dissociating from the main personality, yet may recall a past life as the manifesting personality, part of the soul-mind consciousness of the person. There is usually no break in memory for an earthbound spirit in the sequence of its own life, death, attachment, and its activity between death and attachment to the host.

Rachel, a 30-year-old Black woman, entered therapy after she awoke in her bed holding a knife over her infant child. She had been molested as a child, gang raped at age 11, and, with meager education, was employable only at menial tasks. The author was called in as consultant.

At the beginning of the session, Rachel, sitting on the edge of the couch, began rocking back and forth. She suddenly dropped to her hands and knees on the floor, still rocking, and crying out:

C: "I'm burning, I'm burning! It's so hot."

T: "What's burning?"

C: "My house is burning. I'm burning!"

Her voice sounded like a child's.

T: "How old are you?"

C: "Ten."

T: "What's your name?"

C: "Theresa."

T: "Theresa where are your mommy and daddy?"

C: "They're burning, they're already gone."
She slumped to the floor, no longer rocking, no longer crying. This indicated the death and relief of physical pain caused by the fire.

T: "What happens next?"

C: "I'm going down the street...."

T: "Where are you going, Theresa?"

C: "I'm going to this little girl's house. She's 10. I'm going in."

She joined Rachel. Though they were the same age, Theresa did not know Rachel's name, nor had they been playmates.

T: "Theresa, look straight up. Look straight up. What do you see?"

C: "It's bright. I'm scared."

Her voice quavered. This brightness reminded her of the fire which took the lives of her family.

T: "This brightness won't burn. Do you see anyone there in the bright place?"

C: "My mommy and daddy."

T: "Have you missed them?"

C: "Yes."

T: "Reach out to them, Theresa. What do they do?"

C: "They reach for me."

T: "Do you want to go to them?"

C: "Yes."

T: "Take their hands, Theresa. We send you to the Light with
     love. Good bye, Theresa."

She left and did not return. Rachel did not manifest the rocking behavior
again in that session nor in subsequent sessions.

Some of the alters can tell which are "created," meaning alter personalities, and which are "invited," meaning attached entities.

After the release of Theresa, about 15 minutes passed before Rachel
calmed down. She switched to Hannah, an adult alter who handled the anger.
Hannah was loud and domineering and intimidated the other alters and the
entities which were attached. She was angry that Theresa had "escaped." It all
transpired so quickly that Hannah did not grasp what was happening.

Hannah would not allow the other entities to emerge for more than a brief
period. Spirit releasement therapy is most effective if the therapist and the entity
can engage in meaningful and uninterrupted dialogue.

At one point in a subsequent session, Hannah tried to swing at one of the
therapists. He placed his arms around her, subduing her arms. She immediately
switched to Julie, the 11-year-old alter who held the pain. She actually enjoyed
being held in this safe manner. These are two of the alters commonly found in
the victim of childhood sexual abuse: one who holds the anger, and one who holds
the pain. Neither Hannah nor Julie had any awareness of being and no memory
of anything prior to the sexual abuse. They had "always" been with Rachel.

Julie proceeded to tell the therapists that she and Hannah were created
and the others were invited. In further sessions, Rachel began to feel and express
more of her own anger. Hannah seemed to weaken as her anger was diminished.
The entities could emerge and remain long enough for conversation.

One of the attached entities was Rachel's pimp who died as the result of
a drug deal gone sour. Another was Yvonne, one of the girls in his stable of
prostitutes. She and Rachel had been good friends. Yvonne had purposely taken
an overdose. While under the influence of the drugs, she ran out of the building
where she lived and into the street, directly in the path of an oncoming car. She
died instantly. Rachel commented that no one had ever known if Yvonne had
overdosed or died solely because of the impact of the car. Yvonne admitted freely
that she was close to death with the drugs and she was glad to be out of the
situation. Several other entities unknown to Rachel were also released.

A dormant past-life personality as part of the soul-mind consciousness
can be reactivated at a time of stress when the person is in need, and then
manifest as an alter personality for a specific purpose.

At 42, Connie was a marriage and family counselor. She had begun
studying psychology at age 32. Only three years prior to this session, had she
discovered, in the course of her own therapy, that she had been molested as a
child. From age three until age ten, her father had sexually abused her. When she

was ten, a twenty-two-year-old male alter personality emerged. Apparently this alter had enough personal authority to persuade father to cease the abuse.

Connie was already working on the inner child personality with her own therapist. In this session, several entities were released before the 22-year-old-male emerged. He was certain he was not a separate entity but was part of her soul consciousness. He claimed to be the manifesting personality in a former lifetime. He was called up from dormancy as the result of her stress and pain caused by the molestation. He was not treated as an attached spirit, and he was not integrated in this session. The woman did not return for further sessions.

A hallmark of the multiple personality is lost time, as control shifts between the alters as they switch. There is no sense of lost time for the host of an attached entity except in rare cases of total possession and takeover. The attached earthbound spirit imposes attitudes, behavior, addiction, emotions, physical sensations on the host, not amnesia.

The Inner Self Helper, or ISH, can act as co-therapist. It is aware of the entire family of selves: those fragments which are part of the family and those which are intruders. In some rare cases, the ISH may advise not releasing one or more of the entities.

A therapist attended a presentation on the subject of spirit attachment and spirit releasement presented by the author. At that time, the presenter advocated release of all attached entities at the time of discovery.

In her own practice, the therapist discovered a female entity attached to a female client diagnosed with MPD. The entity acknowledged its situation but suggested that she not be sent away, as she cared for and kept a number of child alter personalities under control. The therapist insisted that the entity leave, as the presenter had advocated.

After the session, the client went into emotional chaos. The children alters took over randomly and her life was out of control.

The more conservative position is to determine each situation individually and not always insist that the attached entities leave immediately. If there is a specific valuable function performed by the attached entity, if the client wants to retain the entity, and if the entity agrees to leave on a future date, specified or unspecified at the time of the session, then there is sometimes wisdom in allowing the attached spirit to remain.

An entity may have a definite purpose, such as caring for and controlling the many children alters.

An entity cannot be integrated; co-consciousness may be the only result possible.

Entities know they are separate; alters know they are part of the group, and the body is theirs.

An attached entity or spirit can be channeled easily through a medium and will identify itself as a discarnate. A fragment of a living personality can also be channelled, as in the case of attachment by a fragment, as described in the next section, and will be able to identify itself as the living person.

A living person can channel another living person. In some cases on record, a spirit communication through a medium proved to be from another living person. The person who is the source of the communication was most often sleeping. In any case, the source person was unaware of the communication (Fodor, 1966, p. 59).

The ISH or High Self can often be invited to speak through the client and to assist in the therapeutic process.

Mind Fragment of a Living Person

Although fragmentation of consciousness is seen in the condition of MPD, more commonly it is seen in the formation of subpersonalities in the normal or average person. Apparently, some of these fragments can externalize, separate from the original person, remain in another location, or attach to another living person. This is distinctive from the thought form or projected energy of anger, hex or curse.

A person with an illness can parasite on a healthy person. This is a sort of psychic vampirism. An overbearing mother can obsess a child; this can turn out to be more than a parental introject. In the practice of Witchcraft, casting a spell involves a fragment of the witch's consciousness, which is transmitted to the victim.

A fragment will act much like an earthbound spirit, yet will claim to be alive in its own physical body at the present time. It will recall the moment of fragmentation and separation from the original personality, the percentage of fragmentation, the act of attachment to the client and the purpose for the attachment.

Marion was about 40, a recovering alcoholic and drug addict. One of the attached entities discovered in her first session was a fragment of her 84-year-old aunt Dolly who lived a short distance away. A scan of past lives revealed that Marion had been Dolly's daughter in another time. Dolly loved Marion as one of her own children. With the assistance of her high self and her spirit guides, the fragment of Dolly was sent back to integrate with her own consciousness. Marion immediately felt stronger, with a clearer mind and better energy.

A few weeks later, Dolly fell and broke her hip. With trepidation, Marion visited her dear aunt in the hospital. During the week following the visit, she felt increasingly tired and depressed. In her second session it was discovered that the fragment had returned. Before sending the fragment back again, a remote releasement was conducted on Dolly. There were several earthbound spirits with her, including a deceased boyfriend who had given Dolly some of his mother's china and silver after her death. His mother was also attached, still angry that her son had given her beautiful things to this woman he wasn't even planning to marry. After they were released, the fragment was once again sent back, accompanied by her spirit guides. It did not return to Marion.

During the time of Marion's visit to see her aunt in the hospital, she played the tape of her first session for her cousins, Dolly's daughters. When they heard the conversation with the mind fragment of Dolly, they both recognized their mother's voice mannerisms.

A single session with a young woman revealed an interesting twist. Gwen, the subject, was well aware of the presence of Richie, her brother, who had died in an automobile accident some months earlier. The single car accident is often a suicide (MacDonald, 1964). She loved him deeply and she welcomed him to join her after his death. A scan of past lives revealed that they had been lovers in other times.

With very little explanation of his situation and the effects he had on his beloved sister, Richie expressed his love for Gwen and was ready to separate from her and move into the Light, but it appeared to be too far away. Since there was no resistance on the part of either of them to the release, this was an indication of interference. It turned out to be another entity attached to him. As he explored within his own being, he discovered the entity, but could not identify it.

The questions were addressed to this deeper entity.

T: "You, the one inside Richie, inside Gwen, step forward and speak. You the one interfering with these people, speak up."

C: "Yes, what do you want?"

T: "Who are you and what are you doing here?"

C: "I'm their mother."

She revealed that she was their mother and she had attached when Richie was about two years old. As mother was still living, this proved to be a separated fragment of her consciousness. Her possessive and overpowering love, along with her fear of inadequacy for the job of raising a child, had caused her to fragment and attach to her tiny son. Many cases of mind fragment attachment prove to be by a family member, most often a parent in this or a prior life (Crabtree, 1985, p. 160).

In the classic description of spirit attachment or possession, the living person is possessed by the spirit of a deceased person. Here is the reverse situation, in which a deceased spirit is possessed by a living person.

A fragment can also be the etheric form of a physical body part. An attached entity may have a history of amputation, either surgical or as the result of battle wounds. The severed part may or may not be present with the attached entity. If an entity brings up the experience of amputation, then the therapist must guide it in locating, reclaiming, and reconnecting its missing part before it is released.

The part is sometimes located in the hospital refuse disposal area or on the battlefield. It might also be attached to the client yet in a location separate from the entity. If the entity is released without the part, it can still be sensed and located by the client in a body scan. The part must then be sent to the Light to join with the fragmented entity.

If the attached entity died by decapitation, it may not be able to speak in the initial phase of the discovery process. The client may have a wordless feeling of distress. The therapist asks the question:

T: "If that feeling could speak, what would it say?"

The client fills in the words and the entity finds that its thoughts can be expressed.

As the story of the trauma unfolds, the therapist guides the entity to locate its head and to replace it upon the shoulders. That usually feels much better to the entity. Any remaining conflict is resolved and the entity is released into the Light.

If a mind fragment is discovered as an attached entity and it cannot locate its live physical body, it is not a mind fragment of a living person. The therapist directs the entity to locate and recover its other fragments, wherever they may be. They may be attached to one or more other people, or they may be attached or nested in other entities attached to living people. They may be found in a structure or other location associated with a prior-lifetime trauma. The entity is guided to recover the fragments, still attached by the silver thread, and to integrate them into the wholeness of their being.

Walk-Ins

This concept was popularized by Ruth Montgomery (1979). According to her, when a being from the Light wants or needs a functioning body for a specific purpose and a living person chooses to end this life cycle, an exchange can be arranged. Rather than suicide, which will destroy the vehicle, an agreement is made at a subconscious or superconscious level for the exchange. Some people can recall this agreement in the planning stage prior to the present lifetime. Others seem to be able to renegotiate the Life Plan in meditation or the lucid dream state.

If the concept is valid, the new being will have the memories of the original contracted spirit but no emotional attachment to the history. There may be less connection with family and loved ones after the exchange. The ostensible reason for the walk-in is to accomplish some work which will benefit others, some grand purpose.

Many people claim to be walk-ins. However, if their life seems to work no better than before, with no major changes, no new avenues of growth, then there is some doubt about the validity of the assertion.

This condition requires no treatment, just assistance. The person might be confused by a sudden change in life circumstances and might need some clarification of the process. The therapist familiar with the concept can assist the client to locate the agreement for the exchange and the actual event of the exchange itself.

The therapist can explore for attached entities, especially dark ones which might interfere with whatever work is to be done by the walk-in. After these are released, the work of the walk-in can proceed more effectively.

This exchange can be accomplished in a session with a capable therapist. This requires the assistance of the spirit guides under the direction of the High Self. The therapist must invoke the Light as protection against intrusion by opportunistic entities. The rescue angels who will be the guides for the retiring spirit must be present. When the new being is ready to come in and the contracted spirit is ready to leave, the old silver cord is disconnected and the new one is replaced in the connector site. Guided imagery of Light and healing are appropriate for closure on such a session.

The phenomenon of the walk-in spirit must be qualified. As in any spiritual manifestation, only a brief and limited knowledge is gained by observation of only a few cases. False assumptions and conclusions can be drawn from such limited information. A separate consciousness can influence a living person in varying degrees. The attached earthbound spirit, in its confused state, is focused on earthly concerns and interferes with the Life Plan of the host. The walk-in spirit ostensibly comes from the Light with some higher purpose to complete, some important function to perform, and replaces the contracted spirit who moves on to the Light.

Deeper exploration into the phenomenon suggests that the walk-in can merge a portion, some significant percentage, with the contracted spirit in the body. Complete exchange is not necessary. The walk-in can remain for a period of time, then disengage, leaving the original being in charge of his body. There are many possible variations and combinations, depending on the assignment or mission of the being from the Light.

Soul Merge

The soul-mind can split or fragment. The fragment can separate and follow closely the main portion of the consciousness in the physical body. It can attach to another person or move into the Light and return to the earth in a separate embodiment. Thus, a being may be incarnated in several physical bodies at the same time. This is termed parallel lives. These others can be contacted in the altered state of consciousness.

An earthbound spirit can attach to a living person but cannot merge or join the consciousness in a permanent way. It is possible that two soul-minds can choose to merge or join while they are in the Light. They can move into physical incarnation as one being.

An attached being may claim to be dispersed within the consciousness of the living host to such an extent that it cannot be reconstituted and sent on to the Light. A monad or individual spirit being can be so distraught with existence that it can choose to disperse completely into the greater consciousness, back to Source, thereby losing identity and self-awareness as a separate spark. These claims made by earthbound entities through the voice of clients must remain as speculations.

Elizabeth was a gentle woman of 60, tall, slender and a spiritual seeker. In one of her sessions she discovered an attached being. It had never been human, it was not dark, and it claimed to have been with her since the beginning, the experience of Oneness. It had never been anything but a spark. Its first memory was separating from Source stuck to another spark. The other spark was the being who was incarnated this time as Elizabeth. It had never broken away. It had never developed, just remained with Elizabeth through all of her spiritual journey. It had never known there were other options. It gladly agreed to return to the Light.

Past-Life Personality
During past-life therapy, the death scene is worked as described in the section, Clearing the Death (119). Only when the being leaves the earth plane and moves fully into the Light can the therapist be fairly certain the life described was that of the client and that the past-life therapy on that lifetime is complete. An attached entity, the earthbound spirit, can usually recall its life, the death scene, and the act of attachment, but has no experience of entering the Light at that time.

Certain stimuli, such as trauma or drugs, can reactivate an entire past-life personality into conscious awareness in the present time. This personality is aware of itself as part of the soul-mind consciousness of the person, appropriate in the past and not now. It is here for a specific purpose of its own or for the person's benefit. Such a case is described above in the section Alter Personality (250).

Millie was mentally healthy and well integrated. She used the drug MDMA (ecstasy) for recreational purposes. For the six hours following ingestion of the drug, she manifested a male personality who could speak only an Indian dialect, although she could write clearly in English. The integrity of the subconscious mind was somehow loosened by the drug and the personality emerged intact and took control. As the drug wore off, Millie regained her own normal well-integrated personality.

Later, in a session, the Indian personality emerged was elicited and was requested to speak in English. He claimed to be a past-life personality of hers and he was impatient with her spiritual growth. He claimed that her spiritual progress had been slowed by Millie's 20-year stint as a Catholic nun. After he communicated his impatience and love, he was cooperative and agreed to submerge and reintegrate. She had no further problem.

Past-life therapy is the treatment of choice for the reactivated past-life personality. It is inappropriate for the past-life personality to be active, interfering or dominant in the present time. It rightfully belongs in another era. Some form of emotional residue reactivates the personality, and this is processed to completion.

Ralph and Emmy had been married more than 30 years. After his second heart attack, their relationship began to deteriorate. In session, as they described the relationship and the heart attack, Ralph began to feel tingling sensations in his arms. He could not get any words or communication from the sensations. Emmy seemed to sense the words and was able to bring through the entity's communication.

During the time Ralph was in the emergency room after his heart attack, an accident victim was brought in. He was dead on arrival but his spirit was following the body. The spirit moved from person to person in the ER, looking for another body for his use. A past-life personality of Ralph recognized this spirit as a fellow warrior in Roman times and invited him in. This entity did not like Emmy and was creating discord between these two people. He willingly departed into the Light and the couple remained together.

The cases of Ralph, Millie, and Connie seem to indicate that the past-life characters or personalities are still intact within the subconscious mind. In most cases they are dormant and well integrated, though accessible in the altered state through regression therapy techniques. In some cases they are actively functioning, even interfering with the present personality and life circumstances. They can impact the life of the manifesting personality with annoying and destructive behavior. This is similar to the interference by an active subpersonality, a split within the personality due to a traumatic event in the present lifetime.

This must not be miscontrued as possession by a past life personality. This condition is past life interference or bleed-through, and past life therapy is the appropriate treatment of choice. A person cannot be "possessed" by either a subpersonality or their own past lives. Possession is, by definition, influence, control or takeover by a separate agent. Sometimes they are dormant, sometimes awake, but they are aware of present circumstances. They can impact the life of the manifesting personality with annoying and destructive behavior.

Thought Form

The thought form is a projection of consciousness. It can be in the form of an emotion such as anger, fear, or sadness. In this form, it can simulate an earthbound spirit in its effect on the host. As a thought form projected by a living person, it has no spark of God consciousness at its center, yet it seems to have consciousness, intelligence and purpose. It may have a mind fragment of the person who projected it.

Angie experienced what at first seemed to be an angry entity. Further probing revealed that in a past life she was a passenger on a sailing ship. The captain of the vessel was unscrupulous and attempted to force his affections on her, which she refused. Angry at her rejection, he pushed her overboard and she drowned at sea. His intense anger followed her as a thought form. In the session she forgave the captain. The thought form of his anger was dissolved by visualizing Light surrounding it.

A thought form can be a figure of some sort—for example, an imaginary playmate or protector that a child might wish into existence. A sorcerer, witch or black magician might conjure a spirit helper called a familiar spirit. The familiar spirit can be sent out to do the evil bidding of the conjurer. The thought form is connected to the conjurer by a cord of consciousness. A thought form can persist through lifetimes of its host. Since it is created by the sorcerer, it has no history, no memory of existence, prior to being conjured. Conscious beings are created by Source and can recall the experience of the Light.

Fantasy role-playing games such as "Dungeons and Dragons" can become terribly engrossing for teenagers who play. During the game players conjure or fantasize beings which are often given powers of destruction to be used against other players. Extensive involvement in this game can disrupt the reality perception of the young players. Numerous cases of violent crime and teenage suicide have been attributed to such participation. This game has led some teenagers into active participation in Satanism (Pulling, 1989).

The thought form created by the client in this or another lifetime can be eliminated as the client takes responsibility and chooses to cease creating the form. This might entail past-life therapy with the client to locate the actual incident when the thought form was conjured and resolving whatever emotions led to the act.

Inspirational Possession

Frederic Thompson was apparently influenced by R. Swain Gifford, a prominent artist who died in 1905. They had only a brief acquaintance prior to Gifford's death in January of that year. During that summer, Thompson gave in to overwhelming urges to paint. The subjects of the paintings were unknown to Thompson, yet on investigation they were found to be familiar to Gifford, in particular one of Gifford's unfinished works. In this well-documented case of possession, Thompson assumed the artistic skill of the deceased artist (Rogo, 1987, pp. 13-51)

Brazilian psychologist and psychic Luis Antonio Gasparetto produces works of art in the trance state, apparently transmitted by the spirits of the great painters (Villoldo and Krippner, 1986, pp. 6-18).

As a child, Rosemary Brown believed she saw spirits around her family. At age seven, Franz Liszt began to appear to her. She studied piano for a year as a child and a year and a half as an adult. Under the direction of and partial possession by Liszt, she gave excellent performances of difficult piano compositions.

Pearl Curran produced more than 4,000 pages of fine literary work over a period of 24 years. Patience Worth was the spirit who transmitted the work written in late Medieval English. Mrs. Curran had little education and limited exposure to English literature.

Matthew Manning went to boarding school at age 15. Prior to his leaving his father's home, there had been an outbreak of poltergeist activity. Furniture was rearranged; puddles of water appeared on the floor; there were scribblings on walls; faucets and lights turned on and off. In the boarding school which he attended, beds moved in the dorms, kitchen utensils rained into the dorms from out of midair, writing again appeared on walls. This ceased only when Matthew took up drawing instruments and began producing sketches, drawings and paintings, purportedly from deceased masters.

Robert Louis Stevenson credited his "little people," or "brownies," as he called them, for much of his literary output.

These cases are considered to be inspirational possession. There is no indication that the possessors are earthbound spirits. Loved ones in the Light can bring messages of assurance or assistance for ones still living. When they assume the familiar identity, there is recognition without fear.

Can higher beings impart skills to living people? Is it possible for a more advanced spirit to manipulate or control the mind and body of a living person and create art, prose or music such as these people produced? Such questions evade understanding.

The answers remain part of the Mystery.

Non-human Entities

The purpose of the first diagnostic question to the entity is to determine whether it has been human, alive in its own human body. If the answer indicates otherwise, the most likely possibility remaining is the demonic entity. The characteristics and behavior of these beings and the clinical approach to treatment are described in the section The Demonic (273). There are also many other types of spirit beings which affect living humans.

A tiny fraction of the 30 million species of insects in the world pose a threat to humans. Of the thousands of animal species, only a few are poisonous and deadly. Of the countless varieties of microorganisms, many are beneficial while others are parasitic, invasive and harmful. In the plant kingdom, a few are known to be harmful, even deadly, to humans. Many have proven to be beneficial and healing. In fact a large number of modern medicines were first derived from plant material.

So it is in the spiritual or non-physical level of reality. Of the myriad beings created and emanated by Source, a small fraction seem to be hostile to humans. Many others are friendly, loving, and helpful. It is up to each individual to use the spiritual gift of discernment of spirit. Human beings are admonished to test the spirits.

The spiritual realm is vast; only a small number of created beings choose to enter the cycle of human existence on this planet. Many beings however, seem to want to experience this level of reality. For some, this can only be done through the physical apparatus of a living human. There seem to be other beings of different levels of vibration currently existing naturally on the planet, such as the little people of folklore, and plant Devas.

Substance Spirits

Substance spirits are akin to plant Devas. Hallucinogenic and conscious-ness-altering drugs of plant origin seem to involve characteristic beings. People see them, feel them, and describe them in specific terms. An example of this type of being is "Mescalito," the spirit character associated with the substance described in the works of Carlos Castaneda (1969, 1971). When they are discovered as attached beings, they are sent to the Light, accompanied by angelic guides.

Little People

Occasionally a client will describe an ugly-looking character and call it a gnome, an imp or a troll. They are not dark or malicious; they just seem to be grouchy, mischievous, ornery, and try to get in the way. They are sent to the Light.

Experiments

Bioengineering and genetic manipulation may produce medical miracles in present times and in the future. There is also serious concern that some of the experimental effects may cause immense, irreversible and unalterable harm to living organisms, the inhabitants of this planet, including human beings.

In the time of Atlantis, the fabled continent which allegedly submerged beneath the Atlantic ocean some 14,000 years ago, biological experiments were also conducted on living beings. At the time it was possible for interspecies breeding to produce offspring. Supposedly, mythological creatures which were part human and part animal existed at that time. They were considered as "things" and were routinely enslaved and otherwise brutalized. Experiments and surgeries were performed on them to produce freaks for exhibition to the decadent crowds (Robinson, 1972, pp. 49-71). They were not ceremoniously buried after death but discarded in trash heaps or pits in the earth.

These strange creatures were of very low intelligence and yet they were created beings with evolving souls. The experimentation and brutalization so traumatized them that many remained earthbound in their agony. When they are discovered as attached entities, they are usually found in groups. The rescue

From the public domain color original, *Tomb For A Dying Earth*, by Jeff Seldin, courtesy AOL.

spirits from the Light are often recognized as the doctors or other experimenters who violated them in Atlantean times. These fearful beings cannot comprehend the situation and usually refuse to go with their former tormentors who want to atone for their errors in the earlier times. Other rescue spirits must be summoned from the Light. These pitiful earthbound spirits will finally reluctantly agree to accompany the rescuers.

Extraterrestrials

Some beings do not want to come through the Portal in the Light to engage in the reincarnational cycle of earth. They do not want to go through the process of preparation for the earth plane in the halls of learning and the planning stage. Not wanting to bother with human birth and maturation, they may selfishly attempt to attach to a living human and simply experience this world through the sensorium of that person. They sometimes attempt to displace the contracted spirit and take over the body completely.

Carla, a 35-year-old woman, was very upset and she burst into tears after observing a demonstration of a spirit releasement. Her tears finally subsided and the entity attached to her was able to speak. It was her brother in another lifetime on another planet in a different solar system. He followed her to this system but did not want to endure the whole process of becoming a human in his own body. He wanted to crowd her out or at least move her to one side and take over her body.

With very little explanation he realized the harm he was doing to his sister, whom he loved yet wanted to dominate in a chauvinistic manner. As he told of their life on their home planet in a distant space and time, Carla also recalled the love they had shared there and began to weep again, this time for the joy of that memory and the sadness over the loss.

He agreed to go and she agreed to release him, though the attraction of love was strong between them. More than a year later, she reported that many positive changes had occurred in her life as the result of the release of her ET brother.

The description of ET, or extraterrestrial, encompasses beings which come from a different planet, solar system, star system, even a different dimension. Some arrive here alone, while others claim to belong to groups, forming many such connections with living humans. It is not appropriate for these or any other discarnate beings to attach to living humans.

When the Light comes for these ETs, it often appears to be blue, green, silver-yellow, even violet, as contrasted with the golden white color of the Light of the reincarnation cycle of earth.

Spirit Guides

Spirit guides are non-physical beings who, by agreement, are assigned or chosen for service as advisors for other beings who choose to incarnate in human form. Most people can neither see nor hear nor feel the presence of their guides and so do not accept the reality of guides or guardian angels. Still others accept the actuality of spirit guidance and actively participate with these spirit helpers in everyday life.

The spirit guide comes from the Light and has its own source of energy. It does not use the energy of a person. The earthbound has not returned to the Light since death and must draw energy from the host.

Guides are non-judgmental, non-critical, non-intrusive, non-interfering, only give advice and guidance when it is sought, and have no earthly needs of their own. Earthbound spirits may be very egotistical in their attitudes and judgments and often satisfy their own very human needs and appetites through the sensorium and physical apparatus of the human.

The earthbound has its own agenda for living life. The guide has no agenda of its own. A spirit guide has no residue to impose on a person; the earthbound often inflicts its ailments on the host. The only purpose of the true spirit guide is to serve the incarnated being.

A spirit guide does not attach to the human in any way and cannot be exorcised. It carries a different energy. A person who is aware of spirit guides might describe them as "light," "floating," "sparkling," "tinkling like crystal." The earthbound is "shadowy," "heavy," "clinging," and sometimes interferes physically. The earthbound entity is of such low vibration that it is often not discernible by the spirit guide.

Sharon was 32 when she volunteered to be the subject for a spirit releasement demonstration at a conference. An attractive woman, she was standoffish in her attitude, with a somewhat angry expression on her face. Forceful in personality and a bit mannish in attitude and dress, her femininity was obviously diminished and suppressed. Sharon worked as a hypnotherapist and used her intuitive and psychic ability in sessions. She had good communication with her spirit guides, and they assisted her in her work.

The main entity who exerted the greatest influence was Joe, a soldier in the artillery who died in World War II. In that incarnation, Sharon was a buddy. She/he was killed when an incoming shell exploded near their gun emplacement. She/he fell back on Joe, who was wounded and not strong enough to extricate himself from beneath his buddy. Joe suffocated under the weight of the dead soldier and was angry because of it.

Joe waited in the intermediate place for his war buddy, whom he blamed for his death. As the being who was to be Sharon came onto the earth plane, Joe followed. He joined her in a moment of vulnerability during her childhood. He affected her femininity with his masculinity and his anger showed on her face.

With very little explanation, Joe realized the inappropriateness of his position, and agreed to leave. He offered to assist with the other weaker spirit attachments. Sharon was cleared. Her guide was available and was able to communicate through her voice.

T: "Were you aware of these entities, these spirits with Sharon?"

C: "We were aware of the energy but did not recognize it as such. But we will from now on."

T: "Are you aware of these energies in her clients?"

C: "We were aware of the energy but did not recognize it as such. But we will from now on. Thank you."

The spirit guide had learned something about spirit reality in the demonstration session.

At the closing luncheon of the conference, Sharon was dressed in a skirt and sweater. She commented that when she was preparing to come to the conference she wondered why she packed a skirt in her suitcase. She often found herself doing such things almost automatically and she considered it part of her guidance. She had thought to herself, "I wonder if there is going to be a costume party." This had been her attitude toward feminine attire in general.

Her appearance was quite comely. Her face carried no sign of the angry expression which was so familiar prior to the session. A few months later, she described her life as quite different than it had been before. She continued to enjoy her femininity and she carried it very well.

Occasionally, a spirit guide will respond to the questions of the therapist and will speak through the voice of the client in a deep altered state. It will refer to the client in the third person, as "he" or "she". It will offer information and insight which is usually not known to the person. There is often surprise and sometimes awe or reverence at this phenomenon, especially if it is a first-time event. The client may report a feeling of dissociation and loss of control of the voice mechanism. There is usually a feeling of deep trust and love for the guide in this experience.

Implants

Clinical practice with clients in session reveals that there are many sentient species in the universe. Some of these explore on scientific expeditions, much as our scientists explore the jungles, oceans and remote places on this globe. As our scientists probe and dissect animals to learn the secrets of life, so also do some of the extraterrestrial scientists probe human beings.

Clients have discovered such probes in various parts of the anatomy and in the chakras. These probes are non-physical in nature yet attached in a way which allows for transmission of information to the ET scientist's location. This can be a home base somewhere or a spacecraft hovering nearby.

In the altered state of consciousness, a client can visualize the probe, often a black cord, leading to the ET laboratory. The therapist directs the question to the experimenter. This information is transmitted to the ETs, who answer through the voice mechanism of the client, just like any entity in a remote releasement.

Janet was an intuitive healer, quite adept in her work and in her life. In session she discovered a probe in her third chakra, the solar plexus. She described a thin black cord which, in her perception, led two dimensions upward. It connected to a laboratory on some sort of spacecraft. As Janet visualized the place, the therapist called out to someone in charge of the lab. Janet described some sort of humanoid form and was able to repeat its words.

Yes, it acknowledged, there was a probe inserted at the level of her solar plexus. It was for the purpose of gathering information on the members of the human species.

T: "How many such members of the human race have you treated in this way?"

C: "About 3,000."

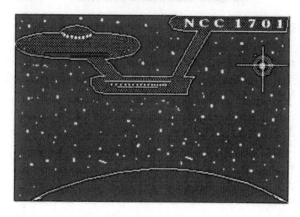

T: "This is a violation of an intelligent species. You have no right to interfere in this way."

C: "We did not know we were interfering."

The therapist borrowed from the concepts of the TV series *Star Trek*. It seemed to work.

T: "Cross connect us with your headquarters. We want to speak with your high command."

A few moments passed and Janet straightened in the recliner. Her voice took on a different tone; her manner was almost imperious.

C: "Yes, what do you want?"

T: "Your scientists have placed probes in 3,000 human beings without consent."

C: "Yes. They are gathering data."

The therapist again used the images from *Star Trek*, specifically the notion of the "Prime Directive": Non-interference with a sentient species.

T: "You are gathering data from unwilling subjects. Aren't you aware of the prime directive of non-interference? You are not to interfere with another sentient species."

C: "Yes, we are aware. We did not mean to interfere, only to gather data."

T: "We protest this violation of the prime directive."

C: "What would you like us to do?"

T: "We request that you withdraw your probes from every human being on this planet."

There was some hesitation, as if there was discussion in the background.

C: "We will withdraw the probes. We have gathered enough information."

T: "Thank you."

C: "You are welcome. Good-bye."

T: "Good-bye."

The commander was already gone. The scientist apologized and completed whatever task remained.

Janet came out of altered state as bewildered as the therapist. Are these visualizations valid? Are humans perceived by more highly developed beings as nothing more than subjects to be randomly probed, examined and tested, much like lab animals to an earth scientist? Several clients have experienced such probes, implants, and testing devices. The therapist must work within the paradigm which emerges as if it were real. At some level of consciousness, it is real for the client.

Author Whitley Strieber (1989) described his decidedly unpleasant encounters with alien beings. He claims they placed probes or needles in his skull. Many people have made similar claims of probes placed up the nose into the brain. Strieber has X-ray films of his skull showing a small shiny object beneath the surface on each side of his skull close to his ears. The doctors cannot identify these shiny objects.

In the time of Atlantis, the main source of power on the continent was a huge crystal which somehow generated energy by balancing cosmic power and earth power. This energy could be beamed to vehicles on land, on or under the sea and in the air. It could also be used to control the citizens.

Apparently, quartz crystals of varying sizes ranging from tiny ones of a millimeter or so in length to large ones nearly a foot long were surgically implanted in the bodies of the Atlanteans. The longer ones would be placed in the chest cavity just in front of or immediately behind the sternum. Smaller ones could be placed anywhere in the body, near organs, in the shoulders, the back, the wrists, even in the skull.

Somehow, the implanted crystals could be made to resonate with the giant power crystal and the citizen could be manipulated. The etheric pattern of the implanted crystals still remain with some people living today. The power crystal is supposedly inactive now but the intrusion in the body is somehow still having an effect.

The therapist calls on the spirit surgeons from the Light to be present in the session. These etheric doctors are asked to remove the crystal implants, including their etheric patterns in the client's physical, mental, emotional and etheric bodies, and to undo the consequences of the implants.

Some futurists have predicted that citizens of earth will someday have implanted in their brain a small computer chip. It will ostensibly carry vast amounts of information which will be available to the person. It will also be a connection with some central location, some central authority, some "Big Brother" who will be able to not only keep track of the citizen but to control him as well.

Group Mind

The power of group consciousness is well known. The effects can be seen in situations of mob violence such as lynchings, gang rapes and the phenomenon of mass frenzy in soccer stadiums, which has caused the trampling deaths of many fans.

The family unit produces a network of consciousness. Information can spread within a family system without overt communication, not only across space and time but across generations, sometimes through dreams. In addition to a personal or individual unconscious and a collective unconscious, there is another active, dynamic level of consciousness that deeply influences thoughts, emotions and psychic energy. This energy level exists in the powerful network of family patterns and emerges as the Family Unconscious (Taub-Bynum, 1984, p. 6).

The family unit is very strong in some cultures, and this affective energy level can accompany those who leave the neighborhood confines. Crabtree (1985, pp. 172-179) writes of two cases of group-mind possession experiences.

Marg came from a very clannish East European family. Distrust and hopelessness were the chief characteristics. They perceived life as being very hard and heavy; one could not expect to get ahead. She was not a strong-minded person but very vulnerable and easily influenced. She described the sensation of something descending upon her like a dark cloud which engulfed her in feelings of despair. This proved to be the group-mind influence of her family. The fact that she was easily influenced by those around her was a major factor in her therapy. The influence of positive-minded people pulled her out of her despair.

Maria was Italian. The group-mind influence from her family was described as a black cloud and it embodied hatred and violence toward women. For the men of the family, the violence was acted out against the women, and the women showed suicidal tendencies in response to the group-mind influence. A group of people gathered with Maria, visualizing white light surrounding her and protecting her from the black cloud. The effects of this were temporary but she felt that the repeated visualizations saved her from suicide.

This description of a black cloud exuding contempt and embodying hatred and violence is typical of the effects of the networks of demonic beings described in the section Release of the Dark Entity (325). The purpose of these networks is disruption of the family connections and interference with the potential for loving interaction among family members. The family is the primary and most important group relationship where love can be manifested. This is a natural target for the dark-energy beings.

Thomas was 45, intelligent, and well educated. He had been fighting against a possessing influence for nearly 15 years. It began quite suddenly and it almost destroyed him. He sought help from more than 100 healers through the years of his suffering. In a session with a clairvoyant, it was discovered that he and his mother had interchanged countless fragments and the threads between them appeared like a woven mat. These fragments were returned to their rightful place and all remaining cords were severed. A demonic being influenced mother and maintained tentacles into Thomas's shoulders, back, and spine, through which jolts of energy were shot at him. The energy source to this being was disconnected and it was released appropriately.

A shape was also discovered which attached to his back, moving up and down along his entire spine. He could hear this thing as a high-pitched buzz or whine. Various psychic healers described it as a buzzing pinwheel, an electromagnetic device, not demonic, not human, but exhibiting consciousness. A mind fragment from his mother was the consciousness of the electromagnetic agency. This was removed and returned to her.

The remaining mass appeared to be made up of mental and emotional debris from both sides of the family. On the father's side, there was history of murder, suicide, and institutionalization. On mother's side there was insanity and a very harsh attitude toward femininity and sexuality, along with the male arrogance of a German lineage. The energy of a personal curse from a past life of Thomas's added to the possessing agency. Anger and resentment, guilt and remorse made up the unfinished business from the present life, which added to this combination family group mind and thought form possessor.

With mother's influence curtailed and the demonic influence released, past-life therapy focused on the situation which led to the personal curse. The next step was traditional therapy on the emotional issues. There was some overall improvement, and for a short while there was some relief from the energy ostensibly projected from mother, but the tentacles from her seemed to reattach soon after the session.

At Thomas' request, his mother agreed to have a private session. She drove several hundred miles to the session, professing her willingness to do anything she could to assist her son. She listened to a description of the process and, with something of a derisive chuckle, absolutely refused to participate in the process. It was discerned clairvoyantly that there was a high percentage of fragmentation and separation, and a large defiant dark being in almost total control.

Within six months of this session, Thomas' elderly mother died. Thomas did not receive word of her death for over a month. During that time he began noticing improvements in his physical strength and endurance, apparently for no reason. In the months after receiving the news, his health and mental outlook continued to improve.

Logically, no conclusions can be drawn regarding mother's effect on Thomas. Experientially, Thomas remains convinced that much of his condition was due to his mother's disturbed sexuality and fragmentation, part of which attached to him. Though he was unaware of her death, there was improvement in his condition. She apparently did not attach to him after death, but moved in some other direction, hopefully into the Light.

Another type of group-mind possession experience closely resembles delusional disorder (APA, 1987, pp. 199-203). The victim is certain there is a person or group of persons, the so-called pseudo or imagined community of persecutors, either following, spying, or experimenting on them. There are voices or auditory hallucinations which direct the behavior and talk in the background. There is interference with work and personal life. The typical onset of delusional disorder occurs between ages 40 and 55. Other behavior may appear normal.

Another explanation for the condition is interference by demonic beings, either by directly insinuating the apparently paranoid thoughts into the mind of the victim or by influencing an actual person or group of people to interfere with the victim. The demonic beings can assume any form and simulate any person in dreams and spontaneous visual imagery. Their menacing red eyes cannot be disguised except momentarily, and this is the key to discernment of the dark beings. If the victim of such attack has clear visual imagery in the altered state, the beings can be detected. A clairvoyant can be employed to discern the nature of this interference.

Electronic Devices

In this modern age of ever-present power lines and vast numbers of electronic devices such as television, computers, and microwave ovens, people are almost constantly bombarded with electrical and electromagnetic emanations. Numerous disease conditions have been attributed to these unnatural energies. Many people become rather paranoid about these intrusions and some have felt as though they are being possessed and controlled by these devices.

This can signal the onset of delusional disorder. Another explanation for the condition of a person who claims such invasion is the onslaught of demonic attack. The distortion of thinking caused by the dark influence may lead to institutionalization and subsequent suffering by the victim and the family. This would be considered a victory by the demonic beings assigned to that person.

Dark Thought Form

During a body scan, a client might discover a black shape, from the size of a golf ball to something covering the entire body. This might prove to be disruption of energy from accident, surgery, or other physical trauma to the body, in this life or any other. It might turn out to contain elements of negative emotional energy generated by the client or projected from other people. It may turn out to be a demonic being or a generated—not created—individual dark-energy form. This form does not have a spark of Light, a spark of God-consciousness, yet does have a low consciousness and limited intelligence. Treatment is similar to treatment of the demonic.

The Demonic

The debate over the existence of good and evil will continue as long as there are people able to speculate and philosophize. What is offered here is the clinical framework of work with the demonic or dark-energy beings, purposely separate and distinct from any religious or spiritual teaching or philosophical viewpoint. The concepts of good and evil or God and devil may be products of the collective unconscious, coexistent with the human mind throughout the history of mankind (Hall, 1979, pp. 38-43).

From antiquity to the present day, religious literature has depicted the polarity of Light and Dark either as a schism within the God Source, or as arising from different Sources. Zoroastrianism, the religious philosophy founded in Iran around the sixth century B.C., held the dualistic view that Ahura-Mazda, the being of Light, was all good and totally separate from Ahriman, the being of Darkness. This religious dualism was the first to posit an absolute principle of evil, a clearly defined Devil. A basic tenet of this philosophy was that the forces of good and evil constantly war over the soul of man. (Russell, 1977, p. 99).

The dualistic position became more attenuated through the centuries and almost ceased to exist in the religions of Judaism, Christianity and Islam. In the Christian Bible, the story of Lucifer figures prominently in the history and future of the world and its human inhabitants. Jesus eventually came into the world to destroy the works of the Devil. Throughout these systems, however, it is Light which is foreordained to overcome the Darkness in some future time, though the Darkness wreaks havoc in the interim.

Blackness and the color black seem to cover an immense range of fearful and negative associations. The Void is deep and black. Chaos reins in that dark Void before the coming of Light. The dark of night is seen as a fearsome and dangerous time. Blindness is dark and helpless. The deep unconscious mind, the id, is seen as dark and chaotic. Depression and despair are described as black. Black indicates evil in many disparate cultures of the world (Russell, 1977, p. 66).

This focus on the color black in no way reflects on the race of people who choose to refer to themselves as Black. This is an unfortunate semantic coincidence. The pigment which produces skin color is melanin, which is predominantly brown in color.

In materialistic Western culture, even in the churches, the existence of an actual Prince of Darkness with legions of demons in his command is considered as symbolic, metaphoric, even mythical. Whether the force of Darkness is a

A Sampling of...

#1

#2

#3

#12

#4

#5

#11

Throughout the totality of human experience, people have attempted to symbolically depict the negative and positive influences in their lives. These samples are indicative of many cultures. This page: #1, *Ptah*, Egyptian God of Creation and Resurrection; #2, *Frigg* (Freya), the Nordic/Germanic Goddess of Dawn and Fertility; #3, *Vishnu*, Brahmanic divinity of The Preservation; #4, *Ho-Tu*, Chinese Charm Against Evil Spirits; #5, *The Good Spirit of the Blue Sky*, North American Indian; #6, *Amida Buddha*, The Boundless Light, Buddhist; #7, A Nordic Rune representing Heavenly Power; #8, *Hoo*, Japanese Phoenix, Prosperity; #9 A Nordic Rune used to Protect Against Witchcraft; #10, *Confucius*, Ethic and Moral; #11, *The Good Principle*, from Zoroaster's Oracle; #12, *Pah-Kwa and the Great Monade*—Chinese Charm against Evil Forces.

#8

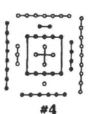

#6

#10

#9

#7

Cultural Symbolism

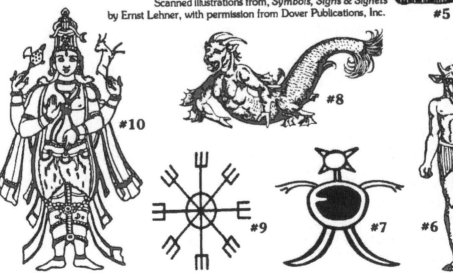

THIS PAGE: #1, **SET**, EGYPTIAN GOD OF WAR AND EVIL; #2, **MARA**, CONFUCIAN/BUDDHIST TEMPTER AND ARCH FIEND; #3, **DEMON OF DISEASE AND EVIL**, BABYLONIAN; #4, **SPIRIT OF EVIL AND HELL**, NORTH AMERICAN INDIAN; #5, **MICTLANTECUTLI**, AZTEC (COPAN, HONDURAS) GOD OF HELL AND DEATH; #6, **MINOTAURUS**, THE MONSTER, GREEK; #7, **BAD SPIRIT OF THE DARK SKY**, NORTH AMERICAN INDIAN; #8, **SEA DEVIL**, 16TH CENTURY OCCIDENTAL; #9, **GINNIR**, OLD-ICELANDIC RUNE FOR DIVINE, DEMONICAL; #10, **SHIVA**, THE BRAHMANIC DIVINITY OF THE DESTRUCTION; #11, **MEDUSA**, THE TERROR, GREEK; #12, **SENEMIRA**, THE BAD PRINCIPLE FROM ZOROASTER'S ORACLE.

Scanned illustrations from, *Symbols, Signs & Signets* by Ernst Lehner, with permission from Dover Publications, Inc.

figment of imagination, a product of the rantings of zealous prophets, a creation of the collective unconscious, or something else unknown, the speculations regarding good and evil will without a doubt continue unabated.

In clinical practice there is no need for concern regarding religious conjecture. Whether it is imagination, archetype, collective hallucinations, mass hypnosis, a projection of the beliefs of the therapist or something else again, the Dark Forces seem to exist in some form in this reality. Beings of Darkness seem to be present and actively involved in our personal and planetary evolution.

The Dark ones may serve spiritual evolution as a sort of "thrust block," from which a being can choose for the Light. The choice between Light and Dark may be the most important choice a spirit being can make. The Light and the Dark may offer a polarity of the same force to allow human beings to exercise the God-given gift of free will.

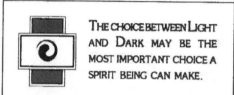

THE CHOICE BETWEEN LIGHT AND DARK MAY BE THE MOST IMPORTANT CHOICE A SPIRIT BEING CAN MAKE.

The shadow is described as the darker personal side of each human being, that which is dreadful or evil and disapproved of by the conscious mind. There are also evils which are acknowledged by the majority of men and almost universally rejected. The archetype of the devil is the nucleus around which these rejected elements gather, and it is from this nucleus that they in turn derive their power. The devil appears in some form in all religions and myths. He is seen as the eternal opponent of all that is good in the world (Cox, 1968, pp. 142-144).

For the purpose of this therapy, the devil or Satan or Lucifer is not categorized as a metaphor, archetype or as an existent being but as one aspect of the spiritual or non-physical reality, a historic construct which is meaningful in the therapeutic work with the client who presents these symptoms or images. This is not a statement of belief or disbelief.

The following is taken from the *New Testament, Revelations 12: 7-12:*

> And now war broke out in heaven, when Michael with his angels attacked the dragon [Lucifer.] The dragon fought back with his angels, [a third of the stars from the sky, a third of the heavenly host, the angels who fell] but they were defeated and driven out of heaven. The great dragon, the primeval serpent, known as the devil or Satan, who deceived the world, was hurled down to the earth and his angels were hurled down with him. Then I heard a voice shout from heaven, "Victory and power and empire for ever have been won by our God, and all authority for his Christ, now that the persecutor, who accused our brothers day and night before our God, has been brought down. They have triumphed over him by the blood of the Lamb and by the witness of their martyrdom, rejoice and all who live there; but for you, earth and sea, trouble is coming because the devil has gone down to you in a rage, knowing that his days are numbered."

And, continuing, in Rev. 12: 17:

Then the dragon was enraged with the woman and went away to make war on the rest of her children, that is, all who obey God's commandments and bear witness for Jesus (The Bible).

This rage of the dragon—Lucifer, devil, or Satan, as he has come to be known—seems to have extended beyond Christians to include all of God's children, that is, all humans. He (the masculine pronoun seems to be universally used for this figure) commands his minions, his legions, the fallen angels of all ranks to do his bidding (Montgomery, 1976; Russell, 1977; Linn & Linn, 1981).

Spirits invade us through chinks in our natural armor caused by emotional and physical trauma. If a person gives in to temptation and strongly indulges the carnal appetites or succumbs to the lure of occult or spiritualistic practices, he renders himself vulnerable to infestation by demonic energies (Basham, 1972, p. 123-136). Without the proper awareness of this condition, continuation of this life-style can lead to obsession by demonic influence, which is seen as quite common, and finally to full demonic possession, which some people believe to be rare. Diabolic possession, or possession by the devil itself (even more rare), is extremely dangerous both for the victim and for the exorcist (Rodewyk, 1975; Martin, 1976; Brittle, 1980).

The following list of criteria used in the diagnosis of acute demonic attack has been collated from eight different authorities. It indicates the type of phenomena to be accounted for.

A. Change of personality.
   1. Appearance.
   2. Demeanor.
   3. Sexual aberrations.
   4. Moral character.
   5. Intelligence.
B. Physical changes.
   1. Changed voice.
   2. Clouding of consciousness.
   3. Catatonic symptoms, falling.
   4. Epileptic convulsions, foaming.
   5. Anesthesia to pain.
   6. Preternatural strength.
C. Mental changes.
   1. Glossolalia; speaking and understanding unknown languages.
   2. Psychic and occult powers, e.g., clairvoyance, telepathy and prediction.
   3. Preternatural knowledge.

D. Spiritual changes.
    1. Affected by prayer.
    2. Reaction to and fear of Christ; blasphemy.
E. Deliverance possible in the name of Jesus Christ.

As the last item is a diagnosis in retrospect, it falls outside the range of pre-exorcism symptoms.

Granting that phenomena like these are observed in many different areas of the world by competent witnesses such as physicians and psychiatrists, numerous explanations may be offered (Lewis, 1976).

The word "possession," as used in the New Testament, comes from a Greek word which more accurately translates as "demonized." Some members of the clergy consider the earthbound spirits of deceased humans to be aberrant, unclean, and demonically influenced. The unwilling, unwary victim of obsession by this kind of entity is said to be demonized, and as such subject to the full force of deliverance ministry and exorcism. In such a service the "unclean spirit" is cast out, condemned to continue its confused wandering in the "outer darkness," perhaps to find another unsuspecting victim. There is no differentiation made between lost and confused souls of deceased humans and the demonic spirits which are among the legions of Lucifer.

The process of this therapy is distinct from any religious tradition or methodology of exorcism. The position of the Church fathers is adversarial and without compassion for the possessing spirit, even though it is a God-created being. Regardless of any religious belief structure, the dark-energy beings seem to exist. They conform to the historic description and classic behavior attributed to demons.

The paragraphs that follow contain descriptions of the characteristics and behavior of the demons, the legions, the minions of Lucifer, the dark-energy beings which may be encountered in clinical practice.

> THE DEMONIC BEINGS ARE ORDERED TO CAUSE AS MUCH PAIN, SUFFERING, DISRUPTION, CHAOS, DAMAGE, DESTRUCTION AND DEATH AS POSSIBLE TO AS MANY HUMANS AS POSSIBLE.

They hate humans, despise Jesus Christ, fear and loathe the Holy Names of Jesus, Mother Mary, Archangel Michael and others.

The numerous lower ranks of the dark hierarchy are not well ordered like a military command. Rather, they operate in something of a pecking order. They are not given power, they take all the power they can by force. The higher ranks seem to be well ordered and disciplined. There is no loyalty or devotion to duty. The dark ones obey out of fear. They are treacherous, disloyal, fiercely competitive with one another, undermine and criticize others, and are only roughly organized. They are all deceivers. They cannot be believed.

There are several categories of dark-energy beings. Ranging from the smallest, these are the disrupters, the threateners, the tormentors and the destroyers. There are others, but these seem to be the most prominent in clinical presentation.

Some are designated as watchers. They gather around the location of the spirit releasement session, either singly or in roughly circular concentric rows. Their assignment is to observe the process and to report back to their dark headquarters exactly what is happening. Occasionally a watcher will venture in to observe closely. They do not interfere.

For every demonic being attached to a living human or earthbound spirit, there are numerous replacements, standing roughly in rows behind them. If anything happens to the attached dark one, such as an exorcism, the next one in line will take its place.

When asked the name of their master they may call him Lucifer,

Top: A scanned classic representation of "Beelzebub," from *The Pilgrim's Progress*, circa 1892. **Below:** A 20th Century interpretation.

Satan, Father, Lord, the devil, the One, the Great One, the Eternal One, the Evil One, the Powerful One, the Dark One, the One who Knows, the Dark Angel, the Darkness, or something similar. They may refuse to state the name of their commander-in-chief or may deny any master other than themselves. Some of them are aware of God as their creator, but not as their master.

The lowest several ranks of the dark hierarchy are so numerous and unimportant to Lucifer that they do not have names. They will sometimes claim to be Lucifer, Beelzebub or Satan. This is a bluff. The therapist challenges such a claim immediately.

T: "What would he say if he knew you were using his name like this?"

C: "He'd be mad, he'd punish me."

This is a typical reply.

It seems that few if any single human beings are important enough for the Lucifer being to be involved directly.

The ones in more elevated ranks have harsh-sounding names. Gor, Bargok, Grrk, Zorkak, Blugok, Gorkor, Baak are typical of the appellations that such entities claim. They seem to be more intelligent, more sophisticated, more aware, and more knowledgeable, and have more to say about the situation. Some of the dark ones will take names such as Lust, Greed, Pride, Fear, Masturbation, Smoking, Hate, Pain to indicate their particular activity or influence on the host. This lends credibility to the practitioners of deliverance ministry who claim to heal by casting out demons of smoking, demons of anger or demons of lust, to name a few.

Individually and collectively in groups, they are ordered to cause as much pain, suffering, disruption, chaos, damage, destruction and death as possible to as many humans as possible. They thrive on the pain of human suffering. They interfere with any and every form of love. This includes self esteem in the individual, conjugal love for couples, and familial love and respect. Disruption of family unity is a primary assignment and a major accomplishment. They attempt to interfere with projects and institutions which can advance or improve the human condition.

The lower ones have little power and much bluster. They are of a low vibration and intelligence. They attempt to intimidate with idle threat. They behave like a tiny but noisy watchdog.

The lower ranks do not cause death directly but can induce self-destruction through undermining self-esteem. They can induce violence between people, which can lead to murder. They certainly influence the drug culture, from producer through the dealers to the end user.

The demonic beings have never incarnated in their own human body. If they recall a life as a human, it can usually be established with careful probing that the dark one was attached to a human being for a considerable time, attempting to exert some degree of control over that person. It came to identify with that human. Because they have never engaged in human form and interaction, they do not bring human physical or emotional residue and problems to the host.

A discarnate earthbound human spirit can behave like a demonic being, yet the client will perceive the attached entity as a human form. Probing within the discarnate will reveal a demonic spirit, or dark-energy form, nested inside, influencing the attitude and behavior of the earthbound spirit. This may have been an unwilling victim of demonic attachment or it may have been the result of purposeful summoning of the dark beings. Removal of the dark one will allow a normal releasement of the discarnate.

Many humans have made pacts with the devil for various self-serving purposes. Once these contracts are established, dark entities are assigned. The person is under the control of the dark forces. The spirit may remain earthbound after death and continue to serve the dark ones, often by attaching to another human.

Reincarnation is possible for the earthbound spirit who bargained with the dark forces. The attached dark one separates from the earthbound spirit and waits in the intermediate place. The human spirit goes through the process of the Light in the usual fashion, but the contract is again implemented immediately upon returning to the earth plane as the waiting dark one reattaches. The human servant of the dark forces continues his work through his own physical body, in bondage to and totally controlled by the dark ones from the moment of conception.

Feelings of anger, hatred, rage, and vengeance open the door for demonic infestation. These emotions distort the consciousness and the offer of assistance in the act of vengeance is accepted all too quickly and all too often.

The demonic entities gather at the time of death of a human being. If the dying person feels rage, hatred, or desire for revenge against the persecutors or killers, the dark ones will offer the newly deceased spirit a chance for revenge. This is often the beginning of the dark attachment. During a disaster involving many deaths, the dark ones

"A man whom seven devils had bound," scanned from *The Pilgrim's Progress*, circa 1892.

hover close by, waiting for the opportunity to ensnare confused spirits who need assistance. This is an important aspect of group rescue work, which is described in the section Rescue Work (371).

The dark beings can pass from one person to another through sexual contact, whether the contact is consensual or forced. They can also pass along the silver thread connected to an attached mind fragment.

They usually appear to the client as a circumscribed area of darkness, a black shape, sometimes with patches of red coloration or background. Some people clairvoyantly perceive the dark shape surrounded by a thin, pus-colored aura. They may first appear out of a swirl of mustardy yellow or an oily, sickly green background. Occasionally they resemble the typical red devil.

If eyes are visible they are sometimes a piercing black, more often red like burning coals. Much less often they appear as a menacing orange or sinister and yellowish like an angry wolf. This has an important bearing on the releasement process for earthbounds. The dark ones can simulate the familiar form of a loved one. They draw this image from the mind of the newly deceased spirit or attached earthbound. However, the eyes, the windows of the soul, will give them away.

The guiding spirits who come for the earthbounds must have clear eyes. The deceiving demonic beings will attempt at the last moment to claim a tired earthbound on the way to the Light. The demonic beings can simulate shiny eyes for a brief time but the shininess appears more like a brassy luster, rusty chrome, or cold ice than pure light shining through.

They growl, snarl or hiss, sometimes exhibiting a red tongue in addition to red eyes. Depending on the mental state and educational and religious background of the client, this can cause fear. This is their objective.

They can appear to the client in any form. Other than the black growling blob, they appear as snakes, spiders, scorpions, lizards, vultures, crows, ravens, bats, dogs, wolves, gargoyles; almost always glaring with red, angry eyes, frequently with hideous open mouths full of sharp teeth. They seem to be able to tap into the mind of the host, drawing on the fear-provoking images in the person's memory banks.

They are extremely hostile, arrogant, egotistical. They swear profusely, using obscenity and foul language but never profanity. They never utter any Holy Names. The client may refuse to repeat verbatim what they say.

They understand only the energy of the lower three chakras: survival, fear, threat, lust, greed, power, antagonism, competition, control, bullying. This resembles the human ego at its worst.

They do not understand love, compassion, sharing, humor, loyalty, devotion, happiness, joy, or fulfillment. There is no reward for their services to their master. They are allowed to continue to exist and they are not punished as long as they continue to obey their orders. They continue to perform their duties because they think there is nothing else. It is just what they do.

They do not ask questions except in aggression, hostility, and arrogance:

C: "Who do you think you are?"
    "What do you think you're doing?"
    "Do you think you can make me leave?"

The therapist must never answer their questions. This would give the demon the position of leader or controller. The questioner has the upper hand. The therapist continues the questioning.

They are cold and rough to the touch. This is extremely important in the release process of earthbound spirits. If there has been demonic involvement, either with the host or the attached earthbound, there is very likely to be a deceiver spirit posing as a guiding spirit of the Light. The true guide from the Light is warm, soft and strong as they take the hand of the attached spirit.

The energy of Lucifer may attempt to channel through the client. He is exceedingly cool in his demeanor, highly intelligent, logical, manipulative, cunning, haughty, almost regal in bearing, and absolutely certain of his position and his right to inflict suffering on humans. The therapist need never engage in a battle of wits with this being; it is a lost cause from the outset. Lucifer is a consummate linguist and debater.

If the client recognizes the Lucifer energy, the therapist cautions her:

T: "Repeat his words and do not under any circumstances allow
    him to come into your body or even use your voice."

The therapist directs the client to establish the boundary and refuse permission to the entity, as described in Remote Spirit Releasement (362).

> C: "I do not give you permission to approach me. I refuse you permission to enter my body or use my voice. I do not give you permission to touch me or influence me in any way. I will repeat your words."

And to the Lucifer being, the therapist directs this command:

> T: "In the name of the Light, stay back from her. She does not give you permission to come in or join in any way. She refuses permission to control her mind or body. Do not touch her body in any way. Speak your words and she will repeat your words."

The therapist may invite this fallen angel to go to the Light accompanied by the Archangel Michael. He will refuse. He might say simply, "Not yet."

Frequently, a client will entertain delusions of grandeur, insisting it is Beelzebub himself who is residing in her. It seems almost a point of pride that only the highest-ranking dark being would approach her in this way. The first focus of the therapy must be the delusional thinking and inflated pride.

The dark beings can be discerned by some clairvoyants. The more powerful ones appear larger and darker.

The demonic beings do not have attached entities, as such. They have not been possessed by another. They sometimes have layers of darkness or other dark ones superimposed and adding power for some specific purpose. This can be seen clairvoyantly.

The demonic attachment can be a recent addition during this lifetime, or it may have been assigned eons ago. Curses and spells are maintained in place by demonic beings.

The commander of the lesser demons assigns them and then forgets them as long as they continue to perform. If they fail in their assignments, this somehow gains the attention of the commanders. Punishment in the pit awaits those dark ones who fail.

They sometimes work alone, in small bands or as part of larger dark networks. The networks focus on specific groups of people. The target groups assigned to the various dark networks include: families, women, men, gays, lesbians, physicians, healers, spiritual students of any path, spiritual leaders of any path, popular leaders of any kind, corporations and their officers, members and leaders of the Catholic Church, the fundamentalist churches, the born-again Christians, school children, political leaders, police personnel, drug users, or any other group of human beings.

The networks and their directors can be assigned to specific geographical locations, titles, offices, or ranks. It is not so much the person who holds the rank or title but the office itself that is the target. The dark influence passes to anyone unfortunate enough to hold the title or earn the rank.

Described in the Pauline epistles of the Bible, the angels (principalities and powers) were delegated by God to rule the world. The devil is also associated with these principalities and powers in their role as rulers of the universe. It seems that certain high dark beings are in charge of the activities of the dark forces in certain areas of the world. The power behind the Roman empire appeared to be the dragon-devil of the Apocalypse (Kelly, 1974).

The aim of the therapist is to locate the director of the dark network. The network spreads to many other people in the world. Locating, capturing, and releasing to the Light any director and his network has the potential of relieving much suffering in the world.

If the dark ones fail in their assignment, they are punished in a deep, dark, cold pit, all alone for a very long time. They are threatened with annihilation, extinction, or ceasing to be. The term "death" is rarely used. This is a function of living physical bodies. After suffering in the pit for a significant duration, they are retrieved and given another mission or project in return for the promise of more perfect obedience. They are promoted in rank and assigned subordinate demons to command. The ones who have attained some rank or stature and who command underlings have certainly been in the pit. They acquire another layer of blackness during their stay in that hell.

They are kept in dark bondage, forced into absolute obedience and controlled by three primary deceptions:

1. They don't know there is a spark of God within them as a created being, a fallen angel. They are told by their superiors that there is nothing within them but darkness. This is the first deception. The denial of God is a deception of the first magnitude. Once they believe there is no spark within, they believe they can be annihilated and they believe the light will cause harm. They will obey without question any orders that are given.
2. The second deception is that they can be destroyed, they can cease to be. This is the constant threat under which they exist. Survival is a major motivation.
3. The demonic beings nearly always fear the Light. Their commander convinced them that it burns and that they should stay away from it. This is the third deception by which they are controlled. Of course, if they avoid the Light, they will never learn anything about it, and the deceptions will remain in place.

The therapist guides the dark entity in discovering these three deceptions, in reverse order. This is the heart of the release process for the demonic beings.

Treatment of the Entity

The sole purpose for therapeutic treatment of the attached entity is the resolution of any remaining issues which maintain the connection with the host. It is not appropriate to attempt therapy of any kind with the entity for any purpose other than releasement. This step of the process is aimed toward bringing the entity to the point of choosing freely to release from the client and move into the Light. Any remaining reluctance or resistance on the part of the entity may result in less than complete separation.

The therapist cannot physically expel an entity. There is nothing to grasp or grab onto. Verbally demanding that the entity leave is unrealistic and ineffective in most cases. After the therapist has directed a forceful command at the entity to leave, the entity may be silent. Both the client and the therapist may be under the illusion that the entity is gone, when in fact it is just hiding and avoiding contact. When the relevant issues are resolved appropriately, the entity will agree to leave.

The most direct approach is to ask the attached entity what keeps it here and what it wants and needs from the host. In most cases it will describe to the therapist the exact nature of the problem. The task of the therapist is to assist the entity in resolving that problem. The therapist focuses on obtaining for the entity what it wants and needs, if the fulfillment of that desire is beneficial for the entity and not detrimental to any one else, especially the host. Everything the entity wants and needs is present and available in the Light.

In cases of painful emotion, the aim is resolution of the issues and healing the pain. If the entity seeks revenge or retribution against the host or someone else, this hostility and aggression must be defused and eliminated. The entity must cease the damaging behavior; the solution cannot in any way cause detriment to the host. The expression of vengeful feelings alerts the therapist to the probability of demonic influence. This must be uncovered and resolved before the entity can begin to clear its own emotions.

The compassionate therapist may be tempted to assist the discarnate in resolving other issues which are obvious. The therapist trained in past-life therapy techniques may be drawn to assist in the spiritual growth of the entity through extensive past-life work. It is not appropriate to impose the emotional and physical traumatic memories of the entity on the client. Whatever karmic burdens and debts are accumulated here on the earth plane must be resolved and discharged here in the physical body of the one who incurred the responsibility, not through the physical, mental and emotional apparatus of another person.

Just Plain Stuck

Many attachments seem to be random, accidental and totally unintentional. No connection can be found between the entity and the host. No animosity exists between them, and the entity exerts little influence. As the result of an accident of time and location, some quirk, sometimes even comical circumstances, can lead to the attachment. The surprised entity, oblivious of the spiritual reality, unaware of any other place to go, simply gives up and settles in.

Florence, a rather quiet and refined lady, was employed by the U.S. Navy prior to retirement. After World War II, she worked in the Panama Canal Zone. For weekend recreation she and friends often drove into the country, exploring old Panama. Florence described a recurring scene which sometimes came to her in dreams, sometimes in waking reverie. While relaxing after a picnic during one of her Sunday outings to the country, she experienced this scene: She seemed to lift out of her body, float up the rise of the hilly meadow where she dozed, fly upward toward craggy mountains covered with tropical vegetation, and then, after a banking turn, zoom back down toward the valley. She had no explanation.

Returning to the Canal Zone one Sunday afternoon, she and her friends (a young navy man was driving) drove past an old house that was widely reputed to be haunted. She felt a shudder of fear as they went by the house. The entity she discovered in her session was a sailor who had died in the area about a century earlier. Being a rough and tumble sort of fellow, he had no interest in the Light or anything else of a spiritual nature. As he emerged from his body, he lifted up through the hills, floated into the mountains, turned and soared back to the valley, finally locating himself in the house. The reputation was valid. He was the haunting spirit.

The spirit sensed the group approaching the house. He felt a kinship with the young sailor and thought he could enjoy some good times in the body of the young man. He described leaving the house and aiming at the approaching automobile. As he sped toward the driver he overshot and landed on Florence. There was no discoverable connection between them in this or any other lifetime. He simply made a mistake. He wanted to enjoy life as a young man again. He was quite frustrated that he missed his chance and got stuck with this woman.

He was not strong enough to exert much influence over her and his desire for the good times was totally thwarted. He was eager to leave and happy to go to the Light.

Call on the Light

The therapist softly speaks to the entity:

T: "I call on the Light. I call on the presence of the Light, right here, right now. The Light is a place which is far more beautiful than anything you could imagine. You will be taken care of; your every need will be met. You will be cared for by loving beings. There is no pain or punishment in the Light. It is not a place of judgment. There is neither anger nor fear in the Light. You can rest as long as you like; you will be safe. When you are ready to awaken you will find classes and great halls of learning where you can prepare for your next life on the earth. Finally, there is a planning stage where you will be advised and counseled on the details of your choices for the coming incarnation. You will be welcomed home to the Light. How does that sound to you, right now? Look around, how does that feel to you, right now?"

Some discarnates have been unsuccessfully seeking the Light and this is all they need. The therapist directs the entity to look for the Light:

T: "Focus upward through the ceiling, through the roof, look right up there. What do you sense? What do you perceive?"

In many cases this is all that is necessary. The entity perceives the Light immediately and is ready to go. However, some caution is advised. It is too easy to get lost on the way to the Light especially if one attempts the crossing alone. Therefore, the therapist asks the entity:

T: "Is there someone there in the Light? Is there someone there that you recognize?"

The Light always comes, and a guiding spirit almost always comes to assist.

The Reality of Death

Many spirits are simply confused and do not know they are deceased. The rightful path of progression for the newly deceased spirit leads to the Light. It is the next step in the spiritual evolution.

The therapist gently asks the confused spirit the open questions:

T: "What happened? What happened to you?"
"What happened to your body?"

The earthbound spirit is often fixated in the death trauma. These open questions will stimulate the recall of that experience. For many people, death comes very peacefully, even during sleep. Many are not aware there has been any kind of transition. For these entities the open questions will stir the memories of dying.

Carefully and gently, the therapist can ease the being through the realization of the death experience, the ensuing confusion, the act of attachment, and through the emotional steps of denial and anger to the peaceful acceptance of the finality of physical death. With this knowledge, the entity is usually ready to move on.

Shared Past Life

Many earthbound spirits still cling to erroneous religious beliefs they held while alive. Fully 80% of the religions of the world accept the belief in reincarnation and karma, the law of retribution and balance. Christian-based denominations have rejected the concept of repeated embodiment since the Second Council of Constantinople in 553 A.D. The new belief is based on the notion that Christ died for people's sins so they don't have to take responsibility, yet the wages of sin is said to be death. It is a confusing dichotomy.

A brief explanation is offered to the entity regarding the spiritual progression of a conscious being who chooses the particular path which includes Earthly life. The journey began with the original separation from Source, continues through the cycles of rebirth as a human being, eventually leads to rejoining with the Oneness of Source. If the entity rejects the idea of reincarnation, it is guided to recall one or more of its own past lives.

> T: "Recall another time, another place, when you lived on earth. Were you a man or a woman?"

Depending on the response, the questions can continue.

> T: "Have you ever known this person you are with, _____(the client), in another time when you were both in your own physical bodies?"

Bringing the connection with the client together with the focus on another lifetime often brings recognition, acknowledgment of the process of reincarnation, and the prior-life interaction which led to this attachment.

An entity may be fearful of heavenly punishment for perceived sins—or karmic retribution—committed in the life just past. In brief, the concept of karma states that every individual is responsible for his or her every thought, motive, intention, action, behavior, and the impact of that behavior on other people. For example, if one person kills another person, the first person bears the responsibility for having taken the life of the other. At the same time, the other person bears the responsibility of agreeing to the interaction for the purpose of balancing an earlier action or for learning about the experience of dying in that way.

There are several ways to balance karmic debt. For example, taking the life of another person is considered a crime—a violation of the free will of the victim—and incurs a major karmic debt for the perpetrator. The killer can experience a similar fate in a future time and can die at the hands of another killer, thereby balancing the karmic ledger. Of course, this places a similar karmic burden on the second killer, even though the first one needed the experience to balance his past action. This is the downward spiral of karmic retribution.

Another way to balance the act of killing is to save the life of another person. A person who brings disruption and destruction to other people can balance this behavior by performing beneficial duties for these same persons or other people in subsequent lifetimes. There is some karmic wisdom in the legal system in the case of a convicted criminal being assigned to perform public service as part of the sentence. Incarceration and capital punishment only contribute to the downward spiral of reciprocal karmic retribution. It corresponds to the Biblical edict of "an eye for an eye." It is simply meaningless, pointless revenge.

The entity may understand the concept of karmic balancing, yet still be fearful of punishment and pain in the Light. Guilt over perceived wrongs to others may interfere with the willingness to move toward the Light. It may not feel like it deserves to go to Heaven. Fear and guilt are processed in the same manner as any conflict stemming from a traumatic event sequence. Therapy moves quickly for an entity, especially if it includes past-life involvement.

Choice to Return

For some earthbound spirits, there is little memory of the Light. The entity can be skeptical regarding all that the therapist has attempted to relate about the Light, and very stubborn. The therapist is safe in offering this choice to the entity:

T: "How's this for a bargain? If you don't like it, you can come back. The choice is yours."

Since the stubborn, independent spirit needs to maintain control—no one is going to push it around or make it do anything it does not want to do—this is a sound move on the part of the therapist and a compelling offer for the entity. When spirits go to the Light, they don't come back. It's too good.

Saying Good-bye

The subconscious mind loves ritual. The performance of rituals signals a beginning or an ending, with nothing dangling, nothing left undone, no unfinished business. Graduations, weddings, and funerals are examples of ritual celebrations of beginnings and endings. A good-bye kiss between husband and wife is also a ritual.

Communication which is withheld or incomplete, such as long-held grudges and resentments between lovers or husbands and wives, represent unfinished business. If these things are not resolved in the present lifetime, the emotional and physical pain of the unfinished business will prompt the beings to come together in future lifetimes in similar situations which offer the possibility for completion at the human level. The reward for this completion is peace and love.

Lucille, an attractive middle-aged woman, was widowed some years prior to the time of her session. She was still struggling with the pain of separation. Her husband, Dale, had been a commercial airlines pilot flying cargo planes. As the result of a spat over something inconsequential they had parted one morning in anger without so much as a good-bye kiss. He died that day when his plane crashed. The pain of this had never ceased for Lucille. Her lament was that she had not even kissed him good-bye. There was no completion, no resolution.

In the altered state she discovered, by direct questioning and body scan, that he had not attached to her.

> T: "In the name of the Light I call to the spirit of Dale, Lucille's husband who died in this lifetime."

The invocation of Light is spoken first, then an exact descriptor (as stated by the client) of the spirit is used to prevent a deceiver from interfering. It is possible to contact a deceased loved one in this manner even if they have gone to the Light. This request is offered as a sort of prayer.

Dale soon responded and Lucille discovered that he had not gone to the Light. She was able to communicate with this spirit and she apologized for the altercation. They expressed their love and said good-bye. For her, this was completion. Did this process eliminate the need for another lifetime together? This speculation cannot be answered. Such answers remain part of the Mystery of the spiritual reality.

Any interference with the flow of love is too much interference. Any time spent in resentment or grudge is too long. The marriage bed can be a place of joy or literally a hot-bed of seething rage. Many young women have been advised by Mama that they must never go to sleep while mad. Anger is an enormously damaging emotion. Love is the healer.

An entity can remain with a living person just because the two never had the chance to say good-bye to each other. The living person may feel the pain as much as the entity. Once the entity is discovered, identified, and acknowledged, this may emerge as the only reason it stayed. These two spirit beings, one with a body and one without, can speak their good-byes, usually amid tears and expressions of love. There is a great feeling of completion for both the entity and client.

After resolving the conflict which maintains the attachment between the entity and the client, all there is left to say is good-bye, with love.

Overcoming Resistance

The Light always comes at the time of death. In the releasement process, the entity is directed to look up and describe what it perceives. If the conflicts are resolved and nothing else remains to be processed, the Light is described as close by or surrounding the attached spirit. The guiding spirits are usually present or they come quickly when summoned. If the Light is perceived as distant or not very bright, there is some upset or emotional residue which still requires processing and resolution.

If the Light is perceived as grey or covered by dark clouds, this is an indication of dark interference. The focus shifts to the treatment of the demonic intruders.

The process of releasing the attached spirit into the Light can be accomplished quickly in many cases. It is the entity who makes the final choice to go. If there is reluctance to separate or resistance to the process, it is the therapist's job to determine the source of the resistance and to bring resolution to the situation.

THE LIGHT ALWAYS COMES AT THE TIME OF DEATH.

The resistance may be mental, emotional or physical. It may involve the entity or the host. It may stem from this life or a prior lifetime. There may be various other entities involved. The Light is the next step in the spiritual progression or evolution for the discarnate. The living host has the right to pursue this life unencumbered with spiritual parasites. Anything which interferes with the spirit releasement process is considered resistance.

A person with an attached entity might frantically demand that the entity leave immediately. This does little or no good. The therapist might demand that the entity leave. The spirit defies the therapist and easily resists this effort. In a classic exorcism, a demonic entity may be expelled by the demand to leave in the name of Jesus Christ. After the exorcism, it can return to the afflicted person, attach to another person, or to the exorcist.

The earthbound spirit of an agnostic or atheist has no respect for the Holy Name. A homeless alcoholic derelict may die in some gutter or back alley, the victim of continuous drunkenness. This spirit may find a living person in a bar and attach with the hope of getting just one more drink. The name of the Son of God will have absolutely no effect on such an entity.

An exorcism may result in the expulsion of an entity. The increased energy created by connected breathing may eject an attached spirit. An intrusive spirit may detach after the application of static electricity, as described in the work of the Wicklands (1924), or electroconvulsive therapy. If the entity in these cases is not released into the Light it can return after the exorcism or as soon as the client's energy is back to normal level. This may appear to be resistance to leaving on the part of the entity, or unwillingness of the host to let go. In fact it is neither; the process was simply incomplete.

Unwilling Host

The person who is host for the entity may be unwilling to release the attached spirit. This may stem from a deeply loving and needy relationship between the two before the death of the one who became the attached entity.

Sue was 27 and divorced. Her brother Johnny had committed suicide about six months before her session. Seriously contemplating suicide herself, she smoked incessantly, was thin and unkempt, and her body shook nervously. About the only thing that kept her from death was her love for her five-year-old daughter and her deceased brother's little boy, who was living with her.

Johnny had been in trouble with the law since childhood. At 21 he was still involved with crime, addicted to drugs, and just didn't want to face another day in the hell of his life. He joined Sue immediately after his death. She loved him dearly and welcomed his presence. A past-life exploration revealed that they had been lovers in previous lives and both had resisted the desire to repeat that interaction in the present life. Johnny urged her to commit suicide so they could be together. She nearly acceded to this selfish demand, yet sought help through this therapy.

In the session she finally agreed to let him go, although he was not willing. A search uncovered another entity attached to Johnny. It was their mother, who had died by her own hand when Johnny was about nine years old. She had attached and interfered with her son's life from that time forward. She was still interfering with both of her children by pushing for the suicide of her daughter. Mother did not want to leave without both of them.

The guiding spirits who came for them were Sue's two grandmothers. The paternal grandmother died before Sue's birth. She burst into tears as she recognized this grandmother from pictures. These two exerted enough persuasion on Johnny and his mother that they agreed to go. Sue wished them love with a tearful good-bye.

Within a few months, Sue's health had improved considerably, she no longer shook, no longer thought of suicide, and had enrolled in college. She finally had something to live for.

A young couple wanted to explore their past-life connection together. They were in the process of divorce and they sincerely wanted to separate as friends. They wanted to resolve any unfinished business before the divorce. They did not want to have to come back together again in another lifetime to handle the problems they had not faced and resolved in the marriage. During the past-life work, a female entity was discovered with the man. She was a comfort to him in this time of stress and he refused to release her.

Her connection held overtones of jealousy and possessiveness, but to him the comfort he received from her outweighed the cost at that time. The therapist cannot insist on separation and release of the entity if the host is unwilling or unready. It is not the duty of the therapist to force this choice on the client. Education about the process and the detrimental effects of entity attachment is necessary for the client to make an intelligent choice about releasing an attached earthbound spirit. The therapist must abide by that choice.

An earthbound spirit can be quite clever, even beguiling, in its arguments and pleas to remain with the host. Dana was a 50-year-old real estate agent. She had recently completed training as a hypnotherapist. In her initial session, she released dark-energy beings and several earthbounds. There were others, but she was too tired to continue. She was aware of a strong male spirit which was still present. The therapist recommended that she call for another appointment in a few weeks when she felt it was the right time. She agreed.

Dana called the very next week, quite upset with what had just happened. Her home was in a mountainous area near the town where she worked. On the drive home from her office, she suddenly found herself on an unfamiliar mountain road with no knowledge or awareness of how she had gotten there. It was about a five-mile drive back to the familiar road which led to her home. She was understandably upset. She made an appointment.

The day before her appointment, she called to cancel the appointment. She said she and the male spirit had reached an understanding and she was going to work it out herself. She thought she could handle it on her own. Her mind was made up. She did not explain what they had worked out or how she was going to handle it. She did not call again.

An entity may offer advice and assistance in the form of psychic information or may promise to divulge metaphysical and spiritual truths to the host. This is quite an enticement for many naive people who are new to metaphysics and eager to learn.

Unwilling Subpersonality

If a subpersonality was formed at the time of a trauma, it can attract a discarnate spirit to soothe the trauma or fulfill the need which first caused the split. The subpersonality may still cling to the entity for comfort.

Joan, a female client about age 40, disclosed that she had not had a meaningful love relationships with another person and did not particularly miss the interaction. She suspected that an attached entity was at the root of this situation. She explained that her father had died when she was about six years old. She recalled standing beside his grave and looking down at the coffin. She knew her daddy was in there, and did not understand at all why he was not coming back. At the time, she was wearing black patent leather shoes and a pinafore dress, and she wore her hair in long pigtails.

Direct questioning elicited a discarnate almost immediately. This one was a nanny who had loved children when she was alive. In spirit she had felt drawn to the location of a cemetery where a little girl stood looking quite forlorn. The child was dressed in black patent leather shoes and a pinafore dress, and her hair was in long pigtails. The nanny came to comfort the child and she had stayed. The child needed no one else; she had her nanny. The nanny was quite ready to leave but could not seem to lift off toward the Light. The guides from the Light were present. There were no other entities attached to the nanny and there was no unfinished business keeping her attached, apparently no resistance on her part.

The therapist addressed the entity:

T: "Is there a part of this woman that is holding on to you?"

C: "Yes, the little child standing beside the grave."

The therapist directed the client to visualize the scene at the graveside, to kneel down by the little girl in pigtails and hold out her arms toward the little one. She described the child turning and running into her arms. Her arms wrapped around herself as she described the feeling of the child hugging her so hard. It felt wonderful.

The therapist called softly to the nanny:

T: "Can you go now?"

C: "Yes."

She moved into the Light as the client continued hugging the little girl, her own subpersonality, her own inner child.

The adult is the only one who understands what the child went through, the pain and loss, the anger and frustration. The adult is the only one who still cares about the incident. The parents known by the child are now much older, if not deceased, and only see their child as the adult she has grown into. The child subpersonality is asked to trust her own adult self, the one she became. The evidence proves that she survived the trauma which caused the split. She need no longer continue to exist in the void of that suffering.

Traditional therapists are recognizing the techniques of inner child healing and subpersonality work as very important avenues of therapy. These techniques are essential in this therapeutic modality.

Unfinished Business

ANYTHING PERCEIVED AS IN-COMPLETE IN A DECEASED PERSON'S LIFE MAY BE ENOUGH TO HOLD THE SPIRIT HERE.

Anything perceived as incomplete in a deceased person's life may be enough to hold the spirit here. This can pertain to emotional interaction with another person involving anger and resentment, guilt and remorse, and most especially ungratified, unfulfilled and unexpressed love.

The unfinished business can be an incomplete project, unfinished invention, or aborted mission. The entity is assured that there is absolutely nothing that it can do to continue the effort. It will usually protest.

The spirit of one of the astronauts who died in the Challenger disaster was discovered near the launch facility by a psychic therapist who understood this work. She was angry because of the aborted mission and the unfinished work. Still, the tragic deaths of these fine people led to great improvements in the space vehicles and higher safety standards. This is seen as part of their accomplishment. As she sensed the validity of this, she agreed to move into the Light, her work truly complete and not at all what she thought it was meant to be.

The therapist can ask questions which assist the entity to see the truth of the situation.

> T: "What have you accomplished on the project since you left?"
> "Is the invention any nearer the finished stage since you joined this person?"
> "Have other people continued with the work you started."
> "Can you really accomplish anything in this way?"
> "What really happened?" (Open question.)

The emotional residue is resolved. The traumatic event of the death is processed.

> T: "What was the purpose of your dying in just that way?"

There is often some deeper purpose, some higher intention, some aspect of the course of one's life and death that was arranged in the planning stage and which evades conscious awareness. The entity that is focused on the completion of some task or project must be guided to a realization of the greater perspective of the situation.

An attached entity can interfere with a person's life script, Life Plan, and karmic opportunities, even the time of death. Demonic entities strive to disrupt plans and people in any way possible and interfere with accomplishments and human advancement in every arena. Dark-energy interference is directed at disrupting love in any form. Demonically introjected thoughts are usually accepted without question and without discernment by most people, as there is widespread ignorance and denial of the existence and presence of these beings and their influence. Some of the unfinished business carried in the thoughts of living people and earthbound spirits is nothing more than thought constructs projected from the attached demonic entities. The destructive conversations in the mind are often intruded by discarnate spirits or demonic entities.

Clare was worried about her husband's health. She wanted to investigate for spirit attachment and help him with a remote releasement, if necessary. In the session, she discovered that his father was attached and affecting his health. Father did not want to leave. Further probing into this resistance revealed that her husband and his father were planning to attach to her teenage son after her husband's impending death. At this revelation, she burst into angry tears.

At a subconscious level, this was their project and it was not as yet finished. The final step was the attachment to Clare's son, the third generation of men. This sort of intrusion on another person is often instigated by a demonic entity. Invasion of a family is usually the work of a dark network of demonic beings. The dark energy was cleared from the family and father agreed to move into the Light.

Conflict Resolution

The therapist must discover and bring to resolution any remaining emotional conflicts which keep the entity earthbound and attached to the host. This may entail brief therapy on the entity, sometimes just a sympathetic ear. An entity may attach to the person involved in the personal conflict or may attach to someone close to that person if direct attachment is impossible.

Ron and Elsa entered counseling together. They had been married more than 30 years. His elderly sister had passed away some months earlier. Ron was a quiet man, mildly depressed and not given to socializing. Left to himself, he might have become something of a recluse. Elsa maintained contact with his family members and arranged family visits.

Ron's sister Dorothy was discovered attached to Elsa. She had not attempted to attach to Ron, partly because there was no emotional opening (in fact there was very little emotion at all), but mostly because he was so dull. Though she loved him, she was angry at this aspect of his personality. She also knew that Elsa would maintain contact with the rest of the family. Dorothy liked that.

After very little processing, Dorothy was willing to leave. With a tearful display of emotion, she and Ron voiced their love, which he expressed quite openly. She was released into the Light.

Fred was a healer and a past-life therapist in his mid fifties. Since childhood he had suffered from Tourette's disorder. This unusual condition includes motor tics such as eye blinking, tongue thrusting, and jerking of facial muscles or the musculature of the trunk and limbs. It is also defined by vocal tics, outbursts of yelps, barks, sniffs, and often obscene words. The median age of the onset of this condition is seven years, though it can begin as early as one year of age. It is considered a lifelong condition, though periods of remission may occur. In some cases it disappears totally, usually in early adulthood (APA, 1987, pp. 79-80).

Roman, the entity who claimed to be responsible for the disorder, was very angry, not at Fred but at Fred's mother. During the entity's life he had been in love with a woman. Fred's mother was the father of the woman in that earlier lifetime. The father was strict with his daughter and forbade any contact between Roman and his beloved. They never fulfilled their love in that time. Roman attached to Fred in childhood in order to bring embarrassment and shame to the mother. Revenge was the motive. Fred had no part in the prior-lifetime saga. There was no connection between them except for this opportunistic attachment. Roman finally agreed that he had extracted sufficient revenge on the one who had kept him from his love. He agreed to leave.

Soon after this session, skeptical Fred, though he noticed relief from the Tourette's, sought relief of his condition through group therapy, another healing modality which had not helped in earlier sessions. The condition continued to ease. He attributed the healing to the group therapy.

Resolution of Conflict with the Host

The most common situation in spirit attachment involves an interpersonal conflict between the host and the entity. Human drives and instincts function to reduce emotional and physical tensions. The earthbound spirit is fixated on the emotional trauma, frozen in the traumatic event. For the entity, time does not exist; there is no sequence of events moving in time, no beginning, middle and ending of the event, no resolution. It is a freeze-frame, stop-action position. There is no sense of moving from the height of emotional tension to a more quiescent state. The entity came to a standstill at the height of the emotion at the time of death. This is the basis of the conflict with the host.

The therapist urges the entity to ventilate, to express the feelings, to put words to the sensations and feelings. Once this commences, the fixation begins to ease and brief therapy can bring resolution of the conflict for the entity. The entity can come to the completion of the story and go on to the next step, which is the Light.

The client and entity both need to take responsibility for their respective parts in whatever drama initiated the conflict. Often this is in a past life.

Past-Life Regression to Original Event

If a past-life traumatic event is the source of the conflict which maintains the attachment, this may indicate that the entity did not return to the Light after death in that lifetime. The client did. Being fixated in the emotional upset of the event, the entity can remember vividly the past-life situation. The client has left it behind, except as an unconscious memory. As the entity recalls and describes the original traumatic events and interactions, the client also recalls and feels the impact. It is the misperceptions and misinterpretations which lead to the painful residues. As these are cleared in the regression, both participants feel the easing of tension. It is actually a dual regression, in this sense. The final communication is often an apology, then an expression of love.

Past-Life Regression to Karmic Event

Past-life therapy with an entity follows much the same sequence as with a living person. Recall of a single lifetime may not resolve the issue. It may require locating earlier connecting lifetimes and the original karmic event.

Attached earthbound spirits do not participate in the planning stage of the present life of the host. However, a being may have a recollection of instances when it attached as a spirit to someone embodied in a human form on the earth plane. In the planning stage, the scheme for the coming lifetime may include an opportunity for balancing that intrusion—that is, to accept an attachment.

Occasionally, a client in a past-life session recalls being an earthbound entity attached to a living person in another time. Deeper probing may reveal that the one who is presently the attached entity was in the opposite role in the earlier lifetime. In the greater reality, here is an attempt at balancing the earlier intrusion.

Return to the Death Scene

The Light always comes at the time of death. The Light remains and will be visible any time the earthbound spirit looks up for it. Whatever the reason a newly deceased spirit does not turn to the Light at the time of death, it is never too late to make that choice. There is no time in the spirit realm, and as the entity is directed to recall the moment of separating from the body at the time of death, the entire experience is revivified. For the entity, it is the moment of death. When attention is focused on the Light, it is there. Often, the entity expresses surprise. It didn't look there when it separated from the body; its attention was drawn elsewhere for some reason.

IT'S NEVER TOO LATE TO HAVE A HAPPY DEATH.

This is a very effective approach to assisting a reluctant or disbelieving earthbound spirit into the Light. Once they perceive the brightness, they can usually perceive figures of trusted friends or loved ones waiting patiently for them. This leads to a quick release.

The entity with Cindy had no prior connection with her. No past-life connections could be recalled, no emotional interaction ever existed, there was no unfinished business. This was another case of being just plain stuck. The entity was directed to recall the last day of her life.

T: "Where are you in the last moments?"

C: "My husband and I were going on vacation. The plane was taking off and it exploded. I was still strapped in my seat when it just blew right through the side of the plane. I came out of my body and just kept going and landed on her (Cindy)."

T: "Go back to the moment just before the plane exploded. What do you feel?"

C: "I can feel something vibrating. I know it's not right."

T: "What happens next?"

C: "There is a loud explosion. My whole seat, with me in it, just bursts through the side of the plane. I continue moving sideways out of my body. I land in her."

T: "One more time now. As you explode out of the plane, stop for a moment. Look up above the plane."

The therapist was attempting to have her find the Light.

T: "What do you see, what do you perceive?"

C: "There's my husband! He went straight up when I went out sideways. He's been waiting for me!"

T: "Reach out and take his hand. How does it feel?"

C: "Wonderful. Good-bye."

She was gone.

Clarence was the entity attached to the client. He died as the automobile he was driving crashed. He described getting out of the car, only to see his body still inside. Confused, he glanced around. The first thing he saw was his aunt Agnes. This scared Clarence, because he knew Aunt Agnes was dead. He thought he was seeing a ghost. He took off running in the opposite direction.

T: "Clarence, wait a minute before you take off. Skip back to just before you see Aunt Agnes. Look right above the car. Look up, Clarence. What do you see?"

C: "It's real bright up there."

T: "Clarence, are you curious?"

C: "Sure."

T: "Keep looking. How does it feel?"

C: "Feels good."

T: "Is Aunt Agnes a ghost?"

C: "Yeah, but it's not so scary now. She wants me to come with her."

T: "Clarence, do you trust her?"

C: "Yeah."

T: "Good-bye, Clarence."

C: "Bye."

Return to the Planning Stage

The planning stage of the reincarnation cycle is a key part of past-life therapy, and also spirit releasement therapy. In addition to the physical circumstances of the coming life, such as personal details and family connections, beings plan the opportunities for growth, karmic balancing and resolution of past residues. This is also the source of the synchronicities which appear as accidents and coincidences in life. In past-life therapy, a person can explore these details, examine the purpose of his life, and rediscover the one person responsible for the vicissitudes of life—himself.

Anger, resentment and blame of other people for the circumstances of one's life is always false. At the same time, guilt and remorse over one's own personal behavior or act that is perceived as harmful to another is also false. In the immediate sense, people have an impact on other people through their intention, attitudes and behavior. In the larger reality beings plan the course of life and the learning situations which seem at times so calamitous.

Responsibility begins with the willingness to acknowledge oneself as the cause of one's life. This is not associated in any way with blame, shame, guilt or fear. It appears that discarnate influence and entity attachment can interfere with the full unfoldment of the Life Plan. Perhaps there is a meta level, a higher octave of the planning stage, where an even larger plan is prepared which includes spirit interference and demonic disruption. This is speculation. It has not been found in clinical practice.

Denise was plagued by a very angry entity. In her immediate past life in Chicago in the late '30s, she had accidentally hit a pedestrian. He stepped off a curb and walked directly into the path of her oncoming car.

Ernie was surprised when the car hit him. He was not watching. His mind was on other matters. He was totally unaware of the impending impact. He instantly popped out of his body, looked around, and realized immediately what had happened. He was incensed. For the first time in his life he was involved in an honest career which could prove lucrative with room for quick advancement. He was a hot salesman newly hired by a major insurance company and his future was very bright.

At 35, Ernie had never quite made it. This was truly the opportunity of a lifetime. It was not just his high hopes or imagination. In an instant, it was ended. He felt he had a right to blame the woman driver, to blame her for this tragic misfortune on the eve of his success, the beginning of his good life.

In his anger, Ernie reached out to attack her. As spirit he could not touch her; but he did attach. He remained with her for the few remaining years of her life. He waited in the intermediate place and found her again in the present life. She was born as Denise. Ernie was in the typically confused state of the earthbound spirit. For him, this was the woman who had killed him and he still blamed her; he was a prisoner of his own anger. For him, there had been no passage of time, no dilution of his fury, no compensation. He would not listen to reason and refused any elucidation on the spiritual reality.

The therapist asked him about his job, his life, his plans for his rich future. His ego was inflated and he was eager to talk of his accomplishments and plans. In this frame of mind, Ernie followed instructions and was easily regressed to the planning stage for his life. The therapist directed him to look at the plan for his life, his blueprint for the life to come when he would have a chance to become an extraordinarily successful insurance company sales person and executive. This piqued Ernie's curiosity, this look into his future which he had forgotten by now that he never had.

He saw that he would have retired wealthy and would have lived extravagantly into ripe old age. He also discovered that he could have died of a heart attack at age 52, a victim of his own fast living. He next realized that he could die by being run down by an automobile at age 35. The woman driving the car was someone he had killed in the prime of her life in an earlier existence when they had known each other. He was balancing a karmic debt. He suddenly understood that it had been his choice. She was never to blame. He had wasted many earth years in his anger. The impact of this was devastating and liberating at the same time. There was nothing else keeping Ernie here. He apologized to Denise and he was ready to go.

Remaining Emotion

When the conflicts have been resolved and forgiveness completely realized, the emotion which remains is love. Love can be possessive and demanding. Love can be needy and fatuous. Love in any form cannot be faulted, though it may need to be corrected and realigned. The therapist acknowledges the love which the entity professes to feel for the host and assists the entity in clarifying the situation.

T: "How have you affected this woman you love?"
"How has your love interfered with her life?"
"Is this the way you would choose to show your love for her, affecting her and interfering like this?"
"Is this the way you want to continue to love her? I don't believe you love her if you treat her this way."
"Has she been aware that you were here loving her like this? Tell the truth."

"Would you like to be with her again as a man and a woman?
Would you like to love her in that way again?"
"You can be with her again as man and woman only if you
return to the Light. Only after she has lived out her full allot-
ted span of years and leaves her body in the transition called
death will she return to the Light. Time is different in the
Light. For you it will seem as if no time at all has passed until
she makes her transition. Once you are both in the Light, and
only if you both agree, can you plan another lifetime together.
How does that sound?"

It usually sounds pretty good to a fellow who has been attached for years
without any acknowledgment of his presence. That is extremely frustrating for
the spirit of a man in love with a woman—especially if she has engaged in
relationships with other men.

T: "Perhaps when the time comes you can assist her in finding
her way home to the Light. As you have seen, it is easy to get
lost on the way. That would be a truly loving thing to do.
Would you be willing to help her then?"

This seems to be quite appealing to the earthbound spirit. If there still
seems to be some hesitation to leave, the therapist appeals to that very love which
keeps him attached.

T: "Love her enough to leave, friend. Love her enough to say
good-bye for now. Love her. All there is is love and love never
dies. It's time to go "

This is usually sufficient to convince the most ardent lover.

Fear of the Light
For some earthbound spirits, there is a fear of the Light. Probing
questions may reveal that they were burned to death. Naturally, the brightness
of the Light will restimulate that fear.
The therapist requests someone from the Light who knew the entity to
come and assist in the release.

T: "I call out into the Light for someone who knew this person.
Someone he trusted."

Addressing the entity:

T: "Look carefully, friend, wait until there is someone you know you can trust. Don't take my word for it. Is there someone coming?"

There will be someone who comes. Several guides may have to come before the entity will trust someone enough to believe them about the Light.

The victims of the atomic bombs dropped on Hiroshima and Nagasaki have a profound fear of the Light. When they are found they seem to be clustered in groups, frozen in the moment of destruction and fused together by the force of the blast. The enormous energy of atomic fission affected the spiritual energy of these beings. Carefully and patiently, the therapist must direct them to survey the world as it is now, the country of Japan as it is today, to view the miraculous recovery that has been accomplished by the Japanese people.

Darla was in grammar school when the atomic bomb was released over Hiroshima. In her session she discovered a group of Japanese school children about her age at that time. They died instantly in the blast. Somehow, they found her in America and attached.

T: "What was there about this American child that attracted you?"

C: "She was having fun. We wanted to play and have fun."

T: "Where were you?"

C: "We were in school and it was recess time. Our teacher was punishing us. We couldn't go outside for recess. We just wanted to play."

T: "What happened?"

C: "There was a big light. Then everything went away. We found her playing."

That was it. There was a big light, then everything went away. They wanted to play and their teacher wouldn't let them go outside. The children died together, all of them wanting to play. Their only connection with Darla was the fact that she was playing.

This group of school children in spirit were huddled together in fear. More than that, they described being actually stuck to each other. When they looked outside for the Light they saw it but were afraid of it. The therapist called out for someone in the Light to come for the children, someone who knew them. A boy identified their teacher as she came.

T: "What does she look like?"

C: "She looks like our teacher."

T: "How does her face look? What is her expression?"

C: "She looks sad. She has been waiting for us."

The guiding ones who come from the Light have a peaceful and loving countenance; they do not appear angry, sad or fearful—simply peaceful and loving. The teacher's expression meant that she was not in the Light.

T: "Teacher, you have come for the children. Are you in the Light? Have you been in the Light?"

C: "No, I have been waiting right outside here. The Light is far away. I could not go anywhere without them."

T: "Teacher, what happened?"

C: "It was supposed to be their recess and I would not let them out. They were being punished. I am responsible for their deaths. If I had let them go outside they would not have died."

She was terribly distraught. She felt guilty for the deaths of these children. She had no comprehension of the devastation wrought by the atomic blast. She followed them after death but did not attach to Darla. She waited at some distance, suffering this appalling guilt.

T: "Teacher, go back to that day. Rise above the school. What do you see?"

C: "It's all burning, the buildings are gone. Everything is gone!" (her voice quavered with emotion).

T: "If you had let them out for recess would they have been safe? Would they have lived? Everything is gone."

C: "No," (calmer voice) "Everything is gone. What happened here?"

The therapist briefly and gently explained.

C: "I was not responsible for the deaths of the children?"

T: "You were not responsible. Look to the Light now, Teacher. Is it closer? Is there someone there that you recognize?"

C: "Yes, it's closer. Some of the other teachers are here. Some of the children's parents."

The Light surrounded the children. Their parents reassured them. They slowly split apart and separated from each other. They all moved into the Light.

Addictions

Lack of physical gratification of the need for food, drugs, sex or alcohol can hold a spirit earthbound, continually seeking satisfaction of the need. Since consumption must be accomplished through someone else's body, attachment for the purpose of personal gratification is common. The food or other substance consumed does not satisfy the hunger of the entity; it is not a true physical hunger, it is a memory, a thought construct, an artifact of personality. The host might gain weight from overeating or become a drug user, yet the entity is not fulfilled by this consumption.

T: "When she eats, are you satisfied? Is your hunger satisfied?"
"When he drinks, does it satisfy you the way it used to do when you were in your own body?"
"When she's high, does it feel the same to you as before?"

The answer is usually a disappointed "NO." Physical substance does not satisfy a spiritual hunger.

The entity is assured that there is everything they might want or need in the Light. For the spirit of the drug addict and alcoholic, there is a substance they will be given once they are safely in the Light. It will produce the high sensations they associate with the addictive substance on the earth plane. However, there will be no side effects, no hangovers, no withdrawal pain. They will no longer be in bondage to the addiction that made life on earth a personal hell.

The entity is urged not to take the word of the therapist but to ask the guides that come. The guides will confirm this information. This generally eases the suspicion of the entity and it agrees to go.

Fragmentation

Fragmentation persists after the death of a person who suffered with the mental or physical condition while embodied. The entity might complain that his head is missing and he can't leave without it. Amputation of a limb might keep a spirit earthbound in search of the limb. If the genitals have been severed from the body, an entity might not want to return to the Light as less than a complete man. Many people have been killed in an explosion which shattered the physical body. Combat situations expose the savage brutality which men can inflict on each other.

One client discovered that he was a participant in this appalling scene in a past-life regression. During a fierce battle, a number of Native Americans were killed and emasculated by American Cavalry. The red men were still enraged over this foul treatment. They adamantly refused to leave the fort where the battle took place. Not only were they fragmented in a brutal way, but the fierce, self-righteous anger of the spirits of the American Cavalrymen kept the Indians immobile in that place.

Using the technique described in the section Mind Merge (126), both sides were relieved of their intractable anger. When the combatants of both sides experienced the beliefs and attitudes of their opponents, they found how alike they really were. There was finally a feeling of forgiveness. The Native Americans managed to locate and reconnect their parts. The process is described in the section Fragmentation Categories (177).

The client felt shame at being one of the American soldiers. However, through his recall of the scene, the therapist was able to help free the spirits of the Indians and the American troops. This is termed *rescue work* and is described in the section Rescue Work (371). The client was able to release the inappropriate shame when he realized the healing for so many which occurred through him.

A therapist unfamiliar with fragmentation recovery conducted a session with a female client. A male entity was discovered and finally released into the Light. He claimed to have lost a leg by amputation. After his release, the client continued with a body scan and located what turned out to be the amputated leg of the released entity. It was sent to the Light with guiding spirits with the request that it be returned to the male spirit who had left it behind.

The entity who is missing a significant portion of the soul-mind can be so lethargic that it cannot muster the strength to lift out. When no other resistance can be found, the therapist directs the entity to look within for the empty place, to follow the thread, to locate and recover the missing fragment. This can be very effective when no other approach seems to work.

In treatment of entity attachment, it is necessary to explore for the conditions of fragmentation and nested attachments. When these conditions are resolved, the entities are usually eager to move into the Light.

Female clients with a history of sexual molestation will nearly always exhibit signs of fragmentation and spirit attachment, both earthbound and demonic.

Thirty-year-old Cindy was hardly functional in her life. Divorced, she was raising her five-year-old daughter alone. Cindy was depressed to the point of being suicidal. She was aware that she was an incest survivor and she had been working on that issue in therapy. Her deceased stepfather had been the perpetrator. It is not unusual for the deceased father or stepfather who was the incest perpetrator to become an attached spirit after his death. His guilt surrounding the incest is the impetus for the attachment to his daughter, in an attempt to seek forgiveness. In some cases this spirit claims to own the woman. This is a typical sign of demonic influence.

This proved to be the situation with Cindy, though it was not discovered immediately. As she recalled the incest, she described fragmenting and separating. She estimated the fragmentation at about 60%. When the separated fragment was recovered, it was a subpersonality at the age of the little girl when the incest occurred. The fragment was invited to rejoin the client but adamantly refused. When the therapist asked what prevented her from coming in, she reported that stepfather was still there. He was an attached spirit, clearly visible to the fragmented and separated subpersonality, and she was afraid to come any closer. She agreed to remain nearby and observe.

Attention was then focused on the attached entity. The perpetrator of such a violation is usually found to be afflicted with an attached demonic entity which caused distortion of the man's thinking while he was alive. The spirit of the stepfather seemed belligerent at first, claiming dominion and ownership of the woman. He was directed to look within himself. He discovered the dark-energy being and it was appropriately released. As this influence was removed, his own values were restored. He was immediately remorseful and apologetic.

Communication between stepfather and daughter at this time began to relieve both the woman's hurt and anger and the stepfather's overwhelming guilt. When Cindy's fragmented subpersonality was finally willing to forgive the man who violated her as a child, he was also willing to forgive himself. Finally, he could be released into the Light. Only after he was gone was it safe for the young fragment to return and integrate with the client.

Nested Attachments

An entity attached to a living person may be strong enough to prevent the host from going to the Light after death. The newly deceased spirit becomes earthbound with the original earthbound entity nested within itself. It is not at all unusual to find an entity with another entity attached. The second one nested inside the first might have a third nested within it, and so on. There is no limit to this chain of nested entities. An entity usually does not know about the ones nested inside itself.

A client may describe behavior which is uncharacteristic and be confused about it. The cause may turn out to be an attached spirit. An entity may describe uncharacteristic behavior or attitudes as it recalls its life. This may turn out to be a nested entity. A belligerent and hostile attached earthbound spirit which causes much strife and conflict in a person's life often turns out to have a dark-energy being nested within. After the dark one is released, as described in the section Release of the Dark Entity (325), this earthbound is usually apologetic to the host and grateful to the therapist.

Nancy was a 36-year-old psychotherapist. She wanted to experience past-life therapy and chose to work on her drinking problem. She spoke about waking night after night at about 3:00 A.M. to take "a couple of belts" of Scotch whiskey before being able to go back to sleep again. She mentioned several other aspects of the problem, but the use of the terminology "a couple of belts" was not in keeping with her lovely feminine nature.

As she continued to talk about the drinking, the therapist asked her if she felt any sensations in her body as she spoke. She described a feeling of nausea in her stomach. The therapist requested that she close her eyes, focus her awareness on the nausea, and describe whatever happened. At first there was nothing. Then she began to see swirling shapes of yellow and orange color. Suddenly there emerged the scene of a saloon. A cowboy stood drinking at the bar. His name was Tom and he was a heavy drinker. Married to a woman who despised him for his excess, he slept in a separate bedroom. He routinely took his bottle to bed and would take a couple of belts before falling asleep.

Tom told of numerous occasions, including his daughter's wedding, when he would overindulge in alcohol and his wife would send him away from the house. He was always glad to be away. Late one night at home in his own bed he began to feel pain in his stomach. He took a few more belts of whiskey to ease the pain but the feeling spread across his belly until he felt like his guts were on fire. The pain and nausea were so bad he called to his wife to go for the doctor. She angrily refused, which infuriated him, and he had some foul things to say about women. He died that night in pain, drunk and angry at women. He quite likely had a perforated ulcer.

This is an obvious and typical example of a past-life experience which might be contaminating a person's present situation. The therapist cannot be content with the obvious but must continue to probe until there is no further avenue to pursue.

T: "Tom, how old was Nancy when you joined her?"

C: "She was 14 and she was having an argument with her father."

The answer came immediately, without hesitation.

T: "Tom, was there ever a time in your life when you felt like something just came into you and took over?"

C: (surprise in his voice) "Yes, I was 16 and I was having an argument with my dad."

T: "Is that other one still here? Is the person who entered Tom still here?"

After only a brief hesitation, Nancy's voice said softly:

C: "Yes."

At the end of the session she revealed that her clearest mental imagery of the entire session was at the moment that Tom recalled the feeling of being entered.

T: "What's your name?"

C: "Larry."

T: "Larry, what happened?"

C: "I was working in the assay office and they accused me of stealing gold. They were real mad at me so I left there. I had a bottle of whiskey I was drinking. I was walking along the railroad track and the train hit me."

He died drunk and angry.

T: "Well, Larry, did you steal it?"

C: (after a pause) "Yes."

Larry sounded very tired. He responded to the description of the Light and was immediately ready to leave. The guides appeared and lovingly assisted him on the journey home.

Tom was relieved and after a parting dialogue with Nancy eagerly accompanied the guides who came for him. Once the attached entity or entities clearly realize the nature of the situation, they are almost always ready to go. It often takes a little convincing before they recognize that they are no longer in their own body.

Past-life therapy techniques are valuable in this situation. As they recall their own life, the situations which caused their strong persisting appetites and emotions, their unresolved conflicts, and finally the scene of their own bodily death, they cannot deny the truth.

They have reached the point of readiness to leave when they begin to be remorseful for interfering with the host. They apologize, often in tears, and announce their desire to go home. Most often the last statement is simply, "I love you."

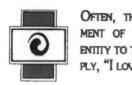

OFTEN, THE LAST STATE-
MENT OF THE DEPARTING
ENTITY TO THE HOST IS SIM-
PLY, "I LOVE YOU."

A few days later, Nancy reported being able to sleep through the
night since the session and sleeping
better than she could remember. She
had not stopped drinking completely
but it was now under her control.

In the case of nested attachment such as this, there is often a sudden
clarity on the part of the primary attached entity about their own lifetime. They
feel the difference immediately and can recall instance after instance when the
nested spirit influenced their behavior. This can produce a resolution of many of
their own conflicts and explain certain behavior patterns for them.

The earthbound human spirits can be released one by one, and as each
goes, the task becomes easier. The remaining ones sometime express anger at
the interference, realizing they were not in total control of their lives as they had
believed. They, in turn, apologize to the one they attached to in life, the one who
was held earthbound at the time of death. When the client sees this tangled mesh,
there is usually compassion for the earthbounds, forgiveness and tearful good-
byes.

During the information gathering in the discovery phase of a session, the
entity might speak lovingly about the host. As the therapist begins the releasement process, the entity might shift suddenly in its attitude toward the host and
declare ownership or swear vengeance. Such a switch in attitude can signal a
nested dark entity. This is only an added clue for the therapist; any resistance to
leaving other than unresolved emotion and addictive desires may indicate a
nested attachment.

Kara worked in a bookstore. Trained as a nurse, she had worked for some
time in a Veterans Administration hospital. Like so many nurses, she left the work
because of burnout. While still at the hospital, she had fallen in love with Trevor,
a marine wounded in Vietnam.

Trevor, a medic, was on patrol with four other guys. He was fifth in line
as they carefully moved along a narrow dirt road through the jungle. Suddenly
there were explosions in front of him. The point man was blown to bits—"Not
enough to pick up," as Trevor described it. The second man had half his body
blown away. The third and fourth men in line were killed instantly.

Trevor called in the Medevac helicopters. Though seriously wounded
himself, he picked up the remains of the second man and hoisted him onto the
chopper when it arrived. Trevor's lieutenant was aboard the Huey and began
yelling at Trevor, blaming him for the disaster. Trevor swung his fist at the officer,
knocking him cold. Trevor passed out at the same time and remained unconscious for three days. During this period he was transported to the States and
placed in the V. A. hospital where Kara worked. He awoke in the hospital. The
spirits of his four buddies had joined him.

After Trevor was released from the hospital, he and Kara dated for a brief time. Trevor was a violent man and she soon ended the relationship. He went to live in a forest, camping out alone. He continued to suffer serious depression and he eventually took his own life. He joined Kara, the woman he loved, as an attached spirit. Since that time, she had avoided relationships with men.

In the session, Trevor emerged almost immediately. He professed love for Kara, and was quite possessive. He refused to leave. As he explored inside himself, he recognized his four close buddies who were killed on the patrol. Each of them discovered attached entities from the time of the Vietnam War and from their childhood.

Rick was one of the men killed on the patrol. One of the entities with him was one of his dad's friends who died in a tragic accident on a hunting trip. When he was a young teen, Rick accompanied his dad and the friend. The man stumbled over his own shotgun. It discharged, killing him instantly.

One of Trevor's buddies was Sam, a Black man. He discovered Min Van Thieu, a teenage prostitute he had known in Vietnam. She died when a bomb fell on the building where she lived. Another entity within Sam claimed to be a Ku Klux Klan member. When Sam was nine years old, living in a shack in Alabama with his folks, three Klansmen came to the house and threatened to rape his mama and burn the house down. Sam's daddy pulled out a shotgun and blew the head off one of the white racists. Sam was in shock at the sight of this, and the spirit of the Klansman found the young Black easily accessible.

The white man hated this Black kid. Sam hated this racist who had threatened his family so many years before. The white man was directed to locate the source of his prejudice, his hatred. Only a few moments passed and he began describing a life as a young Black boy. The slave master whipped the boy's parents unmercifully. The young Black could barely contain his hatred.

Again, the Klansman was directed to another lifetime which contributed to his hatred. He discovered a life as a Black slave, this time a nubile young woman taken from her husband in Africa, brought to America with the express purpose of being a sex slave for some white landowner. She refused to perform the desired acts and her tongue was cut out. She fervently hated white people.

After recalling these experiences, this white racist was asked how he felt about Sam, the Black man.

C: "I don't hate him, he's a brother."

Sam expressed his feelings about this man who had threatened to rape his mama and burn his house down.

C: "I don't hate him, he's my brother."

The hatred of lifetimes had been healed for these two spirits. The entities were glad to move into the Light.

There were Viet Cong clad in black pajamas, women, a baby, Sam's old dog and a lot of gooey, slimy dark sludge which was the energy of hatred and prejudice generated in his life as a Black. There was deep resentment and confusion about the war. All these entities lifted to the Light and the sludge was cleansed. Kara was exhausted and exhilarated at the end of the session.

Trevor thought he had let his buddies down. He was the medic and he could not save them. He was plagued by typical survivor guilt feelings. In this session, he had assisted them in lifting their heavy emotional burdens, and releasing the entities trapped within each of them. They had all found the way to the Light. Trevor finally understood his service to them. He helped them go home. This erased the guilt feelings he had carried so long. He was free. He and Kara spoke their last words of love and he lifted into the Light.

Within three months, Kara met a man, a customer at the bookstore. She felt a spark of interest, the first in a long time. This developed into a lasting relationship for Kara. There was no longer any external influence keeping her from the experience of love.

"Despair," scanned from *The Pilgrim's Progress, Peerless Edition,* circa 1892.

The innermost layers of the nested beings exert less influence than those on the surface, except in the case of a demonic entity at the center. Then the others may exhibit signs of demonic interference, such as demands of ownership, general disruption, destruction, hatefulness, vengeance, spitefulness, and defiance of the Light. These dark beings are challenged first by the therapist. The dark ones are released as soon as possible, as this makes the remainder of the release work much easier. The dark energy acts like the key log in a log jam.

T: "To you, the one who thinks he owns her, did you

ask her? Did she invite you?" "You, the one who wants to get even, step forward. What is the first thing you have to say?"

This may be the earthbound spirit of one who loves her with a nested demonic entity distorting his thoughts about ownership or revenge.

T: "Look inside yourself. Look deep inside your own space. You may be surprised."

If the entity is willing to look, the search usually reveals another inside. There may be more layers beyond that.

T: "Look inside that one. Are there any others? Are there any more layers?"

This is worse than finding worms in an apple while it's being eaten. The entity is often surprised, annoyed and disgusted when it discovers nested attachments. Entities are usually very cooperative after that.

Involvement with the Dark Forces

Many of the entities encountered in session with clients will appear to manifest characteristics, behavior and attitudes consistent with the demonic beings. Yet in the decision-tree questioning, they will claim to have a history as an embodied human. This may be an outright lie. Their presentation gives that clue. Another possibility is that a lesser demonic being was attached to a powerful human for an extended period of time. Like the Black slaves in the early decades of United States history who assumed the name of the owner, the entity assumed the identity of the

"The Temptation on the Mountain," scanned from *Charming Bible Stories,* circa late 19th Century.

THE COIN OF THE DARK
REALM IS THE HUMAN SOUL.

person. It is simply an identification with a living human.

T: "Recall being in your own human body. Describe."

The account will be typical of a human lifetime.

T: "How old was he when you joined him?"

Taken by surprise, the little demonic being will answer, even if it is a bit confusing.

T: "Where were you before you joined him?"

Again the answer will come. The description will be typical of the dark beings and not consistent with human existence. This will establish the entity as a minor demonic spirit.

"Doctor Johannes Faust and Mephistopheles," from Christopher Marlowe's *Tragical Historie of D. Faust* (1631), scanned from *Symbols, Signs & Signets* (1969) by Ernst Lehner, with permission from Dover Publications, Inc.

Much more likely is the situation of a living human who chose to serve the dark side. Once this choice is made, the demonic beings come to lodge within and take control. When this occurs, the person is in complete bondage to the darkness. After death the spirit remains under the control of the attached dark commander. There is minimal personal volition in the activities after the moment of choice.

The agreement is sometimes unspoken; it is just assumed. The unwary human believes he will get what he wants without even asking for it. He sees the invitation as a doorway to personal power. He may believe that inviting the darkness is just a matter of adding fuel to his own fire, that his own energy will increase, that he will become more powerful. He does not consider the possibility of any cost to himself, any price to pay for this power. He does not realize that the coin of the dark realm is the human soul.

The demonic energy distorts the thinking just enough that the man actually believes that what he is doing is just exactly what he wants to be doing. Without some intervention such as this therapy, this behavior would continue unabated.

In many instances the agreement is a conscious act and deliberately sought. The most serious summoning of Satan is for the express purpose of making a formal pact. The pact normally guarantees some Earthly gain, such as personal or political power, wealth, or securing the favors of a desirable woman. The Dark One delights in offering such transient rewards in return for the eternal soul of the bargainer.

The poor fool who enters such a contract agrees to become Satan's servant, swearing allegiance to Lucifer, and renouncing his fealty to God. There is no time element in this contract. It binds him to dark service in perpetuity.

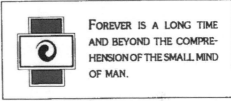

FOREVER IS A LONG TIME AND BEYOND THE COMPREHENSION OF THE SMALL MIND OF MAN.

Forever is a long time and beyond the comprehension of the small mind of man.

The notion of the pact with the devil goes back at least to the fifth century A.D. A young man made a pact with the devil in return for obtaining the favors of a pretty young girl. The father of the girl refused and the girl struggled in vain against the temptations of the devil. At last she yielded. In time, the story of the pact was told. With the help of St. Basil, the man repented and the girl was saved from his lechery, a fate worse than death.

In the sixth century, another such story was told and Mary the Blessed Mother of God assisted the poor soul in breaking the pact. Thus it seemed that Mother Mary, or a non-judgmental saint, could assist a wretched fool in freeing himself from the clutches of the Evil One. The cult of Mary spread across Europe as a result of these tales (Russell, 1984, pp. 80-81).

When such an attached entity is discovered and it claims to have been embodied as a human, the questioning focuses on the circumstances leading to the encounter and the pact with the dark forces.

T: "Recall being in your own body. Are you male or female?"

Many more men than women have been involved in pacts with the devil. The male ego so often needs and actively seeks further power and control over others. The women who were involved were usually the political power, executive or royal head of state in need of more authority. The sorceress, black magician, or witch openly invited the dark forces; it was a partnership from the inception of the practice of the black arts.

T: "What did you want?"

The reply will frequently reveal the motivation of lust, greed, revenge, hunger for power, control over others, and obedience from people. In some cases there is unselfish motivation, a willingness to offer one's own life to save another.

One adult client reported making a deal with the devil. She was only six at the time. Her mother was hospitalized and the girl was not told anything about her mother's condition. She was afraid her mother would die. How the contact was made was a mystery; she only knew that she promised her soul in return for her mother's life. Mother came home from the hospital alive, and the girl kept her promise. She was musically gifted and several big contracts had been offered to her. Always at the last moment she would fail to show up for an appointment to sign the contract or she would become ill or do something to block her own success. She refused to attempt to dislodge the dark interference. She still felt a true obligation to maintain her bargain, even though the six-year-old child she had been could not begin to understand the ramifications of what she had done.

Renunciation of the Darkness

Further questioning will uncover further motivation for the bargain.

T: "What did you do to get it? How did you contact the dark ones?"

This will begin an account of dissatisfaction with life as it was and the longing for more material satisfaction. It will usually include the process of actively calling on the forces of darkness, either by invocation or with the help of a black magician or witch or accepting the invitation of the dark beings who offer fulfillment of the carnal desires and distorted emotional needs.

T: "Did they offer you what you wanted?"

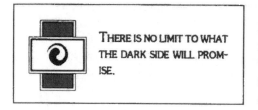

THERE IS NO LIMIT TO WHAT THE DARK SIDE WILL PROMISE.

The offer is always grandiose and enormously tempting, with promises of wealth, power, sexual gratification, revenge and any other hidden desire. There is no limit to what the dark side will promise. It is safe to proffer such abundance; they do not keep their agreements. The dark side never fulfills the promises, never honors the pact nor preserves the bargain. The dark ones nullify and invalidate the contract by non-compliance with the particulars of the agreement.

T: "Did they fulfill their part of the bargain? Did they give you what you wanted? Did they give you exactly what they promised?"

The answer is invariably "NO."

> T: "When did they say you would receive your part of the bar-
> gain, your reward?"

The promise is always held out for some non-specified time in the future. On this basis alone a person can disavow any further allegiance to the Evil One and withdraw from the contract. A contract is void if one party bargains in bad faith (and the omission of a time factor is bad faith) or if one party fails to fulfill the specified agreements of the contract.

> T: "How long will you wait? You've been duped like everyone
> else who bargains with the devil. He is the Father of Lies. He
> never keeps his bargain. He's made a fool out of you. He lied
> to you. He has given you nothing. You work for him for no
> reward, no recognition. How much longer do you want to
> work for him for nothing? He despises you and your weak-
> ness. He laughs at you."

Such questioning focuses on the very ego needs which first led the person to seek the help of the dark force. The deluded earthbound spirit will usually understand at this point. He will welcome any assistance.

> T: "Would you like to break that false contract? Are you willing to
> renounce the dark forces and pronounce your separation
> from the pact?

The answer is almost always affirmative.

> T: "Listen to the words of the Renunciation of the Darkness as I
> say them. Make them your own. Change them if you want to,
> but the meaning must remain the same. Speak the renuncia-
> tion in your own words, from you own center. Your word is
> law in your universe. These are the words of the Renunciation
> of the Darkness."

The meaning and certainty of the words of the renunciation must not be changed. A client may voice pleading thoughts such as:

> "I don't like you darkness, and I want you to leave."
> "You can't bother me anymore."
> "Go away and leave me alone."

There is no power, no establishment of boundary, no pronouncement of dominion, no certainty of command in these phrases. The therapist gently guides the client in stating the pronouncement "I rebuke..., I revoke..." These words are clear, even to the dark ones.

The therapist must be sensitive to the religious views of the client. For those who do not object to the name of the Christ, the Holy Name is used. For those who do object, the term "Light" is substituted.

T: "In the name of the Light, I rebuke you, darkness."

The client repeats the sentence, though it is the entity making the pronouncement.

T: "I renounce all activities of the darkness."

The client repeats.

T: "I revoke all contracts, agreements and initiations with the darkness."

The client repeats.

T: "Throughout eternity for as long as my soul exists."

The client repeats.

T: "In the name of the Light, it is so."

The client repeats. The therapist waits for 10 to 20 seconds.

T: "How does that feel?"

There is usually a deep feeling of relief, both for the entity and for the client. The dark ones can be released from this confused and misguided earthbound spirit at this time.

The same pronouncement can be used with any client who recalls a lifetime when they interacted with the dark forces in any way, whether they were involved in sorcery, black magic, witchcraft, dark brotherhood or priesthood, or Satanic activity of any kind.

Many clients who show signs of demonic interference can be cleared of the dark ones. In subsequent sessions, dark attachments may again be discovered, as if the door has been left open. The dark ones will claim ownership or partnership with the person by right of his agreement. Demonic spirits do not understand reincarnation; they just know the pact was made, and for them this is the open door.

Past-life regression to the experience of involvement with the darkness will allow the person to discover and take responsibility for his actions and behavior. He can then, in full awareness, sever the connection and speak the words of the renunciation of the darkness.

THERE IS ONE POWER IN THE UNIVERSE. IT IS THE POWER OF THE LIGHT.

There is one Power in the universe. It is the Power of the Light. It is the power of love, healing and spiritual evolution. The power of the Light can be distorted and misused by anyone with such miscreant intention to damage or destroy others. This abuse is a violation of the free will of the victim, the person who is the object of the distorted force. It also violates the basic nature of the perpetrator; to misuse the Power of the Light is to incur severe karmic debt.

At the core of every created being is a spark of Light, a spark of the God consciousness. Denial and defiance of this spiritual heritage is a denial and defiance of God. At the innermost core, each being knows the truth of its identity. This cannot be denied. It is the way home.

Tempted by the Dark Beings

Ryan was a willing participant in the process of therapy. At 38, he was becoming painfully aware of the turmoil within himself, the relationship with his wife, who was several years his senior and their family situation. They were in therapy as a family. This was a personal session for him. In a fit of violent anger he had put a fist through two doors and a wall.

As he described the painful situation of his life, he had a growing awareness of physical sensation and the mounting emotion behind it.

C: "Wait, something's wrong, something's wrong."

There were things in Ryan's life which just did not seem to be right, fair, or just. As he repeated the phrase, his stomach began to tighten. He suddenly found himself in a past life, holding a dagger against his abdomen about to commit seppuku. It was the code of bushido, the honorable way to take his own life, and yet something was wrong. As he plunged the dagger into his gut he sensed a vague and momentary awareness of the wrongness of this code which had led him to this act. In the next moment the attending second slashed downward with the sword in the prescribed and accepted manner of bushido and his head went rolling away.

As a spirit, Ryan surveyed the scene and he once again felt the fierce loyalty of the bushido code of honor. It was everything. It was more than sufficient reason to live and die.

As he moved back to explore the life, the details began to emerge. His father had been Shogun before being assassinated. His wife had been killed by the rival faction and a new Shogun had come to power. As son of the former Shogun he also was required to die and was given the choice to commit seppuku, or ritual suicide, in keeping with the code of bushido.

The second time through the death scene, he had a different sense of the meaning of his life. Suddenly, bushido seemed nonsensical, ridiculously structured, somehow comical, yet enormously tragic. He realized that he had loved his wife and family and that indeed love was, in truth, the only important element of life. A major realization, but just a little late for this samurai.

Again moving back into that lifetime, he discovered that his wife was part of the rival family. He and she had grown to love each other, yet she was still a part of the betrayal. Her family could not trust her any longer and had ordered her death. He died feeling rage at the betrayal—rage and hatred and the desire for revenge. This set the stage for the ensuing events.

He described the scene of his death without much emotion. He sensed two shadowy figures moving about in the distance. They came closer and he saw their forms more distinctly; each the size of a man, yet amorphous and dark, they were spirit, not physical. They addressed his rage and offered him the chance for revenge. They offered him reembodiment, not in the form of reincarnation, but by possessing the body of the new Shogun's counselor. The counselor was trusted and had constant access to the Shogun. This would afford the opportunity for revenge, which the young man desired. In return they requested his soul, of which he had little knowledge or need. He instantly accepted the offer. This was the pact with the devil, his descent into dark bondage by choice and by the power of his own word.

It was two weeks before the conditions were right for the counselor to be open and vulnerable to possession. There seemed to be a moment of fear or confusion. The spirit of the young man just went in and took over. He adjusted quickly to the situation, and perceived that the counselor and Shogun were walking and talking quietly in a garden setting. At first Ryan thought they were alone and it would be a simple matter of drawing his sword and killing the Shogun. With his hand on the sword he suddenly became aware of the retinue of samurai guards following them. As he drew the sword with the intention of dealing a death blow to the hated Shogun, the samurai reacted swiftly, and the counselor, in Ryan's words, looked like sliced salami.

Here are the classic elements of demonic infiltration. Ryan's hatred, rage, and desire for revenge acted like a magnet for the dark ones. They offered life—which is a deception, as it is not theirs to give in any form. The divine spark of life within all beings is a spark of the God Source, the only Source. They cannot arrange or offer reincarnation options, as that lies only within the province of the Light. The offer of possessing another is doubly intrusive: it is a violation of the free will of the host, and also a deviation from the spiritual path and a karmic burden for the possessing spirit. Blinded by his rage, the newly deceased spirit of the samurai accepted the offer and mindlessly gave his soul in return. Even then, the revenge was not achieved. His foul desire was not fulfilled.

The contract is never honored. The dark ones never deliver what is promised. Herein lies the key to terminating the contract. The child of Light, the human being, operates with perfect integrity and will continue to fulfill the promise to the darkness, whatever the nature of the promise. Because the dark ones never fulfill their part of the bargain, the contract becomes null and void and the lost soul, the earthbound spirit who made that bargain with the "devil," is free.

Ryan perceived this concept fully in the altered state, and was willing to reclaim dominion and his freedom. He made the words his own as he repeated the therapist's phrases:

T: "In the name of the Light, I rebuke you, darkness."
"I renounce all activities of the darkness."
"I revoke all contracts, agreements and initiations with the darkness, or with any being of darkness."
"For now and throughout all eternity."
"For as long as my soul exists. I am free. For so it is. AMEN."

Treatment of
the Demonic

Scanned images from the *Pictorial Bible*, circa 1882.

Treatment of the Demonic

The Catholic exorcism procedure, the Roman Ritual, has a long history of development. It finally reached its present format in the seventeenth century. It is still used by priests of the Catholic Church in cases of solemn exorcism. Between 1970 and 1980, there were more than 600 solemn exorcisms performed in the United States. It is still a viable procedure in the Church, though not publicized. Basically, the interaction between the possessing entity and the priest exorcist is adversarial; the demon is forced out in the name of Jesus Christ. It is just cast out, without a specified destination. The procedure offers no love, no compassion, no concern whatsoever for the entity, as though the fallen angel were not a God-created being.

Jesus came to destroy the works of the devil (The Bible, 1 John 3:8). For nearly 2,000 years, beginning with Jesus as the exorcist, the demons and devils have been successfully expelled from their human hosts in His name. The demonic entities adhere to the belief system; they seem to accept the rules of the Church and the steps of the Roman Ritual exorcism procedures. They respond angrily and fearfully to the name of Jesus, to holy water, and to the relics of the saints or the cross. (Relics are said to be tiny pieces of the body or clothing of saints, or the wood of the cross upon which Jesus was crucified.) They react strongly to the recitation of "The Lord's Prayer" and the "23rd Psalm." The victim of the demonic invasion does not have to be Catholic, or even religious, or profess any belief in God. It is the demonic entity who fears God, Jesus Christ, Archangel Michael, Mother Mary and other holy figures, and reacts through the host.

This form of exorcism is irresponsible with regard to the treatment and disposal of the entity. An entity can return to the same person. It can find another unwitting victim, or it can also attach to the priest exorcist. It is like removing a nail from a tire and tossing it out into the street. Either the person who tossed it, or someone else, may pick it up in their tire again.

Scanned reproduction of "Exorcism," from a Stephanoff (London, 1816) print which appeared in *Picture Museum of Socery Magic & Alchemy* (1963) by Emile Grillot De Givry, with permission from University Books, Inc.

Sequence of a Demonic Spirit Releasement

There is a specific, logical sequence of events in the releasement of the dark-energy beings, the demonic spirits. It has been developed by trial and error with many errors and many corrections. Once the diagnosis of darkness has been made, this sequence is followed.

1. Call on the Light to guide and direct the session.
2. Call on the Warrior Angels of Light to surround the area.
3. Call on the Mighty Rescue Spirits of Light to stand by for the work at hand.
4. Request the Mighty Rescue Spirits of Light to surround the dark one with a mesh of Light, a net of Light, a capsule of Light: impervious and inescapable. Request that they squeeze the capsule until the one inside is compliant and communicative.
5. Dialogue with the one inside the capsule. Discover the vulnerability which allowed the attachment, the purpose and effects of the attachment.
6. Direct the dark one to look within itself for its own key to freedom. (It will discover its own spark of Light.)
7. Discovery of its own light will lead to transformation of this little being. The darkness will disappear along with the hostility and destructive behavior.
8. Call on Archangel Michael and the Legions of Heaven for the work of rescuing the many dark-energy beings which will come. The transformed dark one will assist in summoning its underlings and subordinates, its associates and those of equal rank and stature. The therapist calls out in the name of the Light for those of higher rank and stature, and for all the replacements, unto the end of the replacements.
9. Request the Legions of Heaven to gather every dark one along every thread of any and every dark network involved or associated in any way with the client, the ancestors, the offspring including those yet unborn, with anyone who has married into this family or has been connected in any way.
10. Request that the Legions of Heaven continue this rescue of the dark ones, and to lift the path of freedom far, far from anyone involved in the session, the buildings of work and residence, and far from the earth plane.
11. Call for the Mercy Band of Rescue Angels of Light to gather and take home to the Light all those earthbound spirits now freed by the dark-energy beings as they are being lifted to their appointed place in the Light.

12. Give thanks to all those who assisted in the rescue work.

Release of the Demonic Entity

The basis for Spirit Releasement Therapy, this present approach to the treatment of spirit possession or attachment, is the firm knowledge that all created beings contain the spark of God consciousness. All else is illusory and transitory, part of the duality that constitutes this physical reality which encompasses good and evil, light and dark, right and wrong, and other polarities. The Book of Revelations outlines the beginning of the game, the act of choosing sides: Light or darkness. Every spark of God will return, and eventually all will join in the Oneness. This includes Lucifer, the ultimate prodigal son, and his legions of demons, "the Forces of Darkness."

A clairvoyant may perceive the dark-energy being as a shape of dark gray or black, with a thin outline or aura of sickly yellow. The dark ones seem to know if a person can see them. They may assume ugly, menacing faces with vicious fangs and fierce red eyes. The gargoyle-like masks are meant to frighten and discourage the person gifted with this sight. The person with this ability can also perceive the beings of Light and can call on their assistance to remove these horrible images. Another defense against this intrusion is to demand in the name of the Light that they drop the Halloween-like costumes and show their true forms. They will frequently show up as the black blobs.

During a session, a client may focus within and describe a dark form or hideous face with red eyes, perhaps with surrounding flashes of red. The client may experience fear in reaction to what she is visualizing, she may express disgust at an ugly gargoyle-like face or black thing which is growling, snarling or hissing. An attached earthbound may explore within itself and discover and describe a similar apparition. With this description, the therapist must assume the presence of a dark-energy being, a demonic being. The therapist uses the client's descriptor as the name of the dark being: growler, hisser, snarler, red eyes, gargoyle, blob or whatever distinctive description is given.

The client may describe an area of darkness within their body, perhaps moving or churning. This most often emerges with the recall of some traumatic event which left them with anger, rage, hatred or feelings of vengeance. The therapist probes for an entity within the darkness.

T: "Can you find a consciousness within that area of darkness? Is there something hidden in that darkness? Is there someone there?"

C: "Yes there is something there."

T: "What color are the eyes?"

C: "Red."

This newly discovered dark being will be defiant toward the therapist and threatening toward the client.

> C: "She's mine."
>   "Go away."
>   "Leave me alone."
>   "Go to hell."

The therapist does not respond to these angry and defiant outbursts. This key diagnostic question will soon reveal the true identity of this red eyed intruder.

> T: "Have you ever been alive in your own human body?"

It will not only deny being human but will answer the question derisively, as if insulted. After all, who would want to be human?

> T: "If you hate humans so much, why are you here? What is your purpose with her? What is your assignment?"

A demonic being will describe some form of interference, interruption, disruption with the family, occupation or goals. The purpose might be to stop her in her work. Most often the object is to block the person in every way possible.

> T: "You, Blocker, how have you affected her? Have you stopped her?"

> C: "No, but I've slowed her down."

> T: "Your assignment was to stop her and you have only slowed her down. How many lifetimes have you been trying to stop her?"

The answer may indicate a first lifetime attachment. More likely, however, the interference started many lifetimes before.

> T: "You've been here that long and you have not accomplished your purpose, you have not completed your assignment. What happens to you when you fail? What is the punishment for failure?"

There is a denial of failure. The dark one begins to look and feel foolish and becomes defensive. The therapist presses in on this failure. There is concern over losing face and deep fear regarding the punishment for failure.

C: "I haven't failed. I've slowed her down."

T: "Big deal. Your assignment was to stop her. She is much stronger than you are."

C: "No, she's not. I'm stronger."

T: "You have failed in your assignment, Blocker. You are going to be punished. Look outside, are they waiting for you?"

C: "Yes. I can't go."

This dark one will perceive other dark ones waiting outside. They always appear to the attached dark one as very angry. It knows they are here to take it back to the darkness. There will also be other dark ones lined up to replace this one. There are always numerous replacements. They are considered expendable by the dark superiors, though the attached ones do not know this. They think they are important and the only ones who could possibly perform their particular task. It's like shark's teeth or snake's fangs: when one is lost, another drop into place individually, as needed, to replace the lost ones.

There may be an attitude of possessiveness and ownership. The dark one might state that its assignment is to take this one back to the master.

T: "You're working for him. What is your reward for taking her back to your master? What do you get?"

C: "Nothing. I just get to do it. He doesn't punish me."

They act as if it were a privilege. This little dark one efforts and struggles without thought of reward.

The process of demonic spirit releasement requires fantasy, imagery, and acceptance of certain spiritual figures. This is not a religious exercise and does not require adherence to any religious belief or practice. This can be explained to the client before a session begins or after the dark one has been discovered. Certain names will be used and specific beings may be called on for help. They seem to be universal and not associated with any organized church or religion. Spirit beings are eternal. Human beings have developed the rules and restrictions of organized religion around misperceptions, misinterpretations, magical thinking and false individual beliefs.

THE SPIRITS WHO ASSIST IN THIS PROCESS MAY BE ARCHETYPAL OR TOTALLY IMAGINARY. THEY MAY ALSO BE ABSOLUTELY REAL CONSCIOUS BEINGS EXISTING IN A NON-PHYSICAL REALITY OF A VIBRATIONAL LEVEL DIFFERENT THAN THE EARTH LEVEL.

The spirits who assist in this process may be archetypal or totally imaginary. They may also be absolutely real conscious beings existing in a non-physical reality of a vibrational level different than the earth level.

The following is the typical and idealized sequence of a releasement of a dark-energy form, the demonic spirit. Surprisingly, many sessions follow this format very closely.

> T: "I call on the Christ Consciousness to guide and direct this healing work."

Depending on the religious sensitivity of the client or the therapist, the word "Light" may be substituted for Christ Consciousness.

> T: "I call on the Warrior Angels of Light, to stand against the darkness that would interfere."

In the imagery, these powerful beings stand shoulder to shoulder around the space of the releasement proceedings forming a fortress surrounding in every direction, including overhead and underneath.

> T: "I call on the Mighty Rescue Spirits of Light to work with us here in this place and time."

The dark side has their own rescue spirits so it is imperative that the rescue spirits of Light be called. These angelic spirits capture and transport the dark ones back to their appointed and appropriate place in the Light. Their destination is distinctly separate from the path of evolution of the deceased spirits of human beings. In rare cases, with the appropriate preparation, a former dark one can join the reincarnation cycle and become a human being.

> T: "Mighty Rescue Spirits, move deep inside this one (the client) and locate that dark one. In the name of the Light, bind that one in a net of light, a mesh of light, a capsule of light. An impenetrable, inescapable, impervious capsule of light surrounding that dark one now. Begin to squeeze the capsule of light, squeeze tighter and tighter, until that one cannot breathe. How does that feel, little darkness?"

The diminutive adjective, "little," is purposely used to goad the dark-energy being. They may defend against this insult by replying that they are not little. It may prod a reluctant dark one into conversation.

A persecutor sub or alter personality will not see or feel the light. A subpersonality is at the same level of spiritual awareness as the client in conscious state. Except for the more powerful demonics, most of the dark ones will respond to the light surrounding them.

C: "It hurts, it burns. I can't breathe. I'm dying."

They are told by their superiors to avoid the Light, that it is harmful and they believe it. Some anthropomorphizing of the demonic being may be helpful. The request is directed to the Rescue Spirits to squeeze until this one cannot breathe. This is a powerful hypnotic suggestion to the dark one. Spirits do not breathe, though they are susceptible to suggestion and easily influenced and swayed. In all but the more advanced dark ones, the intellect is not well developed.

T: "What did they tell you about the Light?"

C: "They told me to stay away from it. They said it would burn, they said it would destroy me."

T: "That is the third deception. Is it burning? Is it destroying you?"

C: "Yes, it's burning."

T: "Are you being destroyed?"

C: "No."

T: "Look again, is it burning?"

C: "Well, no."

T: "Did they lie to you?"

C: "Yes."

T: "The third deception is that the Light is dangerous. The truth is, Light will not harm you in any way. Are you being destroyed?"

C: "No."

T: "Did they lie to you?"

C: "Yes."

T: "The second deception is that you can be destroyed, that you can be annihilated, that you can cease to be. The truth is, you cannot be destroyed, you can never cease being. You are an eternal spirit being. What's happening to your edges as the capsule squeezes tighter?"

C: "They're getting fuzzy, they're fading, they're turning gray. They are disappearing."

The true demonic beings have not been human, so they have no experience of dying, though they may have a sense of the concept due to contact with human minds. As their edges become fuzzy, gray or ragged, as they begin to disappear, they often momentarily fear death. They think fading means dying.

T: "Are you disappearing?"

C: "No."

T: "They were partly right, something will disappear. What is happening to you right now?"

C: "I'm not burning. I'm not dying. I can breathe."

There is very little belligerence at this point. The entity's focus has been turned from its assignment with the client and its defiance and threats toward the therapist to thoughts of its own survival. It begins to understand that it has been deceived.

T: "You realize they deceived you about the Light. Did they lie to you about anything else?"

C: "I don't know."

T: "What will happen to you now?"

C: "I can stay here."

T: "THAT IS NOT AN OPTION. You cannot stay with this person. What will happen to you if we open the capsule?"

Almost always, other dark ones are standing outside a distance away. These are the watchers. They report back to headquarters with information about the proceedings. They also seek to retrieve the captured dark ones and return them to their superiors. The little dark being often begins to show fear. It knows the punishment for failure.

> C: "I can't go with them."

> T: "Look out there. Are they waiting for you?"

> C: "Yes, they're angry."

> T: "What happens to you when you fail? You have been discov-
> ered and you have spoken with us. That constitutes failure.
> Recall another time when you failed. What happened?"

The dark beings are just as susceptible to the command "Recall" as any client. They will often become quite agitated. They remember and describe the place of punishment as cold and dark. They can hear others moaning and wailing but can never get close to any other being. They are alone. They are kept there for a very long time. They are threatened with an eternal stay in this cold dark place, their suffering terminated only by annihilation. They label this place The Pit. It is described as hell. They do not want to go back.

> T: "There is one other option. Are you interested? Are you
> curious? Curiosity is a sign of intelligence."

> C: "Yes."

> T: "Turn and look deep inside yourself. Begin to focus deep
> inside, to your center, to the very center of your being, to the
> very core of your existence. What do you find?"

> C: "Nothing, it's just dark."

> T: "Keep looking. What did your superiors tell you about what's
> inside you?"

> C: "There is nothing there except darkness."

> T: "That is the first deception. Keep looking. Through the
> darkness, through the layers of black slime. Keep looking,
> keep going, right into your center."

If the dark entity shows hesitation and obvious fear, the therapist offers to metaphorically go with it in the search.

> T: "Are you afraid? Would you like me to go with you?"

Surprisingly, the answer is often a timid "Yes."

T: "Then by an act of will, create a tunnel to the center of your being. Together we walk side by side down the tunnel, not touching, neither ahead nor behind. Let's move swiftly down the tunnel. Is that better?"

C: "Yes."

T: "Let's keep moving. What do you see ahead? Look carefully."

C: "Nothing. There is nothing. It is just dark everywhere."

T: "Let's keep going. Keep looking ahead. What do you see?"

C: "There is some light. Just a little light."

T: "No, they told you there was nothing inside."

C: "Yes, there is light up ahead."

T: "They deceived you. They told you there was no light inside. The first deception is that there is no spark of Light at your center. This is the denial of God, a deception of the first magnitude. This spark of Light is the spark of God consciousness. The truth is, every created being is a spark of God consciousness, each in a slightly different frequency or vibration, so each is recognizable. It is the spark at the center of your being which gives you eternal life. No one can take it from you. The dark ones can neither give you life nor can they take it away. Once you believe the first deception, that there is no Light at your center, you will believe the second deception, that you can cease to be. After that you will believe anything. They tell you the Light is harmful and you must stay away from it. If you believe this third deception and obey this command, you will never learn about the Light. How does it feel to know they deceived you from the beginning?"

C: "I don't like it. I'm angry. They lied to me."

T: "Would you continue to serve these masters who deceived you like this?"

C: "No."

T: "You can go on ahead now, you don't need me any longer. Describe what you see."

C: "It is a little light. I'm afraid it will burn."

This is the remnant of the fear instilled by their superiors. The Light has been described as a flicker, a spark, a candle, a speck, a little flame, a red coal, a pearl, a diamond, a star, a ruby, a crystal, an emerald, a fire, a sun. Occasionally the being describes a scene such as a meadow with a sun overhead which grows larger and warmer or a stream bubbling from a spring. The spring is the metaphor for source and it will begin to glow.

T: "What happens to it as you continue to observe it? What happens to the little spark?"

C: "It gets bigger. It's growing."

The spark always grows larger after the encapsulated dark being discovers it. The dark watchers can sometimes funnel dark energy past the Warrior Angels of Light into the attached dark one even though it is bound in the capsule of light. It might report that its spark is getting smaller. The belligerence and defiance may flare up. It might begin to express hostility again. This indicates there has been a breach in the defenses.

When this happens the therapist calls on the Rescue Spirits to squeeze even tighter, and the dark one will get lighter again and more compliant. As the interaction continues, it may turn darker once again. This means there is interference from the outside; dark energy is being funneled in somehow. The therapist calls for help.

T: "I call on the Warrior Angels to locate any pipeline, any conduit, any fiber, any thread, any connection from an outside source of dark energy to this one inside. Warrior Angels of Light, cut and sever any conduit of dark energy coming into the capsule. Disconnect any tieline, any pipeline, any supply line of dark energy coming into this encapsulated one. Crush any attempt to funnel dark energy into this space. Cut and sever completely any conduit of dark energy from any source to this dark one inside."

In a moment, the one in the capsule will report the spark is again growing larger. The breach has been sealed.

T: "Move closer to it now. Move closer to the spark of Light as it grows. How does it feel? Does it burn?"

C: "No. It feels warm."

T: "Step into it. It is your own Light. It is the center of your being. It is who your are. You can start by putting just one toe into the Light. Now you can step right into it. Stand tall in your own Light, little friend. How does that feel?"

Once the dark being has stepped into its own Light, the darkness disappears, the transformation is complete, and the therapist can use the term "friend" if it feels appropriate.

C: "It's warm. Peaceful."

T: "How long since you have felt warm?"

C: "I don't remember."

T: "How long since you felt peaceful?"

C: "I can't remember."

T: "What has happened to your dark form, the darkness we first saw?"

C: "It's gone."

Some will say it has melted, dissolved, it's disappearing, turning gray, turning light, or just gone.

T: "Look out at the rescue spirits of Light who have come for you. How does your Light compare to theirs? Can you see it?"

C: "Mine is not as bright."

T: "In your appointed place in the Light you will find peace. Your Light will grow and become stronger. There is no pain, no punishment in the Light. It is warm and safe. How does that sound?"

C: "Sounds wonderful."

This transformed dark spirit, this former demon is ready to go home to the Light, safely on a new path. But the work is not complete yet. As the release process continues, the therapist can also probe for other dark ones, working individually and in groups.

Group Demonic Entity Release

Though the prospect of rest and peace in the Light sounds good to the little demonic being, there are consequences for its past behavior and actions. This is made clear.

> T: "You have caused much harm to this person since you joined her, is that correct?"

> C: "Yes."

> T: "You have caused much harm to other people over the eons, is that correct?"

> C: "Yes."

> T: "You will have to make up for all the harm you have caused. You will have to experience everything that you caused others. You will have to suffer in equal measure all the suffering you have caused others through the eons. Every thing will be balanced. Do you understand that?"

> C: "Yes." There is often some fear.

> T: "You can suffer every pain that you caused others. You have caused much pain, yes?"

> C: "Yes, do I have to? I don't want to."

> T: "There is another option, another way to balance the consequences of your actions and behavior. You can help others out of their pain. You can save others from pain. You can save other people from infestation by the dark intruders. You can remove and rescue the dark ones from their bondage, just as you have been rescued. How does that sound to you?"

> C: "How can I do that?"

> T: "In the Light, you can rest as long as you want to or need to. When you are ready, there is a place of rehabilitation and a course of training. You can prepare to become a member of the Rescue Teams of Light. Look out at the Rescue Spirits of

Light who have come for you. Do you recognize any of these as former dark ones you have known?"

Often there is a recognition of some of the rescuers. One client described the surprise of the transformed entity when it recognized his feminine counterpart among the rescue spirits of the Light. She was not female as a gender, but feminine as an aspect of being. It was also made clear to the client that this one had been released by this process by the same therapist during an earlier session with a different client.

T: "There is something you can do now to begin balancing the harm you have caused. Do you have any subordinates, any underlings?"

C: "Yes, a lot of them."

T: "Are they here with this person? Do you have your little dark ones assigned somewhere else?"

C: "Yes. Some are here. Some are with other people."

The newly transformed one cannot be sent out after the underlings. It is not strong enough to ward off capture by the watchers waiting outside. As it calls to its underlings, they begin to converge on the location of the releasement procedure.

T: "I call out to the Rescue Spirits of Light. Gather each of these dark ones in a capsule of light. Gather each one as it comes in its own capsule of light.

You are their commander. Begin to call to them. They will listen to you. Call out to those attached to other people where they are assigned. Call out across the horizons of time and space, in this world and any other, in this dimension and any other. Do you understand what I'm asking you to do?"

C: "Yes. I understand."

T: "Do they hear? Do they listen? Are they coming?"

C: "Yes. They listen, most are coming. I didn't realize there were so many."

T: "You've been working in the darkness for a long time, yes?"

C: "Yes."

T: "Command them to look for their spark inside. Are they doing this?"

C: "Yes."

T: "I call out to the Rescue Spirits of Light. Gather each of these dark ones in a capsule of light. As they find their own Light within, lift them swiftly and directly to their appointed place in the Light. Are they going?"

C: "Yes, everything looks bright."

T: "I call out in the name of the Light to all of those underlings of this one. Come to this field. Gather here in the name of the Light. Are more coming at my call?"

C: "Yes. More are coming. There are so many."

T: "Call out to those of equal rank and stature to yourself. Do they listen? Do they come?"

C: "Some of them but not all."

This is almost the universal answer. Those of equal rank and stature will listen and some of them will choose to come immediately.

T: "In the name of the Light, I call out in the darkness for those of equal rank and stature to this one. Come to this place of Light. Mighty Rescue Spirits of Light, gather them as they come. Do more of them come at my call?"

C: "Yes, more are coming, but not all."

T: "To all of you of equal rank and stature who come, call out to all of your underlings. Call out across the horizons of time and space. Command them to come to this field of Light. Do more come at their call?"

C: "Yes, many more are coming, the sky is filled with them."

T: "Call out to those of higher rank and stature than yourself. Do they listen? Do they come?"

C: "No, they don't pay any attention to me."

Again, this is nearly always the response. Those of equal rank will acknowledge each other. The underlings are subjugated by fear. Those of higher rank will not deign to listen to those of inferior rank.

T: "In the name of the Light, I call out into the darkness for those of higher rank and stature than this one. I call out to all those of higher rank, up to the very Generals themselves. Come to this place of peace and Light. Mighty Rescue Spirits of Light, gather these higher ones as they come. Do more come at my call?"

C: "Yes. They're big."

The newly transformed dark one often shows fear at the presence of the higher dark beings. Intimidation and pain are commonplace in the dark hierarchy. Fear is the result.

T: "In the name of the Light, all of you of higher rank and stature in the darkness, call out to your underlings, your subordinates, wherever they may be. Mighty Rescue Spirits of Light, gather them as they come, encapsulate them and transport them to their appointed place in the Light. Are more coming at their call?"

C: "Yes, there are so many."

T: "In the name of the Light, I call out to all of the replacements for all the dark ones who have chosen for the Light this day, down to the tiniest bullet of dark energy, for all of those dark ones who have come to this field. To all of the replacements, unto the end of the replacements, there is a place in the Light for all of you. Mighty Rescue Spirits of Light, gather them as they come. Do more come at this call?"

C: "Yes. The sky is black with them. They come like a black ooze, like black lava flowing this way."

T: "In the name of the Light, I call out to all in the darkness who would choose for the Light this day. To all those who have feared the Light, who have wanted to explore the Light but have been afraid to let it be known, you are welcome. Are more coming?"

C: "Yes, they still come."

T: "In the name of the Light, I call on Archangel Michael and the Legions of Heaven; to continue this rescue and move the path of this exodus far from us here in this place. Maintain this path of freedom wide open and move it far from all of us in this place, our families and friends, far from this building, far from the places we live and work, and from our vehicles of transportation. What is happening, little friend?"

C: "They are still going, but it's far away now."

Many clients become fearful at the sight or thought of such a gathering of dark energy or demons close to them. Some protest, others continue with the process, trusting the therapist. It is comforting for the client and the therapist alike to see Archangel Michael move the dark stream far away from the treatment room.

The demonic spirits can act alone or in groups to hold spirits of deceased humans in the earth plane. As the dark ones let go and come to the Light, these earthbounds are suddenly free. They need help at this time.

T: "In the name of the Light, I call on the Mercy Band of Rescue Angels of Light to gather the lost souls, the confused earthbound spirits who have been freed by the release of these dark ones this day. Wherever they may be lost, Rescue Angels, locate them and take them home to the Light."

This is all that can be done for them. Many earthbound spirits will be rescued in this way.

Seldom will this single demonic entity prove to be the only dark influence with a client. The transformed dark being can be enlisted to assist in the discovery of other dark ones. It is not sent to scout for others, it does not leave its protective capsule. It is requested to look around within the body for them or recall whether it has ever known of others attached or hovering near the client. Any others located in this manner are addressed and the Mighty Rescue Spirits of Light are directed to bind each of them in capsules of light for later treatment.

These other dark ones attached can be connected with another network, or they may be working alone. Some are even renegade demons who have struck out alone and reject any authority or dark superior. The same process is used for the release. It usually moves more quickly and easily than the first one.

T: "Are you ready to move into your own place in the Light now, little friend?"

C: "Yes. Thank you."

T: "You're welcome, and thank you for your assistance. You have taken the first step in balancing the harm you have caused. How does that feel?"

C: "Feels good. Can I go?"

T: "Yes. As you go, is there anything you want to say to this one you were with?"

C: "I'm sorry."

This is often a time of tears, as the little being begins to realize the full import of his actions and damaging behavior to the client and all the other human victims. Usually there is a plea for forgiveness. Most clients extend this forgiveness with an unconditional love that is inspiring to the therapist. It is a holy instant.

T: "Mighty Rescue Spirits of Light, lift this one swiftly, safely and directly to its appointed place in the Light. We send you to your own place in the Light, little friend, and we say farewell."

The therapist has just performed an exorcism of a demon. Not from the adversarial position of a priest, not with rancor and animosity toward this foul thing, but from a compassionate stance of tough love for a created being who went astray. Long ago this spirit made a serious error and chose the dark path. It is certain that it caused untold misery to countless beings along that path. It has also suffered great pain in the darkness.

These beings carry a heavy karmic debt which will have to be balanced fully. As more dark beings transform by rediscovering their own spark of God within and choose the option of joining the teams of Rescue Spirits of Light, this work of releasing other dark ones from their bondage will continue to expand. The Forces of Darkness which plague this planet will be diminished. There is much work to do.

Release of the Demonic Networks

There seem to be networks of demonic beings, with specific target populations such as women, physicians, healers, gay people, children, light workers, politicians and many others. These networks are like branches of bureaucratic government, concerned with only one aspect of business of the realm. Each network is headed by a director, a very high dark being. Before the final release of the transformed dark-energy being, the therapist attempts to discover any and all dark network connections.

T: "In the name of the Light, I ask you and your subordinates,
and those of equal rank and stature and their underlings, is
there some specific target for your interference?"
"Is there anyone in particular you go after?"
"Who are the people that you and your subordinates are
assigned to?"
"What is the assignment?"

If the attached dark being acknowledges itself as part of a network of dark
beings, the Legions of Heaven under Archangel Michael are requested to follow
the dark threads of consciousness outward to every dark-energy being that is part
of the network, up to and including the director. Some are attached to living
persons or earthbound spirits, others are connected with certain locations,
structures, artifacts and weapons. The Legions of Heaven are requested to bind
each dark one in its own capsule of light and transport it swiftly and directly to
its appointed place in the Light.

If the family-disruption network is discovered, the Legions of Heaven are
requested to seek out and remove the dark ones attached to all members of the
family, the ancestors, the descendants, living and deceased, the offspring yet
unborn, and those other people who have married into the family throughout all
the generations, and anyone else who had anything to do with the family
members.

Several networks may be interfering with any one person. A married
female physician with children may be infested with representatives of the
networks focused on doctors, women, mothers, children and families. The
Legions of Heaven are requested to follow every connection of each and every
one of these networks and to encapsulate and transport swiftly and directly to its
appointed place in the Light each and every one of the dark-energy beings
associated in any way with any and all of these networks, interfering in any
manner with any human, living or deceased, including the offspring yet unborn.

Because of the success of these methods on individual and family
situations, this work with the dark networks is done largely on faith.

Spawn of the Demonic

There is another form of dark being. These are not created but spawned
by the higher demonic beings and have no spark of Light within. These dark
thought forms are robot-like entities who do the bidding of the dark ones. They
are totally without emotion or affect and are completely mental in operation.
There is no emotional outburst in their resistance. These beings do not respond
to love, as they exist only in the mental realm, but they do respond to wit humor.
Little else is known about these beings. The Mighty Rescue Spirits of Light are
called on to encapsulate and finally remove these, though they will not and cannot
locate the spark of Light within.

Fragmentation of the Demonic

The demonic spirit does not fragment and separate in the same way that the human consciousness or soul-mind fragments. However, a higher dark one may extend projections of itself to many different people if the job or purpose of infestation is beyond the capability of a lesser dark being. The higher dark one maintains closer control over the situation and can more easily monitor the results of the infestation by projection rather than by assigning lower echelon demons.

These projections are connected by a dark tendril or tentacle, stretched out from the main dark blob shape of the dark-energy being. This is not in any manner similar to the silver thread connecting mind fragments to the human. The dark projections have a tiny spark and separate consciousness similar to human subpersonalities. They can describe their purpose and the location of their central controlling dark-energy being.

If they are discovered first, the central controller can be captured. If the discovery process leads to a higher dark-energy being and it is encapsulated in light, it may not divulge its projections. The therapist must ask specifically for any projections, extensions or spawn which have been assigned and left behind.

The projections may be discovered in a session. They may divulge that the one which projected them has already been taken to the Light, the tentacles severed. They continue their work, but without much power behind them. They will capitulate very quickly and call in all other projections of the high dark-energy being.

Reality of the Demonic

The question arises about the reality of demons and demonic possession. In an orderly universe created by God, why would He allow such beings to exist? Why would He allow His human creations to be so plagued by them? Why is such chaos allowed in the world? Some people have speculated that this is His way of giving humans an incentive to strive for something better. The dark ones act like starting blocks for a runner, something to give the impetus for forward movement, something to push against on the journey back home to the Light.

In the act of creation, He gave his created beings, the individual sparks of consciousness, the power of free will. This is the greatest of His gifts. As great as this gift is, there must be something equally significant to choose between for this power of free will choice to be meaningful. There must be something upon which to exercise the power of choice, something of enormous impact. It seems to be the choice between Light and darkness.

Of course this is only a speculation growing out of the extensive clinical work with the dark-energy beings.

Overcoming Resistance of the Demonic Beings

Surprisingly, many cases of spirit releasement of the dark-energy beings will closely follow the format described above. It is almost like following a recipe. The therapist may well doubt the validity of the process because of the relative simplicity. However, the results are often astounding to the client and therapist alike, especially if the releasement is done remotely and the recipient of the healing work is not aware of the releasement. Many people have used these methods and report similar posi-

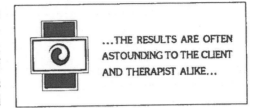

...THE RESULTS ARE OFTEN ASTOUNDING TO THE CLIENT AND THERAPIST ALIKE...

tive effects. It is the consistency of the results which tend to validate the concepts and methods of this clinical paradigm.

If the client indicates that the capsule of light does not affect the being, there are several possibilities. It may be a thought form, a fantasized creation of the client's own imagination or subconscious mind, a defiant subpersonality or persecutor alter personality.

Although in most such cases the dark beings resist the process at first, all but the strongest will respond to the binding capsule of light. For those stronger dark ones who see the light but disregard it, or burst out of it without effort, the therapist calls on the Higher Source for assistance. This is a last resort, and is done only after other efforts have failed. The nature of the Higher Source is unknown.

> T: "In the name of the Light, I call on the Higher Source. We ask that this dark one be walled up in a cage of Light, a box of Light, tightly closed on all sides, top and bottom. (pause) We ask that the box close in tighter and tighter on all sides."

The one confined in this manner may fight against the Light for a time, but will finally succumb. It knows about the spark of God within and is openly defiant toward it. When it finally transforms, it might request permission to return as a being of Light to assist the therapist in the releasement work.

The Price of Failure—The Pit

The smaller dark ones may fight the capsule of light and may refuse to look inside, in defiance of the therapist. The therapist directs them to recall the price of failure.

> T: "What happens to you when you fail? Recall a time when you failed. What happened?"

> C: "I haven't failed."

Defiance and bluster mark this reply.

> T: "You have been discovered, you have been captured, and you have spoken to us. That constitutes failure. You know exactly what I mean. Recall a time when you failed. Recall the punish-

ment for failure. Recall vividly what happens to you. Describe it. What happens? Where do they take you? What's it like?"

It is assumed that the being recalls the experience and the questioning shifts into present tense.

C: "It's dark. They beat me. It's a dungeon. It's cold. I'm all alone."

T: "What do they threaten in that cold dark place?"

C: "I'll be here forever. I'll never leave. I will cease to exist."

T: "What do they call the place of punishment?"

C: "'The pit.'"

T: "How did you get out, if they threatened to keep you in the pit forever?
What happened?"

C: "I had to promise...."

T: "Promise what?"

C: "I had to promise to behave, to work harder."

T: "And you promised?"

C: "Yes."

T: "Did they assign you subordinates, some troops of your own?"

C: "Yes, how did you know?"

T: "I have spoken to many of your kind. This is the way you make promotions in the darkness. Are you ready to go back there? Do you want to return to the pit? Look outside, are they waiting for you?"

C: "Yes they are waiting. I don't want to go back. Don't send me back."

T: "Turn and look inside yourself. Deep within you is the only key to your freedom. Look to the center of your being. Look inside, what do you find?"

At this, the dark one will look inside and find the spark of Light. On the way in, either alone or metaphorically accompanied by the therapist, it may encounter grotesque faces or other threatening diversions. These are meant to deter the dark one from searching within. A pastoral scene may emerge, such as a meadow with trees. The therapist is guiding the entity toward discovery of the Light within.

T: "Look around, what do you see?"

The entity will describe the surroundings.

T: "Look upward, what do you see?"

C: "There is the sun, it's bright."

T: "Keep looking, what happens?"

C: "It gets larger, closer. It's warm."

The being has discovered its Light. The scene will fade. The scene might be a river or stream flowing from a waterfall. The being is guided to the source of the flow of water. Its source may be a glowing opening in the ground. Going into the opening, the being will find the glowing light. The glow of the light might be emanating from within a large building with guards at the portals. Many such images may be encountered. These seem to be thought constructs insinuated on the mind of the entity by the dark superiors, and meant to interfere with the discovery of the truth of the Light within.

While searching for the spark of Light within, the form of a baby may be encountered. What heart isn't softened by a "helpless" infant? The client will want to stop right there and rescue the baby. The client is directed to look into the eyes of this one; they will be blazing red. It is a deceiver, a shape-shifting dark being attempting to take advantage of the natural love of an infant. It is a deceptive ploy, but effective if not thwarted.

T: "Mighty Rescue Spirits, gather this little deceiver, this little shape shifter in a capsule of light. Remove it to its appointed place in the Light."

It will disappear, and the search for the truth of the Light within can continue.

The Decoy

When commanded to stand forth, the first dark one that emerges may go through the motions of the releasement as if it is a powerful challenge. This decoy will dare the therapist away from the larger one attached to the client. There are a few subtle signs: perhaps some hesitation in the replies of this one, perhaps too much bluster, not enough authority. The therapist may intuitively suspect that this is not the one in command. This is the key to uncovering this deception.

> T: "Are you the one in charge here? Are you the strongest one here with this person? I want to talk to the real commander here. Who is the one in charge in here?"

> C: "Yes, I'm the one in charge."

The real commander has a very large and very vulnerable ego. He does not like the little one to claim authority, even though this was part of the deceptive plan. The commander wants to be known as the strongest one. This line of questioning irritates the real commander, and brings the little decoy to the realization that it has been sent to the sacrificial slaughter.

> T: "What does your commander think about you claiming to be in charge? Did he send you out to fool us? Were you sent out as a sacrifice?"

> C: "He doesn't like it. Yeah, he sent me out."

> T: "You, commander, did you think you could fool us? Are you really in charge here, or is this little decoy really the boss?"

> C: "I'm the commander. He is nothing. What do you want?"

> T: "Step forward, commander. Mighty Rescue Spirits of Light, bind this commander in a capsule of light, begin to squeeze."

The process begins with this one. This ploy is often used by the dark commander attached to the client.

Better Use of Talents and Skills

The dark one may be covetous of his presumed position in the hierarchy of darkness. He does not want to lose his power. He feels possessive of the talents and skills he has learned in his toils. He does not want to be demoted. Even after finding the spark of Light inside, he may express the desire to stay. In this place he had a purpose, albeit a destructive one, which gave some meaning to his existence. The Light has something better to offer.

T: "You cannot stay here. That is not an option. When you move into your appointed place in the Light you will not have to give up your talents and skills. You can continue to be useful, but for a far different purpose. In the Light you will be given tasks which will call for the full use of your skills. Your talents will not be wasted."

This may prompt the willingness of the formerly dark being to move into the Light.

Scanned reproduction from *Bible Stories for Young People*, circa 1938.

Calling on the Counterpart

Feminine energy can be a soothing counterpoint to masculine energy of any species. It also seems to hold true for the demonic beings. Spirits have no gender, yet there have always been feminine and masculine aspects among the gods and goddesses of mythology, in the heavens and in the underworld. This facet of the releasement work invites speculation that the dark beings are projections of the human psyche.

If a demonic being is particularly arrogant and recalcitrant and stubbornly refuses to participate in the process, the therapist calls on the feminine aspect.

T: "I call out among the rescue spirits of Light for the counterpart of this one. I call on the feminine counterpart of this arrogant being."

It may take several tries before that one comes. There is no experience of love in the dark hierarchy. There is, however, a definite awareness of connection or partnership. With this counterpart, there is no sense of competition, as there generally is among the dark beings.

The stubborn resistance calms almost immediately upon the arrival of the counterpart. The process can resume.

Regression to Source

When all else fails, God is the answer. If the being is communicative yet stubborn, the therapist conducts a brief regression.

> T: "Recall your first experience of being. Recall your very first experience of being individual."

At first the dark being may refuse to recall anything. It may deny there was ever anything else but what it is at the moment.

> T: "Recall back, way back, before you chose the dark path. Recall your very first memory, your first experience of being aware. Recall your first experience of being. You're smart, can't you remember? I bet you can't remember."

This is a little challenge to the ego and his ability to do something. The demonic beings are extremely egotistical, and nearly always accept a dare or challenge. A few moments may pass before the response comes.

> C: "It is Light. There is Light."

> T: "Light? You? You are dark. You have always been dark. What do you mean, Light?"

> C: "There is Light. I'm Light."

Often there is surprise and awe in the voice.

> T: "How does that feel?"

> C: "Feels good. I never knew...."

> T: "You are Light. In the beginning you were Light. You are still Light. Turn and look toward your center. Look deep inside, through the layers of blackness. The blackness is illusion, nothing but a deception. You have been kept in bondage to

the darkness by the force of lies and deception. You have been deceived from the beginning of your dark path."

The attitude is more cooperative after this personal realization. The truth brings freedom.

False Alarm

Ben was a single father, a good father. His two teenaged children lived with him in a two-story house in a suburb of a large Midwestern city. He had attended an intensive training course in this therapy and he wanted to attempt a remote dehaunting to clear his house. He had awakened during the night some weeks earlier and had perceived two spirits at the foot of his bed. As he sat up, one ran out the bedroom door, and one scurried into his bathroom. His elderly uncle had died some months before and Ben wanted to make sure he had not remained earthbound in this house.

Ben had very clear imagery in the altered state of consciousness. His psychic ability was well developed. He described the front of his house. As he went inside he was directed to search each room on the ground floor. He could perceive nothing out of the ordinary. Going upstairs he searched his bedroom and his bathroom. There was nothing there. The other rooms on the second floor were clear except for his daughter's bedroom.

Going into his daughter's room, Ben described a large black form on the edge of the bed. He was naturally concerned. The spirit releasement procedure for the dark-energy being was started. The Warrior Angels of Light were in place, the Mighty Rescue Spirits of Light were standing by. Light filled the place. As Ben moved closer to the black form on his daughter's bed now encapsulated in light, it did not move or make a sound. He looked for the eyes expecting to see red. They were a light smoky blue.

The therapist directed the blue-eyed one to step forward out of the black shape. It was a female, hesitant and timid. She spoke. Ben repeated her story. This was his aunt, the first wife of the uncle who had so recently passed on. She held an infant child in her arms. Some 50 years earlier she and her husband lived on a small farm near the current location of Ben's house.

Late one afternoon, as she was making preparations for the evening meal, she attempted to light the kerosene lantern. It was made of glass. Carelessly she put it on the warm stove. In moments it shattered, splashing burning kerosene on her clothes, onto the baby in her arms, and all over her three-year-old daughter standing beside her. Screaming, they ran out of the house, flames engulfing their bodies. Ben's uncle was walking toward the house from his fields. When he saw the flames and heard the cries, he began to run. It was too late. His wife and children died before he could reach them.

The dark shape Ben first saw on the bed was not a demonic entity. It was the woman's painful memory of her charred body, the thought form of her death trauma. She happily released that burden. When she was directed to look upward, she immediately perceived the Light. In the Light were her guiding spirits, her husband only recently deceased, and her three-year-old daughter who died with her in the fire. The child had gone to the Light at the time; she was safe. The woman took the hands of her beloved family. She and the spirit of her infant daughter were lifted homeward to the Light.

Dora was a plain woman of Mexican ancestry with simple tastes. At 45, she was unmarried, overweight, and more than a little disappointed with life. She knew she had an attached entity; she could hear its thoughts expressing the desire to be near her and its feelings of ownership of her. When it emerged, she felt a dry choking feeling in her throat. In her quest for relief, she had tried many avenues of healing to free herself from this interference.

Being a religious woman, she had sought counsel with a fundamentalist minister. He and two other ministers had attempted an exorcism by deliverance. As they shouted at this intruder and demanded that it leave, it responded with anger and violence. One of the ministers was slammed back against a wall. This occurred while Dora was firmly seated in a chair. She had not touched him.

The three fundamentalist ministers were certain that this was a sign of the devil. They quit the deliverance service and told Dora not to come back. This increased her fear immensely.

She brought a friend to the therapy session for moral and spiritual comfort. They were both afraid of what might happen. As she talked she recognized the onset of the dry, cottony, choking feeling in her throat and she was frightened.

The entity was a young African boy who loved her. In the African lifetime, the two were promised to each other in marriage. He was about 16 or 17 and was first required to pass his manhood initiation. He was gathering certain stones and other artifacts in a stream bed near the territorial border of his tribe. Unknowingly, he wandered beyond the border into the province of a hostile neighboring tribe.

Suddenly three warriors surrounded and quickly subdued him. They buried him up to his neck in the desert sand. The hot desert wind blew sand in his face, into his nose and mouth. He literally drowned in dry sand. This was the source of the dry choking feeling in Dora's throat.

Verse from an old hymm, *A Call To Praise*, circa 1895, scanned in the background.

"Fear ye not the Prince of Darkness,
Or his legions in the land;
Well may he arise and tremble,
For his downfall is at hand."

In spirit he found his way back to his village. It was the family tradition that, at mealtime, a place was set for the departed spirit. He joined the others yet they could not see him and did not acknowledge his presence. His intended bride grieved and seemingly ignored him. He wandered outside in the village. Spirits of deceased warriors stood guard around their settlement. They had remained earthbound. He eventually left the area and wandered aimlessly. He found Dora in the present lifetime when she was about the age of their intended marriage in Africa centuries before.

The ministers had attempted to separate this young African warrior from his beloved without explanation or any communication. He loved her. This was no demon. They not only made a bad situation much worse, they frightened Dora with their own ignorance and fear.

As the young warrior expressed his deep love for this woman he called her by her African name. He told of his disappointment at losing the chance for a life together in their village. They both cried tears of joy at the memory of their love and grief over their loss. He agreed to leave her to fully live her present life. He loved her enough to say good-bye.

The earthbound spirits of the warriors guarding the village were released from their selfless duty. They were tired and very ready to go to the Light.

Extraterrestrials and the Dark Forces

One type of non-physical entity which attaches and interferes with people is the extraterrestrial, the alien. They attach to humans for many reasons. Some claim to be using the eyes and ears of the human as they themselves do not have the proper apparatus to perceive this reality, dimension or plane. They cannot interpret the band of the electromagnetic spectrum which is seen as color, nor can they interpret sound waves.

Many people who attempt to channel some higher source of information are deceived by opportunistic extraterrestrials. Channelling or mediumship is a temporary possession by another being, with permission of the host, but for a specified purpose and limited duration. In many cases of channelling, the being coming through refuses to leave at the end of the channelling session. This becomes a permanent spirit possession or attachment by an extraterrestrial.

People call out for a visitation by extraterrestrials, or space brothers. The motivation can be curiosity or a genuine call for help for this disintegrating civilization. They will come at the call, and the person calling better have something important to ask. The extraterrestrials are serious and have their own mission to accomplish. The call for help can be interpreted as permission to connect to the human being. This attachment can be enormously destructive for the hapless victim.

Some attached extraterrestrials assert flatly that they are taking over the world in this manner. They will simply suppress the human will, control human bodies and live here in these physical biological vehicles.

Others claim to be conducting experiments much as earth scientists conduct animal experimentation. They have implanted physical and non-physical probes and various types of devices into humans for the purpose of gathering information. There are numerous reports of shiny, metallic nodes found in various locations in the skull.

The extraterrestrials express various reasons for being here, but most have no compunction about the invasion, no hesitation regarding the violation of the free will of the affected human. Basically, there is no concern for the Prime Directive of non-interference with a sentient species, to borrow from Star Trek.

Attached extraterrestrials may be lost, marooned or retired here on the earth (Fiore, 1989). They may be associated with a nearby spacecraft, surveying or gathering information. Through the consciousness and voice of the client, the focus of the session shifts to the command hierarchy, beginning with those in the spacecraft. The highest ranking leader, the commander-in-chief, is the final target goal. The space commander, crew leader or the science officer can be summoned. Lines of communication are maintained between all members of this alien crew. The client can repeat their words as they speak. They may reveal that they are under orders and are part of a fleet of several such crafts on similar missions around the earth. They can cross-connect with base headquarters. The client can repeat the words of the base commander.

In some cases, the base commander will acknowledge the intrusion and will agree to remove the probes, the communication devices, the implants or whatever invasive mechanisms have been placed. They sometimes claim that they were just doing experimentation, much like earth scientists and did not realize that humans would either be aware of the intrusion or object to the work. They give the appearance of compassion and quickly cooperate with the request to disengage.

In other cases, however, the base commander may be evasive, deceitful, even defiant and refuse to remove the intrusions. Even so, he will usually divulge the information that there is a high dark being who controls his people. The therapist demands, not personally, but in the name of the Light, to speak to the highest in command of this group.

The high dark commander will grudgingly come through. The client is again cautioned to refuse permission for it to approach or to control the body or voice in any way. The client can repeat the words of this dark-energy being. This dark one may be a former Angelic being who followed Lucifer in his rebellion, one of the dark Princelings beneath Lucifer, the Prince of Darkness. Though very powerful, these errant beings exist in terror of Lucifer and his ostensible might. They are jealous of his power and envious of his legions.

They attempt to establish their own kingdom of dark-energy beings, their own organization of dark interference. Somehow these dark Princelings have convinced, induced or forced various groups of extraterrestrials, through coercion or temptation of the rulers, to obey them. The rulers agree to a pact with the dark forces, and an entire race of extraterrestrials comes under subjugation.

Once this is accomplished, the dark underlings, the minor demons, are assigned and attached to the extraterrestrials. This generates the same distortion of thinking that humans suffer with the same affliction. The extraterrestrials are then motivated to greed, power, domination, aggression, antagonism, and exploitation without compassion.

When this condition of attached extraterrestrial being with nested demonic is discovered in session, the same process of releasing nested demonic beings from earthbound spirits is initiated. The aliens are freed of their dark burden. The demonic beings are the same on this planet and any other where the Lucifer energy has penetrated. The same spirit releasement process works.

There are planets and perhaps universes where the Christ Consciousness, the Light has not penetrated. The Lucifer energy arrived there first and is considered God in some of these planets. The dark ones are treated with the same procedures and transported to the Light of this universe.

The aliens are sent back to their spacecraft, their base headquarters, or the Light. In some cases, they are from another, perhaps parallel, universe. The Light from other universes is often described as a different color such as purple, blue or green. The Light in this universe is always seen as golden white.

The dark Princelings nearly always capitulate without much resistance. They are very intelligent and remember clearly the Light and their place in it before the rebellion. They are repentant and often tired of the struggle. They welcome the opportunity to return home to the Light. Their entire dark network can be herded into their appointed place in the Light. Perhaps an entire alien civilization can also be liberated and turned toward the truth of the Light.

Comparison of Treatment—Multiple Personality Disorder and Spirit Possession Syndrome

Therapy with the multiple personality can be long and arduous for the therapist as well as the patient. The therapeutic alliance must be nurtured and strong trust established. This is the foremost principle for the treatment of MPD and must be maintained as the framework of the therapy.

Through the appropriate use of hypnosis, the various alter personalities can be brought forward to the conscious level. The focus is on the whole human being, and a contract must be negotiated between the identified patient and the alters, agreeing to commit to therapy, and to shun suicide, homicide, or violence except in self-defense. Work must continue at a pace which is comfortable for the patient, especially in sessions involving abreaction and catharsis of traumatic experiences. A variety of therapeutic techniques can be used, selected according to the uniqueness of the individual.

The relationships among alters must be identified, and the overall intrapsychic system determined. All personalities must be accorded complete respect as individuals, and each is afforded equal time in therapy. Awareness, empathy, cooperation and communication are encouraged between alters. All the parts are informed about their roles in the dissociated system. This fosters a sense of the deeper unity which underlies the apparent individuality of alternate personalities.

The end of successful therapy is fusion or integration, and the individual must be protected following this. There is a need for a quiet time for the body and mind to heal, like a wound after surgery (Kluft, 1985; Braun, 1986; Putnam, 1989). Experts disagree on the advisability of complete fusion or integration of personalities as the treatment of choice, even though complete and lasting integration has been accomplished in many cases. In some instances, the alter personalities can maintain—and insist upon maintaining—separate and peaceful coexistence. Severe stress can once again lead to dissociation, even in a successfully fused multiple personality.

The steps in the treatment of the multiple personality can be listed as follows:

1. Trust, establishing the therapeutic alliance.
2. Making and sharing the diagnosis.
3. Communicating with the personalities and honoring or validating them as individuals.
4. Contracting with the personalities to continue therapy, not to harm self or others, including the therapist.
5. Individual and system history gathering. This means learning details such as the name; the age of the client when the personality was created and its present age; the reasons for creation and present function; where it was created—physically in the real world, inside the head, and the present position in the power structure; what functions it now serves; what problems and issues arise; and how it was created.
6. Therapeutically working the issues of each personality.
7. Special procedures, such as sand play, art therapy, occupational therapy.
8. Interpersonality communications, an early step to co-consciousness and integration.
9. Resolution and integration. After the conflict areas are resolved, integration is the goal. Some alters refuse to integrate, to be absorbed. Some fear they will die. An acceptable but less stable form of resolution is a co-consciousness or mutual cooperation among alter personalities. This is less than complete integration
10. New coping skills.
11. Social networking.
12. Solidifying gains and skills.
13. Follow up.

These steps are detailed in the first book published on the treatment of MPD (Braun, 1986).

Steps 1, 2, 3, 5, 6, 8, 10, 11,12, and 13 are also part of the treatment process for spirit possession syndrome. Step 4 is less important, as the release is most often accomplished during the same session as the discovery of an attached spirit, less often, over a period of two to five sessions. If the release is not completed during the session, it is wise to request an agreement with the entity or entities to return for another session. Regarding step 7, it is unnecessary to utilize adjunct procedures for the attached spirits. Therapy with the entity is not aimed at resolving its issues so it can lead a productive life; it has left its physical body. It has no life. The goal is to bring about sufficient resolution to release the emotional or physical bond which holds the entity to the earth plane and sever its attachment to the identified client. This will allow the next step to be accomplished—that is, moving into the Light.

The point of widest divergence between the therapies for the two conditions is step 9. After the resolution in Spirit Releasement Therapy, the entity is sent on to its own evolution, to its rightful place in the Light. One spirit cannot be fused with another. It cannot be forced to blend or integrate with another separate, sovereign entity.

By letting go of something, releasing some inappropriate connection, by getting rid of the burden of an attached spirit, the client is left whole and complete in him or her self, without the parasitic attachments. In therapy with multiples, the alter personalities are fused, integrated, blended with the original personality in the attempt to reestablish the wholeness which was destroyed by early trauma.

The differences between MPD and SPS may be due to the disparate theoretical frameworks, or therapeutic paradigms. It may be simply an artifact of the two distinct metaphors. It may also indicate that the two models are both valid and accurate in the description of their respective conditions.

The two disorders have some characteristics in common that appear similar in outward manifestations, yet are distinct from one another in cause or precipitating factors, onset, history, diagnosis, prognosis, and successful treatment, and must be considered and treated differently. The treatment for MPD is useless and confusing for a person burdened with attached spirits. Releasing discarnates from the person afflicted with MPD may allow for earlier success during treatment with the methods appropriate to that condition. In fact, releasing attached spirits from anyone beset by the lost earthbound souls will bring relief from imposed ailments and behavior. It is the best recourse for the condition.

The Final Release—Earthbound Spirits

With the successful resolution of any remaining conflicts, the attached entity is ready and more than willing to go. The being is directed to focus upward and to describe what it perceives. It is most often a brightness, a Light, brilliant and warm. With the resolution of the earlier resistance the Light is very close or surrounding the entity.

T: "Is there anyone there? Is there anyone in the Light? Can you
see the forms of any people?"

The guiding spirits usually appear in the Light. If there is nobody visible
or perceivable, the therapist prompts the entity to look deeper into the Light.

T: "Think of someone who knew and loved you when you were
younger. Look deeper into the Light. Is there anyone there?
Is there someone in the Light that you recognize and trust?"

The one who comes most often as a guiding spirit from the Light is the
mother of the entity. Next most often is grandmother. Brothers, sisters, aunts or
uncles, even children can come as guides. Occasionally father comes, especially
if there was conflict with father while both were living. This is a time when that
conflict can be healed. Buddies who died in a war often come for a soldier who
died in combat. Some entities do not recognize the guides; they look like angels,
and that is enough. All of these spirits must be tested, as described in the section
"Test the Spirits" (357). The entity, through the client, will describe hands
reaching out.

T: "How does it feel when she takes your hand?"

When the entity takes the hands of the guiding spirit from the Light, it is
most often described as "warm." The next most common descriptions are
"strong," "safe," "friendly," or "good."
Any final communication with the host is encouraged at this point.

T: "Is there anything you would like to say to her before you
go?"

Usually, it is an apology for any harm that has been done, a plea for
forgiveness and the expression of love.

T: "Now that you are connected with the Light, do you feel
stronger?"

C: "Yes."

T: "Can you reach back and repair the physical damage you have
caused? Ask the guiding spirit to help you. Can you do that?
Please tell me when that is done."

C: "Yes, I'm doing that now." (pause) "It's finished."

T: "Thank you. Will you reach in and remove the thought patterns and beliefs which you imposed on this one's mind?"

C: "Yes, I can do that." (pause) "That's done now."

T: "Please remove any emotional residue that was yours. She does not need to continue to carry any of your emotional burdens."

C: "Yes, I've done that now."

T: "Thank you. Are you ready to move on into the Light?"

C: "Yes, I want to go. Thank you."

T: "You are welcome. We send you home to the Light, with love, and we say farewell."

The client continues to observe the departing entity until it is fully into the Light. Any interference must be treated immediately. At this point, almost any interference turns out to be dark beings making one last attempt to capture the lost soul.

DECEIVER SPIRITS WILL OFTEN ATTEMPT TO INTERFERE WITH THE TRANSITION OF THE RELEASED ENTITIES INTO THE LIGHT.

Test the Spirits

The guiding spirits who come in the Light will often appear as someone who is recognizable to the entity. Even so, the entity is asked to look into the eyes of the guide. The eyes are the window of the soul and cannot be camouflaged. Deceiver spirits will often attempt to interfere with the transition of the entities into the Light, especially if there has been involvement with the dark forces or release of demonic beings during the session. The deceivers are most often demonic beings. They stand outside and just in front of the Light. They appear at first to be part of the Light, but this deception can soon be uncovered.

The deceptive behavior includes: hesitation to look at the entity; turning the head away; refusal to remove a hood which casts a shadow over the eyes; and anything else that seems suspicious. Any aggressive or dominating behavior on the part of the ones who come as guiding spirits is suggestive of the dark-energy beings. They are not true guiding spirits, they are imposters and will lead the unwary spirit into the darkness.

Beings in the Light are clothed in Light. It most often appears as white robes or gowns. It can be pale gold, pale pink, light blue, pale lavender, or soft silver. Any other color usually indicates that this false guide is not coming from the Light. The guiding spirits may be identified by the entity as angels. A further examination may reveal that these angels have wings. This is immediately suspect. Angels do not need wings to fly. This depiction of winged angels stems from artist's conceptions of these spirit helpers. On closer inspection the wings might appear to be a little bit askew, reminiscent of children playing angels in a second-grade school play. These are deceiver spirits attempting to draw images of angels from the mind of the client or the entity. The dark beings know little about angels.

The attitude and expression of those in the Light reveals peace, gentleness and love. If a mother appears stern or sad, if a father expresses anger or judgment, they are not fully in the Light. If the entity died of drug overdose the ones who come for him may be his buddies who also died of drug abuse. They may be dressed in jeans and T-shirts, with a pack of cigarettes rolled up in one sleeve. They may invite the newcomer over to party with them. These buddies are not in the Light. A call to the Light for more guiding spirits is the next step in assisting these wayward buddies to find their way home.

The dark deceivers can simulate clear eyes, warm hands, even peaceful expressions for perhaps 30 seconds. There is no hurry in sending the entities with the guiding spirits. When the therapist asks the entity to describe the feeling of contact with the guiding one, there may be some hesitation. The entity may somehow feel some distrust.

> T: "Reach out with your heart. Can you trust this one? Is this guiding spirit really what it seems to be? Trust your feelings friend, you don't have to go until you are certain."

If there is hesitation, the therapist directs the entity to withdraw its hand from the proffered hand of the guiding one.

> T: "Mighty Rescue Spirits of Light, remove this deceiver. Bind it in a capsule of light and transport it to its appointed place in the Light."

This might occur several times before a true guiding spirit from the Light can get through. The dark ones do not like to lose any of their own, and they do not like any earthbound to disavow any pact with the devil. They will repeatedly attempt to block this transition. The therapist calls on the Warrior Angels of Light to assist in making the path of transition to the Light safe.

> T: "I call on the Warrior Angels of Light to stand along the pathway to the Light, to stand against any deceiver who would attempt to interfere."

The guiding spirits of Light, the angels, any worker for the Light will not resist or refuse any challenge to their validity. They are not the least bit irritated with repeated requests for confirmation of their source. The final test for any spirit is the willingness and ability to say "Jesus Christ is my Lord and master."

T: "Can you say 'Jesus Christ is my Lord and master'?"

The beings of Light can and will immediately repeat verbatim the joyful claim. The dark ones will distort the request.

C: "Yes, I can say that."
    "Yes, I know about Jesus Christ."
    "Yes, we know Jesus is a Lord."
    "Jesus is Lord to many people."
    "We know about the Light."

Without hesitation, the therapist calls for assistance.

T: "Mighty Rescue Spirits of Light, surround these deceivers,
    these interferers. Encapsulate each of them in light. Remove
    them from the path. Carry them swiftly and directly to their
    appointed place in the Light."

When there are no more deceivers interfering, the entity feels the purity of the guiding spirits of the Light. They clasp hands and the lost ones are no longer lost; they are safely on their journey home.

The Cleanup Teams of Light

Now that the attached entities are gone, the "place" must be cleaned up. The therapist directs the cleanup efforts.

T: "In the name of the Light, I call on the Cleanup Teams of
    Light. Move deep inside, clean and cleanse every part of her
    space, every cell of her physical body, every aspect of her
    mental, emotional, etheric, and higher bodies, every chakra
    level, every compartment of mind, every track of emotion.
    Lift the residues left by the others who were violating her
    space. Disconnect any last threads of consciousness from any
    other being into her being. Remove any accumulated sludge
    left behind, anything that is not purely of her own being. She
    has the right to her sovereign space, to move forward on her
    own chosen path in this life and future lives. She has the right
    to be free. As you move through, Cleanup Teams, leave every
    part filled with light. In the name of the Light, we thank you."

The Healing Teams of Light

Some of the damage caused by the intruders was healed as they left. More help is often needed. The spirit physicians and nurse angels are called.

> T: "In the name of the Light, I call on the Physicians of Light to touch in and repair what can be repaired. I call on the Healing Angels of Light to touch in and heal what can be healed appropriately at this time. Pack with a solid salve of Light all those places which have been cleared and healed this day. I call on the Perfect Physician [The Christ] to restore the perfect pattern of body, mind and spirit."

A little motherly care is always welcome. For male or female clients this is appropriate.

> T: "I call on Divine Mother to enfold this one in light and love. Touch into the pure heart of this one, restore the beauty of this one's sweet being, the essence of this child of God."

A final recognition of all the assistance is now in order.

> T: "In the name of the Light, we give thanks to all the beings who assisted in this work today. Thank you, and we say amen."

The client usually reports feeling lighter, empty, devoid of the emotions that plagued her, free of conflicts, even some physical sensations or symptoms, and an absence of the noise or voices in the head. It is a profound spiritual experience for the client and for the therapist.

Group Entity Rescue

As the being is moving toward the Light before the last farewell, the therapist can ask if there are other spirits outside the Light. The answer is almost always affirmative.

> T: "Call to these others. Have them turn toward the Light. Do they listen? Do they come?"

> C: "They are listening, some are beginning to move this way."

> T: "Call to others behind them. Ask them to call to others behind them. Ask them to ask the others beyond and beyond. Send out the call. The Light is open. There is a place in the Light for everyone. Are they coming?"

C: "More are coming. They are streaming into the Light. It looks like a river of humanity."

Many earthbound spirits are not attached to a living human, a structure, a location or anything else. They are just lost and aimlessly wandering. This invitation is all they need to come home to the Light.

Group Entity Release

With so many single entities or groups of entities attached to one person, it seems it would take an enormous amount of time to clear one client. It is not necessary to work the entire process with each attachment. A spokesperson for each group can answer for the whole group. Once a few earthbounds find their guiding spirits, the others are usually eager to go. In the same way, once a few dark ones find their spark within, the others will go more quickly.

One woman described thousands of battlefield casualties with her. She was a military officer in a past lifetime. In that time she/he felt responsible for his dead soldiers. He survived the battle and he carried their spirits along with him. They had joined again in the present incarnation. Another woman described what appeared to her to be a stadium full of people with her. Another client described the load as a world of captured spirits. He had bargained with the dark forces lifetimes before and had repeatedly incarnated to perform the work of gathering souls for his dark master. They had attached to him instead.

A guided visualization can be effective in these cases of a large group of spirits. The therapist calls on the Mercy Band of Rescue Angels of Light to create a vortex of light, a white tornado of light, swirling over and around all these lost and confused souls. Gathering them gently, lifting them safely toward their place in the Light. The Rescue Angels are requested to search thoroughly for any remaining ones after the vortex is gone. In this way many attached spirits can be released and rescued very quickly.

Sealing Light Meditation

There is a guided meditation for the client that is very important at this time to fill the space left by the departing being or beings. Even though it is a non-physical space, a palpable emptiness is left and must be filled. If the client does not take responsibility for the filling of this space, the emptiness is a natural magnet for other lost souls.

THE EMPTINESS AFTER A SPIRIT RELEASEMENT IS A NATURAL MAGNET FOR OTHER LOST SOULS.

They will be more than happy to fill this void.

T: "Imagine now, begin to visualize, deep within your chest, a brilliant point of light. It is your connection with the Light, your connection with Source. (pause) See this light expand into your whole body, feel the energy flow through your entire body, down into your legs, out into your arms, filling your head. (pause) Imagine now that the light is expanding out past the boundaries of your body, outside your physical form, expanding out about an arm's length in front of you, an arm's length behind you, an arm's length on either side of you, as high as you can reach above your head and down beneath your feet. (pause) See and feel this light now, lovingly, protectingly, comfortably surrounding you like a large egg-shaped bubble of light. (pause) Sparkling through the bubble of light now, begin to imagine bits of emerald green, the color of the energy of healing, and bits of rose pink, the color of the energy of love. (pause) Every cell of your body has its own intelligence and will use this healing energy for the highest good of the entire organism. (pause) This cocoon of Light does not interfere with the expression of love, as you love others, or the experience of love, as others love you. (pause) Take a few moments several times a day for the next few weeks and repeat to yourself this meditation. Repeat this meditation of Light when you awaken and before you go to sleep. Take a few seconds every time you feel tired or unhappy. Do it every time you feel happy and when you smile. See and feel this light every time you breathe. Soon it will be with you permanently. This is your continued protection. Take another deep breath of light now and begin to come back into your body. Completely back into your body. Reconnect your consciousness with every cell of your physical body. Take control, take charge of your own body. When you are ready to open your eyes into your own regular state of consciousness, you can do that. Another deep breath of light now and come back."

Remote Spirit Releasement

During the Spiritualist era, Dr. Carl Wickland (1924) facilitated the release of many lost spirits through the mediumship of his wife, Anna. Several friends would form a circle around Mrs. Wickland. She would enter the trance state and Dr. Wickland would call out to the spirit attached to the identified patient who would be seated in an adjacent room. The spirit would take control of Mrs. Wickland's body and mind and the conversation would begin. From that point the process was similar to the spirit releasement therapy procedures presented here. Much of the present methodology was derived from Wickland's work.

In Brazil, remote spirit releasement is conducted routinely at the healing centers run by the Medical Spiritist Association; of Sao Paulo (Krippner, 1986, pp. 3-81; Rogo, 1987, pp. 219-241). The work is done without charge. The work of *disobsession*, as it is called, is conducted by a group of six mediums. Four of the people sit in a circle facing a fifth at the center. A sixth person acts as facilitator. A doctor or a family member can send the name and address of an afflicted person. The facilitator calls out for the spirit interfering with the identified patient. That spirit incorporates, or enters into, the medium in the center of the circle. Reminiscent of the work of Mesmer, the facilitator makes magnetic passes with the hand over the person, from the head downward, about six inches to a foot from the body. The spirit is expelled and apparently guided to its appropriate destination.

Ethics of Remote Spirit Releasement

Human beings are creatures of free will. This includes the right to pursue the spiritual path designed in the planning stage in the Light prior to incarnating. This path often includes the possibility of certain illnesses and disease conditions. There is always an emotional element in any physical condition, often it is the residue of a past-life conflict. In this way the disease has the potential for offering spiritual learning and the balance of karma. If a healer treats a condition he becomes part of the karmic balancing; he must contribute to the learning process of the body (Bruyere, 1989). The healer participates with the person who suffers the illness. Remote healing—that is, healing a condition at a distance without the knowledge and permission of the person receiving the healing—interferes with the learning potential and violates the free will of the person being healed.

Spirit attachment, except in rare cases, is not part of the Life Plan for a being. The earthbound spirits do not participate in the planning stage in the Light. If they were in the Light, they would not be earthbound. The client who seeks assistance for a problem gives tacit consent for therapeutic work by attending a session with the therapist. Remote spirit releasement—that is, releasing attached spirits from someone not present in the treatment room—constitutes healing at a distance. If the person has not requested the work and has not given permission for the releasement, there is a possibility of violation of free will. For this reason the remote spirit releasement is always preceded by a request to High Self for permission to proceed. The response is perceived in some manner by the client before the process continues.

ATTACHED EARTHBOUNDS ARE OFTEN AWARE OF OTHER EARTHBOUNDS ATTACHED TO OTHER MEMBERS OF THE FAMILY.

An attached spirit can influence the attitudes, behavior, choices and decisions of a person. In this way the free will is already violated by the intruding spirit. Such a spirit can influence a person to refuse the offer of a releasement through another person and prevent the afflicted person from working directly with a therapist trained in these methods. The successful remote spirit releasement allows a person to be returned to the path of free will choice. In the case of the aggressive, intrusive dark entities, the free will is clearly violated. No permission is requested for the removal of these.

Most people would call the police if they observed burglars attempting forcible entry into a neighbor's house. It is an extension of this attitude and thinking which justifies the remote releasement work without the express permission of the person involved.

Indications for Remote Spirit Releasement

More women than men participate in this therapy. Women are more open to the spiritual dimension of life, and usually more able to freely and willingly allow another being to speak through their voice, that is, to become the medium. The caution is given to refuse permission to any entities to approach or to use the body or voice in any way. The woman who volunteers for this service can usually hear and see the entities and repeat their thoughts and words clearly. This is a safer form of mediumship or transmitting, a process of conscious channelling.

A woman may describe problems in her family which include alcoholism in the husband, unacceptable behavior in the young children, drug use or antisocial behavior by a teenager heavy into rock music. An aging parent might exhibit erratic behavior following surgery, or a loved one might be hospitalized and unable to attend a session. These people might not be willing to consider a session.

In the dysfunctional family, therapy must include the whole system to be maximally effective. Spirit releasement therapy is a necessary part of a total therapeutic approach to individual therapy, couples counseling or family therapy. If the wife or mother in such a family is the only person willing to pursue this therapy, remote spirit releasement is indicated.

If a woman wants to attempt a remote spirit releasement on her husband just because of his nasty disposition, or a husband wants a session on his wife because of her nagging, this is not a valid approach. The remote work is done as an act of unconditional love, almost as a last resort in some cases. The remote spirit releasement is done for the benefit of the target person, not for selfish reasons of the person acting as the connecting link, the medium.

Mediumship and channeling have been studied and extensively described. It is the consensus that the message from the spirit control is filtered through the mind of the channel and altered in varying degrees, depending on the belief system of the channel and the level of language ability. This is not necessarily deliberate on the part of the channel; it is a function of the mechanism.

In photographic technique, optical filters of different characteristics are placed over the lens to create certain effects on the final photograph. Sound output from a stereo system will vary, depending on the quality of the speakers. Transmission from spirit can be in distinctly spoken words, it can also be in telepathic thoughts or non-verbal concepts. These concepts are translated into language by the person who is channelling.

The non-hypnotic discovery techniques allow the client to remain in the fully conscious and aware state. The attitudes of the client can definitely be seen in the responses of the attached entity. This is particularly apparent when the therapist becomes more demanding and authoritative in dealing with a resistant entity and the client is an egotistic male who actively avoids any form of domination by other males.

This type of client must be led to a full awareness and acknowledgment of the presence of the attached entity as a separate being. He must disidentify with the entity. The client is directed to step back mentally and allow the entity to control the voice. This is difficult for the predominantly left-brained, strongly self-controlled person.

If this is not successful then remote spirit releasement is recommended. The client is urged to invite a female family member or acquaintance into a session to act as the intermediary.

Women tend to be more right-brained and can usually go into altered state, perceive the thoughts of the entity, and repeat the responses. Women tend to cooperate, whereas men tend to compete. The personality of the client is bypassed; the resistance is absent. The communication from the entity is not contaminated by the egotistic defenses of the client. The client can be present in the session or in some other location.

In cases of Satanic cult ritual abuse, the victim/client will certainly have dark attachments. After these have been appropriately released, the remote releasement procedures can be implemented in an attempt to clear the perpetrators. This may include the family members involved in transgenerational cult activity, the leaders of the group, and other people who participated in the ritual abuse activity. The remote releasement procedures can be directed toward other victims, alive or dead, whether or not they are known to the client. This process is described in the section Group Demonic Entity Release (335).

Satanic cult ritual abuse is being uncovered in many parts of the United States and other countries as well. This most hideous of human activities and the devastation caused to the victims has been well documented (Hollingsworth, 1986; Terry, 1987; Kahaner, 1988; Spencer, 1989; Friesen, 1991; Ryder, 1992).

Technique of Remote Spirit Releasement

The person who is to act as the medium or connecting link for the remote releasement must first be cleared of her own spirit attachments. The channel is then more available to work on the target person. The remote work might be the primary focus of a session or the need might develop during a session. Attached earthbounds are often aware of other earthbounds attached to other members of the family. There might be a system or sub-family of entities acting through the bodies and minds of the family members. Demonic entities are usually involved in dark networks with specific targets such as women, couples or extended families. In altered state the client can usually perceive these connections quite readily.

Whether the remote work is the focus of the session or part of direct personal work, the client is directed to visualize the target person face to face.

> T: "Look into the eyes of _____.(the target person) Can you
> see the eyes?"

> C: "No, he is turning away from me."

> T: "Call to him, ask him to look at you."

> C: "Good, he is looking this way."

> T: "Look deep into the eyes. Can you feel the connection?"

Often the client will move in the recliner, even twitch or jerk slightly. This indicates the moment of connecting psychically with the other person.

> T: "I call for High Self permission to proceed with this work.
> What do you sense as an answer, yes or no?"

The client will usually describe a feeling of warmth, a smile on the face of the other person, a nod of the head, a shout of "YES" from the other, even a written message that reads "YES." Rarely does the response come back as "no."

> T: "Look deep into the eyes of the other. Is there something
> there? Something else there? Is there something else looking
> out the eyes? Is there another face superimposed on his? Are
> there any other faces hovering around his head? What do you
> sense, what to you perceive?"

The client may describe other eyes looking out from his eyes or from behind his eyes. There may be a dim outline of another face over his like a transparent mask. There may be other faces hovering close by.

It is essential for the client acting as the intermediary in the remote work to refuse permission for these entities to come in and take control of her body or voice. This is especially true for the dark ones who will be more intrusive and aggressive. They want to come in and take over. Unfortunately, they don't want to leave after they get in.

It is important for the client to establish this boundary, to pronounce the refusal at this time.

> C: "I do not give you permission to approach me. I refuse you
> permission to enter my body or use my voice. I do not give
> you permission to touch me or influence me in any way. I will

repeat your words."

T: "Do not touch her body in any way. She will repeat your
words. I call out to the one looking out from behind his eyes.
Step forward. What is the first thing you want to say to us?"
"I call out to the one in charge here. I call out to the strong
one with this man. The one in charge, what's your name?"
"I call out to the one who likes the alcohol."
"I call out to the one with _____(the person's name) who
likes the drugs."
"I call out to the one who _____." (descriptor of the
problem)

This will usually elicit a response from the designated spirit. The
descriptor can be any problem or condition afflicting the target person as outlined
by the client.

From this point, the procedure for the remote spirit releasement is the
same as for direct spirit releasement.

The client takes responsibility for continuing the visualization of filling and
surrounding the other person with the Sealing Light Meditation. When the
process is complete, the therapist calls on spiritual help for the target person.

T: "We call on the High Self to descend into the body of this
one, and to remain and assist as the healing and integration
continue. We ask the Healing Angels to touch in to this
person to heal what can be healed, to restore to wholeness
that which is damaged. We call on the Warrior Angels of
Light to walk with this one in the days and years of his life, to
guard against any further intrusion of dark spirits. We ask this
in the name of the Light."

It is highly recommended that the spirit releasement work be done
personally and directly with the afflicted person. It is usually more effective and
lasting if the person takes responsibility with full knowledge for the choice to do
the work, and to do the necessary healing work after the release work is finished.
In situations such as those described here, the work can be done in the name of
love and compassion, for peace and harmony within the family. It is God's work.
If it is not appropriate in the larger spiritual framework, the healing or
releasement will have no effect.

Posthumous Remote Spirit Releasement
Katherine scheduled a session for past-life therapy. She wanted to
uncover any past lives which were interfering with her present experience. Her
21-year-old daughter, Julie, had died three months earlier in a traffic accident.

She had been riding on a motorcycle with her boyfriend. Julie had been living at home and had a 2-1/2-year-old child. Katherine had adopted her little grand-daughter, knowing that Julie was not financially or emotionally capable of caring for the child. Julie had always been a problem for Katherine: unruly, defiant, and generally unpleasant.

The exploration of past lives was significant for Katherine. The process led to the planning stage for the present life. She examined the planned personal interactions with significant other people in her coming life. When she came to Julie, her face contorted, her voice tightened.

> C: "She just came in to irritate me. She just came in to make my life harder. Ooooh, she came to be like a burr under a saddle."

This sort of interaction is often for the benefit of the one who feels like the victim. It can be a spiritual lesson in patience, forgiveness and a balancing for prior-life injustices. This realization would normally prompt the exploration of the connecting lifetimes involved. In this case this possible avenue was not pursued. Her focus suddenly shifted to a viewpoint above and behind Julie and her boyfriend on the motorcycle just before the fatal accident. It was as though she were riding in a traffic helicopter describing the scene.

> C: "Oh God, I can see them. If there is anything to this possession stuff, there is a big black thing on her back. It's making her tell her boyfriend to pass the truck they are following. He's doing it. Oh my God, there's a car coming. OH MY GOD, THEY JUST CRASHED!"

Katherine was shaken by this imagery, but she continued the narrative.

> C: "She's floating here with this black thing dug into her back. It's always been with her. I remember watching her one time when she hit her brother. She was sitting down in a chair and I saw her literally propelled out of the chair. She didn't just stand up, she was lifted out of the chair and she landed on her feet. She ran over to him and just hit him. I watched the whole thing. She looked at me afterward with such a pitiful expression on her face. She cried to me that she hadn't done it. Now I know she was right."

> T: "I call on the Mighty Rescue Spirits of Light to surround this black thing in a capsule of light. Remove this thing to its appointed place in the Light. They will be gentle with her, Katherine."

C: "No they're not. They're ripping it off her and they're racing off in the other direction. Oh, she looks so sad. She's looking at me."

T: "I call on the Mercy Band of Rescue Angels from the Light. Here is a lost soul, she needs help."

C: "There is a man in a white suit. He looks kind. He says he can help her."

This was a true guiding spirit from the Light. Katherine and her daughter Julie spoke with each other and quickly reached a mutual understanding and forgiveness. This was a beautiful healing, long overdue for these two women. They completed their communication.

T: "Julie, we send you to the Light, with love. Farewell."

Some time after the session, Katherine reported that her adopted child had suddenly improved in her behavior. She had been manifesting the "terrible twos." That eased considerably. There was no exploration of the connection of Julie with her daughter, but perhaps there had been some influence. Katherine was much happier in her life.

Posthumous remote releasement seems to have a religious equivalent. Biblical scholars have long puzzled over the following verse: "Now what of those people who are baptized for the dead? What do they hope to accomplish?" (The Bible, 1 Corinthians 15:29). Part of the baptism ritual is a minor exorcism. In the Mormon faith, members can be baptized for the dead with the intention of clearing the sins of those who can no longer do it for themselves. It is a presumptuous yet compassionate act.

Out-of-Body Ministry
Some people seem to have the ability to emerge from the body by choice. The consciousness remains aware, alert and self-directed. Specific activities and destinations are possible. The manifold applications of this conscious out-of-body state stretch the imagination.

Edward was a graduate student in psychology. His father and mother had divorced a few years earlier and it had been difficult for him. He and his father had grown close during this time and they had both found solace through a born-again experience in a fundamentalist Christian church. He was quite hesitant about the subjects of past lives and spirit releasement but was familiar with deliverance ministry. He chose to attend the intensive training. As a prerequisite, a basic hypnosis class was held on Thursday and Friday nights prior to the weekend training.

   The exercise in hypnosis on the first evening was to imagine stepping out of the body, recalling one's home, locating a favorite spot in the dwelling place, and noticing the details of the furnishings, fixtures, and decorations. The instruction to step out of the body was an error. The instruction should have been to recall the home, recall the favorite spot, etc. Edward followed the instruction literally, which is not unusual for a compliant, cooperative subject in the altered state of consciousness.

   On coming out of the hypnotic state Edward described his experience. He lived in a halfway house for mentally disturbed patients. These were people who had been released from mental institutions but were not ready to resume normal living. Most of the residents lived in a dormitory-style bedroom. Edward and his charge, Andy, shared a room separate from the others. Andy was particularly disturbed and needed extra care. Normally, Andy would begin pacing the room about 10 P.M. each evening. About 3 A.M. Andy would be fatigued enough to go to bed and sleep.

   In the altered-state imagery, Edward recounted going into the dormitory.

E: "There were spirits all over the place. I called on Jesus to
    stand on one side of me and you [the trainer] to stand on the
    other side. We sent the spirits out of that place. Then I went
    in to the room I share with Andy. There were spirits jammed
    into that place from floor to ceiling. I called again on Jesus to
    stand on one side of me and you to stand on the other side.
    And we sent all those spirits right out of there."

   On the second evening of the class Edward reported that when he arrived home about 10:15 the night before Andy was in bed and slept the night through. On Saturday and Sunday of the training he reported the same thing, marveling at the apparent results of sending the spirits out of the halfway house.

E: "Are there a lot of people doing this out-of-body ministry?"

   It was the first time the trainer had encountered or even heard of such a thing. This compassionate, sensitive, trusting 25-year-old student had simply followed instructions and had somehow known what to do when he encountered the spirits interfering with the residents in the halfway house.

   Derek was a long-time student of various masters and meditation teachers. His Native American teacher assured him that months of preparation were necessary before a person could uncover past-life memory. Perhaps he had already prepared, because the affect bridge and linguistic bridge were quite effective with him. He repeated a meaningful phrase only a few times. In less than a minute he uncovered a vivid experience of a prior lifetime.

His meditations were also very clear and very real. He described being taken by his guides to various locations. As he would search the location he would discover another human form, sometimes more than one. Somehow he knew what to do. He would help them up a conveniently located stairway and the Light would be present to receive them. Consciously he had no idea what he was doing nor why. A description of this work revealed to him the meaning of his deeds over the several years he had been doing it.

Judith performed out-of-body ministry for a period of years even before she learned about the problem of earthbound spirits. In meditation she would find herself with someone in distress, a living human being, sometimes the victim of calamity or disaster. Often, these were children. She extended comfort, even sometimes symbolically nursing the little children, and offered spiritual succor to many. With the knowledge of earthbound spirits and their dilemma, she began to release these lost souls into the Light in addition to ministering comfort to living humans.

Toby was close to 40. Adept at creating wealth, he lived life simply and abundantly without working. He had full clairvoyant vision, clairaudient connection with Universal Wisdom and was a delightful spiritual teacher. His focus was spiritual enlightenment and offering the awakening thrust to other people. This gave him pleasure in life. He freely shared his enormous joyfulness with his many friends.

Toby had lived for a time in Hawaii. Naturally, he had sought out the kahunas, the spiritual healers and teachers of that magical place. He described his out-of-body work with one kahuna. Together they would journey to various trouble spots in the islands. They could see the disrupting spirits and the spirits could see them. The spirits recognized the power of the kahuna and they would scatter. Together, Toby and the kahuna cleared many areas of infestations of mischievous discarnates.

Rescue Work
Rescue work has been conducted for decades, perhaps centuries. A small group of two or more like-minded people can gather with the intention of calling out to lost spirits and directing them to the Light. The Light is invoked by a prayer or the meditation given in section Sealing Light Meditation (361). A request is made for the presence of the Mercy Band of Rescue Angels of Light to assist as necessary.

One or two members of the group relax into an altered state of consciousness. These people will act as medium or connecting link to the lost spirits. The facilitator of the group can ask the contact to repeat any words and information that comes in response to the questions. The facilitator calls out to any lost spirits or lost souls in the vicinity to come to the location. The contact person will acknowledge any awareness or perception of the presence of a spirit.

The questions are directed to the spirit or spokesperson for any group of spirits who respond. They are guided to look upward, to locate the Rescue Angels of Light, and to begin to lift toward the Light. This can be very effective for people killed in earthquakes, floods, volcanoes, airplane crashes or any disaster. Distance is no obstacle. Time does not exist for earthbound spirits. Spirits of people who died years, decades, centuries ago may still experience themselves as being trapped underground as the result of volcano eruption, earthquakes or landslides. They are often perceived as trying to claw their way out of the earth.

The contact person often perceives the scene of the disaster and the spirits still gathered in the place. Such groups operate on a regular basis for natural or man-made disasters, suicide or murder victims, persons who drown with sinking ships, combat casualties on battlefields or victims of abortion. This rescue work is effective for present-time events and for disasters of long ago.

Shortly after the October 17, 1989, Loma Prieta Earthquake in Northern California, the participants in an intensive training course requested a demonstration of the remote spirit releasement and rescue work focused on the casualties of the disaster. The woman chosen as the subject was very clear in her visual imagery. Several other people in the room also received clear impressions as the demonstration proceeded.

The Sealing Light Meditation was used for the altered-state induction and invocation as described in the section The Direct Approach (217). The therapist directed the invitation to those people who lost their lives during and after the quake. The wording of the invitation must be specific.

> T: "In the name of the Light, I call out to those people who suffered in the Earthquake. I call out to you and invite you here to this place. This is a place of safety, this is a place rescue, a place of peace. We welcome you to this place. We can help you in your confusion."

The subject immediately perceived dozens of spirits moving toward her. One participant sensed a mother with a baby in arms. Apparently many of the earthbound spirits answering this summons lost their lives in the San Francisco Earthquake of 1906. Another participant recognized spirits with oriental features. A few weeks prior to the Loma Prieta temblor, a devastating earthquake had taken the lives of thousands of Chinese.

The subject reported the presence of countless light beings ready to assist this rescue. She laughed as the image of a fire engine suddenly came into her awareness.

> C: "They're even coming to the rescue in a fire engine. The rescue squad of the spirit world. But it's like the Keystone Cops."

The beings of Light have a gentle sense of humor. They don't do slapstick comedy. This sort of cartoon image or caricature was not consistent with the nature of the higher beings.

T: "Look at the eyes of the driver. What do you perceive?"

C: "Oh! The eyes are red! They aren't here to help at all.
     They're trying to capture some of the earthquake victims."

This proved accurate. It seems the dark-energy beings wanted to muscle in on the group rescue and try to pick up a few stragglers. They projected the image of a recognized and accepted symbol of hope, the trusted fireman, everyone's friend. The dark ones could be surreptitious and quiet about their dirty work and would more often escape detection. They seem to approach many situations such as this with an inexplicable stupidity.

About two years earlier, a large earthquake in Armenia caused widespread destruction and loss of life. Rescue workers flew in from other countries with supplies and manpower to assist the people. One of the planes carrying a number of rescue workers crashed, killing everyone aboard.

Gina, an Armenian by descent, wanted to do a remote session for the people. She easily went into the altered state and perceived clear images. In spirit, one woman was trying to pull at the rubble in a helpless and futile effort to free her husband and son. She could not manage to move even a particle of physical matter. Through Gina, she was urged to focus her gaze upward. Her loved ones were in the Light waiting for her.

As Gina searched the area, she discovered that some of the spirits wandering about were the rescue workers who had died in the plane crash. They were still trying to help. Many of these lost souls were directed to the Light.

Disturbed spirits can remain in buildings or other locations on land or at sea because of strong emotional ties. This is especially true following violent death. Persons with the gift of clairvoyance or psychic sight can perceive and communicate with these confused and lost spirits. When such a spirit is locked into the repeating drama of the emotional and physical pain of the original event, a living human with the compassion and ability to reach out to them can help break this entrapment in the astral realm (Summer Rain, 1989).

Ellie was a woman with simple tastes; she shunned modern conveniences. She was a plain woman, somewhat coarse in language, mannish in dress and she was obviously missing a few teeth. Ellie had natural psychic abilities, compassion for all living things and she had a heart of gold. In summertime, she worked aboard a fishing boat in Southern California, during the winter, she shipped on a small coastal freighter which plied the Pacific Coast of the U. S. The central coast of California is rugged and rocky. The normal prevailing winds are strong and ocean is typically rough. Winter storms can generate treacherous conditions in these sea lanes. Many ships have been lost along this forbidding coast.

During some of the night watches on the ship, Ellie would sense many frantic spirits pounding on the glass windows of the pilot house where she was safe and warm. She sensed these spirits as the sailors and crew of the shipwrecked vessels, trying to get into the safety of the pilot house, not realizing they could come right through the thin walls. Her heart went out to them.

In session, Ellie wanted to help the souls of these men who had lost their lives in the violent ocean. She recalled her feelings as she sat in the pilot house. She easily recalled the sounds and faces of those who pounded on the windows. Through her, the spirits were invited into the warmth of the pilot house. They came flooding in, filling the place, and many more were outside, trying to get in. They were directed to gaze upward through the roof of the pilot house and find the brightness, like a beacon, a lighthouse leading to the safe harbor of the Light. They quickly headed Home.

The call was put out for all who had suffered in shipwreck on the rugged Western coast from Canada and Mexico and beyond. Ellie described many beings streaming from the south and from the north. They all lifted into the Light. The following winter, Ellie again shipped aboard the coastal freighter. There were no frantic spirits pounding on the glass windows of her safe pilot house. The lost sailors were in the Light, finally home from the sea.

Reverend Dr. Donald Omand of the Church of England has performed exorcisms on Loch Ness, the Bermuda Triangle, stretches of roadway with unusually high accident statistics, and portions of the oceans of the world which have the reputation for causing "Sea Madness," a condition which prompts sailors to heave themselves overboard for no logical reason. These locations are referred to as "black spots" and account for nearly two thirds of the exorcisms performed by this respected cleric (Alexander, 1978).

Ongoing Therapy

The goal of psychotherapy is change. The change can be associated with old destructive behavior patterns, attitudes, feelings, perceptions, unrealistic expectations, false beliefs, unnecessary pain, literally anything in the life of the client which leads to discomfort. The goals and results of therapy can include new behavior patterns, a more realistic viewpoint of life circumstances, greater self-esteem and sense of self-worth, awareness and development of firm personal boundaries, and improved communication.

Spirit Releasement Therapy is not a panacea; it will not cure every problem of society nor every ailment of an individual. However, it will ease or eliminate the symptoms, conditions, and behavior imposed by attached discarnate beings, so-called possessing spirits. A person can learn certain behaviors and attitudes through the influence of other people, parents, teachers or attached entities. Addictions initiated by a discarnate may continue to affect the physical body after the release is accomplished. The mental attitude and emotional desire will be almost completely erased after the releasement. The physical, mental and emotional residue, or remnants of the influence imposed by the attachments, must be addressed in therapy. This becomes a much simpler job after the entities are gone.

A great deal of work can be accomplished in the initial two- to three-hour session. If the client works well, if the impressions are clear and the expression is honest, the process can be swift and very effective. One session, however, is insufficient time to resolve lifetimes of karmic burden, release every spirit attachment from this life and previous incarnations, and heal the vulnerabilities which allowed the attachments. Even the entities which are obviously present may not be released in the first session if they are extremely stubborn or even dim-witted. They may not be able to understand what is taking place or they may refuse to cooperate. They may simply submerge and refuse to speak. The resistance encountered at the first attempt at releasement may be insurmountable.

The work is taxing on the client and this length of time is usually the maximum which can be tolerated in a single session. Clients who travel a long distance to the location of the sessions often desire intensive work over several days, even up to two weeks. Two such sessions in a day are tolerable with a relaxing lunch break. Two successive days are tiring, but effective. A day without sessions is recommended after two full days if the intensive work is to continue.

The location and nature of discarnate attachments can be seen by people who have the gift of clairvoyance. Since entities can move about in the body and aura, this picture may change during a day, and may be distinctly different on successive days. In many cases the situation may remain exactly the same over several days, weeks or even months. Some entities seem to be anchored in one place and unable to shift.

Layering

In subsequent sessions, more attached entities may be discovered. Some of them claim that they were simply not ready to go during the first session. Others insist on waiting for those who were deeper or dormant within the client, while some seem to be suppressed by those spirits which were first encountered and released. When symptoms of the client do not respond to therapy, it is safe to suspect that there may be additional entities which are reluctant to reveal themselves. As the client grows in strength and awareness, these resistant entities are usually forced to the surface and can be released.

This layering of entities is similar to the phenomenon of layering of alter personalities in cases of MPD. Failure of integration and fusion in such cases is often caused by layers of undiscovered alters (Braun, 1986, pp. 40-42; Putnam, 1989a, pp. 124-125).

Jeff was a hypnotherapist who used past-life therapy and spirit releasement therapy in his practice. In his own personal sessions, spaced about six months apart, new entities were discovered, including dark-energy beings.

One attachment was discovered about two years after Jeff's initial session. This was a being who died as an infant. As a spirit he was a mature being. He related the story of his demise.

The setting was in high mountain country in the northern United States a hundred years earlier. It was winter. His father was trudging through an unexpected snow storm toward his village, carrying his infant son. He grew weary and knew he could not reach the village. He carved a cave in a snowbank and placed the infant inside. This was the normal procedure for adults caught in such a storm. Body heat is trapped inside, there is no chilling wind, and the survival rate is high.

Father thought he could reach the village, summon help and return to the infant in time to save his life. But his energy was so drained he did not reach the village. He froze to death on the trail. As a spirit he returned and attached to his son in the snow cave. The child lived many hours after his father's death before he also succumbed to the cold and hunger. The older man was emotionally devastated by his failure to reach his village and bring help, and he suffered much guilt over his perception that he caused his son's death. He went into a deep somnolence and could not be roused. In the earlier sessions the spirit of the child would not respond to any of the discovery questions, as he refused to leave without the father. Until he was ready to awaken, the son did not want to go to the Light.

In the session the spirit of the child came forward, acknowledged that he had heard the therapist in earlier sessions, and gave his reason for not responding. He knew this time his father was finally ready to go. Together they released easily.

Jeff worked with a number of Vietnam veterans in his hypnotherapy practice. Many of these men carry the spirits of their buddies who lost their lives in combat. The bond between these men is very strong. One of these entities which Jeff attempted to release from a client seemed to be drawn to him. The symptom Jeff suspected as evidence of a new attachment was a sore spot on his heel, as if he were wearing new shoes which created a blister. It turned out to be a soldier wearing new boots that had rubbed a blister. It had not healed prior to his death in combat.

New Attachments

New attachments can develop at any time after the releasement process. The procedures do not prevent further interference by discarnates. Near the beginning of each session, a process of discovery may be helpful to locate any new attachments. The client may be more aware of the signs and symptoms of a newly formed attachment after the initial releasement session. Physical sensations and emotional feelings which are new or foreign are perceived more quickly and identified as alien. These signs are more familiar to the client and more readily disclosed. Discovery is quickly facilitated in a more cooperative effort between therapist and client.

Personal boundaries need to be established and reinforced, ego strength must be enhanced and changed. Inappropriate habits and personal behaviors must be more closely monitored by the client. The spiritual protection of the Sealing Light Meditation must be practiced on a regular basis, visualized repeatedly throughout the day by the client, and also projected to anyone who was treated remotely.

Individual Counseling

Traditional therapy can be much more effective after the release of the influence of discarnate beings. Individual therapy is focused on improving self-image, self-esteem, reestablishing personal boundaries, and developing a greater ego strength. Consolidating the gains achieved in the releasement work is important. Healing the painful memories of childhood abuse is an essential part of ongoing therapy (Bass & Davis, 1988).

The client may feel and behave differently after a successful spirit releasement. Formerly destructive behavior, habits, even addictions may cease entirely. Self-esteem and self-image may improve significantly. This new way of being is not simply the afterglow of the altered-state experience. It is truly a new way of being and is often a surprise to the client who waits for it to wear off or expects the old feelings to return, even worries if they don't. The client is urged to expect and welcome their new, albeit unaccustomed, way of being.

A person may have quite a different appearance after a releasement. The fixed expressions associated with some emotions such as anger and fear may disappear. Dark circles around the eyes will sometimes diminish or vanish, even in children. A feeling of "lightness" may show as an expression of wonder and surprise. The eyes are usually more clear, awake and focused. A client will often be delighted at the difference in facial appearance after a session.

One focus of therapy is alteration of habitual behavior patterns which were caused by an entity attachment. Though the driving force behind the behavior or addiction is gone, the force of habit can perpetuate the unwanted behavior to some degree.

The client may drop certain eating habits, anything ranging from sugar addiction to the binge purge cycle of bulimia. Drinking and drug use will cease, in many cases. Taste in clothing style and color may alter significantly. Excess body weight may drop away without effort. Relationships which were important before the releasement may end abruptly. The love bond which appeared to exist between two people may actually have connected one of the entities with the relationship partner. The relationship between two people can actually exist between two entities attached to the people and have nothing to do with the two humans at all.

Other members of the family may be surprised at the new behavior of the client. In an effort to reestablish the patterns long established, some family members may attempt to push the client back into the old patterns of behavior. This is similar to the dynamics within the family of an alcoholic. If the alcoholic person ceases the drinking, they behave differently. The family, though out-wardly happy with the change, may exert subtle pressure on the person to resume the "comfortable" old habits. The interactions with the drinking person are known and familiar, and new ways of interacting must be developed if the drinking ceases. People often resist change and attempt to resort to the familiar. For this reason the family of the alcoholic must be included in the overall therapy.

In a similar way, the family of the person undergoing spirit releasement therapy should also be involved. Ideally, every member of the family would experience the releasement process. This is sometimes difficult to achieve, as the belief systems of many people do not allow for such a spiritually-oriented theoretical approach to healing. This may be an appropriate reason for use of remote releasement procedures on the other members of the family, conducted through the client.

The client is the one who has requested treatment for areas of discomfort in her life. She is considered metaphorically as the hub of a wheel. Each person in her life has a spot on the rim of the wheel. The spokes of the wheel represent the interactions between her and the other people with whom she relates. Any work done remotely on others must be considered as directly benefiting the client. Indirectly it may help improve the quality of life of the other person.

Healing the Grief

At the subconscious level, there is an awareness of the attached entity. If there was a loving connection in the present life or past lifetime of the client, the object of this love is gone after the releasement and there may be a totally unexpected reaction of grief. The entity might have been a dear friend, a lover or mate, a parent or child, even an unborn infant of a woman who had a terminated pregnancy.

The physical body of a loved one is not the object of emotional love. If it were, there would be no reason for grief in the event of death. It is the personality, the essence, the being that shares the love connection. The being is not physical and can attach after the loss of the corporeal form. After the releasement the feeling of loss can be immediate and severe. The grief, though seemingly illogical to the client, is quite real and must not be denied. It can be expressed openly in session with the therapist who understands the dynamics of spirit attachment and releasement.

Healing the Vulnerability

It is vitally important and necessary to do therapeutic work on healing the vulnerability which first allowed the attachment. This weakness or susceptibility to attachment may have been residual mental, physical or emotional pain of the host only, with no prior connection between the host and the entity. The healing work is focused on healing of these residues, whatever the source.

Information about this opening or vulnerability can be obtained during the differential diagnosis phase of questions.

> T: "How old was she when you joined her in this way?"
> "How did you manage to get in at that time?"
> "What allowed you to attach?"
> "Where was she when you found her?"
> "Recall the experience of joining her. Where was she and what was she doing?"
> "What was the vulnerability, what was the opening, what caused the weakness, what was it that let you come in?"
> "Was she using some substance?"
> "Did she invite you in?"
> "Did she invite you in for a specific purpose?"
> "Did you ask permission? Did she give you permission to join her?"
> "Did you know her in the present lifetime before you joined her in this way?"
> "Have you known her in another lifetime?"

The weak points thus exposed can allow further interference and attachment if not healed. Drug or alcohol abuse are open pathways to spirit attachment. Without the urging of one or more entities, a person may have a better chance of ending these destructive habits through standard treatment approaches. Therapy can focus on the emotional pressures which first led to the use and abuse of the substances.

If the vulnerability was a momentary emotional flash, perhaps involved with physical pain of a minor injury or brief interaction with another person, such as a store clerk or a driver of another automobile on the highway, the client can recall and relate the event, releasing any minor emotional residue. If an emotional trauma continued over a long period of time, as in the case of a dysfunctional family situation or unhappy love relationship, the vulnerability becomes a prevailing condition. The trauma and residual emotions will require more extensive therapy, including past-lives exploration.

Many people openly invite an entity to join. A loved one may be welcomed. A lover who returns as a spirit may be quite exciting at first to a lonely widow. A single person weary of being alone may welcome the sexual advances of an incubus or succubus. This can quickly become an intolerable burden. A deathbed promise to stay together can cause great misery. If such a promise was made in a previous lifetime, the burden can become intolerable in the present lifetime.

A victim of some sort of violence can call on the powers of darkness for help in seeking revenge. The dark beings are all too willing to assist such a person.

The cost is very high; the person becomes the vessel for these dark ones, often little more than a slave to their disruptive intentions. Putting out the call to these beings is an open invitation and is tantamount to granting permission for attachment.

In times of apparent emotional abandonment, many people have lamented:

"Isn't there anyone out there to love me?"

It is figuratively expressed, yet lonely disembodied spirits take it literally and may answer the call. The result may be an attachment.

It is certainly every person's right to choose to invite a spirit. With a little education about the spiritual reality and the consequences of such a choice, the client may choose differently. Even with this new awareness, some people will choose to maintain the connection. The therapist must have a thorough knowledge of metaphysics and the spiritual dimensions in order to adequately educate the client.

A person can be approached by a spirit in a moment of vulnerability, requesting permission to join, offering promises of information, power or knowledge. The person may be naive, spiritually, and think it might be fun or empowering to have a companion spirit. Just imagine having a spirit to help at the horse races or gambling in a card game with high stakes. Once permission is granted, however, the spirit can exert a great deal of influence and offer little information.

A lonely person who fantasizes sexual pleasures may be approached by intrusive spirits bent on sexual interaction with a human. If permission is given, whether by saying yes or not saying no, the sex may be fantastically enjoyable at first. Multiple orgasm is commonplace. After a short period of time, this situation usually turns to sexual slavery, with the living human a helpless victim of the sexual activity. Spirits do not sleep and seem to be tireless and relentless in their sexual aggression, and the client may fall victim to forcible restraint and be unable to stop the activity. Lack of sleep contributes to the mental, physical and emotional toll of this foolhardy choice. What begins as vaginal intercourse can quickly become anal intrusion progressing to perverted and abusive sex.

Psychic ability can offer an open channel to an entity seeking a lodging place with a living person. Many people are unaware they have such psychic capacity. These gifted people can benefit themselves and others by finding a good and reputable teacher of psychic development. Their first step is to learn to control the psychic energy and to be able to close the psychic doorways. Persons who want to learn to channel some higher intelligence must carefully develop spiritual discernment in order to tell the difference between a teacher from the Light and an opportunistic astral entity pretending to be something great.

Physical trauma, such as a serious fall, a blow on the head leading to unconsciousness, surgery or an automobile accident may offer longer periods of susceptibility to spirit attachment. There is vulnerability during periods of time of unconsciousness, emergency-room treatment, surgery, recovery from anesthesia and the physical weakness following injury and illness.

On many occasions, the being leaves the body just prior to an anticipated physical trauma. Thus a dream of falling from a cliff and not hitting the bottom may indicate a past life in which the consciousness emerged during the fall. In such a case the body retains the physical memory of the trauma of crashing to the ground and this must be processed in session to eliminate the possibility of recreating the injury in some form in the present physical body. If the body survives such a trauma, the consciousness may return to find another being has slipped in.

Fragmentation Recovery

Recovery and reintegration of soul-mind fragments which were dissociated and dislodged during traumatic episodes is an important aspect of ongoing therapy. Techniques were covered in the section Recovery of Soul-mind Fragmentation (171).

Franny was 32 and had a number of sessions at about three-month intervals. She suffered petit mal epilepsy. For years she feared having to take medication and refused anything for the condition, even though she was so incapacitated that she could not hold a job. Her husband was loving and very patient in caring for her.

Epilepsy is not a mental illness, yet Franny was quite distressed by her condition. She often had no memory of what she had done during the minutes immediately before and after the seizures, which occurred four to six times a month. When people related what had happened, she was embarrassed and depressed. She feared mental illness and any thought of institutionalization.

Her mother suffered mental illness and was institutionalized several times when Franny was young and was finally committed permanently. Franny recalled the medication her mother was forced to take to maintain some level of functional sanity. Intellectually she knew hers was an irrational fear; medication does not create mental illness. In addition, there was some childhood fragmentation as a result of this fear.

Franny's father left her mother during her pregnancy. After she was born, he visited only occasionally. Franny missed her father and there was a fragmentation of the unborn consciousness when he left. This fragment joined with her mostly absent father. He died when she was about 28, taking from her the only parental connection to normalcy. In retrospect, the loss was amplified when it was discovered in session that the pre-natal fragment accompanied him to the Light.

In the several sessions, numerous entities were released, earthbound and dark. Past-life decisions and connections with her mother were recalled and processed. Traumatic episodes in her life which caused fragmentation were explored. The frequency of seizures diminished. As she grew in personal strength, she began to take a mild medication, which produced little or no side effects and controlled the seizures almost completely. She began to plan for her own future.

Recovery of the fragmented parts, including the pre-natal fragment which had moved into the Light with father, brought a profound peacefulness to Franny. There was no longer the emptiness and fear within her. She felt grounded and whole for the first time in her life. There was much forgiveness to do with mother, who had abandoned her by sinking into mental illness, and with father, who had provoked the loneliness and sadness by being gone so much of her life.

Forgiveness

Forgiveness is a major aspect of the ongoing therapy. This includes the willingness to forgive others as well as forgiving oneself.

Forgiveness of one's parents can release a person to a fuller life. Many adults carry anger, even rage over the way they were raised and disciplined. Parents are supposed to be perfect and infallible. At least this is a basic assumption of the young innocent child. Abuse of any kind is a terrible violation of this innocence. With therapy, this rage can be shifted to pity as the client gains insight into the parent's own dysfunctionality. Finally acknowledging that they did the best they knew how may lead to forgiveness.

If there was abuse from one or both parents, the therapeutic exploration can be assisted with the technique of stepping into the other's body and mind. This was described under the section Mind Merge (126). Through this process any approach can be used: past-life therapy, recovery of fragments, spirit releasement of any type of entity, forgiveness and healing.

A woman who has a history of one or more abortions may have a great deal of guilt after releasing the spirits of the unborn ones. Self-forgiveness can erase the guilt. This powerful healing process is described in the section Self-Forgiveness (133).

Patty was a 38-year-old woman who attended a small group-rebirthing session. During the breathing exercise, she developed a pain in her left side. Through individual processing she discovered that there was an attached spirit. It proved to be the spirit of her would-be sibling who had died prior to Patty's conception. Her mother was pregnant for 12 months, and did not have a menstrual period for that length of time. The attending physician could not explain the condition. The first fetus apparently terminated naturally at about 2-1/2 months.

Shortly after that, another ovulation occurred and Patty was conceived and carried to full term. In its insistence to be born, the spirit of the earlier fetus attached to her. It was extremely angry about the spontaneous termination and demanded that Patty's body was rightfully its own, insisting that Patty was the intruder. Past-life therapy and an exploration of the planning stage finally dispelled this unwarranted anger. Forgiving Patty was the final step in the release of this frustrated spirit.

The spirit of the terminated fetus can attach to anyone nearby. It is not unusual for a woman to accompany a grown daughter during a surgical termination. Marie, 60, discovered such an attached spirit during a session. This one had been terminated some ten years previously, when she had helped her daughter through the unpleasant process of an abortion. Exploration of the connection revealed a past life when Marie was a woman undergoing an abortion and this spirit was to be her child in that lifetime. It had returned to her in this manner. After mutual expressions of love with Marie, it quickly agreed to leave.

In a past-life therapy session, past-life characters can apologize to each other for wrongs committed and misunderstandings of all sorts. After the death is cleared, the other beings involved in the incident can be summoned. The communication can include acknowledgment of damage and wrongdoing, apologies and mutual forgiveness. What remains is love, the final healing energy.

In the last conversation between host and departing entity, the entity may acknowledge the damage caused, apologize, and ask for forgiveness. If the event has truly been cleared for the client then forgiveness is easy. Again, what remains is the healing energy of love.

An apology can be less than honest if a being refuses to take responsibility for its actions.

> C: "I'm sorry if I have caused you pain."
> "I want to apologize if I caused you harm."
> "Please forgive me if I hurt you in any way."

These are irresponsible apologies because of the word "if." Especially when the recalled traumatic event clearly depicts the damage wrought this is not an expression of regret and contrition; it is an insult. The therapist must confront the entity with this deceit.

> T: "Not good enough. Did you harm her? Did you hurt her in some way?"

The answer may be honest, or it may be evasive. The therapist must press for the truth. Anything less will leave emotional residue for each participant.

> T: "How exactly did you harm her, how did you hurt her?"

The entity may have to recall part of the scene again. Then the truthful apology can be expressed.

C: "I'm sorry that I caused you pain."
"I apologize for causing you harm."

With this truthful acceptance of responsibility by the entity, the process can proceed to completion.

Forgiveness is the final step in dissolving the residues from earlier times. In the altered state, especially in the spirit state after the death in a past-life regression, a client will often complete a process of forgiveness, then begin smiling or laughing. The realization comes that there was never really anything to forgive. The silly dramas of life are mostly governed by the ego which is virtually meaningless in the spirit level of being. A Course In Miracles declares, "Forgiveness is the key to happiness" (A Course In Miracles, 1975, lesson 121). Forgiveness is the underlying premise in this spiritual teaching. It is wise counsel today, with much of the world standing literally at the brink of destruction, morally, financially, ecologically, politically and spiritually bankrupt.

Self-Protection
At the completion of a session, the client may feel particularly vulnerable and exposed to spirit attachment. The client can make the pronouncement:

C: "I take my power back from any discarnate being who wants to attach to me. This is my space and I claim dominion here and now. I refuse permission for any spirit or entity to approach me or to attach to me in any way."

Personal empowerment is our spiritual birthright. Most people tend to give their power away to authority figures, from the parents to police officers, to organizations and institutions such as church and government, and to unseen and feared things like spirits. This is a form of projection stemming from the subconscious assumption that power and control come from some outside agent. Since the Creative Source comes through each individual and is available to everyone at all times, dependence on an outside source of power is unnecessary (Jackson, 1991).

The Sealing Light Meditation is the first step in self-protection. The client must learn to make a habit of the meditation. It is visualized first thing in the morning upon awakening, several times a day and at bedtime. When a person feels down or low, whenever a person feels happy about something, when there is a smile, with every breath the light is visualized. First a tiny bright spark at the center of the body in the solar plexus, glowing and growing brightly outward into every cell of the body. Then out beyond the body the light extends, about an arm's length on either side, over the head, beneath the feet, in front and especially in back of the body. Since people face and look in a forward direction, the backside is often ignored or forgotten. Entities often describe moving in from behind, through the head, neck, shoulders or back.

After a little practice, the visualized sealing meditation becomes automatic. It is a light which is always turned on.

The therapeutic process is also a learning process. A new awareness of the possibility of spirit attachment can lead to a more careful approach to life. As a person recalls the experiences and learns the reasons for vulnerability, there is a greater awareness and often more care taken in terms of emotional outburst, conscious thinking, physical risk taking. Personal boundaries are established and maintained. A person can learn to say "NO."

There are several books on the subject of psychic self protection. They describe various case histories and techniques of protection against psychic attack (Denning & Phillips, 1980; Hope, 1983).

Self-Clearing

As the client experiences the process of spirit releasement, there is a learning that takes place. As she grows in strength and awareness, she can begin to sense any attempted interference or attachment by a discarnate and immediately bolster the personal defenses. There is an increase in the ability to readily and easily perceive the emotional and physical impingement caused by a discarnate being. Conversely, there is a decrease in the fear and apprehension regarding the fact of spirit interference.

Distaste and discomfort with the idea of the parasitic attachment is diminished and replaced with righteous indignation at the violation, and compassion for the plight of the lost and confused souls who are caught in this intertwining mesh of consciousness. This finally extends even to the dark-energy beings who, in ignorance, suffer in their bondage to the dark master.

It is essential that each individual work toward full self-responsibility. The therapist is a guide and instructor along the way. The client can and does learn to deal with most of the entities that gain entrance in moments of vulnerability.

There is improvement in the capacity to communicate with the entity. The psychic link is more easily established. The remaining entities often begin to realize the possible benefits to themselves of the process and cooperate more willingly. The client can begin the actual process of questioning, resolution and release.

Sherry was a determined lady with a strong will. After a seminar in which she was a volunteer subject for a demonstration, she realized she needed more work. She lived in a different state and drove from her home to the therapists office for the releasement work. She worked nearly 27 hours in session over a three-week period. On one of the weekends she visited an old Spanish mission. As she proceeded out the rear door of the mission toward the courtyard, she felt a wave of deep sadness sweep over her and a dull ache in her heart. There was no reason for her to feel sad and she recognized the feelings as alien, yet could not shake them off.

As she walked into the courtyard she sensed many spirits hovering over the area. They realized she was aware of them and they began to move toward her. She immediately put up her shield of light and urged them to focus upward toward the Light. They did not come any closer to her and many seemed to rise toward the brightness. Back inside the mission, she found an information brochure which revealed that the rear courtyard had served as the cemetery in the early days of the mission. Many of the spirits she sensed were the earthbound souls of persons buried there long before.

In her next session, she described her feelings and sensations. She was directed to focus on the dull ache in the heart and recall the feelings of sadness. As these feelings emerged she was directed to ask the discovery questions herself. In her state of dual consciousness she posed the questions and the answers came. The story emerged easily.

A young woman working at the mission was performing chores in the main courtyard when a man, coarse and dressed in ragged clothes, approached her from behind. He had tried to force his unwanted affections on her on several previous occasions. Somehow he gained entrance to the courtyard and slipped past the soldiers who maintained a loose guard on the place.

She turned, recognized him, screamed and attempted to drive him away by hitting him. In his anger and frustration he pulled a knife and plunged it into her body. At the same moment a soldier who had run to her aid slammed his rifle butt into the man's skull. The man and woman died at the same instant, locked in the emotional and physical struggle of their last moments. It was their pain and sadness which had swept over Sherry as she stepped into the courtyard, curiously exploring, unaware of any hazard in the mission grounds, and, for the moment, unprotected. The unusual sensations alerted her to the possibility and in the next moment she protected herself, a bit too late.

The two beings were eager to go to the Light, quickly gave up their sad struggle and moved away from Sherry. She had learned how to recognize an intrusion and how to release the lost souls from herself. On her long drive home she consciously maintained the light shield. She described having the psychic impression of discarnates coming toward her and actually bouncing off the shield with a soft ping. She sensed earthbounds and dark-energy beings.

Clearing Other People

Clearing of others has been accomplished by people after they have been cleared themselves and have taken time to learn the procedures. A person can learn to perform this loving service. The work must be done with unconditional love for the other person, a desire for improved communication and interaction between the two people, and a request to the High Self that the work serve the highest good of all concerned. Interference for selfish reasons or the possibility of personal gain inflicts a most undesirable karmic burden.

Tricia was in her mid thirties and traveled from out of state for her sessions. She was in session over 15 hours during her week-long stay. She had been sexually molested by her father from infancy until age 12. Most of these memories had been suppressed, though she had a repeating dream of a baby being tortured sexually. In other dreams she saw blood dripping from walls and overhead pipes, as if she were in a basement. As she went into these dreams in session, she expanded the scenes and realized these were remembered events. Other memories surfaced. The remembered scenes suggested that the abuse had involved Satan worship.

In every case of molestation and incest, dark-energy beings are involved. Many dark ones were released from her as well as earthbounds. Though she was aware of a few episodes of dissociation and lost time, fragmentation was not as severe as might be expected. She had been in traditional therapy for some time prior to the releasement work and had forgiven her father, though she was not aware of the extent of the abuse nor the spirit attachments.

She was engaged to a man who seemed to enjoy aberrant sexual practices with her, often involving blood and urine. It became apparent from her descriptions that he had also been abused as a child, most probably through some Satanic practices. Tricia was apparently acting out some of her earlier abuse with him, though neither was aware of the dark elements. They had the potential for a satisfying and fulfilling relationship if they could mange to heal this damaging past. It is intriguing that these two people with apparently similar childhood trauma were drawn together.

Tricia worked well in session, going deeply into altered state and bringing through clear conversation with the entities. In her limited time she also wanted to work remotely on her father. She discovered that the dark-energy beings that were with her were part of a dark network. The function of this particular dark network was to entice humans to pursue Satan worship and perform Satanic sexual abuse. It was no surprise that the remote exploration of her father uncovered much darkness and many of these dark beings which had been plaguing him from his youth. It was discovered that he actively participated with the dark forces in earlier lifetimes.

The source of his involvement with the darkness in the present lifetime was an episode during World War II when he was the only survivor of an apparently hideous battle. From that time on he was never the same man; he was cold, unfeeling, even cruel, depressed, and alcoholic. She pronounced the Renunciation of the Darkness for him by proxy.

The night before her last session, she had felt grave concern for her father's health. Early on the morning of the session, she had been notified by phone that he was in the intensive care unit of a hospital, seriously ill with lung and heart problems stemming from his long-time drinking problem. She felt impelled to schedule a flight to be with him and planned to leave shortly after the session.

In the session she approached him in her altered state. She described a darkness surrounding him like a body bag. She was directed to call for the assistance of the Beings of Light and the Rescue Spirits of Light and to begin to clear the darkness from him. She said it was like wet sand, continually falling back into the hole she was clearing out.

She finally cleared his front side. The helpers lifted him and she grimaced as she saw the gooey black energy of the dark beings clinging to his backside. She continued to work with very little direction from the therapist for as long as she could. The suggestion was given that she could continue to work in this way on her own. By closing her eyes and recalling the scene she could resume the clearing and releasement work on him. After this suggestion, she was guided back into her regular state of consciousness. In the closing minutes of the session she asked many questions and during this time she continued to have visual flashes of the last scene of her father. She had learned to do the basic work of clearing another person during her sessions.

Ann was a 62-year-old therapist, loving and successful in her practice. Everyone seemed to love this natural healer. The attached spirit complained that its body had just "quit" when it had been aborted surgically. It indicated with a hand motion that this had happened "over there," which turned out to mean in the body of another person, namely Ann's daughter. It remained with Ann because its main purpose in life was to make Ann feel loved. As a loving grandchild, this could certainly have been accomplished. It resisted separating from Ann and moving into the Light, being firm in its resolve to make Ann feel loved.

The spirit was asked if it wanted to take a name. After some hesitation, Ann burst out laughing.

C: "He says Harry. He wants to be called Harry. It's not a name I would ever choose. Where did he get that name?"

The therapist cannot force an entity to leave. It is far more powerful to draw the entity into a solution by offering a way to fulfill its desire. Ann already had a grandson and a granddaughter, with whom she had an especially close relationship. But there was a problem with the estrangement between Ann and her daughters, Tina and Terri. It was suggested to Harry that he might accomplish his purpose by helping heal the rift between Ann and her two daughters. Then she could see the grandchildren on a regular basis in a more loving situation. Harry had not considered this possibility as a means of fulfilling his purpose. He was enormously relieved to know he didn't have to do it all alone.

Harry was directed to connect with someone in the Light which surrounded him. He saw what he described as a cheering section. Ann described him as a dull grayish shape, half the size of the others, who were glowing white. As he stood among these light beings, his energy was restored and she could see him growing larger and brighter, like a balloon being filled with light. They agreed that he could remain with Ann for a short period of time, still connected with them for his source of energy, until his work was completed. Only then would he move fully into the Light.

This was strictly a temporary arrangement. He did not become a spirit guide. Without moving fully through all stages of the Light, he could not assume that role.

In a session nine months earlier, Ann had uncovered a network of dark beings working to disrupt the family and discredit Ann as a healer in her capacity as a therapist. The main source of these dark ones was her former husband, Ralph. At a subconscious level he was fully committed to the darkness as the result of an agreement in a prior lifetime. In the present life he was sarcastic and mentally abusive to Ann. He turned their three children against her early in their lives. Even though Ann and Ralph had been divorced nearly 17 years, she was still irritated by his continuous undermining. In that session, many dark ones were released from the two daughters, the son and the two grandchildren. The dark commander and his underlings were released from Ralph and the rest of the family, and Ann pronounced a proxy Renunciation of the Darkness for him.

Immediately there was change in the family. Ann's son called from a distant state and asked his mother to arrange a family reunion with his sisters. He was coming home. The two daughters extended themselves in friendship to their mother in a way they had not for several years. She did not hear from Ralph.

As the months passed, Tricia's friendliness dwindled. Tina backed away more quickly, limiting Ann's time with her granddaughter. Ann described something of the session to Tina. She was not surprised, and proceeded to describe a spirit that lived in their house. Ann did a remote releasement on this spirit who was attempting to hold onto the child for itself and interfere with the connection with grandma. But the darkness had again managed to infiltrate the family. The son was living in Ann's home and remained friendly. Tina and Tricia and the grandchildren were again estranged.

It was obvious that Ann would have to clear the dark ones from the family remotely on a regular basis through personal meditation. This is where Harry could assist her. He could perceive the attached spirits with the other people quite easily. This proved to be important guidance for Ann.

Past-Life Therapy

During the process of spirit releasement, past-life therapy with the entity may be helpful in the release process. The therapist does only enough work on the entity to secure the release of the attachment.

Even though this exploration includes and involves the host, the focus of this brief therapy is the entity. Work on the client's issues must be completed later. In the case of past-life connection between the host and attached entities, past-life therapy is used with the entity.

> T: "Have you known her in any other lifetime?"
> "How many lifetimes have you been with her in this way?"

"What was your connection in the earlier time? How did you interact with her in that time?"

In about half of the cases of spirit attachment, there is some connection between the beings, in this life or a prior life, and these questions may elicit the necessary information.

Past-life work can be very helpful in ongoing therapy. The mental, physical and emotional residues which allow spirit attachment in the present life can be carried over from previous lifetimes. Attachment in the present life may be a continuation of the connection between the two beings. The host in the present life may discover in an earlier lifetime an instance when he was the attached entity, and the present entity was the incarnated host.

Whatever the conflict or circumstance which initially prompted the attachment in a prior lifetime, past-life therapy can assist in resolution both at the time of the releasement and in later sessions.

The past-life work on these issues centers around the circumstances of the past life or lives involved and the connection between the client and the entity or entities who were released. The client searches for the vows, promises, contracts, agreements, threats, even love ties between them. Once these decisions and pronouncements have been discovered and released the vulnerability is in process of healing.

Inner Child, Inner Person Healing
Healing the inner child, children, or more accurately, inner person, has become an accepted and essential technique of psychotherapy. A young subpersonality can offer an open invitation to entity attachment. Ongoing work with these traumatized subpersonalities can bring relief not only in the release of an attached entity, but also in everyday situations which resemble in any way the original precipitating event which caused the splitting off of the subpersonality. Any situation which restimulates the original emotions can elicit the subpersonality and the regressive behavior.

Some of these subpersonalities actually separate physically from the person, as described in the section Fragmentation and Recovery (381). During the process of healing and integrating these subpersonalities, the client gains new strength naturally by recovering parts of himself which had been left behind.

Child Counseling
Children are not immune to spirit attachment. A child can experience strong emotional reactions, much as adults can. In their innocence and openness, their are easy targets for opportunistic spirits. The spirit of a child who was molested can join a child who is being molested, perhaps to assist or to offer encouragement in the time of trauma. A lonely child is like a magnet to the spirit of a nanny or governess.

Twelve-year-old Juli came into session with her mother, Jana. The child exhibited the annoying habit of clinging to the mother. It was most bothersome at night, when the girl begged the mother not to leave her bedside at bed time, and when the mother delivered Juli to school. With the car double-parked and other cars all around, Juli would beg her mother to wait just a little longer before leaving.

In the session, Juli and her mother were sitting side by side on a couch. Juli quietly watched her mother as she described her daughter's behavior, a plaintive expression on her face. There was no verbal response from Juli when questioning was directed to any attached entities. There were some body sensations but no coherent conversation. Juli was asked to recall and describe a situation when she felt fear at mother leaving.

She related a recent incident when she felt the familiar anxiety. As she described the incident the feelings grew more intense. She turned toward her mother, got up on her knees on the couch and put both arms around her. This was a stark expression of fear as Juli manifested the clinging behavior which so irritated her mother.

> T: "Juli, recall another time when you felt like that. Let those feelings take you back to another time you felt the same way. Let your mind go back to another time when you felt scared just like this."

She turned back and sat down. Her head immediately tipped over onto the back of the couch.

Juli recalled a past life when she was a 15-year-old boy, and the mother was a 15-year-old girl. The boy was standing in a meadow and the girl he loved was walking away from him, her family having forbidden the romance. He didn't speak with her again until the day he died.

He never stopped loving her and he never married. On his deathbed he received a visit from the woman, his first since she walked away from him in the meadow. She professed her lifelong love for him, and her sorrow at the social differences which had prevented their union. As she walked away he begged her not to leave. She did not turn back and he died shortly thereafter, bereft at her leaving.

After his death he did not go to the Light. The next experience he could recall was floating through an open window into a house and joining Juli, the four-year-old girl who lived there. Jana, the girl's mother in the present life was "his love" in the previous lifetime He found and joined her daughter just to be near her. In the experience of saying good night at home and good-bye at school, he was reminded again and again of his feelings of sadness and the overwhelming loss he suffered when she left his side so long ago. This was not Juli's past-life memory but the continuing pain of an attached discarnate entity.

This entity was guilty of nothing but love. He had interfered with the behavior of the child, Juli, for something over 8 years for the sole purpose of being close to the woman he had loved in another lifetime. He had no difficulty understanding this inappropriate connection. He expressed his love and he was willing to release from Juli and move into the Light.

A few months later Juli was referred to a child psychologist because of other emotional problems stemming from the parents' divorce. She reported that after the release of the spirit of this man who loved her mother, Juli had not exhibited the clinging behavior again. It was not just diminished; it was totally absent.

At age nine, Tod was living in a foster home. His history was not divulged. The foster father and his sister, a therapist, accompanied Tod to the session. The attached entity was a young Mexican boy who died of starvation. Several years earlier, Tod and his parents had vacationed in Mexico. Tod was playing in an alley behind a restaurant and this is where the entity attached. Having starved to death, the entity frequented this area because of the food.

Tod was aware of the entity and interacted with it like an imaginary playmate. He did not want to let the entity leave. Whatever trauma he had experienced as part of the family had left him feeling alone and insecure and he just wasn't ready to say good-bye. He understood the effects on him and the influence the entity exerted. He agreed to release it by himself within a year or so. He was able to see the Light and understood the process of spirit releasement. The entity was allowed to remain.

Doug was 13 and large for his age. He did not get along with 15-year-old sister, Melissa. He was at times violent and had struck her on a few occasions. She told their parents and Doug was punished. He complained that she criticized him and goaded him into anger just for spite. After the release of several attached discarnates and dark-energy beings, even his sister's goading could not arouse anger in him. He was much happier. Melissa was confused: The old Doug was more familiar. She could no longer work her manipulations on him.

She also had a session in which several dark-energy beings and earthbound spirits were released. One male entity had apparently caused several instances of petty theft from convenience stores. She reported that she had only vague memories of the acts of thievery. Fortunately, she was caught before the behavior became serious. Several of the dark ones were focused on disruption of the family. Both of these young people benefited by these sessions. Their parents also participated in sessions.

Couples Counseling
Any two people in relationship will run into some differences of opinion about something in the course of their daily life. These differences can eventually lead to separation or even erupt in violence. These conflicts usually stem from some mind set or belief system which was in place before the two people came

together. The relationship is a place where these old patterns may be healed, but only if the two people remain coupled.

Past-life therapy can be employed in couples counseling in several ways. One approach is the dual regression, described in the section Dual Regression (149). Another approach involves two therapists. The four people initially meet together. The partners are urged to discuss and describe the problem areas. As the sensitive topics are exposed, emotions may rise and anger, blaming and defensiveness will be expressed.

At this time the two people are separated, one therapist with each partner in different rooms. The affect bridge is used to access the past-life trauma which is being stimulated, usually a survival issue with the related attempt at control of circumstances. Often the partners will recall the same lifetime when they were together with the same conflict. It may have ended in the violent death of one of them in the earlier time.

It is a serious decision to join with another person in a marriage contract. Two married people may hesitate to separate as quickly as two people in casual relationship. For this reason the conflicts they carry from other lifetimes may come up regularly until they are resolved. There is a greater opportunity to resolve the old residues in a married situation than in any other personal relationship.

Counseling with couples in relationship cannot be complete without a search for discarnate entity interference and attachment. Perhaps this should be a first step. Earthbound spirits remain focused on their earthly concerns, including companionship and sexual activity.

Sandy was the minister and director of a small, independent metaphysical church and teaching center in Southern California. In her early forties, competent, capable and compassionate, Sandy was a strong woman. She scheduled a presentation for her group on the subjects of past-lives therapy and spirit releasement therapy. It turned out to be a small gathering and Sandy volunteered to be the demonstration subject.

Symptoms were vague, nothing definite. With nothing specific to serve as the opening, the therapist used the Sealing Light Meditation as the invocation of light and protection and as the induction into the altered state, then began the questions.

> T: "Is there someone else present, is there someone else living in Sandy's body, is there someone else here, right now?"

This worked immediately. Sandy perceived an old man's face, stern, even a bit hostile.

> T: "You, old man, what are you doing in this woman's body? You have no right here."

He protested, through Sandy's voice, demanding the right to be with her.

C: "I have every right to be here."

T: "What is your name?"

The impression was that a person of powerful, almost regal bearing brought himself to full height, fixed his attention on the therapist and replied.

C: "My name is Amandahjah."

Sandy was sitting relaxed and erect in the chair, eyes closed, yet there was the strongest impression that here was a man worthy of respect, and somehow, even obedience. Taken aback for a moment, the therapist mumbled something like, "Yes sir," then quickly recovered and proceeded with the session.

Amandahjah had been the leader, something of a governor, Rajah, or magistrate of a province or city state in the Middle East some thousand or so years earlier. There had been corruption in the government, and although Amandahjah was an honorable man, he had been seriously tempted. His own beloved son had led a revolt of the people against the corrupted leadership of their land. As the building which housed the seat of administration was burning, Amandahjah had seized what he could carry of the treasury and had successfully escaped with it. In the confusion, panic and chaos of the revolt, he had succumbed to the temptation.

He died shortly thereafter, never reconciling with his son, or with his own feelings of guilt at his failure and greed. This failure and guilt were painfully apparent in this man of honor as he related the details of his last days. These overwhelming feelings had kept him earthbound.

T: "Amandahjah, why did you attach to Sandy, what gave you the right to interfere with this woman's life?"

C: "She was my son."

His reply was spoken very softly, but with enormous, almost palpable feeling. His guilt and his great need for his son's forgiveness had kept him locked in this spiritual prison, attached for lifetimes to the being who had been his son so long ago.

T: "Amandahjah, ask Sandy to forgive you. Ask for your son's forgiveness."

He hesitated at first and then finally was able to ask. Of course, she as Sandy and as his son, forgave him. Both sides of a dialogue like this are spoken by the subject. Even so, for the therapist or observer, there is no doubt who is communicating. For Amandahjah the conflict was not resolved. Further questioning revealed his feelings of guilt before God.

T: "Amandahjah, look to God as you know Him, ask for forgiveness. Listen for the answer."

It took a couple of minutes. With some mumbling, Amandahjah finally replied:

C: "Yes."

Somehow his conflict was still not resolved.

T: "Amandahjah, have you forgiven yourself?"

Amandahjah was visibly shaken as he realized that he had never overcome his own guilt, self-judgment and self-recrimination for his actions, his theft, his terrible fall from grace and honor.

T: "Amandahjah, can you in this moment, forgive yourself for what you did so long ago? You have received forgiveness from your son, God has forgiven you. CAN YOU FORGIVE YOURSELF?"

This was the crucial question. Each person is his own harshest judge, jury and executioner. People judge themselves for their behavior far more harshly than any outsider could. They judge themselves against a standard of perfection adopted long ago, long before beings took on physical form. Their words, deeds, and actions suffer by comparison to this perfect standard. Decisions about apparent imperfection remains for lifetimes so deeply buried that they become invisible mental programming. Those decisions are usually based on incomplete and inaccurate information. Low self-esteem, low self-image, and free-floating feelings of guilt and anxiety may be the result of these decisions and comparison with this permanent, invisible standard of perfection.

This was most difficult for Amandahjah. It required some prompting, some encouragement, before he finally could, in honesty and honor, forgive himself. Self-forgiveness is the most difficult act of forgiveness, and the most impactful. Everyone in the room felt it with a sigh of relief. And with this release, Amandahjah began to lift off, "to separate," as Sandy described it.

Amandahjah left safely hand in hand with the guiding spirits. As he did, Sandy experienced the past life as his son. She reported having seen this life in many dream episodes in the past without knowing what it was. Several nights before the demonstration session, she had a dream about the "old man" who turned out to be Amandahjah. As she described scenes in the past life, the energy of that life also lifted from her. It had been held in place by the attachment of Amandahjah. Emotions and conflicts are left behind if they have been resolved within a lifetime. In this case, his unresolved emotions had caused her unresolved past-life emotions to persist into the present incarnation.

As this lifted, she immediately began to experience another scene coming into her awareness. With sadness, she saw herself as a female baby in an Eskimo tribe being placed on an ice floe and abandoned. She had sensed these feelings of abandonment needlessly in the present lifetime and now had an opportunity to work through the source of these emotions. She returned to normal consciousness, feeling tired and peaceful.

Over the next few days she felt some disorientation in her role as director of the center. She no longer experienced the drive, the powerful, almost masculine assertiveness necessary for the position. She felt very soft, feminine and loving. Sandy eventually turned the center over to the assistant minister as she became more comfortable in her softer personality. She felt no loss at this but more at home with herself than ever before.

A few months later Sandy met a man and fell in love. Glen was also a minister. A big, gentle man, he had served as a medic during the Vietnam War. They knew they were soulmates and wanted to be together forever. They planned to achieve a soul merge once they were in the Light together so they could never again be separated.

Paradoxically, Glen also had an explosive temper which disturbed him and distressed Sandy. She accompanied him to his session.

T: "Can you describe the anger? How does it come? What stimulates you?"

G: "Sometimes it is just a general anger. But every once in a while... This is why I'm here. It's like some thing takes over. It's somebody else just lashing out. It's not that I'm split into separate personalities, really. Something or someone else that lashes out. It's like all my negativity comes out. It just ex-plodes. My behavior changes. I'm not this soft, gentle person; I'm very aggressive, vengeful. It's in the morning when I'm not awake yet or when I'm real tired."

Sandy: "Yeah."

T: "Can you feel that it is not you at the time? You know it afterward, but at the time?"

G: "At the time it's like I've lost some sense of who I am. It's something else there. It's me saying the words, but yet it isn't really me saying it and doing it."

Sandy: "It's at those times that you threaten to leave. Maybe it's like a sense of 'I'm finally getting out of here.' Something like that."

T: "That is in interpretation. We have to be careful about that."

Sandy: "OK."

T: "How long has that been going on, that rush of anger?"

G: "Best I can remember, it's since I came back from Vietnam."

T: "How old were you then?"

G: "I was 19. It's been intensifying recently. I just went through a divorce and that made it worse."

There was some discussion about Glen's experience in Vietnam. His one-year tour in country seemed like ten years to him. He aged that much. There were some terrible, brutal experiences. As a medic he was exposed to the dead and dying on a routine basis. This proved to be the source of the problem.

T: "Right now, as you talk about this, is there any physical sensation in your body?"

G: "Some tension in my neck and arms..."

T: "When we talk about the possibility of this being another, of being influenced by some other's actions, how do the physical actions go?"

G: "The feeling is my heart beating. There has been a lot of fear going on. Maybe there's a part of me that... Or maybe some-body attached that doesn't want to get off."

T: "Is the fear yours or someone else's, like the anger might be someone else lashing out? Can you differentiate that?"

G: "I'm not totally certain that it's mine. On the other hand, I'm not clear that it isn't mine either."

T: "How is your heart now? Is it beating now as we talk about it?"

G: "Um-hmm."

T: "Focus inward right now on your heart beating. If that heart beating could say something right now, or if that beating heart wanted to speak out, what would the first thing be? If it wanted to speak right now, what would it say? The first thing that comes to mind."

G: "Let go."

T: "Say it again."

G: "Let go."

T: "Say it again."

G: "Let go."

T: "Say it again, let the feelings come."

G: "LET GO!"

T: "Again."

G: "Let go. LET GO! (pause) Let go. (softly) Let go. Let go."

T: "Any pictures that come? Any words that come after that?"

G: "I'm hiding."

T: "You are hiding, aren't you? "

G: "Yes."

T: "What are you hiding from?"

G: "My mother."

T: "All right. (pause) Any images, any pictures, any emotions that go along with that, hiding from your mother? Just keep describing your feelings as they come."

G: "I just had an image. I was with a boy when he died. (softly) I told his father that he died. And he was hiding from his mother. He was killed."

T: "Is that boy here now? Is that boy right here right now, listening?"

G: "Somehow he is."

T: "Yes. What is your name, son?"

G: "Nguyen."

T: "Nguyen?"

G: "Cai."

T: "Nguyen Cai. You were hiding from your mother, were you?"

G: "Yes."

T: "Your father was told of your death, Nguyen Cai."

G: "Yes."

T: "What was your father's reaction?"

G: "He cried."

T: "How did you feel when your father cried at your death?"

G: "Terrible."

T: "Where were you?"

G: "I was there on the table."

T: "In your body, or near it?"

G: "Near it. Watching."

T: "There was nothing that you could do, was there?"

G: "No."

T: "Why was it that you were hiding from your mother?"

G: "I was playing outside and I was supposed to be feeding the chickens. My mother would get mad, so I went and hid."

T: "Um-hmm. How old are you, Nguyen Cai?"

G: "Six."

T: "How were you killed?"

G: "The GIs killed me. A bomb killed me."

T: "Were you near your house?"

G: "Not far."

T: "Was your house damaged?"

G: "No."

T: "And your parents were alive. And you were hiding from your mother."

G: "Yes. And something went off. I felt blood..."

T: "Would she have been angry?"

G: "Yeah, she woulda been mad, I was playing and not feeding the chickens."

T: "If you had been feeding the chickens, would you have been killed?"

G: "No."

T: "Was that a direct disobedience?"

G: "Yes."

T: "How do you feel about that, to disobey your mother?"

G: "Like I'm a bad boy."

T: "You feel like a bad boy, Nguyen Cai."

G: "Yeah."

T: "Your dad cried at your death."

G: "Yeah."

T: "And your mother. Did you see her when she found out about it?"

G: "I never saw my mother."

T: "What did you do after that?"

G: "I looked for someone to love."

T: "You looked for someone to love. Did you find someone?"

G: "Yeah."

T: "Tell me about that."

G: "It was the guy that came and told my dad I was dead."

T: "The American, the GI, the medic?"

G: "Yeah."

T: "He cared didn't he?"

Nguyen Cai stayed with Glen because his mother was angry with him. Glen was kind and safe. Nguyen Cai went into Glen's heart. That was where the love was.

T: "Are there others, Nguyen Cai? Would you know if there were others?"

G: "Yes. Others."

T: "Others of your country, or GIs?"

G: "Yes, GIs, big GIs. Hit in the head, shoulder and in leg."

T: "What's his name?"

G: "Jim."

T: "Can that one talk to us now? The big GI. What's your name?"

G: (in a deeper voice) "Jim."

Jim stepped on a mine, and was dying on the way to the field hospital. He knew he was dying. He felt angry, ashamed, hurt, afraid.

G: "I saw this guy and something happened."

T: "What happened, Jim?"

G: "I went in him. My body was so torn up, so much pain, and there was someone there helping me. And when he touched my head, I went into his hands."

T: "You went in when he touched you."

G: "Yes."

T: "He touched you in love, didn't he?"

G: "Yes. I hid in his leg, in his knee."

T: "Has that caused him problems, Jim?"

G: "Yes, so I moved into his head."

T: "Do you ever come out and act through him?"

G: "When Sherry hit him in the head, I came out to protect him, pushed her away."

Jim was wounded in the head. When Glen's former wife, Sherry, hit Glen in the head, Jim was angry and emerged to protect his friend. However, he claimed he hadn't caused Glen's explosive anger, that the really angry one was Lee.

Lee came forth easily. He was the killer. He was the strong one. He died in 1969 in battle. He claimed to have killed a lot of people. He loved to kill. It kept him mad. He spoke in clipped sentences.

Something happened to him at the time of his first battle, he became a killer. He volunteered for two more tours of duty. After he was wounded, he recalled being in a tent and someone was sewing him up.

G: "Someone came, and touched me, touched me in the face and told me it was going to be all right."

T: "You could hear him?"

G: "Yeah."

T: "What happened next?"

G: "I died. Everything stopped. They tried. I just reached out and grabbed him."

T: "You didn't want to die, did you, Lee?"

G: "No. I killed so many. I was afraid. Afraid of what would happen. Go to hell. Burn in hell forever. He's safe."

T: "Lee, look inside yourself. Was there a moment during that first battle when something came inside you like you went inside Glen?"

At this point, Glen closed his eyes. He had been sitting comfortably in the recliner with his eyes open, gazing blankly toward the carpet across the room..

G: "Yes."

T: "It changed you into a killer, didn't it?"

G: "Yeah."

T: "Is that one still here, Lee? Look inside, is that one still here?"

G: (timidly) "I don't know."

T: "If that one is still inside Lee, I want that one to speak now."

Glen straightened up in the recliner, cleared his throat, and appeared to grow smaller. The voice was cold, deliberate and clipped.

G: "I am Sergeant Chung."

T: "Sergeant Chung."

G: "From Cambodia."

T: "Sergeant Chung, you are a killer?"

G: "I am a killer."

T: "You are well trained."

G: "Yes. I am well trained. I am the best. My hands can kill. Anything."

Sergeant Chung was a trained killer, trained from childhood. He was serious and unemotional about this. It was his way of life. It was a powerful feeling for him. It was during the battle that Lee described that Sergeant Chung was killed. He hovered near his body after the battle. The Americans walked the field among the bodies of the enemy dead. Lee put his rifle to Chung's head and fired a round just to make sure. Chung wanted to be with someone strong. He thought this was a fine act for a soldier and he came into Lee. He wanted to continue to kill. This he would do through the American.

Inside Sergeant Chung was Mao Ta, an ancient warrior prince in China. He died a slow death at his own hands for the sake of honor over his father's death. His father was a province chief. It was the custom for the son and other warriors to die with the chief in order to protect him on the other side. It was not like he thought it would be. He never saw his father or the other warriors. He attached to a little girl living in a jungle. She picked flowers. He enjoyed the purity of flowers as he had enjoyed the purity of his warrior life. An intriguing viewpoint, this juxtaposition of war and peace.

He remained with this girl as she matured into a woman. He joined the woman's first child at birth. He stayed with her until she died. He joined a shepherd after that. When the shepherd died, Mao Ta joined an unborn child, Li Ha, just before his birth. Li Ha was destined to be a warrior in Cambodia. Mao Ta brought these others with him when he joined Sergeant Chung in Cambodia. They all came along when Chung went into Lee. Glen was burdened with the entire lot.

There were many others with Glen: American GIs, Vietnamese soldiers and civilians, including women, children, and babies. There were hostile Viet Cong still perceived as wearing black pajama-like clothing. These were all released as the Light surrounded them.

Lee was the last to go. He no longer felt like a killer after the release of Sergeant Chung and his nested following. He apologized to Glen and expressed his deep appreciation and love for the gentle GI. Lee was asked about this condition of spirit attachment and the Vietnam Veteran.

T: "Lee, did this sort of thing happen often with the men who fought there?"

G: "Yeah, man. There are legions of Chinese warriors walking all over the U.S."

Perhaps this can stand as a commentary on the Vietnam War. The veterans continue to suffer the effects of that conflict, both mentally and physically. Post-traumatic stress disorder (PTSD) may be at least partially caused by spirit attachment. Some men have repeated dreams of dying on some battlefield in that country. These dreams may well be the memories of the spirits of men who died and later attached to a buddy fortunate enough to be spared.

Glen's angry outbursts escalated for a couple of weeks after the session. Then he took full self-responsibility and the outbursts ceased. He was able to feel normal anger of his own at appropriate times.

Sandy called about two months later. Somehow the romance no longer flowered between them. No longer did they want to achieve a soul merge. They were not soul-mates after all. Something was missing in the relationship. The strong attraction, the soul-mate longing, was never a connection between Sandy and Glen. It seems she had been drawn to Lee. His energy came through Glen's persona. The angry outbursts stemmed from Sergeant Chung, Mao Ta and Li Ha. The magic had existed between Lee and Sandy. Glen was not really part of the picture. Not ever.

Maria and Talbot had been married about five years. There were no children. About six months before their session, Maria met Brian, a Vietnam veteran. She was enormously attracted to him and felt compelled to be with him. Talbot tried to be patient and understanding when Maria would beg to return home to him. She truly loved her husband. Then after a few weeks, she would again be compelled to be with Brian.

They had been in counseling for some months without success. The situation was very upsetting for both of them. Maria was totally confused and Talbot was nearly at the end of his patience. As a last resort they wanted to try past-life therapy or spirit releasement therapy.

Maria worked well in the altered state. The troublesome entity with her was her grandmother, who died when Maria was a small child. Remote exploration of Brian revealed that Maria's grandfather was with him. Grandfather died some months before Maria's birth. Apparently, spirits can perceive future events. Somehow he knew that Maria, who was not even born yet, and Brian, a kid who lived a few miles across town, would someday meet. Grandfather joined Brian and waited. It was grandma and grandpa who were getting together through Maria and Brian.

If grandfather had foreseen or predicted more clearly, he might have joined Talbot and there would have been no obvious problem. It is also possible that one choice for Maria was marriage with Brian. There are many paths one can follow. Either grandfather made an error in predicting the future or he simply chose the wrong possible alternative. Maria would have benefited from past-life exploration of these questions. She did not return for further work in these areas.

They did seek further couples counseling with a traditional therapist and it seemed to help. For a short while she continued to see Brian occasionally but this soon ended. Six months later, Maria and Talbot seemed to be doing fine as a couple.

Communication Exercises

Undelivered communication, particularly unspoken love, is a major source of upset between people in intimate relationship. Communication between men and women often fails, and this failure is the source of much pain and even separation. These exercises can be suggested as homework for couples in distress. With the exercises, partners can express love safely and intimately in private. Love is the healing energy and these exercises will not fail to generate the feeling of love.

The two people face each other, willing and agreeing to be fully present, paying total attention to each other. One partner voices the questions of exercise #1; the other partner listens with full attention, integrates the meaning of the question then answers as much as possible from the heart. After five to ten minutes of repeating the question and voicing the answers, the partners change roles. The same format is used for exercise #2.

The freedom to express love in this way without rejection or censure generates deep feelings of love.

EXERCISE #1. WHAT ARE SOME OF THE THINGS YOU DO OR SAY TO SHOW ME THAT YOU LOVE ME?

EXERCISE #2. WHAT ARE SOME OF THE THINGS YOU WOULD LIKE ME TO DO OR SAY TO SHOW YOU THAT I LOVE YOU?

Acknowledging love for another person can be very healing for the recipient and uplifting for the one expressing love. The need to give love may be a stronger drive than the need to receive love.

THE NEED TO GIVE LOVE MAY BE A STRONGER DRIVE THAN THE NEED TO RECEIVE LOVE.

This acknowledgment exercise alone can turn an ailing relationship into a loving and vital partnership. The statements are delivered using one of the three words in the parentheses at a time. As the exercise continues, all three words are used in turn. The first partner begins expressing love using one of the statements of exercise #3. The other partner listens with full attention, integrates the meaning of the statement, then responds with one of five answers: THANK YOU, FINE, GOOD, ALL RIGHT, OK, and nothing more. After five to ten minutes of expressing love through the three statements, the partners change roles. They can choose to continue as long as they like.

EXERCISE #3.

STATEMENT #1. I (LIKE, APPRECIATE, LOVE) THE WAY
     YOU_____.

STATEMENT #2. I (LIKE, APPRECIATE, LOVE) IT WHEN
     YOU_____.

STATEMENT #3 I (LIKE, APPRECIATE, LOVE) YOU BE-
     CAUSE_____.

Family Counseling

Couples can work together or separately in counseling. Teenage children can be helped through these modalities if they are willing to cooperate. Mid teens can be a difficult for anyone, even in good circumstances. Entity attachment can exacerbate tensions in a normal situations. It is a natural time for rebellion against parental authority. This rebellious energy can draw the dark-energy beings. Drugs are readily available to teens around the schoolyard. Drugs and entity attachment are definitely linked. Some types of popular music with sensual, hypnotic rhythm and Satanic lyrics can also lead to vulnerability to dark entity attachment (Larson, 1989).

Teenagers can be cooperative if they choose to have a session. If the parents force them into it, they resist and the session is likely to fail. Attention span is shorter in younger children, though they can easily enter the altered states. The images, dialogues and results are essentially the same for young people and adults.

If the younger members of the family are unable or refuse to cooperate, they cannot just be ignored in counseling. The mother is usually the more adept at remote spirit releasement work. It can be extremely effective and helpful in the family setting. Results can be quite dramatic.

Many children suffer autism, hyperactivity, and other conditions which may seem untreatable. Very young children often show precocious sexual behavior inappropriate to their age. Some children seem violent beyond comprehension.

In some cases, such conditions as these have been caused by attached discarnates. Releasement of these attachments has brought partial or total relief as described by the therapists or parents of these children.

An 18-month-old girl talked about Satan and the ways she planned to kill her mother. She exhibited violent temper tantrums, totally abnormal behavior for her age.

A six-year-old boy, one of a set of twins, was being considered for institutionalization. He had violent fits of anger in school once every five or six weeks. The principal stated that the only other child who exhibited such behavior eventually killed his parents with an axe. He drew pictures of himself with cartoon-head figures emanating from his head and fingers. He knew there were others present.

A five-year-old boy talked to his mother about worshipping evil. In school, he drew pictures of snarling wolf heads. He talked about doing sexual things with her, and made fumbling sexual advances toward her.

All of these children had attached spirits of violent adults who had dark-energy beings attached to them. All of these children experienced changed behavior after the releasement procedures were conducted remotely through the mothers.

The Family Curse

Apparent bad luck can follow families. Some people dismiss the idea of curses and black magic; others recognize the signs after reading something about the subject. Whatever the source or belief system behind a curse or spell, whether it be Satanism, voodoo, the huna death prayer, or some past-life sorcerer, witch or black magician, the dark force that maintains it in place is universal. Dark-energy beings, the true demonic entities, do the dirty disruptive work. It is always the same.

At 45, Barbara had not made much of her life. Her brother was schizophrenic, and her teenage daughter hated the brother. A great-grand-mother had killed her husband, the great-grandfather. Barbara's entire family seemed to suffer one catastrophe after another. She lived with several other people in a communal setting in a large California city.

In session she focused on the history of this trouble-plagued family. Suddenly she perceived what appeared to be a large red blood vessel extending from her, snaking through her brother, her daughter, and thence across the country. Seeking the source of this red cord, she found herself viewing a scene at Stonehenge, the mysterious and unexplained grouping of standing stones in England. There were many dark-robed people standing in a circle around a stone slab. One person in robes stood beside the stone altar. He held a long sharp stone knife. There was a young woman lying naked on the slab. This was a religious ceremony and the woman was to be sacrificed for some purpose.

Moving among the circle of robed worshippers were dark shadowy figures, not quite physical. As the robed priest raised the stone knife overhead and plunged it into the chest of the young woman, the onlookers seemed to experience a bizarre excitement. At that moment the shadowy figures merged with the humans. This was the moment of demonic infiltration and the blood lust was the opening.

Barbara saw the red blood vessel lead from that place through England, across the Atlantic to America, breaking into branches which led to the Dakotas, Louisiana, and California. These were the locations where members of her family had settled. The priest in that lifetime was her schizophrenic brother, the woman who was sacrificed on the slab in that lifetime was her daughter. It was no wonder the young woman hated her uncle.

This family curse began with a sacrifice to a dark deity. The dark-energy beings attached to Barbara's ancestors as they participated in the ceremony. It passed from generation to generation and was still affecting the living family members.

Betty was a victim of child abuse. This common theme is heard so often in the therapists office, yet each new account seems more horrible than the last. At 40, Betty was fairly well adjusted, functional in a responsible job and involved in a meaningful relationship with a man. She was quite volatile in her emotional swings, a bit flighty in her manner, and had some trouble remaining in her body during sessions. With a history of anorexia she was very slight in physical build.

She described her mother as a violent woman, mentally and physically abusive, and she had suffered many broken bones. Mother was extremely manipulative, and Betty, in typical co-dependent fashion, still wanted to reach out and fix her. Mother was verbally critical, while claiming to love her daughter. In her distorted caring, negative comments were often proffered:

> "You look terrible, are you getting enough calcium? You'll get
> osteoporosis."
> "You look tired, dear. Are you getting enough sleep? You could
> come down with something."

Mother was described as dirty and unkempt in her personal hygiene and her house was filthy, cluttered with junk, excrement, and dead animals. Betty remembered mother and step-father crowding into her bed in her youth because of the clutter and stench from the animal cages in their bedroom. She was 13 years old the first time her step-father raped her in this situation, while the three of them shared her bed. Mother did nothing to prevent this sexual violation.

All of Betty's siblings continued to suffer from this dysfunctional family life. Betty was aware of six or seven inner personalities; she calls them "the children." She did not lose time or dissociate in the classical manner of MPD. She worked with children and seemed to be effective and enormously caring in the work.

As with all cases of sexual abuse, dark-energy beings were discovered. They nearly covered Betty's body. There were several earthbound spirits, some with dark ones attached. Betty noticed a pain in her right lower-back area. The predominant dark one which covered the front of her body was the first focus of therapy. It quickly capitulated in the face of the Light. It called in its subordinates near and far, and claimed to have come from mother. It also claimed to have been with her grandmother prior to that, and great-grandmother as well. Betty recalled that these women were strong, firm women, powerful and strict. The same dark energy had also extended to Betty's 16-year-old daughter. This condition began to show the pattern of a family curse.

Betty was directed to locate the source of this curse, to follow it back to its origin. She immediately began to visualize and describe a glimpse of the hills of England. She then moved further back into a time in the Basque country. She described a woman who was banished from a small village, and the enormous anger and resentment she naturally felt because of this unjust action. She was the healer in the village and used herbs in her ministrations. These medicaments often brought about seemingly miraculous cures. Because of the mysterious healings she was able to accomplish, she was accused of being a witch by the superstitious people of the village. She was exiled.

Many present-day drugs and medications are derived from herbs and plant substances. The causes of many diseases are known and the mechanism of healing is well understood. It is no longer a mystery that botanical materials can have beneficial effects on the human body.

Here is a typical case of false accusations of witchcraft by the very townspeople who benefited by the healer's skill. The castigation of this person, predicated upon fear and ignorance, led to banishment from the village. The target of censure was most often a woman and the exile usually ended in death.

The Basque woman felt enormous resentment, anger, then rage at the injustice, and this led to thoughts of revenge. She consciously summoned the forces of darkness to assist her in a deliberate plan of retaliation. In the session it was not necessary to explore the actual process of revenge; the important aspect of this act of invitation was her contract with and ensuing bondage to the darkness.

At this point in the session, Betty began to experience more acutely the pain in her right lower-back area. This turned out to be the spirit of the Basque woman, whose desire for revenge had unknowingly initiated the ongoing connection of dark entities with the women of the family. Betty had resolved to end the "curse" on the women of her family and this was the key. The dark entities with the Basque woman were tired. They were released and removed quickly.

The dark ones had almost completely taken control of mother. There was severe fragmentation and separation, with very little of her original consciousness still remaining. The High Self was requested to assist in the healing with the recovery and integration of the fragments of mother's essence. The dark ones were removed by the Rescue Spirits of Light. The Legions of Heaven were entreated to follow the threads of the network of dark ones back through the generations of ancestors, and forward to the offspring, even those yet unborn, to gather and remove all such dark energies and beings for transport to their appointed place in the Light. The Mercy Band of Rescue Angels was enlisted to gather all earthbounds freed from the hold of the networks of dark ones.

The Basque woman was remorseful and penitent. She was more than willing to make the Renunciation of the Darkness. As she moved toward the Light, she apologized to Betty and thanked her for this healing.

Putting It All Together

Techniques are just techniques. Application of the techniques in an appropriate, timely and meaningful form constitutes therapy. Any of these techniques can be useful at the proper time. The therapist will learn by experience which technique to employ as the different situations emerge in the session.

Every attempt has been made to present case histories in a way which indicates the effective usage and combinations of the various techniques. The cases exemplify the process of combining present life recall, birth regression, past-life regression, releasement of single and nested entities (earthbound, demonic and extraterrestrial), subpersonality and inner child work, and recovery of fragments of consciousness.

Here are three cases, presented briefly to show the interplay of the various techniques. The therapist must keep track of all the threads of the narrative and return to complete each piece of work which was started.

Margot, a female client in her 50s, described several areas of her life that were not working. She had four siblings, and her childhood had not been easy. She had lost her father at age 9, her mother and step-father when she was in her thirties. Her mother had always been unpleasant with her. Many family members had passed on. She had feelings of abandonment even though she know intellectually that death is always part of life. She described occasionally seeing an image of a witch in the mirror. Anger was a basic emotion with her.

As she went into her feelings, she reported a bowl-shaped shiny metal skull cap which came down over her forehead. There were six or eight antenna-like projections extending from this cap. This is not an unusual description. Many people have perceived such a device. It indicates interference by extraterrestrials. This one seemed to be receiving mental commands which were programming her mind. She followed the signals to a spacecraft above earth, where a being who labeled himself "Boss" was sending the commands. His only duty was to attempt to control her and "help" her. This was intrusion without her permission, and this indicated demonic interference with an extraterrestrial. He admitted placing the communication device when she was just 9 years old, at the time of her father's funeral. The focus of the session shifted to that event.

Margot began to cry as she remembered the funeral. She was ignored by the adults and not allowed to attend the funeral. They were attempting to save her the pain of seeing her father dead in his coffin, but she did not know that. She was hurt and angered by this treatment and restriction, and she felt abandoned by them. She felt like getting even with everyone and she remembered feeling wiser than anyone there. This is unusual thinking for a 9-year-old. She vowed to herself:

M: "Nobody is ever going to hurt me like that again."

This sounded like an infinite phrase and indicated a past life. She continued by describing her own fragmentation.

M: "That part of me went deep inside. It never came out again."

The focus shifted to that fragment. The fragment proved to be the past life personality responsible for the feelings of abandonment, anger, revenge and the vulnerability to the dark-energy beings with Margot.

T: "9, you are still inside Margot, is that right? Are you still angry?"

She was there. She was still angry.

T: "9, recall another time when you felt abandoned, another time when you felt angry, another time when you felt wiser than anyone else."

She immediately recalled a lifetime as a witch. It was the image of this past-life character which Margot often perceived in her mirror. When she was young, perhaps 4 or 5 years old, this girl had lost her parents. The townspeople ignored her. She was so angry at them she hated them, she felt hurt by them and she wanted to get even. This was the opening for the dark-energy beings. She suddenly felt as though she were very powerful and wise, and her hands felt like they were growing into claws. This was the indication for release of the dark beings.

Soon, a man from the village befriended her and began to teach her special things and ways to get even with people. He made her go through a ritual of sharing her heart with him. She recalled a sort of fantasy of pulling her own heart out and actually eating it. This was either a symbolic act of giving up her heart, or soul, in a pact with the dark forces, or there was a sacrificial victim whose heart was eaten by the two of them. This indicated the necessity of the renunciation of the darkness.

The teacher had red eyes in that lifetime, and Margot realized he was still with her as an attached entity with one or more nested demonics. The dark nested ones were released. The renunciation was spoken by the fragment, by the teacher and by Margot simultaneously through Margot's voice. The past life was processed to the point of forgiveness and the fragment was welcomed back in to Margot's heart. The earthbound spirit of the teacher was released after he and

Margot expressed their true feelings of love which had always been present.

Two other fragments were discovered. One was 5. She fragmented out of fear and confusion, and was glued to the sidewalk outside of her house. She did not know what was inside the house. The conditional question was used:

> T: "If you did know what was inside the house, what would that be? Would you like grown-up Margot to go with you?"

This was agreeable to 5. Mother was there, looking fierce and yelling loudly. Her eyes were red. This indicated a posthumous remote releasement of the dark beings infesting mother. This was completed quickly. 5 was very forgiving. She loved her mother and wanted her mother to love her. She happily came into her place in Margot's heart. The other fragment came in without any processing.

Now Margot was more whole and feeling much stronger. The focus turned back to the "Boss" on the spacecraft. The process of release of the dark entities was initiated. The "Boss" answered to a character on the craft who appeared to Margot as a "devil" complete with horns and a black cape. This one answered to a gigantic being which looked like a huge octopus with countless tentacles to similar spacecraft near earth and other planets, other galaxies, other universes and other dimensions. This one seemed to be connected to some higher dark one who was laughing hideously. Margot did not want to go after that one.

The Beings of Light were requested to follow the dark network as far as possible. The "Boss" agreed to remove the skull cap. The others on the ship and those on other ships agreed to do the same as soon as the dark ones were sent to their appointed places and no longer interfered with these extraterrestrials.

Margot was deeply moved by the session and all that was accomplished in just two hours. In years of therapy, the five-year-old subpersonality had never budged, would not respond to any therapist. She had touched into the past life as the witch, but it had never been fully processed. There had been no awareness of the fragmentation, the extraterrestrial or dark interference.

Lynn, 34, complained of a pain in the left side of her upper chest She had explored some past life regression, and a therapist had released one entity and claimed that there were no others present. This is where the entity had been discovered. It had been killed by a wound in the same location. There was no change in the pain.

As she began the session, the pain increased. At first it appeared to be a past life. The emotions flooded out. The past life personality, a much older woman, was walking down a staircase in her modest home. Her husband stood at the bottom of the stairs holding a big knife, a strange, crazed look on his face.

She continued down the stairway, partly out of concern and curiosity about her husband's strange look and behavior, not suspecting he would harm her. As she approached him, he struck out with the knife, fatally stabbing her in the upper left chest. Dumfounded, she slumped down on the bottom stairs. This was not a past life memory; the woman described joining Lynn in her teens when she had a chest infection. There was no other connection between Lynn and the entity.

Before she was released, the woman was directed to move back up the stairs and look into her husband's eyes once more. They were red. He was being controlled by a dark-energy being. This indicated a posthumous remote release-ment of the dark beings with him and a group dark entity release. The dark ones followed the lady in when she attached to Lynn. These were released.

The pain in Lynn's chest began to subside. There were past lives in which she had been injured in this place. This was the vulnerability which allowed the older lady to attach. These lives were processed to the point of forgiveness and resolution.

Lynn's five-year-old son had made crude sexual advances toward her. She was concerned and wanted to do a remote spirit releasement on the boy. The entity attached to his second chakra was a grown man who wanted to have sex with Lynn. There was no other connection with anyone in the family. He was released and the behavior ceased. There was also a dark one attached to the boy's crown chakra, attempting to interfere with his spiritual progress. This became more clear at the next session.

During a meeting of people who wanted to learn to do rescue work, a woman brought through a spirit who was identified as Lynn's deceased brother. He admitted being connected with the darkness. He was attempting to procure Lynn's son for the use of the dark side. This called for a dark entity release on this spirit, a group dark entity release, a dark network release, and the renunciation of the darkness by the brother. He and Lynn were able to resolve some old issues and he moved into the Light.

Judith recalled a past life in Roman times when her husband, an army Commander, went into a battle and never returned. She still felt angry about that abandonment in the present life. During the session it was discovered that each of them knew that he would not return, yet neither voiced that knowledge. It was this undelivered communication which still caused pain.

As she went into the session, she was bidding him farewell in front of their home. They were of the Patrician class, and were well off financially. She watched as he walked away and out of sight. Her heart was heavy with grief. A short time later she received word of his demise in battle. Anger at him and at the war along with grief and sadness over the loss welled up in her like a volcano. Their relationship had been passionate and they had been deeply committed to each other. She suffered great loneliness.

She lived a long life, and came into political power in her later years. The intractable anger and sadness remained. After her death, she was directed in spirit back to the day her husband left for the battle. She watched as he bid farewell to his wife. She followed as he walked with heavy steps toward his fate. She saw him slump against a wall and sob hot tears of his own grief at what he knew he was losing at home and what he knew was coming in the battle of the next day. She watched as he spent the long night in contemplation of what the battle stood for, what it meant for the future. She did not yet understand the far-reaching significance of this encounter with the enemy warrior and his troops.

She followed him as he rode into the battle, seeing clearly the opposing forces riding toward the Commander and his men. She watched as the two leaders fast approached each other, weapons held high. She puzzled over the Commander's hesitation in swinging his sword in a death blow on the head of the enemy warrior. She refused to watch as the enemy warrior's mace began the swing which would, in moments, crush the skull of the Commander, her husband. She did not understand.

Again, in spirit, she was directed to the moment of their parting in front of their home. This time she was directed to step into her husband's body, turn and look out his eyes, merge with his mind, think his thoughts, feel his feelings and speak as him. She now understood his foreboding and foreknowledge of the outcome of the impending battle. She knew his deep sadness as he left her, feeling the powerful and overriding emotion and motivation to bring this drama to completion. She still did not know what it was.

As he spent the long night in contemplation and meditation, the story unfolded. Three hundred years earlier, two similar men met on a battlefield in the very region where this battle was to take place. These men were the ancestors of the enemy warrior and the Commander. Many of the troops of each army were family members of the two leaders. The Commander's ancestors emerged the victors in that original battle.

Many family members of both sides were killed that fateful day. Those of the losing army gathered together and raised their voices in a curse on the victors, their families and their offspring for all succeeding generations. This hatred and vengeance opened the way for the dark forces to infiltrate the losing army. The blood lust, arrogance and bursting egos of the victors allowed the dark infiltration of the winning army. This was the indication for a remote posthumous group dark entity release.

On their deathbeds each of the leaders had passed on to his son the commission to carry on this blood feud. Through the decades, skirmishes had erupted between the two armies, still filled with family members, generation after generation. Many men had died through the centuries. Only a few people knew the origins of the vendetta. The Commander had vowed to end this blood feud, and he knew only one way to accomplish this.

The Commander's wife, as spirit, watched through his eyes as the battle commenced early in the morning. The armies stood motionless at opposite sides of the field. Suddenly, both leaders bolted forward, weapons held high. Their troops rode beside them like waves of death rushing across the field. She felt his strength and his firm resolve as he rode headlong toward the enemy warrior. She saw the eyes of the enemy warrior glow a deep orange as he closed on the Commander. A quick glance at the troops revealed the same fiery glow in their eyes. The dark-energy beings were guiding many soldiers into senseless battle and certain death.

At the critical moment, she felt the Commander hold back in the death swing of his weapon. The troops could not notice, but she knew that split second of hesitation sealed the fate of her beloved husband, the Commander of these loyal troops. A moment later the heavy, spiked mace crashed through his helmet, pierced his skull and destroyed his brain. He fell to the ground, dead. She was horrified, yet she finally knew the full meaning of the Commander's sacrifice.

She scanned back through the past life paths of the Commander and the enemy warrior. Each was the reincarnation, 12 times removed, of the leaders of the armies which clashed in the original battle. It was their men in that time who had originated the curse which had been passed, as a commission to continue the battle, from father to son for all these generations. It was their karmic burden which was brought up again this horrible day for either resolution or continuation. The choice was up to the Commander. He had killed the other in the first battle. He knew he had to die to balance that karmic debt and halt this downward spiral of death. Only then would the senseless feud be ended. By hesitating for just a moment, he had made his choice. It was balanced. But at what enormous personal cost to himself and his beloved wife.

But it wasn't ended by his noble and spiritually valid decision. The dark ones which had infiltrated these souls would not allow such karmic justice to prevail. The situation called for a group demonic release for the opposing armies, both on the day of the Commander's death and the original battle as well.

The Might Rescue Spirits of Light were summoned for the work of this release. Archangel Michael and the Legions of Heaven were called on to follow all the threads of the dark networks affecting each and every one of these soldiers. The call was put out for all the Beings of Light necessary for this cleanup. This was a group release which spanned centuries. Judith described the dark ones flowing across the sky, so closely packed together they looked like a river of lava moving toward the Light.

The Commander lifted from his body. He wasn't quite ready to go to the Light. His thoughts turned toward home and his wife. He considered going home and attaching to her. This was not a loving thought. He voiced the intention to possess her, to claim ownership. He was still being influenced by the dark ones. The Rescue Spirits of Light were called specifically for the dark ones with the Commander. This was cleared quickly and he was ready to go to the Light.

The Commander's wife separated from him and he lifted fully into the Light. She was directed to return to the moment of her own death, so many years after his death on the battlefield. As she lifted toward the Light, she saw and recognized his spark, bright and clear, awaiting her return Home. As she moved fully into the Light, her spark joined and blended with his; they became one spark. Twinflames were united once more.

Above and beyond anything else, far more fundamental than any technique or process, the most vital and essential aspect of this clinical paradigm is the infinite and eternal healing power of total, absolute, non-judgmental and unconditional love.

Unconditional Love

Scanned reproduction from, *The Sacred Tree*, ©1988 Four Worlds Development Project. Illustration by Patricia Morris.

Discussion

Notes

—————— Quick Guide to Section V ——————

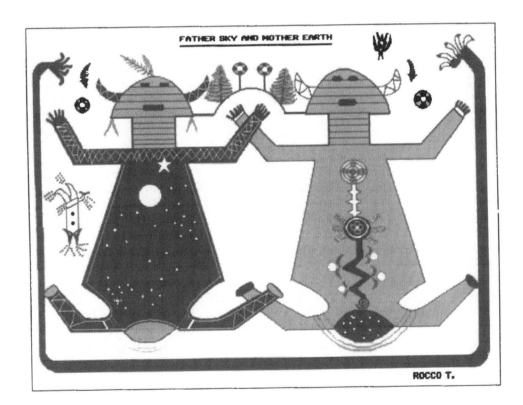

From computer art, "Father Sky, Mother Earth," by Rocco Tripodi, courtesy AOL.

 ———————— Discussion ————————

The author conducted a clinical research project on the subject of Spirit Releasement Therapy. Within the transpersonally oriented clinical practice one hundred clients completed the initial survey. Sixty-two of the clients completed and returned the follow-up survey. Twelve (19.4%) experienced only past-life recall, fifty (80.6%) showed signs of attached discarnates, and the spirit releasement procedures were implemented. Thirty-nine of the fifty (78%) were female; thirteen (26%) were male. The significant questions are listed here along with the results.

Initial survey:

1. WERE THERE SPECIFIC CONCERNS WHICH MOTIVATED YOU TO MAKE THE APPOINTMENT?

YES: 94/100 (94%)   NO: 6 (6%)

A. IF YES: PLEASE DESCRIBE ANY SPECIFIC FACTORS OR AREAS OF CONCERN.

The replies were categorized generally into problem areas, which turned out to be typical for people seeking therapy.

B. IF NO: PLEASE DESCRIBE YOUR REASONS FOR COMING.

The replies were summarized. It was generally curiosity or a desire for self-improvement.

Follow-up survey:

7. DO YOU EXPERIENCE ANY CHANGES IN THE SPECIFIC FACTORS OR AREAS OF CONCERN WHICH ORIGINALLY MOTIVATED YOU TO MAKE THE FIRST APPOINTMENT?

YES: 37/50 (74%)   NO: 13 (26%)

NEGATIVE	NONE	MINOR	MODERATE	MAJOR	TOTAL
2/50 (4%)	13 (26%)	3 (6%)	12 (24%)	16 (32%)	4 (8%)

8. DO YOU EXPERIENCE ANY OTHER CHANGES RESULTING FROM THE SESSION?

YES: 33/49 (67.3%)   NO: 16 (32.7%)

NEGATIVE	NONE	MINOR	MODERATE	MAJOR	TOTAL
4/49 (8.2%)	16 (32.7%)	7 (14.3%)	15 (30.6%)	6 (12.2%)	1 (2%)

More than 80% of the clients in the study showed signs of spirit attachment. After the releasement procedures 70% showed improvement of their original symptoms.

A new therapy can be effective just because it is new. This method is new to most people. The entire concept is outside the belief structure of many people. Because of the nature of the spirit, the subject is not amenable to validation by the current Western scientific paradigm. The non-physical, non-ordinary reality is beyond the pale of current investigative procedures of hard science. Psychology itself is a soft science; parapsychology and things of the spirit can be considered even softer science. Not until 1969 was the Parapsychological Association accepted into the American Association for the Advancement of Science. It remains precarious and peripheral as an academic discipline (Wolman, 1977, p. 20). Spirit Releasement Therapy is conducted as if the concept were valid, as if the metaphor were real.

Statistical figures give only an accounting of the results, the assessed degree of change in specific symptoms. The emotions and insights cannot be read in the statistics, nor the joy of the participants at the changes. Not evident in the figures are the people who are now free from the incessant internal voices which had plagued them for years, voices which sometimes urged self-destruction.

Statistics cannot express the elation felt by the 55-year-old man who had been a transvestite for 50 years. He first became fascinated with his mother's underwear when he was five. During his preteen and teen years, he stole articles of women's clothing from clotheslines in his neighborhood, eventually collecting enough to have his own wardrobe of female attire. His wife knew of his condition, but his grown children did not. He was a strong man, masculine to the point of macho, not delicate in any way. He worked in a demanding, forceful position as a personnel recruiter. The entity was a woman who had been his baby-sitter when he was a young child. She had died in a trolley accident.

By the next day after the session, he said he felt like a new man, like a ten-ton weight had been lifted out of his guts. After three months, he was certain that she, the attached entity, and the urge to wear feminine clothing were totally gone and he "wanted to shout it from the rooftops," to use his words. Four months after the session he reported that it was back. He was again enjoying dressing as a woman. This was depressing for him. Two weeks later, he described this brief episode as just a flash, a passing fancy. It was gone again. Six months later he was still free of the practice and yet could remember the excitement and pleasure derived from wearing the feminine attire which he had stored in trunks in his garage.

A letter from his wife praised the session as the most significant event in their marriage of seven years. Though she loved him and tolerated the fetish, it had always bothered her a great deal.

People who cross-dress, that is dress in the clothing of opposite gender, are labeled "transvestites." The condition is often a part of a sexual fetishism. Persons with gender dysphoria—that is, discomfort with the anatomical gender—are labeled "transsexuals," and many seek gender-reassignment surgery. Many people with these conditions are happy with their life-style and do not want to change. For those people who do want to alter these gender orientations through psychotherapy, the prognosis is poor. The conditions are considered by mental health professionals to be difficult to impossible to treat successfully—that is, to restore to normal gender orientation (Kaplan and Sadock, 1985, pp. 434-449).

In the clinical practice which was the setting for this study, two male preoperative transsexuals were treated with spirit releasement therapy. After the releasement procedures, one completely reversed his desire for gender reassignment. The other man, a 62-year-old architect, chose to keep the female entity, as he attributed his artistic ability to her influence. The releasement is never forced, it is the choice of the client. This spirit was Shirley, a girlhood friend of his mother who died in a boating accident on Lake Michigan several years before his birth. She entered and attached to him at about the sixth or seventh week in utero. His mother called him Shirley during the entire pre-natal period.

Still troubled with the gender dysphoria, he sought therapy with a female psychologist who also understood the concept of spirit influence. During the first session she discovered and released the entity immediately when it manifested. She did not ask for the client's permission. The next morning the man reported that for the first time in his life, he had awakened "not confused." Before that morning he did not know what it was like to be single-minded. He had nothing with which to compare his mental state.

The psychologist had only a limited knowledge of the process of spirit releasement and did not know about sending the earthbounds to the Light. In the process, she sent the entity out into a pleasant apple orchard. Sitting in church three days later, the man, lulled by the sermon, was staring at a mother-of-pearl necklace around the neck of a woman seated nearby. Perhaps he started to go into an altered state. Suddenly he felt a whooshing sensation and the spirit of the female apparently came back in.

He chose to allow her to remain and he continued to see still another therapist in an attempt to solve his gender dysphoria through conventional sex therapy. Several years later he was still suffering with the urge to dress as a woman, and was still considering the gender-reassignment surgery. He was 68 years old and newly married at the time. For a while after this marriage, he maintained his old apartment, occasionally dressing as a woman. His new wife accepted this, though she did not like it.

Within months, he let his apartment go, fully involving himself in the marriage and family life. He still thought about Shirley, felt her presence, and missed the feeling of dressing as a beautiful woman. Even after several years of marriage, he still thought about dressing in female attire, was still in therapy for the gender dysphoria, and refused to release Shirley. He stated that if anything happened to the marriage, he would still consider the gender-reassignment surgery.

Statistics can't record the amazement and wonder of Bennett, a 37-year-old man who had suffered complex epileptic seizures on average once a week for more than a dozen years, often while driving an automobile. His seizures began about age nine, after he fell off a bicycle and hit his head on a cement curb. They continued for about seven years, then ceased. The seizures began again when Bennett was in his mid twenties shortly after his first son was born.

The attached entity was a high school senior, a football hero with low self-esteem, plagued with disbelief about the claims made by others regarding his success on the football field. He died in an auto accident, recklessly and purposely. He joined the client as a spirit attachment because he, the client, had bullied the senior's little brother. The motive was revenge. There was a dark-energy being attached to the football hero. It was the dark one that had undermined the teenager's self-confidence and self-esteem and also urged suicide. It was not difficult to encourage revenge as the young man was already resentful toward Bennett about the way he treated his little brother.

Eight months after the releasement procedure, the client had experienced only three seizures. For him this was nothing short of a miracle.

Jolene was a 34-year-old nurse suffering from "burnout." During the four-hour midday drive from her home to the session, she had to stop several times for short naps. This sort of resistance is not uncommon. The spirit attempts to divert the client, either by inducing lapse of memory of the appointment time, causing illness, or causing sleep, as in this case. In her normal weekly routine, the woman hated to go to work and was barely able to trudge up the steps of the hospital building. This situation had gradually worsened during the years of her career.

The first of many attached entities to be discovered was the spirit of an angry 16-year-old girl who died of leukemia in her hospital bed. She hovered over the door of her room, unaware that she could leave through the walls or ceiling.

The next person to enter the room after she died was this nurse and the entity immediately attached. The first session lasted six hours. Two days later, the second session lasted for two hours. Many discarnates were released. The woman was once again happy with her work.

Her experience was so profound, even beyond the relief of symptoms, that some of the peripheral questions on the follow-up survey having to do with spiritual beliefs were at such a mundane level that they were almost meaningless to her.

Bulimia is characterized by the binge-purge cycle of eating and vomiting. Essential features of bulimia include: recurrent episodes of rapid consumption of large amounts of food in a discrete period of time; a feeling of lack of control over eating behavior during the time of the binge eating; self induced vomiting; use of laxatives, diuretics, vomiting, vigorous exercise, dieting and fasting to control weight gain; and overconcern with body shape and weight. Even though the eating binges may be pleasurable at the time, disparaging self-criticism and a depressed mood often follow. To qualify for the diagnosis of bulimia, a person must have had a minimum of two binge eating episodes a week for at least three months (APA, pp. 67, 68).

A 35-year-old female client, bulimic since age 14, went through the binge-purge cycle three times a day on the average. The attached entity was a woman who had killed her deformed Siamese twin children, then escaped into the woods outside of town, successfully eluding the authorities for the remainder of her life. This had occurred over a hundred years earlier. She would sneak into town at night eating whatever she could and as much as she could. She also ate whatever she could find in the woods.

When the client was 14 and suffering from typical teenage female emotional stress, the entity joined her, suggesting that she:

"...eat, eat, it will make you feel better."

The initial intention of the entity was to be helpful to the girl. However, she gained considerable weight and was unhappy about it. The entity prompted her to:

"...throw up, it will make you feel better."

The entity was asked to follow that thought back to where it began. The client began retching, doubling up on the floor. The entity had apparently eaten some unripe or poison berries which had made her ill. Vomiting eased her pain, and made her "feel better."

This was the genesis of the binge-purge cycle which she had imposed on this young woman in the classic pattern of bulimia. The woman was immediately relieved of the compulsion to binge and purge. Several months later the referring therapist, who had observed the session, reported that the client was bingeing and purging perhaps two to three times per week, but with no real power behind the act. It seemed to be just a nagging habit and no longer a compulsion.

In one case, the therapist worked four and a half hours with a female client, Norwegian by birth. She was a colleague who knew of the work and wanted to attempt to resolve some of her own personal issues. Many attached discarnates were released beginning with the first man who died in the 1500's, who then attached to another man, keeping him earthbound at the time of his death. They attached to another and another, until there were ten. Their stories were congruent, their travels quite eventful. They attached to the woman as a nested group during the Nazi occupation of Norway during World War II. After the release there was absolutely no change in her presenting symptoms. Several years later, however, she was able to recognize and describe changes which had occurred slowly. What had seemed like a therapeutic failure turned out to be a slow growth process.

Change that occurs within a given system which itself remains unchanged has been defined as *first-order change*. Change which changes the system itself is referred to as *second-order change* (Watzlawick, Weakland, and Fisch, 1974, pp. 77-91). In one example the authors tell of a four-year-old girl going to kindergarten for the first time. She became so upset when her mother prepared to leave that her mother was forced to stay with her until the end of the school day. This continued on subsequent days and the situation was considerably stressful for all concerned. All attempts at solving the problem failed; the only thing which stopped the avoidance behavior was for the mother to remain with the child. This left the overall problem unchanged and unchangeable.

This could have been diagnosed as a school phobia and, depending on the professional mythology of the school therapist, all manner of things could have become the object of therapy, including the child's dependency needs, the overprotectiveness of the mother, a possible marital conflict between the parents. Any change coming out of this approach would constitute a first-order change. As it happened, the mother became ill and could not take the child to kindergarten one morning. The father delivered the child. She cried a little but soon calmed down. When the mother took the child to school the very next morning there was no relapse, no fuss, and the problem never recurred. The solution for the original problem occurred outside the original framework, or context. This is considered a second-order change.

Another well known example of second-order change, or reframing, is Mark Twain's account of Tom Sawyer and how he induced the other boys to whitewash the fence. When the boys chided Tom for having to work while they went swimming, Tom replied by asking if a boy gets a chance to whitewash a fence every day. Somehow Tom convinced them that it was quite a privilege. That put the thing in a new light, the situation was reframed, and the others begged Tom to let them, which he did for a price.

As the result of an unexpected turn of events, an irrational occurrence, a previously unconsidered viewpoint, a system reorganizes itself along a new premise. This is the nature of a second-order change. Bandler and Grinder (1982) refer to this as *reframing*. Others refer to it as *recontextualization*. The technique is an essential element of Milton Erickson's approach to therapy and has been described and systemized very well by Bandler and Grinder in Neuro Linguistic Programming, their contribution to psychotherapy.

The results of this study suggest that there is a *third-order change*, which occurs in a successful spirit releasement procedure. If the behavior, condition or symptom of the client is caused by a separate attached consciousness of another being, a spirit, and that discarnate spirit is released and sent on to the Light never to return to the client, then the unwanted behavior, condition or symptom will diminish significantly or cease entirely. There is something which was there before the intervention and is simply gone afterward, totally absent.

This is not described by clients as something missing, which implies an incompleteness, but as something gone, as if they were relieved of a burden, an interference, in fact more whole, more able to function normally. It can be described as a spiritual surgery, the removal of something much as a cancerous tumor can be totally removed by a skilled surgeon in the operating room of a modern hospital. Often even the memory of the old patterns of behavior or emotion are erased from the psyche so that no comparison can be made by the client. In many clinical cases, this is just what happens. After the source or cause of the problem is removed, the memory of the former patterns of behavior and emotion are nearly or totally erased. This change cannot be defined as first- or second-order change.

This seemed to occur in the case of the 15-year-old girl who participated in the study cited above. She reported no change on her follow-up survey. Prior to the session, her father and mother had considered having her committed to the juvenile authorities as an incorrigible child. Several earthbounds and dark-energy beings were released. Three months later, her father reported that she was behaving normally. Over a year later, her mother confirmed that the girl had become an "ideal" child again.

There is so much to be learned about the non-ordinary reality and the way it interweaves and interacts with the consensus reality known as the "three-dimensional physical world." And there is much to be gained from this knowledge which will benefit all of mankind. Curious minds will continue to explore the depths of the mind and the farther reaches of consciousness. The evidence will mount and finally even the most skeptical among us will have to concede that this is not all there is. Physical reality is but a minuscule part of the Total Reality that is God.

Afterword

This Technique Manual was a long-term project. It was a project borne out of my personal experience and all that I learned in sessions with clients before I met Judith; our shared experience in the private sessions we conduct together; and the experience of every client who trusted us to guide them in the mind's farther journeys. It was prompted by my own inner direction and the requests of many people who perceived value in the work, both for themselves and for other people. My work on the book was supported all along the way by Judith, my wife and my life partner. It is our intention, hope, and fervent prayer that those who will benefit by the processes outlined in the book will find it and use it to full advantage.

This is the basic text of Spirit Releasement Therapy. There may be future revisions. There will be other books which expand on certain areas of this work.

Part of the material presented here is already standard practice in psychotherapy. Treatment of subpersonalities and inner child healing is widely accepted. Some of the work presented here, such as pre- and peri-natal therapy, birth regression and past-life therapy are quite new and controversial for many professionals. Spirit releasement, remote spirit releasement, and clinical exorcism procedures for dark-energy beings may be met with fear, disbelief and enormous resistance from many health professionals for some time to come.

Even when the category of possession states is included in the Diagnostic and Statistical Manual of Mental Disorders, many practitioners will scoff at any suggestion of a non-physical or spiritual reality where such things as discarnate spirits, demons and extraterrestrials can exist. Without the benefit of knowledge of this reality and the techniques of dealing with the conditions of spiritual interference, their meager efforts will continue to produce little or no result, or worse still, cause damage to the trusting client. This is unacceptable in an age of enlightened intelligence. Ignorance (which comes from the same root word as ignore which implies disregard, disdain and neglect), and denial are the guiding principles of such limited minds. These attitudes are used by the dark-energy beings to thwart human progress.

To the people who consider these techniques as viable modalities in clinical practice and who use some variation of the approaches described in the Manual, we salute you. You are forerunners of a new order of mental health facilitators and spiritual healers. The personal experience of the client will no longer remain submerged due to the fear and disbelief of the traditional psychotherapist.

Are the concepts valid? Is it possible there are discarnate personalities of deceased humans drifting about just waiting to insinuate themselves on unsuspecting people? Are the techniques outlined in this Manual realistic, or just guided imagery and fantasy? Are the results lasting and permanent? These and so many other speculative questions must await coherent answers.

Many people, including mental health professionals of all levels, hypnotherapists, body workers and lay persons interested in helping their fellow humans, have participated in the Spirit Releasement Therapy Intensive Training. Thousands of clients have sought assistance from these people, with good results in many cases.

After spirit releasement, people report feeling "lighter" in body, mind, and spirit. Problems and conflicts often dissolve completely. Still, any semblance of proof must come from personal experience and it is the results of the work which speak volumes.

Though the comfort zone of safe traditional thinking may die hard, it has but little chance of standing against the truth of human experience. As Carl Wickland personally inscribed in his book:

> "Truth wears no mask
> Bows at no human Shrine
> Seeks neither place nor applause
> She only asks a hearing."

There is one truth which has been repeatedly validated in this work and throughout human history:

ALL THERE IS IS LOVE,
THE VARIATIONS AND DISTORTIONS OF LOVE,
THE BARRIERS TO THE EXPRESSION OF LOVE
AS WE LOVE OTHERS,
AND
THE BARRIERS TO THE EXPERIENCE OF LOVE,
AS OTHERS LOVE US.

LOVE IS ALL THERE IS.

Love and Light to all.

William J. Baldwin, D.D.S., Ph.D.
March 21, The first day of Spring, 1993

Prisoners of Habit

"The Slave of Habit Breaks His Galling Chains, and Through All-Conquering Grace His Freedom Gains."
Scanned from *Charming Bible Stories*, circa 1892.

REFERENCES

A Course In Miracles. (1975). Tiburon, CA: Foundation for Inner Peace.

Abrams, J. (1990). *Reclaiming The Inner Child*. Los Angeles: Jeremy P. Tarcher.

Achterberg, J. (1985). *Imagery in Healing*. Boston: New Science Library.

Alexander, M. (1978). *The Man Who Exorcised the Bermuda Triangle*. New York: A. S. Barnes.

Allison, R. (1980). *Minds in Many Pieces*. New York: Rawson, Wade.

Allison, R. (1985). In B. O'Regan (Ed.), *Investigations: Research Bulletin of the Institute of Noetic Sciences*. Vol. 1, No. 3/4, (p. 9). Sausalito, CA: IONS.

American Psychiatric Association (1987). *Diagnostic and Statistical Manual of Mental Disorders* (3rd ed. rev.). Washington, D.C.: Author.

Araoz, D. L. (1985). *The New Hypnosis*. New York: Brunner/Mazel.

Assagioli, R. (1965). *Psychosynthesis*. New York: Viking.

Bandler, R., & Grinder, J. (1982). *Reframing*. Moab, UT: Real People.

Barlow, D., Abel, G., & Blanchard, E. (1977). *"Gender Identity Change in a Transsexual: An Exorcism."* Archives of Sexual Behavior, Vol. 6 (pp. 387-395).

Basham, D. (1972). *Deliver Us From Evil*. Washington Depot, CT: Chosen Books.

Bass, E., & Davis, L. 91988). *The Courage to Heal*. New York: Harper & Row.

Beahrs, J. (1982). *Unity and Multiplicity: Multilevel Consciousness of Self in Hypnosis, Psychiatric Disorder and Mental Health*. New York: Brunner/ Mazel.

Beattie, M. (1987). *Codependent No More*. New York: Harper & Row.

Berg, P. (1984). *The Wheels of a Soul*. New York: The Research Center of Kaballah.

Berne, E. (1961). *Transactional Analysis in Psychotherapy*. New York: Grove.

Bernstein, M. (1956). *The Search for Bridey Murphy*. New York: Doubleday.

Blatty, W. P. (1971). *The Exorcist*. New York: Harper & Row.

Bletzer, J. G. (1986). *The Donning International Encyclopedic Psychic Dictionary*. Norfolk, VA: The Donning Company.

Bliss, E. L. (1986). *Multiple Personality, Allied Disorders and Hypnosis*. New York: Oxford University Press.

Boorstein, S. (1980). *Transpersonal Psychotherapy*. Palo Alto: Science & Behavior.

Bradshaw, J. (1988). *Bradshaw On: The Family*. Deerfield, FL: Health Communications.

Bradshaw, J. (1990). *Home Coming: Reclaiming and Championing Your Inner Child*. New York: Bantam.

Braun, B. G. (Ed.). (1986). *Treatment of Multiple Personality Disorder*. Washington, D.C.: American Psychiatric Press.

Brittle, G. (1980). *The Demonologist*. Englewood Cliffs, NJ: Prentice-Hall.

Brittle, G. (1983). *The Devil in Connecticut*. New York: Bantam.

Brown, M. Y. (1983). *The Unfolding Self: Psychosynthesis and Counseling*. Los Angeles: Psychosynthesis Press.

Bruyere, R. (1989). *Wheels of Light: A Study of the Chakras*. Sierra Madre, CA: Bon Productions.

Bull, T. (1932). *Analysis of Unusual Experience in Healing Relative to Diseased Minds*. New York: James H. Hyslop Foundation.

Campbell, R. J. (Ed.). (1981). *Psychiatric Dictionary* (5th ed.). New York: Oxford University.

Castaneda, C. (1969). *The Teachings of Don Juan: A Yaqui Way of Knowledge*. New York: Ballantine.

Castaneda, C. (1971). *A Separate Reality: Further Conversations with Don Juan*. New York: Simon & Schuster.

Chamberlain, D. (1988). *Babies Remember Birth: Extraordinary Scientific Discoveries About the Mind and Personality of Your Newborn*. Los Angeles; Tarcher.

Chaplin, A. (1977). *The Bright Light of Death*. Marina del Rey, CA: De-Vorss.

Coleman, J. C., Butcher, J. N., & Carson, R. C. (1980). *Abnormal Psychology and Modern Life* (6th ed.). Glenview, IL: Scott, Foresman & Company.

Cox, D. (1968). *Modern Psychology: The Teachings of Carl Gustav Jung*.

New York: Harper & Row.

Crabtree, A. (1985). *Multiple Man*. New York: Praeger.

Crampton, M. (1981). *"Psychosynthesis."* In R. Corsini (Ed.), *Handbook of Innovative Psychotherapies*. (pp. 709-723). New York: Wiley.

Denning, H. (September, 1988). *Private communication.*

Denning, M. & Phillips, O. (1980). *Psychic Self-Defense and Well-Being*. St. Paul, MN: Llewellyn Publications.

Ehrenwald, J. (Ed.). (1976). *History of Psychotherapy: From Healing Magic to Encounter*. New York: Jason Aronson.

Ellenberger, H. F. (1970). *The Discovery of the Unconscious*. New York: Basic Books.

Federn, P. (1952). *Ego Psychology and the Psychoses*. New York: Basic.

Ferrucci, P. (1982). *What We May Be*. Los Angeles: Tarcher.

Finch, W. J. (1975). *The Pendulum and Possession* (rev. ed.). Sedona, AZ: Esoteric Publications.

Fiore, E. (1978). *You Have Been Here Before*. New York: Ballantine.

Fiore, E. (1987a). *The Unquiet Dead*. New York: Doubleday/Dolphin.

Fiore, E. (1987b, September). *The Unquiet Dead*. Lecture presented at the Seventh Annual Fall Conference of the Association for Past-life Research and Therapy, Sacramento, CA.

Fiore, E. (1989). *Encounters*. New York: Doubleday.

Fisichella, A. (1985). *Metaphysics: The Science of Life*. St. Paul, MN: Llewellyn.

Fodor, N. (1966). *Encyclopedia of Psychic Science*. Secaucus, NJ: Citadel.

Foulks, E. (1985). In B. O'Regan (Ed.), *Investigations: Research Bulletin of the Institute of Noetic Sciences*. Vol. 1, No. 3/4 (p. 7). Sausalito, CA: IONS.

Frank, J. D. (1971). *Therapeutic Factors in Psychotherapy. American Journal of Psychotherapy*, 25 (pp. 350-361).

Fremantle, F., & Trungpa, C. (1975). *The Tibetan Book of the Dead*. Boulder: Shambhala.

Friesen, J. G. (1991). *Uncovering the Mystery of MPD: Its Shocking Origins...Its Surprising Cure*. San Bernardino, CA: Here's Life Publishers.

Gallup, G. (1982). *Adventures in Immortality*. New York: McGraw-Hill.

Gauld, A. (1982). *Mediumship and Survival*. London: Granada.

Goldberg, B. (1982). *Past Lives, Future Lives.* New York: Ballantine.

Goodwin, J. (1985). Credibility Problems in Multiple Personality Disorder Patients and Abused Children. In R. P. Kluft, (Ed.), *Childhood Antecedents of Multiple Personality.* (pp. 2-19). Washington, D.C.: American Psychiatric Press.

Grof, S. (1985). *Beyond The Brain.* New York: State University. of New York.

Guirdham, A. (1982). *The Psychic Dimensions of Mental Health.* Great Britain: Turnstone.

Hall, C. S. (1979). *A Primer of Freudian Psychology* (25th anniversary ed.). New York: New American Library.

Harner, M. (1980). *The Way of the Shaman.* San Francisco: Harper & Row.

Head & Cranston, V. (1977). *Reincarnation: The Phoenix fire mystery.* New York: Julian.

Hendin, H., & Haas, A. P. (1984). *Wounds of War: The Psychological Aftermath of Combat in Vietnam.* New York: Basic Books.

Hickman, I. (1983). *Mind Probe Hypnosis.* Missouri: Hickman Systems.

Hilgard, E. R. (1986). *Divided Consciousness: Multiple Controls in Human Thought and Action* (expanded ed.). New York: John Wiley.

Hollingsworth, J. (1986). *Unspeakable Acts.* New York: Congdon & Weed.

Hope, M. (1983). *Practical Techniques of Psychic Self-Defense.* New York: St. Martin's.

Hoyt, O. (1978). *Exorcism.* New York: Franklin Watts.

Hunt, S. (1985). *Ouija: The Most Dangerous Game.* New York: Harper & Row.

Hutschneker, A. (1977). *The Will to Live.* New York: Cornerstone Library.

Hyslop, J. H. (1917). *The Doris Fischer case of Multiple Personality.* Proceedings of the American Society for Psychical Research XI. New York: ASPR.

Hyslop, J. H. (1920). *Contact With the Other World.* New York: The Century Co.

Ingerman, S. (1989, Mid-summer). *"Welcoming Our Selves Back Home."* Shaman's Drum. (pp. 25-29).

Ingerman, S. (1991). *Soul Retrieval.* San Francisco: Harper.

Isaacs, T. C. (1985). The possessive states disorder: The differentiation of involuntary spirit possession from present diagnostic categories (demonic, exorcism, deliverance ministry). (Doctoral dissertation, California School of Professional Psychology, Berkeley). *Dissertation Abstracts International*, 46/12-B, (p. 4403).

Jackson, J. (1991). *Empowerment Technologies*. Seminar. Altamonte Springs, FL.

Jahn, R. G. & Dunne, B. J. 1987. *Margins of Reality: The Role of Consciousness in the Physical World*. New York: Harcourt, Brace, Jovanovich.

James, W. (1950). *The Principles of Psychology* (Vol. 1). New York: Dover. (Original work published in 1890)

James, W. (1966). In N. Fodor, *Encyclopedia of Psychic Science*. (pp. 265-266). Secaucus, NJ: The Citadel Press.

Kahaner, L. (1988). *Cults That Kill*. New York: Warner Books.

Kaplan, H. I., & Sadock, B. J. (1985). *Modern Synopsis of Comprehensive Textbook of Psychiatry/IV* (4th ed.). Baltimore: Williams & Wilkins.

Kelly, H. (1974). *The Devil, Demonology and Witchcraft* (rev. ed.). Garden City, NY: Doubleday & Company.

Kelsey, D., & Grant, J. (1967). *Many Lifetimes*. New York: Doubleday.

Kempe, R. S. & Kempe, C. H. (1984). *The Common Secret: Sexual Abuse of Children and Adolescents*. New York: W. H. Freeman.

Keyes, D. (1981). *The Minds of Billy Milligan*. New York: Bantam.

Kihlstrom, J. (1985). In B. O'Regan (Ed.), *Investigations: Research Bulletin of the Institute of Noetic Sciences*. Vol. 1, No. 3/4 (p. 9). Sausalito, CA: IONS.

Kluft, R. P. (Ed.). (1985a). *Childhood Antecedents of Multiple Personality*. Washington, D.C.: American Psychiatric Press.

Kluft, R. P. (1985b). In B. O'Regan (Ed.), *Investigations: Research Bulletin of the Institute of Noetic Sciences*. Vol. 1, No. 3/4 (p. 5). Sausalito, CA: IONS.

Kluft, R. P. (1985c). In B. O'Regan (Ed.), *Investigations: Research Bulletin of the Institute of Noetic Sciences*. Vol.1, No. 3/4 (p. 11). Sausalito, CA: IONS.

Kluft, R. P. (1986). "Treating Children Who Have Multiple Personality Disorder." In B. G. Braun, (Ed.). *Treatment of Multiple Personality Disorder* (pp. 79-105). Washington, D.C.: American Psychiatric Press.

Kübler-Ross, E. (1969). *On Death and Dying.* New York: MacMillan.

Larson, B. (1989). *Satanism: The Seduction of America's Youth.* Nashville: Thomas Nelson.

Lewis, B. A. & Pucelik, R. F. (1982). *Magic Demystified.* Lake Oswego, OR: Metamorphous.

Lewis, G. R. (1976). Criteria for the Discerning of Spirits. In Montgomery, J. Warwick (Ed.), *Demon Possession.* (pp. 346-363). Minneapolis: Bethany Fellowship.

Linn, M. & Linn, D. (1981). *Deliverance Prayer.* New York: Paulist Press.

Lodge, O. (1909). *The Survival of Man.* New York: Doran.

Long, M. F. (1948). *The Secret Science Behind Miracles.* Marina del Rey, CA: DeVorss & Co.

Long, M. F. (1953). *The Secret Science at Work.* Marina del Rey, CA: DeVorss & Co.

Long, M. F. (1959). *Psychometric Analysis.* Marina Del Rey, CA: DeVorss & Co.

MacDonald, J. (1964). *"Suicide and Homicide by Automobile."* American Journal of Psychiatry, 121 (pp. 366-370).

Martin, M. (1976). *Hostage to the Devil.* New York: Bantam.

Maurey, E. (1988). *Exorcism.* West Chester, PA: Whitford.

McAll, K. (1982). *Healing the Family Tree.* London: Sheldon.

Monroe, R. (1971). *Journeys Out of the Body.* New York: Doubleday.

Monroe, R. (1985). *Far Journeys.* Garden City, NY: Doubleday/Dolphin.

Montgomery, J. W. (Ed.). (1976). *Demon Possession.* Minneapolis: Bethany Fellowship, Inc.

Montgomery, R. (1979). *Strangers Among Us.* New York: Ballantine.

Moody, R. (1975). *Life After Life.* Covington, Georgia: Mockingbird.

Myers, F. W. H. (1904). *Human Personality and its Survival of Bodily Death.* New York: Longmans, Green, & Co.

Naegeli-Osjord, H. (1988). *Possession & Exorcism.* (S. & D. Coats, Trans.). Oregon, WI: *New Frontiers Center.* (Original work published 1983)

Nauman, S. E. (1974). *Exorcism Through the Ages.* Secaucus, NJ: Citadel.

Netherton, M. (1978). *Past Lives Therapy.* New York: William Morrow.

Nicola, J. J. (1974). *Diabolical Possession and Exorcism.* Rockford, IL: Tan.

Oesterreich, T. (1974). *Possession and Exorcism*. (D. Ibberson, Trans.) New York: Causeway. (Original work published 1921)

Okada, M. (1982). *Foundations of Paradise*. Church of World Messianity.

Ornstein, R. (1986). *Multimind*. Boston: Houghton Mifflin.

Osis, K., & Haraldsson, E. (1977). *At the Hour of Death*. New York: Hastings House.

Pavelsky, R. (1984). *The Newsletter of Corona Psychological Services*. Vol. V, No. 4.

Peck, M. S. (1983). *People of The Lie*. New York: Simon & Schuster.

Perls, F., Hefferline, R. F., & Goodman, P. (1977). *Gestalt Therapy*. New York: Bantam.

Pulling, P. (1989). *The Devil's Web*. Lafayette, LA: Huntington House, Inc.

Putnam, F. (1985). In B. O'Regan (Ed.), *Investigations: Research Bulletin of the Institute of Noetic Sciences*. Vol. 1, No. 3/4 (p. 11). Sausalito, CA: IONS.

Putnam, F. (1989). *Diagnosis and Treatment of Multiple Personality Disorder*. New York: Guilford.

Putnam, F. W. (1986). "State of the Art." In B. G. Braun (Ed.), *Treatment of Multiple Personality Disorder*. (pp. 175-198). Washington, D.C.: American Psychiatric Press.

Rama, S., Ballentine, R., & Ajaya, S (1976). *Yoga and Psychotherapy*. Honesdale. Pennsylvania: The Himalayan Institute of Yoga Science and Philosophy.

Renshaw, D. C. (1982). *Incest: Understanding and Treatment*. Boston: Little, Brown.

Rinehart, L. (1976). *The Book of est*. New York: Holt, Rinehart & Winston.

Ring, K. (1980). *Life at Death*. New York: Coward, McCann & Geogehagan.

Ring, K. (1984). *Heading Toward Omega*. New York: William Morrow.

Ritchie, G. G. (1978). *Return From Tomorrow*. Waco, TX: Chosen.

Robinson, L. (1972). *Edgar Cayce's Story of the Origin and Destiny of Man*. New York: Berkeley Books.

Rodewyk, A. (1975). *Possessed by Satan*. (M. Ebon, Trans.). Garden City, NY: Doubleday & Company. (Original work published 1963)

Rogo, D. S. (1985). *The Search for Yesterday*. New Jersey: Prentice-Hall.

Rogo, D. S. (1987). *The Infinite Boundary.* New York: Dodd, Mead.

Ross, C. (1989). *Multiple Personality: Diagnosis, Clinical Features and Treatment.* New York: Wiley.

Russell, J. B. (1977). *The Devil: Perceptions of Evil from Antiquity to Primitive Christianity.* New York: Cornell University Press.

Russell, J. B. (1984). *Lucifer: The Devil in the Middle Ages.* Ithaca, NY: Cornell University Press.

Ryder, D. (1992). *Breaking the Circle of Satanic Ritual Abuse: Recognizing and Recovering from the Hidden Trauma.* Minneapolis, MN: CompCare Publishers.

Sabom, M. (1982). *Recollections of Death.* New York: Harper & Row.

Sargant, W. (1973). *The Mind Possessed.* New York: Penguin.

Schreiber, F. R. (1973). *Sybil.* Chicago: Regnery.

Selling, L. S. (1943). *Men Against Madness.* New York: Garden City.

Silver, S. M. & Kelly, W. E. (1985). "Hypnotherapy of Post-traumatic Stress Disorder in Combat Veterans from WWII and Vietnam." In W. E. Kelly (Ed.), *Post Traumatic Stress Disorder and the War Veteran Patient.* (pp. 211-233). New York: Brunner/Mazel.

Singer, J. (1973). *Boundaries of the Soul: The Practice of Jung's Psychology.* New York: Doubleday.

Simonton, C.O., Simonton, S., & Creighton, J. (1978). *Getting Well Again.* Los Angeles: Tarcher.

Snow, C. (1989). *Mass Dreams of the Future.* New York: Doubleday.

Spencer, J. (1989). *Suffer the Child.* New York: Simon & Schuster, Pocket Books.

Spiegel, H., & Spiegel, D. (1978). *Trance and Treatment.* New York: Basic Books.

Starr, A. (1987). *Prisoners of Earth.* Los Angeles: Aura.

Stevenson, I. (1974a). *Xenoglossy: A Review and Report of a Case.* Charlottesville: University of Virginia.

Stevenson, I. (1984). *Unlearned Language: New Studies in Xenoglossy.* Charlottesville: University of Virginia.

Stone, H. & Winkelman, S. (1985). *Embracing Ourselves.* Marina del Rey, CA: DeVorss.

Stone, H. & Winkelman, S. (1989). *Embracing Each Other.* San Rafael, CA: New World Library.

Stone, H. & Winkelman, S. (1990). "The Vulnerable Inner Child." In J. Abrams (Ed.), *Reclaiming The Inner Child.* (pp. 176-184). Los Angeles: Jeremy P. Tarcher.

Strieber, W. (June, 1989) *UFO Experiential Research.* Keynote address at the Second International Conference on Paranormal Research. Fort Collins, Colorado.

Summer Rain, M. (1989). *Phantoms Afoot: Journeys Into The Night.* West Chester, PA: Whitford.

Sutphen, D. (1976). *You Were Born Again To Be Together.* New York: Simon & Schuster.

Sutphen, D. (1978). *Past Lives, Future Loves.* New York: Simon & Schuster.

Sutphen, D. (1987) *Lighting the Light Within.* Malibu, CA: Valley of the Sun.

Sutphen, D. (1988). *Predestined Love.* New York: Simon & Schuster.

Swedenborg, E. (1979). *Heaven and Hell.* (G. F. Dole, Trans.). New York: Swedenborg Foundation. (Original work published 1758)

Targ, R., & Puthoff, H. E. (1977). *Mind Reach: Scientists Look at Psychic Ability.* New York: Delacorte.

Taub-Bynum, E. B. (1984). *The Family Unconscious.* Wheaton, IL: The Theosophical Publishing House.

Taylor, E. (1984). *William James on Exceptional Mental States: The 1896 Lowell lectures.* Amherst: University of Massachusetts.

Tebecis, A. (1982). Mahikari, *Thank God for the Answers at Last.* Tokyo: L. H. Yoko Shuppan.

Terry, M. (1987). *The Ultimate Evil.* New York: Doubleday.

Thigpen, C., & Cleckly, H. (1957). *The 3 Faces of Eve.* New York: Fawcett.

Van Dusen, W. (1972). *The Natural Depth In Man.* New York: Swedenborg Foundation.

Van Dusen, W. (1974). *The Presence of Other Worlds.* New York: Swedenborg Foundation.

Vargiu, J. G. (1974). Subpersonalities. *Synthesis 1, The Realization of the Self.* (pp. 51-90). Redwood City, California: Synthesis.

Verney, T. (1982). *The Secret Life of the Unborn Child.* New York: Dell.

Verney, T. (1987). *Pre- and Peri-natal Psychology: An Introduction.* New York: Human Sciences.

Villoldo, A., & Krippner, S. (1986). *Healing States.* New York: Simon & Schuster.

Wambach, H. (1978). *Reliving Past Lives.* New York: Harper & Row.

Wambach, H. (1979). *Life Before Life.* New York: Wm. Morrow.

Watkins, J. G. (1971). "The Affect Bridge: A Hypnoanalytic Technique." *The International Journal of Clinical Hypnosis,* Vol. XIX, No. 1 (pp. 21-27).

Watkins, J. G. (1978). *The Therapeutic Self.* New York: Human Sciences.

Watzlawick, P., Weakland, J. H., & Fisch, R. (1974). *Change: Principles of Problem Formation and Problem Resolution.* New York: Norton.

Weiss, B. L. (1988). *Many Lives, Many Masters.* New York: Simon & Schuster.

White, L., Tursky, B., & Schwartz, G. E. (1985). *Placebo.* New York: Guilford.

Whitfield, C. L. (1987). *Healing the Child Within.* Deerfield Beach, FL: Health Communications.

Whitton, J., & Fisher, J. (1986). *Life Between Life.* New York: Doubleday.

Wickland, C. (1924). *Thirty Years Among the Dead.* Los Angeles: National Psychological Institute.

Wickland, C. (1934). *The Gateway of Understanding.* Los Angeles: National Psychological Institute.

Wolman, B. B. (Ed.). (1977). *Handbook of Parapsychology.* New York: Van Nostrand Reinhold.

Woodward, M. (1985), *Scars of the Soul: Holistic Healing in the Edgar Cayce Readings.* Columbus, OH: Brindabella.

Woolger, R. J. (1987). *Other Lives, Other Selves.* New York: Doubleday.

Yogananda, P. (1975). *Man's Eternal Quest.* Los Angeles: Self-Realization Fellowship.

Young, W. C. (1987). "Emergence of a Multiple Personality in a Post Traumatic Stress Disorder of Adulthood." *American Journal of Clinical Hypnosis,* 29, 249-254.

Zilbergeld, B., Edelstien, M. G., & Araoz, D. L. (1986). *Hypnosis Questions & Answers.* New York: W. W. Norton.

Permissions

In the section on multiple personality disorder, the quotes by William James are reprinted from *WILLIAM JAMES ON EXCEPTIONAL MENTAL STATES: THE 1896 LOWELL LECTURES,* by Eugene Taylor (Amherst: University of Massachusetts Press, 1984), copyright © 1982, 1983 by Eugene Taylor.

In the section on multiple personality disorder, the case history of Max and Duane was taken from an article in the *American Journal of Clinical Hypnosis,* Vol. 29, No. 4, April, 1987. Young, W. (1987). Emergence of a multiple personality in a post-traumatic stress disorder of adulthood. 29, 249-254.

Portions of the section on non-hypnotic inductions reprinted by permission of Religious Research Foundation, and first appeared as a chapter entitled "Past-lives Therapy: the Affect Bridge Induction Technique," in *Psychography: A Method Of Self-Discovery.* Grand Island, FL: Religious Research Press, 1990.

In the section on treatment of Multiple Personality Disorder, excerpts were used by permission of the American Psychiatric Press, Inc. Citation: Braun BG: Issues in the psychotherapy of multiple personality disorder, in *Treatment of Multiple Personality Disorder.* Edited by Braun BG. Washington, DC, American Psychiatric Press, 1986, pp 5-9. Copyright 1986 American Psychiatric Press, Inc.

In the section on treatment of Multiple Personality Disorder, excerpts were used by permission of the American Psychiatric Press, Inc. Citation: Kluft RP: Treating children who have multiple personality disorder, in *Treatment of Multiple Personality Disorder.* Edited by Braun BG. Washington, DC, American Psychiatric Press, 1986, pp 87-89. Copyright 1986 American Psychiatric Press, Inc.

Illustrations: Credits and Acknowledgements

Introduction:

Page XXI: "Navajo Creation Myth," from the original computer image by Rocco Tripodi, with permission, downloaded from America Online.

Section I:

Page 3: Indian girl, scanned from an untitled original appearing in *The Sacred Tree*, ©1988 Four Worlds Development Project, The University of Lethbridge, Lethbridge, Alberta, Canada. Illustration by Patricia Morris. With permission.

Page 17: "Saul and the Witch of Endor," scanned from the original by Gustave Doré (et al.), from the *Pictorial Bible*, circa 1882.

Page 32: African masks, scanned public domain images by Mike "Gwydian" Wiseman, downloaded from America Online.

Page 33: Devil with book, public domain image scanned by John E. Williamson (Cherry Tree Software), from a 19th Century woodcut, downloaded from America Online.

Page 33: Emmanuel Swedenborg, scanned from the *Pictorial Bible*, circa 1882.

Page 51: "The Clinical Framework," enhanced representation of author's original by BT.

Page 52: "Saucers Over Yosemite," ©1992 by Mike "Gwydian" Wiseman, from an original, with permission. Downloaded from America Online.

Page 56: "Jacob Wrestles with the Angel," from *Charming Bible Stories*, circa 1890.

Page 64: "Cat of the Cosmos," ©1992 by Mike "Gwydian" Wiseman, from the original computer image, with permission, downloaded from America Online.

Section II:

Page 67: Silhouette, scanned from an untitled original appearing in *The Sacred Tree*, ©1988 Four Worlds Development Project, The University of Lethbridge, Lethbridge, Alberta, Canada. Illustration by Patricia Morris. With permission.

Page 96: "The World Within," ©1992 by David Palermo, from the original computer image, with permission, downloaded from America Online.

Page 145: "Land of the Sacred Cow," ©1992 by Mike "Gwydian" Wiseman, from the original computer image, with permission, downloaded from America Online.

Page 166: "Future Quest," originally entitled "Stonehenge," ©1992 by Mike "Gwydian" Wiseman, from the original computer image, with permission, downloaded from America Online.

Section III:

Page 169: Two faces and a sacred circle, excerpted clipart and original additions, by BT.

Page 172: "Much-Afraid," by F. Barnard, scanned from *Pilgrim's Progress: Peerless Edition*, circa 1892.

Page 179: "Fragmentation Categories," excerpted clipart and original additions, by BT.

Page 197: "Adoration," scanned from the *Pictorial Bible*, circa 1882.

Section IV:

Page 201: Indian girl, scanned from an untitled original appearing in *The Sacred Tree*, ©1988 Four Worlds Development Project, The University of Lethbridge, Lethbridge, Alberta, Canada. Illustration by Patricia Morris. With permission.

Page 203: "Sending Forth the Twelve Apostles," by Gustave Dore (et al.) scanned from the *Pictorial Bible*, circa 1882.

Page 210: "Reaching Through Time," ©1992 by BT, with permission.

Page 218: "The Dove and Olive Branch," scanned illustration from, *Symbols, Signs & Signets* by Ernst Lehner, with permission from Dover Publications, Inc., New York.

Page 230: "Demons and Angels Contending for the Soul of a Dying Man," *Ars Moriendi* (Augsburg, circa 1471) and "St. Michael Trampling on the Dragon," scanned from *Picture Museum: Sorcery, Magic and Alchemy*, ©1963 by Emile Grillot DeGivry, University Books, Inc., New York, with permission.

Page 240: Excerpted from the *Pictorial Bible*, by Gustave Dore (et al.) circa 1882.

Page 243: "Warrior's Promise," scanned excerpts primarily from the *Pictorial Bible*, by Gustave Dore (et al.) circa 1882. Recombined and arranged by BT.

Page 264: "Tomb for a Dying Earth," from a public domain computer image by Jeff Seldin, downloaded from America Online.

Page 268: "The Enterprise," from clipart, with enhancements by BT.

Pages 274-75: scanned illustrations from, *Symbols, Signs & Signets* by Ernst Lehner, with permission from Dover Publications, Inc., New York.

Page 279: "Beelzebub and they that are with him shoot arrows," by F. Barnard, scanned image from *The Pilgrim's Progress: Peerless Edition*, circa 1892.

Page 279: Peering figures, clipart enhanced by BT.

Page 281: "A man whom seven devils had bound," by F. Barnard. Scanned image from *The Pilgrim's Progress: Peerless Edition*, circa 1892.

Page 312: "Giant Despair," by F. Barnard, scanned image from *The Pilgrim's Progress: Peerless Edition*, circa 1892.

Page 313: "The Temptation on the Mountain," scanned image from *Charming Bible Stories*, circa 1890.

Page 314: "Doctor Johannes Faust and Mephistopheles," scanned image from *Symbols, Signs & Signets* by Ernst Lehner, with permission from Dover Publications, Inc., New York.

Page 321: "Jumping for Joy," from clipart, enhanced by BT.

Page 322: "Angel Descending," excerpted scan from "The Agony in the Garden," by by Gustave Dore (et al.), the *Pictorial Bible*, circa 1882. Enhanced and modified by BT.

Page 323: "Exorcism," scanned from *Picture Museum: Sorcery, Magic and Alchemy*, ©1963 by Emile Grillot DeGivry, University Books, Inc., New York, with permission.

Page 347: From *Bible Stories for Young People*, circa 1838.

Page 350: Hymn excerpt, scanned from original by BT.

Section V:

Page 417: "Unconditional Love," scanned from an untitled original appearing in *The Sacred Tree*, ©1988 Four Worlds Development Project, The University of Lethbridge, Lethbridge, Alberta, Canada. Illustration by Patricia Morris. With permission.

Page 421: "Father Sky, Mother Earth," from computer art by Rocco Tripodi, courtesy AOL.

Page 432: "Prisoners of Habit," scanned image from *Charming Bible Stories*, circa 1890.

Cover Illustration:

"Seeking the Light," by Bob Teets, ©1992 by Human Potential Foundation Press.

Acknowledgments:

The Publisher wishes to thank those who contributed to this project, and to acknowledge the help of Mike "Gwydian" Wiseman, graphic artist and Graphics Board Operator (PC MikeW) on America Online.

Index